W. H. Adams

The merry monarch or England under Charles II - Its Art, Literature and Society

In two Volumes - Vol. II.

W. H. Adams

The merry monarch or England under Charles II - Its Art, Literature and Society
In two Volumes - Vol. II.

ISBN/EAN: 9783744625241

Printed in Europe, USA, Canada, Australia, Japan

Cover: Foto ©ninafisch / pixelio.de

More available books at **www.hansebooks.com**

CONTENTS.

Chapter I.—The Actors of the Restoration.

Chapter II.—The Actresses.

Chapter III.—The Poets.

Chapter IV.—A Couple of Courtiers.

Chapter V.—The Prose Writers.

THE ACTORS OF THE RESTORATION.

THE CIVIL WAR.
SUPPRESSION OF THE THEATRES.
DAVENANT'S MUSICAL ENTERTAINMENT.
GENERAL MONK.
THE RESTORATION.
REVIVAL OF THE STAGE.
THE KING'S COMPANY.
THE DUKE'S COMPANY.
DESCRIPTION OF THE THEATRE OF THE RESTORATION.
ANECDOTES.
THE ACTORS.
CHARLES HART.
BURT.
JAMES NOKES.
JOHN LACY.
WILLIAM CARTWRIGHT.
MAJOR MOHUN.
"SCUM" GOODMAN.
HARRIS.
SCUDAMORE.
ANTHONY LEIGH.
SANDFORD.
SMITH.
CADEMAN.
CAVE UNDERHILL.
JOSEPH HARRIS.
KYNASTON.
BETTERTON.

CHAPTER 1.

THE ACTORS OF THE RESTORATION.

THE CIVIL WAR—SUPPRESSION OF THE THEATRES—DAVENANT'S MUSICAL ENTERTAINMENT — GENERAL MONK—THE RESTORATION—REVIVAL OF THE STAGE—THE KING'S COMPANY—THE DUKE'S COMPANY—DESCRIPTION OF THE THEATRE OF THE RESTORATION—ANECDOTES—THE ACTORS—CHARLES HART—BURT—JAMES NOKES—JOHN LACY—WILLIAM CARTWRIGHT—MAJOR MOHUN — "SCUM" GOODMAN—HARRIS—SCUDAMORE—ANTHONY LEIGH—SANDFORD—SMITH—CADEMAN — CAVE UNDERHILL — JOSEPH HARRIS—KYNASTON—BETTERTON.

As everybody knows, plays, at least the public performance of them, and players, so far as the law could touch them, were suppressed by the Long Parliament in 1647.* Many efforts were made to propitiate the authorities, but all in vain; and during the Commonwealth period, sock and buskin found their occupation gone. Some private representations were given at rare intervals—for instance,

* The ordinance of suppression described "those proud parroting players" as "a sort of superbious ruffians; and because sometimes the asses are clothed in lions' skins, the dolts imagine themselves somebody, and walk in as great state as Cæsar." Some of the actors betook themselves to the wars, mostly on the King's side. Robinson, a player of merit, was fated to encounter the fanatical Harrison, who, when he asked quarter, ran his sword through the hapless actor's body, crying, "Cursed be he who doeth the work of the Lord negligently!".

Cowley's Comedy of "The Guardian" was played at Cambridge; but to the general public the theatre door was religiously kept shut.* A bold attempt was made to re-open the Cockpit in 1648, but on the fourth day a troop of soldiers entered it, drove out the audience, destroyed the stage (in a frenzy of iconoclastic enthusiasm), and arrested the players, who were marched through the streets in their theatre costume, and imprisoned for awhile in the Compter and the Gatehouse. This severe example was accepted as a warning by the members of the despised profession, and to meet the exigencies of the situation Richard Cox invented a new kind of dramatic exhibition, at the Red Bull playhouse, in which rope-dancing was put forward as the *pièce de resistance*, to deceive the authorities, while the taste of the audience was gratified by the performance of what were called "Humours," or "Drolleries"—that is, a combination of the richest comic scenes from Shakespeare, Marston, Shirley, and others, into one piece, disguised under a new title. Thus: "The Equal Match" was concocted from Beaumont and Fletcher's "Rule a Wife and Have a Wife;" "The Bouncing Knight; or, the Robbers Robbed," was an adaptation of the Falstaff scenes from the second part of "Henry IV." These Drolleries were collected by Marsh in 1662, and reprinted by Kirkman in 1672, who, in his preface, says :—

"As meanly as you may now think of these Drolls, they were then acted by the best comedians; and I may say, by some that then exceeded all now living; the in-

* A fine of 5s. was inflicted on any person attending illegal performances; money taken at the doors was to be confiscated and given to the poor of the parish; and any player caught in the act was, the first time, publicly whipped; and afterwards, if he offended, to be treated as "an incorrigible rogue."

comparable Robert Cox, who was not only the principal actor, but also the contriver and author of most of these farces. How have I heard him cried up for his John Swabber and Simpleton the Smith; in which he being to appear with a large piece of bread and butter, I have frequently known several of the female spectators and auditors to long for it; and once that well-known natural Jack Adams of Clerkenwell, seeing him with bread and butter on the stage, and knowing him, cried out, 'Cuz! Cuz! give me some!' to the great pleasure of the audience. And so naturally did he act the Smith's part, that being at a fair in a country town, and that farce being presented, the only master-smith of the town came to him, saying, ' Well, although your father speaks so ill of you, yet when the fair is done, if you will come and work with me, I will give you twelve-pence a week more than I give any other journeyman.' Thus was he taken for a smith bred, that was, indeed, as much of any trade."

The fall of the Long Parliament, by which they had been so cruelly persecuted, was grateful enough to the players, and we may fairly assume that Alexander Brome spoke their feelings in the verses which, in 1653, he prefixed to the collected edition of Richard Brome's Plays. The players, he exclaims, have survived the Parliament:—

> "See the strange twirl of times! when such poor things
> Outlive the dates of parliaments or kings!
> This revolution makes exploded wit
> Now see the fall of those that ruined it;
> And the condemnèd stage hath now obtained
> To see her executioners arraigned.
> There's nothing permanent; those high great men
> That rose from dust, to dust may fall again;
> And fate so orders things, that the same hour
> Sees the same man both in contempt and power;
> For the multitude, in whom the power doth lie,
> Do in one breath cry *Hail!* and *Crucify!*"

The Government could suppress the public theatres, but they could not suppress the taste for dramatic representations, and clandestine performances became of frequent occurrence during the Protectorate. In Lord Hatton, of Scotland Yard, the poor actors found a kindly patron; and not less generous was the Countess of Holland, who erected a private stage at her mansion, Holland House, Kensington. It was necessary that these performances should take place with the greatest precautions, and we are told that William Goffe, " the woman-actor," was employed as "the jackal" to give notice of the different "fixtures," and communicate between actors and audience. At the close of the play a collection was made for the benefit of the actors, whose share was carefully proportioned to their respective merits.

To increase their funds the players resorted to the practice of publishing the plays, which had hitherto been jealously kept in manuscript, and in one year no fewer than fifty were thus given to the public. Many of these have undoubtedly perished, for though the titles are recorded, the plays themselves are not known. And, in 1653, John Cotgrave issued a remarkable collection " of the most and best of our English Dramatic Poems" under the title of "The English Treasury of Wit and Language." In his preface he complains that "the Dramatic Poem had been too much slighted;" and he adds that some, not wanting in wit themselves, had, through this unfortunate neglect, "lost the benefit of many rich and useful observations; not duly considering, or believing, that the framers of them were the most fluent and redundant wits that this age, or I think any other, ever knew."

But with the overthrow of "the Rumps," and the entrance into London of prudent George Monk and his regiments, brighter days dawned for the poor players. Bustling old Rhodes, who had been prompter at the Blackfriars Theatre, and afterwards sold books and pamphlets in a shop at Charing Cross, hastened to the camp in Hyde Park, and wheedled out of the General permission to revive the drama at the Cockpit, in Drury Lane (June, 1660). A similar license was granted to Beeston, who about the same time opened the Salisbury Court Theatre. That Monk's tastes were theatrical we opine from the fact that, when he and the Council of State were entertained by the London Guilds, dramatic representations were always included in the programme, with "dancing and singing, many shapes and ghosts, and the like; and all to please his Excellency the Lord General."

At first the revival of the drama was attended with a good deal of irregular competition; but in 1662 the King took the matter in hand, and settled all disputes by issuing patents for two theatres only—one to Thomas Killigrew, who opened in Drury Lane at the head of the King's Company; and the other to Sir William Davenant and the Duke of York's Company, in Salisbury Court, Fleet Street. The latter afterwards removed to the old Tennis Court in Portugal Row, on the south side of Lincoln's Inn Fields. In 1671, after the death of Davenant, the Duke's comedians betook themselves to the new theatre in Dorset Gardens, built by Sir Christopher Wren, and decorated by Grinling Gibbons. Meanwhile, the King's Company, burnt out of Drury Lane in 1672, found shelter in Lincoln's Inn Fields until Wren provided them with a new house in 1674. Eight years later, on Killigrew's death, the two companies united, and started at the New Drury Lane Theatre, also built by Wren, on the 16th of November, 1682.

Before we put together a few biographical and critical notes respecting the Actors and Actresses of the Restoration, we must say a word or two in description of the theatres in which, and of the audience before which, they donned the sock and buskin. The usual hour of performance, at least in Charles II.'s early years, was three in the afternoon. The house was lighted, partly by the light of heaven, which the open roof—for the pit was not covered over *—freely admitted, and partly by flaring candles, which were trimmed by regular "snuffers." Two rows of boxes † accommodated the King and his courtiers, the nobles, and the wealthier gentry; but the company in the pit was frequently among the best, and thither resorted the wit and the critic, on whose fiat the fate of play and players depended. Thither, too, went the gay gallants of the period, dividing their attention between the fair actresses on the stage and the beauties in the boxes, with a ready glance for a pretty face among the orange girls, who pushed the sale of their costly fruit. When, in February, 1668, Sir George Etherege's comedy, "She Would if She Could," was produced at the Duke's House, the pit was crowded with a brilliant company, including Buckingham, and Dorset, and Sedley, which incontinently condemned the play, much to the dissatisfaction of its author. Our wonder that ladies could attend

* Pepys records, on one occasion, the inconvenience caused by a storm of hail.
† The prices of admission to the boxes seem to have ranged from 4s. to 18d. On the first night of a new piece the prices were sometimes doubled. (See Pepys, Dec. 16th, 1661.)

the performance of so indecent a drama is not much lessened by the fact that they could, if they chose, appear in masks;* but from the comments of Pepys on the charming faces he saw, and so loved to see, we infer that the number who made even this slight concession to decorum must have been very small.

The patronage of the Court was extended to the Stage during Charles's reign on a more liberal scale than ever before or since. The saturnine King, so falsely called "The Merry Monarch," went to the theatre, almost every night, to escape for awhile from the *ennui* which consumed him, and of course was followed by everybody who breathed the atmosphere of the Court. I think the "auditorium" must often have presented a more interesting, and certainly a more entertaining spectacle than the stage. As, for example, on the 20th of April, 1661, when Mr. Pepys at the Cockpit saw the King, and the Duke of York and his recently-wedded Duchess. The play was Fletcher's "Humorous Lieutenant," not very well acted; but Mr. Pepys found great pleasure in seeing "so many great beauties, especially Mrs. Palmer (in due time to be known as Lady Castlemaine and Duchess of Cleveland), with whom the King did discover a great deal of familiarity." Again, on October 2nd, 1662, when Catherine of Braganza made her first public appearance:—"I did go thither," says Pepys, "and by very great fortune did follow four or five gentlemen who were carried to a little private door in the wall, and so crept through a narrow

* " I remember," says Colley Cibber, " the ladies were then observed to be decently afraid of venturing bare-faced to a new comedy, till they had been assured they might do it without insult to their modesty ; or if their curiosity were too strong for their patience, they took care at least to save appearances, and rarely came in the first days of acting, but in masks, which custom, however, had so many ill consequences attending it, that it has been abolished these many years."

place, and come into one of the boxes next the King's, but so as I could not see the King or Queen, but many of the fine ladies, who yet are really not so handsome generally as I used to take them to be, but that they are finely dressed. There we saw 'The Cardinal' [by James Shirley], a tragedy I had never seen before, nor is there any great matter in it. The company that come with me into the box were all Frenchmen, that could speak no English; but Lord! what sport they made to ask a pretty lady that they got among them, that understood both French and English, to make her tell them what the actors said."

On the 21st of November Mr. Pepys took his wife to the Cockpit, and they had excellent places, and saw the King, and Queen, and the boy-Duke of Monmouth, and my Lady Castlemaine, and all the fine ladies. He was there again on the 1st of December—he was always making vows not to go to the theatre for a certain period, and always breaking these vows—and saw acted a translation of Corneille's "Cid"—"a play," he says, "I have read with great delight, but is a most dull thing acted, which I never understood before, there being no pleasure in it, though done by Betterton, and by Ianthe [Mrs. Betterton], and by another fine wench [Mrs. Norton] that is now in the room of Roxalana [Mrs. Davenport]; nor did the King or Queen once smile all the whole play, nor any of the whole company seem to take any pleasure, but what was in the greatness and gallantry of the company."

We fear our dear friend Pepys had a touch of snobbishness or flunkeyism in his character, for when he went to the Duke's Theatre, on December 27th, to see the "Siege of Rhodes," he expresses himself as not pleased with the audience: the house was "full of citizens—there hardly being a gallant man or woman present!" And it was so on New Year's Day, 1663: "the house was full of citizens, and so the less pleasant." But on this occasion, to make some amends, Mrs. Davenport, the actress, was there, in the chief box, radiant in a velvet gown, which was then "the fashion."

At the Cockpit, on the 5th, the Duke and Duchess of York were present, and before all the audience "did show some impertinent, and methought, unnatural dalliances, such as kissing of hands, and leaning upon one another." But these great people seldom manifested much respect for the audience—or for themselves. What a scene is that which Pepys sketches for us as having occurred at the King's Theatre one day in January, 1664:—"How the King, coming the other day to his Theatre to see 'The Indian Queen,' my Lady Castlemaine was in the next box before he came; and leaning over other ladies awhile to whisper with the King, she rose out of the box and went into the King's, and set herself on the King's right hand, between the King and the Duke of York; which put the King himself, as well as everybody else, out of countenance"—this impertinent feat being intended to prove to the world that she had not, as was supposed, lost the royal favour.

On the 4th of October Pepys went to see a foolish play called "The General," and happened to sit near to Sir Charles Sedley, who "at every line did take notice of the dulness of the part and badness of the action, and that most pertinently."

Another time he sees among the company Cromwell's daughter, Mary, with her husband, Viscount Falconbridge, and is much pleased by her gracious looks and modest dress, and by the timidity with which she shrinks from the gaze of curious spectators, putting on her vizard, and keeping it on all the play. But he is more gratified, we fancy, by the sight of laughing Nell Gwynn, who, with her fair locks and bright eyes, shines conspicuous in the front of the house, sometimes filling the soul of Pepys with exultation by condescending to chat with him, and sometimes moving his admiration by the sharp repartees she fearlessly exchanges with the most celebrated wits of the time.

On the 5th of June, 1665, he attends the performance at the Duke's Theatre of Lord Orrery's play of "Mustapha;" but "all the pleasure of the play was" that the King and Lady Castlemaine were present, "and pretty witty Nell Gwynn and the younger Marshall sat next us; which pleased me mightily."

There is a curious entry in the Diary for December 21st, 1668. The King and his Court went to see "Macbeth" at the Duke's Theatre, and Pepys sat just under them and Lady Castlemaine, and "close to a woman that comes into the pit, a kind of a loose gossip that pretends to be like her, and is so, something. The King and Duke of York minded me, and smiled upon me, at the handsome woman near me, but it vexed me to see Moll Davies, in a box over the King's and my Lady Castlemaine's, look down upon the King, and he up to her; and so did my Lady Castlemaine once, to see who it was; but when she saw Moll Davies, she looked like fire, which troubled me."

We have remarked that, on the restoration of the Theatres, their performances began at three in the afternoon; but later hours came afterwards to be the fashion. Pepys notes, on one occasion, that the play was not over until eleven, and that he walked home by moonlight. And in Evelyn's correspondence, when complaining of the frequency of "our theatrical pastimes during the season of Lent," when, he says, there are more wicked and obscene plays permitted in London than in all the world besides, he remarks "that the ladies and the gallants come recking from the play *late on Saturday night* to their Sunday devotions; and the ideas of the farce possess their fancies to the infinite prejudice of devotion, besides the advantages it gives to our reproachful blasphemers."

Strange and exciting was the scene, on the evening of February 2nd, 1679, at the Duke's Theatre, where, blazing with diamonds, and conspicuous by her painted doll-like beauty, sat Louise de Queronaille, Duchess of Portsmouth. Some roisterers, informed of her presence, were seized with a frenzy of morality, and with drawn swords and flaming torches made their way into the pit, shouting curses upon the Duchess of Portsmouth and other persons of honour. A general *melée* ensued, in which the intruders hurled their firebrands among the affrighted actors on the stage, while they pricked and slashed the limbs and bodies of the audience, until they were overpowered and driven out. Instead of punishing the rioters, Charles punished the unoffending actors, and closed the house during the royal pleasure.

Here is another curious incident, recorded by Pepys in 1667—"how a gentleman of good habit, sitting just before us, cutting of some fruit in the midst of the play, did drop down as dead; but with much ado, Orange Moll did thrust her finger adown his throat, and brought him to life again."

It was at the Duke's Theatre in Dorset Gardens, on an April evening in 1682, that Charles, the son of Sir Edward Dering, quarrelled with a choleric young Welshman, named Vaughan, and not having room in the pit to fight it out, climbed on the stage, and exchanged thrust and pass before the excited audience. Dering got the worst of it, and was carried home, bleeding with a wound in the side; and Vaughan was detained a prisoner until the authorities were satisfied that the other offender's hurt was not mortal.

The fine gentlemen of the period would have found time hang heavy on their hands but for the hours passed in the Theatre. When weary of displaying themselves in the pit, or lounging in the boxes by the side of their lady-loves, they resorted to the tiring-rooms of the pretty actresses, and made merry with the paraphernalia of the toilette. One Saturday, in February, 1667, a certain Sir Hugh Myddelton commented with such rude freedom on the dressing processes of the nymphs of Drury Lane Theatre, that Rebecca Marshall sharply advised him to reserve his company for the ladies of the Duke's House since those who served the King did not meet with his approbation. In reply Sir Hugh, an ill-conditioned fellow, threatened he would kick, or that his footman should kick her. On the following Monday Mistress Marshall complained of this insult to the King, who, however, did not at once take notice of it. As she left the theatre on Tuesday evening, after the play, Sir Hugh hung about her, and at last whispered something to a ruffianly retainer, who thereupon followed her closely, and pressed against her with such violence that, alarmed lest he should rob or stab her, she screamed for help. The wretch for a minute or two was abashed; then, picking up some mud and refuse from the gutter, he daubed it about the actress's face and hair, and took to flight. The next day she lodged a second complaint with the King, who, some few days afterwards, issued a decree, prohibiting gentlemen from entering the tiring-rooms of the ladies of the King's Theatre. The prohibition, however, was as unwelcome to the actresses as to the beaux, and in a short time was, by mutual consent, ignored.

Of the audiences of the Restoration, that is, of those audiences so far as they were composed of fine ladies and fine gentlemen, Monsieur Henri Taine furnishes an elaborate picture. "They were rich," he says, "they had tried to deck themselves with the polish of Frenchmen; they added to the stage moveable decorations, music, lights, probability, comfort, every external aid; but they wanted heart. Imagine these foppish and half-intoxicated men, who saw in love nothing beyond desire, and in man nothing beyond sensuality; Rochester in the place of Mercutio. What part of his soul could comprehend poesy and fancy? The comedy of romance was altogether beyond his reach; he could only seize the actual world, and of this world but the palpable and gross externals. Give him an exact picture of ordinary life, commonplace and probable occurrences, literal imitations of what he himself was and did; lay the scene in London, in the current year; copy his coarse words, his brutal jokes, his conversation with the orange-girls, his rendezvous in the Park, his attempts at French dissertation. Let him recognize himself, let him find again the people and the manners he had just left behind him in the tavern or the ante-chamber; let the theatre and the street reproduce one another. Comedy will give him the same entertainment as real life; he will wallow equally well there in vulgarity and lewdness; to be present there will demand neither imagination nor wit; eyes and memory are the only requisites. This exact imitation will amuse him and instruct him at the same time. . . . The author, too, will take care to amuse him by his plot, which generally has the deceiving of a husband or a father for its subject. The fine gentlemen agree with the author in siding with the gallant; they follow his fortunes with interest, and fancy that they themselves have the same success with the fair. Add to this, women debauched, and willing to be debauched; and it is manifest how these provocations, these manners of prostitutes, that interchange of exchanges and surprises, that carnival of rendezvous and suppers, the impudence of the scenes only stopping short of physical demonstration, these songs with their double meaning, that coarse slang shouted loudly and replied to amidst the *tableaux vivants*, all that stage imitation of orgie, must have stirred up the innermost feelings of the habitual practisers of intrigue."

From the audiences we return to the actors.

When Killigrew opened the King's Theatre his company included Bateman, Baxter, Theophilus Bird, Blagden, Burt, Cartwright, Clem, Duke, Hancock, Charles Hart, Kynaston, Lacy, Mohun, Robert and William Shotterel, and Wintersel. He afterwards added Beeston, Bell, Charleton, Goodman, Griffin, Haines, Harris, Hughes, Liddell, Reeves, and Shirley. The ladies were Mrs. Corey, Eastland, Hughes, Knipp, Anne and Rebecca

Marshall, Rutter, Uphill, and Weaver; while at different dates engagements were made with Mrs. Boutell, Nell Gwynn, James, Reeves, and Verjuice. The members of the King's Company were formally sworn in at the Lord Chamberlain's office as His Majesty's servants, and the ten leading actors were not only entered on the establishment of the Royal Household, but supplied with a handsome uniform of scarlet cloth and silver lace.

To the Duke's Theatre belonged Betterton, Dixon, Lillieston, Lovell, James and Robert Nokes; and, afterwards, Blagden, Harris, Medbourne, Norris, Price, Richards, and Young. The ladies were Mrs. Betterton, Davenport, Davies, Gibbs, Holden, Jennings, and Long.

Some degree of reputation attaches to Charles Hart, the grandson of Shakespeare's sister—not to be confounded with that other Hart who served as a major in Prince Rupert's cavalry. He began his professional career by playing women's parts, but after the Restoration asserted his histrionic capacity by his Alexander the Great (in Lee's play), his Cataline (in Ben Jonson's tragedy), and his Othello. He was not less successful as Manly in Wycherley's "Plain Dealer." Rymer refers to him and Mohun as the Æsopus and Roscius of their time. His handsome presence made him a great favourite with the ladies, and we know that he was Nell Gwynn's "Charles the First." In the scandalous chronicles his name is also associated with that of the Duchess of Cleveland. Says Pepys (April 7th, 1668):—"Mrs. Knipp tells me that my Lady Castlemaine is mightily in love with Hart of their house; and he is much with her in private, and she goes to him and do give him many presents; and that the thing is most certain, and Beck Marshall only privy to it, and the means of bringing them together: which is a very odd thing, and by this means she is even with the King's love to Mrs. Davis."

The salary of this famous actor was only £3 a week; but after he became a shareholder in the theatre, his share of the profits brought his annual income up to £1,000. He quitted the stage in 1682, and retired to his country house at Great Stanmore, where he died in the following year, and was buried in the old churchyard.

To Hart's Cataline, in Ben Jonson's tragedy, Burt played Cicero. He was a good actor of solid parts, but did not succeed in characters of much force and passion.

James Nokes, the son of a vendor of toys, played women's parts at the opening of his brilliant career, and even in his later life was famous as "the Nurse" in Otway's perversion of "Romeo and Juliet," and Payne's "Fatal Jealousy." As a comedian few of his contemporaries equalled, none surpassed him: in the unctuousness of his subtle humour he seems to have resembled Munden. He studied character with a keenly observant eye, and reproduced every detail with wonderful truth to nature. Both Court and city delighted in him. Charles II., it is said, first recognized his ability when he was playing Norfolk in "Henry VIII.," and distinguished him to the last with his royal favour. In May, 1670, when the King and his Court went to Dover to meet the Queen-mother, Henrietta Maria, he was accompanied by the Duke of York's comedians, who performed before the brilliant audience the play of "Sir Solomon," founded on Molière's "L'Ecole des Femmes." Nokes played Sir Arthur Addel, which he dressed in close imitation of the costume of the French gentlemen in the Queen-mother's train. To render his equipment the more exact the Duke of Monmouth took off his own sword and belt, and buckled them to the actor's side. His caricature of the airs and graces of the Frenchmen was as perfect as his imitation of their dress, and convulsed the King and his courtiers with laughter—a curious compliment for a host to pay his guests. The Duke's sword and belt Nokes treasured as souvenirs until his death in 1692.*

Colley Cibber says of him :—

" He scarce ever made his first entrance in a play but he was received with an involuntary applause; not of hands only, for these may be, and have often been, partially prostituted and bespoken, but by a general laughter, which the very sight of him provoked, and nature could not resist; yet the louder the laugh the graver was his look upon it; and sure the ridiculous solemnity of his features were enough to have set a whole bench of bishops into a titter, could he have been honoured (may it be no offence to suppose it) with such grave and right reverend auditors. In the ludicrous distresses which, by the laws of comedy, folly is often involved in, he sunk into such a mixture of piteous pusillanimity, and a consternation so ruefully ridiculous and inconsolable, that when he had shook you to a fatigue of laughter, it became a moot point whether you ought not to have pitied him. When he debated any matter by himself, he would shut up his mouth with a dumb, studious front, and roll his full eye into such a vacant amazement, such a palpable ignorance of what to think of it, that this silent perplexity (which would sometimes hold him several minutes) gave your

* This story is told by Downes, in his " Roscius Anglicanus."

imagination as full content as the most absurd thing he could say upon it."

Another of the popular actors of the Restoration was the comedian, John Lacy. He was held in such esteem by Charles II. that he took from the best players the parts to which they had a prescriptive right by the laws of the stage and gave them to his favourite. A first-rate "all round" actor, Lacy was not less admirable as Shakespeare's Falstaff than as the Irishman Teague in Howard's farcical comedy of "The Committee." * All parts came alike to him, but for the beaux and lovers of comedy he was specially fitted by his handsome person and graceful address. He had been, in early life, a dancing-master and a soldier; and his experience in these capacities proved very useful to him on the boards. His position with the public and the King gave him so much confidence that he gave peculiar point in the dialogue he delivered to any satire which hit the vices and follies of the Court, and he seems to have interpolated sarcasms of his own. In Howard's "Silent Woman" he indulged his wit to such an extent that even the King was offended, and ordered the daring actor to be confined in the porter's lodge. On his release, a few days afterwards, Howard offered him his congratulations, which Lacy took very ill, declaring that the speeches put by the dramatist into the mouth of "Captain Otter" had wrought all the trouble, and pronouncing him more a fool than a poet; an epigrammatic way of telling the truth which goaded Howard into striking the truth-teller with his glove in

* Langbaine speaks of him as "a Comedian whose abilities in action were sufficiently known to all that frequented the King's Theatre, where he was for many years an Actor, and performed all parts that he undertook to a miracle; insomuch that I am apt to believe, that as this age never had, so the next will never have his Equal, at least not his Superior."

the face. Lacy, in return, gave the aristocratic dramatist a blow with his cane. Howard immediately carried his complaint to the King, who ordered the theatre to be closed, and thus made all the company suffer for the rashness of one of their number.

In 1671 Lacy played "Bayes" in the Duke of Buckingham's "Rehearsal," and introduced a startling and not altogether happy innovation by mimicking to the life the poet Dryden. The portrait was exact in every detail, but its cruelty was proportionate to its cleverness. Buckingham, it is said, took considerable pains in teaching Lacy.

Lacy died in 1681. Three years later his posthumous comedy, " Sir Hercules Buffoon; or, The Poetical Squire," was brought out at Drury Lane, with a prologue by Tom D'Urfey.* It did not hold the stage, and has long been forgotten. There is a triple portrait of Lacy (executed by Wright, by command of Charles II.) at Hampton Court, representing him as Teague in "The Committee," Mr. Semple in "The Cheats," and M. Galliard in "The Variety."

The visitor to Dulwich College will remember the portrait of William Cartwright, the second of the great benefactors of that noble institution. At his death he bequeathed to it his collection of pictures and his library. Before he entered the dramatic profession he had been a bookseller in Holborn, and in that capacity had acquired a knowledge of books, which explains the valuable character of his library. As an actor, he gained no small reputation, and was particularly esteemed for his Falstaff.

* Lacy also wrote "The Dumb Lady; or, The Farrier made Physician," 1672; " Old Troop; or, Monsieur Ragon," 1672; and " Sawny the Scot; or, The Taming of a Shrew," 1677.

Of another of the Restoration actors the portrait will be found at that famous seat of the Sackvilles, Knowle. Major Mohun, who in his time played many parts—an actor in the peaceful days of Charles I., then, during the Civil War, a gallant soldier on the King's side, and after the Restoration an actor again, and a very good one—was always a welcome guest at the table of the lord of Knowle, the genial Buckhurst. He excelled in such parts as Clitus and Cassius, but played the modern rakes, the Dapperwits and Pinchwifes of the new comedy, with an airy grace and vivacity which none of his imitators could approach. Off the stage he was as lovable as on it he was inimitable. When Nathaniel Lee read to him the part he was to create in one of his swelling dramas, Mohun said, with charming address, "Unless I could play the character as beautifully as you read it, 'twere vain to try it at all."

As a striking contrast to this gracious and gallant soldier-player, we put forward Cardell Goodman, whose unwholesome reputation is summed up in the expressive epithet generally attached to his name, "Scum" Goodman. His theatrical career extended over only twelve years, from 1677 to 1690. Having been expelled from Cambridge University for defacing the portrait of its Chancellor, the Duke of Monmouth, he took to the stage as a means of livelihood, and made his first appearance as Polyperchon in Nat Lee's "Rival Queens." He found a friend and associate in the actor Griffin, and the two poor players shared together their garret, their bed, and their shirt. It is related of Goodman that, forgetful (as he always was) of every rule of honesty and fairness, he wore the shirt one day when it was Griffin's turn to wear it, because he was fain to visit some frail nymph of his acquaintance. To eke out his scanty funds he borrowed horse and pistol, and played on the road the part of a highwayman; but he was arrested and thrown into Newgate, and escaped the gallows only through the favour of James II. His good looks and dashing ways soon afterwards secured him the favour of the Duchess of Cleveland. "This woman," says Oldmixon, " was so infamous in her amours, that she made no scruple of owning her lovers; among whom was Goodman the player . . . and the fellow was so insolent upon it, that one night, when the Queen was at the theatre, and the curtain, as usual, was immediately ordered to be drawn up, Goodman cried, 'Is my Duchess come?' and being answered, no, he swore terribly the curtain should not be drawn up till the Duchess came, which was at the instant, and saved the affront to the Queen."

Scum Goodman, however, was a villain at heart. Annoyed at the presence of a couple of the Duchess's children, and fearing, perhaps, that their portions would lessen his gains, he bribed an Italian quack to poison them. But the plot was discovered, and Scum for a second time became an inmate of Newgate. He was tried for a misdemeanour; had influence enough to save his worthless neck, but was compelled to pay so heavy a fine that it reduced him to poverty. He left the stage in 1690. Colley Cibber says that when he, a *débutant*, was rehearsing the small part of the Chaplain in Otway's "Orphan," Scum Goodman was so pleased that he swore with a big oath the young fellow had in him the making of a good actor.

Goodman, as became a man whose life had been saved by King James, was an ardent Jacobite, and joined in

Fenwick and Churnock's desperate scheme to assassinate William III. He had already distinguished himself as one of the first forgers of bank-notes; nothing, indeed, was too vile for him to engage in. While the details of the plot were being arranged, Goodman, Porter, Parkyns, and other confederates, endeavoured to raise a riot in London (June 10, 1695). They met at a tavern in Drury Lane, and, when hot with wine, rushed into the streets, beat kettledrums, unfurled banners, and began to light bonfires. But the watch, supported by the populace, soon overpowered the revellers, whose ringleaders were apprehended, tried, fined, and imprisoned. They regained their liberty after a few weeks, and resumed their more criminal design. It was discovered, however, and Goodman was then ready to turn informer. To save Fenwick's life, his friends were anxious to get out of the way this all-important witness, and to buy him off they employed the agency of a daring Jacobite adventurer, named O'Brien. "This man," says Macaulay, "knew Goodman well. Indeed, they had belonged to the same gang of highwaymen. They met at the Dog in Drury Lane, a tavern which was frequented by lawless and desperate men. O'Brien was accompanied by another Jacobite of determined character. A single choice was offered to Goodman, to abscond and to be rewarded with an annuity of five hundred a year, or to have his throat cut on the spot. He consented, half from cupidity, half from fear. O'Brien was not a man to be tricked. He never parted company with Goodman from the moment when the bargain was struck till they were at Saint Germains."

What became of Goodman is not known. Probably he perished in a street brawl at the hands of rogues of more nerve than he had, for the man was always a coward as well as a knave.

One of the most popular of the Duke's Company was Harris, whose portrait in his favourite character of Cardinal Wolsey was painted by Hailes, and is preserved in the Pepysian Library at Cambridge. He was a man of versatile talents, a fine singer and dancer, and a good talker, who commanded respect even from the witty and learned company that gathered round Dryden at Will's Coffee-House. He was on intimate terms with Pepys: "I do find him," says Pepys, "a very excellent person, such as in my whole acquaintance I do not know another better qualified for converse, whether in things of his own trade, or of other kind; a man of great understanding and observation, and very agreeable in the manner of his discourse, and civil, as far as is possible."

Then there was Scudamore, who took what is now called, we believe, the "juvenile lead," and played the lover, and the fine gentleman, and the chivalrous knight with a grace and spirit that charmed all beholders. He "created" the part of Garcia in Congreve's "Mourning Bride." In 1700 he married a young lady of £4,000 fortune, who had fallen in love with the gay and gallant actor, though he was then wearing old age and grey hairs.

Reference must also be made to Anthony Leigh, whose portrait is one of those at Knowle, hung there by the great patron of art and letters, the first Earl of Dorset. Cibber speaks of Dominique in Dryden's "Spanish Friar" as his best part, and it is in this part the artist has painted him. "In the courting, grave hypocrisy of the Spanish Friar, Leigh stretched the veil of piety so thinly over him, that in every look, word, and motion, you saw a palpable, wicked shyness shine throughout it. Here he kept his vivacity demurely confined, till the pretended duty of his function demanded it; and then he exerted it with a choleric, sacerdotal insolence. I have never yet seen anyone that has filled the scenes with half the truth and spirit of Leigh. I do not doubt but that the poet's knowledge of Leigh's genius helped him to many a pleasant stroke of nature, which, without that knowledge, never might have entered into his conception." Leigh was on the stage from 1672 to 1692.

One of his fellow-actors was the celebrated Smith, the original of Sir Topling Flutter (1676), Pierre (1682), Chamont (1680), and Scandal (1695), of whom an interesting anecdote is told by Cibber. "Mr. Smith," he says, "whose character as a gentleman could have been no way impeached, had he not degraded it by being a celebrated actor, had the misfortune, in a dispute with a gentleman behind the scenes, to receive a blow from him. The same night an account of this action was carried to the King, to whom the gentleman was represented so grossly in the wrong, that the next day his Majesty sent to forbid him the court upon it. This indignity cast upon a gentleman only for maltreating a player, was looked upon as the concern of every gentleman, and a party was soon found to assert and vindicate their honour, by humbling this favoured actor, whose slight injury had been judged equal to so severe a notice. Accordingly, the next time Smith acted, he was received with a chorus of cat-calls, that soon convinced him he should not be suffered to proceed in his part; upon which, without the least discomposure, he ordered the curtain to be dropped, and having a competent fortune of his own, thought the conditions of adding to it by remaining on the stage, were too dear, and from that day entirely quitted it."

He returned to it, however, in 1695; not to meet with his old favour, for the Whig portion of his audiences resented his well-known Tory sympathies. He died in the following year.

Sandford made his first appearance on the stage in 1661, two years before his colleague Smith, and remained on it two years after his colleague's death, that is, until 1698. It was his peculiar fortune to play the villain— the villain of comedy as well as of tragedy; and the audiences were so accustomed to him in this line that once when he was cast for an honest man, they showed their annoyance by hissing the piece in which he was, to their fancy, so strangely out of place. He was very great in melodramatic characters, and in all was famous for his admirable delivery. The verses of the poet gained an additional attraction from the intelligence and spirit with which he rendered them.

In Hampstead churchyard, though without monumental record, lies Jevon, who, like Lacy, began his career as a *maître de danse*. He was a fellow of infinite fun and fancy, who, in one of Settle's bombastic tragedies, having, according to the stage direction, " to fall on his sword," placed it flat on the stage, deliberately fell over it, and duly " died." At the coffee-house, an angry waiter exclaimed, " You are wiping your dirty boots with my clean napkin! " " Never mind, boy," retorted Jevon, " I'm not proud—'twill do for me." The farce of " The Devil to Pay " is based upon his little play, " A Devil of a Wife," in which he himself acted Jobson.

Cademan, like Cartwright, had been a bookseller, and

when driven from the stage by an accident—Harris, in a fencing-scene, wounded him in the eye, and the wound brought on paralysis of the tongue—returned to his original calling.

Cave Underhill was one of the earliest accessions to Davenant's company. Few actors have surpassed him in length of service; he was on the stage from 1661 to 1710; and none, perhaps, in the exquisite art with which, like our own Compton, he represented the dry and stolid wit, the malicious dunderhead, the uxorious old dotard, or the sourly humorous rustic. His "Don Quixote" was good; his "Sir Sampson Legard" (in Congreve's "Love for Love") better; and his "Grave-digger," in Hamlet best. There is a kindly notice of him in Steele's *Tatler*, 1709, in which he is commended for the naturalness and modesty of his acting, and for the fidelity with which he adhered to the words of his author.

In both these respects Joseph Haines—or Joe Haines, as his friends called him—sinned largely. He "gagged" as the whim seized him; and played always to the audience instead of to his fellow-players. A man of ready wit and easy address, he is the hero of more than one good story. Arrested on Holborn Hill by a couple of bailiffs for a debt of £20, he turned to them with a bow and a smile. "Here comes the carriage of my cousin, the Bishop of Ely; let me speak to him, and I am sure he will satisfy you in this matter." Thrusting his head in at the carriage-door, he whispered to good Bishop Patrick that the two men in waiting were Romanists, who inclined to become Protestants, but had still some scruples of conscience.

"My friends," said the Bishop, "if you will presently,

come to my house, I will satisfy you in this matter." The bailiffs duly waited upon him; an explanation soon ensued; and the Bishop, partly, I think, out of pure benevolence, and partly, perhaps, from a feeling of shame, paid the twenty pounds.

On another occasion, he deluded a simple country clergyman into accepting a situation as "Chaplain to the King's Theatre," and sent him behind the scenes, ringing a bell, and calling the actors and actresses to prayers.

In the course of an excited discussion on Jeremy Collier's " Short View of the Profaneness and Immorality of the English Stage," a critic remarked that the attack was unfair, inasmuch as the stage was a mender of morals. "True," said Haines; "but so is Collier a mender of morals, and two of a trade, you know, never agree."

Haines was once cast by Charles Hart for the part of a Senator in Ben Jonson's "Cataline," Hart himself taking the title-role. Disgusted with the character, Haines deliberately marred Hart's best scene by taking a seat behind him, in a grotesque costume; and, with pot and pipe in hand, grimacing at Cataline until the audience were convulsed with laughter. For this escapade he was rightly punished by dismissal.

Early in James II.'s reign, Haines, to secure the Court favour, announced to Lord Sunderland his conversion to Romanism, and explained that he had been led to it by a vision of the Virgin, who had said to him, "Joe, arise!" For once he met his match. The Earl did not believe in his would-be convert, and remarked that the Virgin, if she had appeared, "would have said 'Joseph,' if only out of respect for her husband!" Haines completed the farce by recanting his pretended conversion on the stage! Holding a taper, and wearing the penitential white sheet, he recited some *à propos* couplets with an effectiveness of delivery which deceived his hearers into thinking they were witty.

The date and place of Haines's birth are uncertain; but he was educated at a school in St. Martin's-in-the-Fields, whence, at the cost of some gentlemen who had admired his precocious talents, he was sent to Queen's College, Oxford. There he became acquainted with Williamson, afterwards famous as Sir Joseph, the veteran diplomatist and Minister of State, who continued his friendship when they had both left college, and appointed him his Latin Secretary on his accession to cabinet office. Haines, however, could not keep a secret, and the revelations he made to his boon companions rendered his dismissal unavoidable. Sir Joseph sent him back to make use of his scholarship at Cambridge; but falling in with a company of strolling players at Stourbridge Fair, he was fascinated by the stir and variety of the theatrical life, and after a brief experience "in the provinces," flashed forth upon Drury Lane stage to become the delight of the town.

Among his best parts were Sparkish in "The Country Wife," Roger in "Esop," Tom Corand in "The Constant Couple," Lord Plausible in "The Plain Dealer," and Captain Bluff in "The Old Bachelor." But in no part which he played did he ever fall below himself; that is, never was he otherwise than airy, sparkling, self-preserved, and inimitable. He was the Charles Matthews of the stage of the Restoration.

His theatrical career began in 1672 and ended in 1701, in which year (on the 4th of April) he died at his own house in Hart Street, Covent Garden.

Before the French custom of giving female parts to women was adopted on the English stage, one of the most popular representatives of female character was Edward Kynaston, who so excelled in this difficult *rôle* that Downes thinks it "disputable" whether any actress that succeeded him produced an equal impression on the audience. Kynaston was a mere lad when, as a member of Sir William Davenant's company, he made his first appearance "before the footlights" in 1659. His success was immediate; and he specially earned distinction, as Downes tells us, by his performance in Beaumont and Fletcher's "Loyal Subject." Pepys saw him in this character on the 18th of August, 1660:—"Captain Ferrers," he says, "took me and Creed to the Cockpit play, the first that I have had time to see since my coming from sea, 'The Loyall Subject,' where one Kynaston, a boy, acted the Duke's Sister [Olympia], but made the loveliest lady that ever I saw in my life. After the play done, we went to drink, and by Captain Ferrers' means, Kinaston, and another that acted Archas the General, came and drank with us." Pepys saw him again on the 7th of January, 1661, in Ben Jonson's "Epicene; or, The Silent Woman." "Among other things here," says Pepys, "Kynaston, the boy, had the good time to appear in three shapes: first, as a poor woman in ordinary clothes, to please Morose; then in fine clothes, as a gallant; and in these was clearly the prettiest woman in the whole house; and lastly, as a man; and then likewise did appear the handsomest man in the house."

There can be no doubt of his good looks; and Colley Cibber tells us * that ladies of quality prided themselves on taking him, after the play, dressed as he was, for a drive in Hyde Park; "which," he adds, "in those days, they might have sufficient time to do, because plays then were used to begin at four o'clock, the hour that people of the same rank are now (1740) going to dinner." On one occasion, the King entering the theatre at an unusually early hour, the curtain did not rise as usual, because the actors were not ready to begin. When Charles sent to demand the cause of the delay, the manager presented himself in the royal box, and humbly pleaded that the Queen was not yet shaved. The oddity of the excuse so tickled the King that he forgot his ill-humour.

As he grew older, Kynaston renounced his female parts, and took his place as a leading actor. It is said his voice had suffered by his early practice in the characters of women. "What makes you feel sick?" said Kynaston to Powell, one day when the latter was suffering from the effects of an over-night revel. "How can I feel otherwise," said Powell, "when I hear your voice?"

In our sketch of Sir Charles Sedley, we have referred to the courtier's cruel treatment of the actor for mimicking him, in dress and action, on the stage. He caused him to be so beaten by his bravos (on the 30th of January, 1669), that he was compelled to keep his bed for a week. He reappeared on the 9th of February, as the King of Tidore, in "The Island Princess," which "he do act very well," says Pepys, "after his beating by Sir Charles Sedley's appointment."

One of his best characters was "Don Sebastian," in

* "Apology for His Own Life," by Colley Cibber.

Dryden's tragedy of that name, in which his "lion-like majesty" was the delight of the town. He also "created," as the phrase runs, "Harcourt," in Wycherley's "Country Wife" (1675), "Freeman," in Wycherley's "Plain Dealer" (1677), and "Count Baldwin" in Southern's "Isabella" (1694). In Shakespeare's kings he made an admirable figure. Cibber remarks of his assumption of Henry IV. that it was truly regal: "when he whispered to Hotspur, 'Send us your prisoners, or you'll hear of it,' he conveyed a more terrible menace in it than the loudest intemperance of voice could swell to."

Kynaston figured on the stage full forty years—from 1659 to 1699. He did not retire too soon, for his memory had latterly begun to fail, and he acted with diminished vigour. At the time of his death (1712), he was probably about 67 years old. He bequeathed to his son a considerable fortune.

The greatest name in the history of the stage, prior to Garrick's, is that of Betterton, whose artistic genius, by common consent, was of the ripest and most comprehensive kind. In his early maturity, Pepys, no incompetent critic, pronounced him "the best actor in the world." In his later years, Steele, in *The Tattler*, declared that "such an actor ought to be rewarded with the same respect as Roscius among the Romans. I have hardly a notion," he adds, "that any performance of antiquity could surpass the action of Mr. Betterton in any of the occasions in which he has appeared upon the stage." Pope speaks of him with an enthusiasm in which he did not often indulge. And Colley Cibber regarded him with an admiration which was tinged with reverence. "I never," he says, "heard a line in tragedy come from Betterton, wherein my judgment, my ear, and my imagination were not fully satisfied, which, since his time, I cannot equally say of any one actor whatsoever. . . A further excellence in Betterton," he adds, "was that he could vary his spirit to the characters he acted. Those wild, impatient starts, that fierce and flashing fire which he throws into Hotspur, never came from the unruffled temper of his Brutus; when the Betterton Brutus was provoked, in his dispute with Cassius, his spirit flew only to his eye; his steady look alone supplied that terror, which he disdained an intemperance in his voice should rise to. Thus with a settled dignity of contempt, like an unbending rock, he repelled upon himself the foam of Cassius." How true an artist he was appears in another passage. "He had so just a sense of what was true or false applause, that I have heard him say, he never thought any kind of it equal to an attentive silence; but there were many ways of deceiving an audience into a loud one; but to keep them hushed and quiet was an applause which only truth and merit could arrive at: of which act there never was equal master to himself. From these various excellencies he had so full a possession of the esteem and regard of his auditors, that upon his entrance into every scene he seemed to seize upon the eyes and ears of the giddy and inadvertent."

This great actor and good man was the son of Charles I.'s chief cook, and was born at Tothill Street, in Westminster, which then enjoyed a more respectable reputation than has since belonged to it, about 1635. At an early age he was apprenticed to a bookseller, but a passion for the stage took possession of him, and when the theatres reopened after the fall of the Puritan party, he easily obtained an engagement.* His success was immediate; for we know from Pepys that his performance of "Hamlet" at the Lincoln's Inn Fields Theatre, in December, 1661, drew thither all the rank and fashion of London. The "Ophelia" on that occasion was Mistress Saunderson, whom he soon afterwards married (1663). As for "Hamlet," the performance was so graceful and yet dignified—the interpretation of the author was marked by such consummate intelligence—the elocution was so perfect—that the audience were stirred into an unbounded enthusiasm, and Mr. Pepys only expressed the general opinion when he exclaimed, "It's the best acted part ever done by man!" Throughout his long theatrical career, which extended just one year over half a century, his "Hamlet" remained one of his finest impersonations. Davenant, who had seen it performed by Taylor, the successor to Burbage, and the inheritor of his "points," taught him the stage traditions, and he himself elaborated the part with unceasing care and study. "When I played the Ghost to him," said Booth, "instead of awing him, he terrified me!" Cibber has recorded some details of his acting in the Ghost scene. "He opened with a pause of mute amazement; then rising slowly, to a solemn, trembling voice, he made the Ghost equally terrible to the spectator as to himself; and in the descriptive part of the natural emotions which the ghostly vision gave him, the boldness of his expostulation was still governed by decency—manly, but not braving; his voice was rising into that seeming outrage, or wild defiance of what he naturally revered."

Betterton was held in such esteem by the King, that he

* His employer, Rhodes, had been keeper of the wardrobe to the Blackfriar's company of actors, and through him he made the acquaintance of Davenant.

sent him to Paris to study the stage scenery used in the Parisian theatres, and introduce into the London playhouses such reforms as he might deem desirable. When the courtiers performed the pastoral of "Calista; or, The Chaste Nymph," before the King and Queen, Betterton was engaged to instruct the gentlemen in their parts, while the tuition of the Princesses Mary and Anne was entrusted to his wife.

From first to last Betterton was in earnest in his profession. "He is a very sober, serious man," says Pepys, "and studious, and humble, following of his studies, and is rich already with what he gets and saves." He did his best with each new part he assumed, whether it was "Bonduca" in Massinger's "Bondman," "Sir John Brute," in Vanbrugh's "Provoked Wife," or "Valentine," in Congreve's "Love for Love." A man of rare ability and judgment, his society was sought by the best wits and scholars of the time. Dryden listened to his witticisms with respect; Cowley, Otway, Rowe, and brilliant Mrs. Centlivre were among his friends; and Tillotson greatly enjoyed his conversation. Everybody knows the anecdote which illustrates the closeness of their intimacy. The great preacher professed himself unable to understand why his friend, the actor, exercised so much more influence over his hearers, over their emotions and sympathies, than he did. "You, in the pulpit," said Betterton, "only tell a story; I, on the stage, show facts." Pope was among his disciples in the actor's old age, and submitted to his criticism his juvenile epic, "Alcander, Prince of Rhodes" — of which Betterton thought sufficiently well to advise its conversion into a dramatic form.

In connection with this great actor—the glory of the stage of the Restoration—two or three good stories are told. With his savings he bought some land near Reading; and one of his tenants coming up to London to pay his rent, during the run of Bartholomew Fair, Betterton took him to see some of its surprising sights. They went into a puppet-show—the owner declining to take the usual admission fees, on the ground that Mr. Betterton was a brother actor! The rustic was so delighted with Punch that he vowed he would drink with him; nor would he be content until his conductor had taken him behind the scenes and showed him that the puppet actors were only "rags and sticks." At night he accompanied Betterton to Drury Lane Theatre, where Dryden's play of "Amphitryon" was performed, the principal* parts by Betterton and Mrs. Barry. Asked, when the curtain dropped, what he thought of them, the good clodpole, who had mistaken them for puppets, replied, "Oh, 'twas wonderful well done for sticks and rags!"

When Colley Cibber first appeared on the London stage, he was unlucky enough, in some small part he played, to put the great master out. Instant inquiry was made as to the offender's name and salary. "Colley Cibber, was it?—and he receives nothing? Then put him down ten shillings a week, and forfeit him five." Well pleased was young Cibber to pay the forfeit, and secure a regular weekly engagement.

When Betterton produced at his own theatre Rowe's "Fair Penitent," with Mrs. Barry as Calista, the part of Lothario was played by the irascible Powell. In

---

* The unsophisticated Berkshire farmer must have been much edified by this lively play, the "gratuitous indelicacy" of which has very properly been censured by Sir Walter Scott.

the last scene Lothario's dead body lies on the bier, under decent covering; and it was usual for Warren, Powell's dresser, to take his master's place, instead of a dummy. On one occasion, forgetting how he was employed, Powell called angrily for his dresser, and at last with such a threatening emphasis that the poor fellow leaped up in a hurry, and ran from the stage. In his flight it so befell that his cloak caught in the bier, which was overturned, along with table and lamps, books and boxes, and even the Fair Penitent herself. The audience broke into a peal of laughter, and the catastrophe became the jest of the town. With a proper sense of what was due to its author, Betterton stopped the play in its full flood of success, so that the public might have time to forget the untoward incident.

Justly resenting the unfair treatment to which he and his fellow-actors were subjected by the proprietors of the theatre, Betterton, in 1695, collected round him a first-rate company, and opened a new theatre in Lincoln's Inn Fields. Congreve wrote for him his "Love for Love," which was produced on the first night, and was an immense triumph. "Scarcely any comedy within the memory of the oldest man had been equally successful. The actors were so elated that they gave Congreve a share in their theatre; and he promised in return to furnish them with a play every year, if his health would permit." Two years passed, however, before he produced "The Mourning Bride," the success of which was even greater than that of "Love for Love." But gradually the new theatre ceased to attract; and no better future attended a theatre in the Haymarket, which some of Betterton's friends and admirers built for him. He had lost most of his fortune in an East Indian speculation into which he had been tempted by his friend, Sir Frederick Watson;* and a "benefit" which was given him in the season of 1708-9 was very welcome to the aged actor. In money for admission he received only £76; but the donations poured in so liberally that the net result was not less than £520. On this occasion he played Valentine in "Love for Love." Next year it was determined that the benefit should be repeated. At the time Betterton was suffering severely from gout; and before he could limp upon the stage was compelled to resort to violent medicines. The part he had chosen was Melantius in "The Maid's Tragedy" (April 10th, 1710), and he performed it with much of his old fire. But the remedies employed drove the gout to his head, and in a few days it proved fatal. He died on the 28th, and was interred with many tokens of public admiration and regret in Westminster Abbey. "Having received notice," says Sir Richard Steele, in *The Tatler* that "the famous actor, Mr. Betterton, was to be interred this evening in the cloisters near Westminster Abbey, I was resolved to walk thither and see the last offices done to a man whom I always very much admired, and from whose action I had received more strong impressions of what is great and noble in human nature, than from the arguments of the most solemn philosophers, or the descriptions of the most charming poets I have ever read."

Cibber tells us that this brilliant actor did not exceed the middle stature; that his aspect was grave and pene-

---

* Watson himself was wholly ruined, and the generous Betterton adopted his daughter (afterwards Mrs. Bowman).

trating; his limbs strongly knit rather than gracefully proportioned; and his voice, which he managed with wonderful skill, more manly than sweet. An ill-natured sketch of him by Anthony Aston—the first of the notorious race of "captious critics"—speaks of his figure as clumsy, with a large head, a short, thick neck, and a corpulent body; his eyes were small, he says, and his face was pock-marked; while he had thick legs, large feet, and short fat arms which he rarely raised above his stomach. Over these personal disadvantages, which, however, Aston certainly exaggerated, his genius completely triumphed; and even our captious critic acknowledges—what the public for half a century gladly recognized—that he was "a superlatively good actor."

Such were the principal "ornaments of the stage" when Charles II. was King. It is the misfortune of the actor that he can bequeath to posterity only a tradition and a name; his work is as fugitive as himself; nothing lives of all that he accomplishes. We have no means of comparing him with his successors, and must take his merits upon trust, in the hope that his contemporaries were not more frequently mistaken in their judgments than we are!

THE ACTRESSES.

NELL GWYNN.
MRS. HUGHES.
MRS. KNIPP.
MRS. DAVENPORT.
MARY DAVIS.

MRS. BARRY.
MRS. BETTERTON.
MRS. MOUNTFORT.
MRS. BRACEGIRDLE.

CHAPTER II.

THE ACTRESSES.

NELL GWYNN—MRS. HUGHES—MRS. KNIPP—MRS. DAVENPORT—MARY DAVIS—MRS. BARRY—MRS. BETTERTON—MRS. MOUNTFORT—MRS. BRACEGIRDLE.

OF all the frail beauties and lewd dames of Charles II.'s Court, the only one whom the public regarded with any tolerance or liking was Nell Gwynn. Perhaps this condonation of her errors was due to the fact that she had sprung, as it were, from the ranks—was "one of themselves;" perhaps it was based upon her good-nature, her frank vivacity, her lively humour. However this may be, it is certain that to the day of her death she was a popular favourite; and the anecdote collectors and annalists, treating her with equal indulgence, have so touched her portrait that even in this later time, with its higher views of womanly purity, a popular favourite she continues still. In comedy and in opera she has proved an attractive heroine; while none of Charles II.'s utterances are remembered with more sympathy than that dying one which expressed his hope that "poor Nelly" would not be allowed to starve.

The ancient world could not agree upon Homer's birthplace, and seven cities claimed him as citizen. Almost as much dubiety attends the birthplace of Eleanor Gwynn. At Hereford you are shown a small mean house in Pipe Lane, as the scene of her birth; but this is disputed by Coal Yard, Drury Lane; and yet another caveat is lodged by Oxford, where, it is said, Nell's father—a " captain," according to one authority, a " fruiterer," according to others—died in prison. As she was indisputably of Welsh extraction, I am disposed to support the claim of Hereford. Tradition relates that at a very early age she ran away from her country home; and, while in her first "teens," gained a meagre livelihood as a vendor of cheap fish. So says Rochester:—

> "Her first employment was, with open throat,
> To cry fresh herrings, even ten a groat."

Nature had gifted her with a fine voice and a sharp wit; and basket in hand she wandered from tavern to tavern, delighting their frequenters by her songs and repartees, and captivating the hearts of susceptible link-boys. For a time she seems to have officiated behind a bar. Listen to Pepys:—" Nelly and Beck Marshall falling out the other day, the latter called the other my Lord Buckhurst's mistress. Nell answered her, 'I am but one man's mistress, though I was brought up in a tavern to fill strong waters to gentlemen; and you are mistress to three or four, though a Presbyter's praying daughter.'" And it may at least be said to the credit of poor Nell that to her "protector" for the time being she was always faithful.

After a temporary passage through the hands of Madame Ross, who kept a notorious bagnio, Nell Gwynn found her way into the pit at the King's Theatre, where she sold oranges and pippins to the gallants, and bandied jests and jibes which, it is to be feared, were not always very delicate. The fresh and piquant beauty dazzled the wondering pit, and soon attracted the attention of the actors, especially of Lacy and the dashing Charles Hart. She lived with the latter for some months, and under his instruction appeared upon the stage of Drury Lane, early in 1667, as "Cydacia" in Dryden's "Indian Emperor" ... "a great and serious part" which, according to Pepys,* she did "most basely." For such characters she was suited neither physically nor mentally; and it was not until she assumed comic characters, in which she could give free vent to her infectious laugh, and show her pretty ankles and tiny feet, and sing with a natural feeling which charmed every hearer, that she became the darling of court and city. Lord Buckhurst (afterwards Earl of Dorset) soon beguiled her away from the scene of her triumphs to keep wild revel with him at Epsom.

Under the date of July, 1667, Pepys records:—"Mr. Pierce tells me what troubles me, that my Lord Buckhurst

* Pepys has several allusions to Nell Gwynn in his 1667 diary. In January he was introduced to her one day, after she had acted Cœlia in Beaumont and Fletcher's "Humorous Lieutenant":—" Knipp," he says, "took us all in, and introduced us to Nelly, a most pretty woman, who acted the great part of Cœlia to-day, very fine, and did it very well; I kissed her, and so did my wife, and a mighty pretty soul she is." Again he writes: "After dinner with my wife to the King's House to see 'The Maiden Queen,' a new play of Dryden's, mightily commended for the regularity of it, and the strain and wit, and the truth; for there is a comical part done by Nell, which is Florimel, that I never can hope ever to see the like done again by man or woman. The King and Duke of York were at the play. But so great performance of a comical part was never, I believe, in the world before as Nell do this, both as a mad girl, then most and best of all when she comes in like a young gallant; and hath the motions and carriage of a spark, the most that ever I saw any man have. It makes me, I confess, admire her." And, again, on the 1st of May:—"To Westminster, in the way meeting many milk-maids, with their garlands upon their pails, dancing with a fiddler before them, and saw pretty Nelly standing at her lodging's door in Drury Lane, in her smock sleeves and boddice, looking upon me; she seemed a mighty pretty creature."

hath got Nell away from the King's House, and gives her £100 a year, so as she hath sent her parts to the house, and will act no more." And on the 14th he writes:— "To Epsom, by eight o'clock, to the well, where much company. And to the town to the King's Head; and hear that my Lord Buckhurst and Nelly are lodged at the next house, and Sir Charles Sedley with them; and keep a merry house. Poor girl, *I pity her; but more the loss of her at the King's House.*" It may be that Nell's brusqueness of manner and freedom of speech offended the fastidious taste of Buckhurst;* at all events, their intimacy was not of long duration. As early as the 26th of August, Pepys writes:—" Sir William Penn and I had a great deal of discourse with Mall, who tells us that Nell is already left by my Lord Buckhurst, and that he makes sport of her,† and that she is very poor, and hath lost my Lady Castlemaine, who was her great friend; she is come to the play-house, but is neglected by them all."

This neglect must have been very transient; for before the end of the year she was again the ornament of the stage and the delight of the play-going public. Her Florimel in "The Maiden Queen," and her Jacinta in "The Mock Astrologer," were particularly admired; and her enlarged experience enabled her to treat serious characters with greater success than before. Her Almahide in Dryden's " Conquest of Granada " (1674) was the talk of the town, and had not been forgotten when Lord

---

* Nell Gwynn seems to have had, however, a real attachment to the accomplished nobleman, whom she called her "Charles I." In that case, Major Charles Hart, the actor, would be her " Charles II.," though it is generally supposed that he had the precedence of Buckhurst. The King was, of course, " her Charles III."

† From what we know of Buckhurst's character, this seems difficult of belief.

Lansdowne, a quarter of a century later, referred to the impression it had produced upon King Charles:—

> "Past is the gallantry, the fame remains
> Transmitted safe in Dryden's lofty strains;
> Granada lost beheld her pomps restored,
> And Almahide once more by kings adored."

In Dryden's play Major Charles Hart, Nell's old lover, played Almanzor; and his relation to Almahide and King Boabdelin being exactly that which off the stage he held towards Nell Gwynn and King Charles, every passage touching upon it was received by the audience with a laughter which pointed the joke.

At the rival theatre Nokes, the comedian, had recently saved a tedious play by wearing an immense hat. Dryden immediately caused one to be made for Nell, of the size of a cart-wheel. She wore it while delivering the prologue, and her quaintly humorous appearance and piquant manners produced quite "a sensation."

It was as Valeria in Dryden's "Tyrannic Love" that the audacious quean completed her conquest of the easy heart of Charles. Dryden, we are told, wrote the part with this result in view, and also the lively epilogue, spoken just as the dead Valeria is about to be carried off by bearers. We transcribe it here; and the reader can easily imagine with what dash and vivacity Mistress Nelly would deliver it. How, suddenly starting to her feet, and assuming an air of mock indignation, she would rattle away at her would-be bearers,—

> "Hold! are you mad? you d—d confounded dog,
> I am to rise, and speak the Epilogue."

Then, with a complete change of voice—a smile, and a pert *moue*—turning to the audience:

" I come, kind gentlemen, strange news to tell ye ;
I am the ghost of poor departed Nelly.
Sweet ladies, be not frightened: I'll be civil,
I'm what I was, a little harmless devil.
For, after death, we sprites have just such natures
We had, for all the world, when human creatures:
And, therefore, I, that was an actress here,
Play all my tricks in hell, a goblin there.
Gallants, look to 't, you say there are no sprites ;
But I'll come down about your beds at night.
And faith you'll be in a sweet kind of taking,
When I surprise you between sleep and waking.
To tell you true, I walk, because I die,
Out of my calling in a tragedy.
O poet, d—d dull poet, who could prove
So senseless, to make Nelly die for love !
Nay, what's yet worse, to kill me in the prime
Of Easter-term, in tart and cheese-cake time !
I'll fit the fop, for I'll not one word say
To excuse his godly out-of-fashion play ;
A play which if you dare but twice sit out,
You'll all be slandered, and be thought devout.
But, farewell, gentlemen, make haste to me,
I'm sure we long to have your company.
As for my epitaph when I am gone,
I'll tend no poet, but will write my own :—
Here Nelly lies, who, though she lived a slattern,
Yet died a Princess, acting in St. Cat'rine."

Thenceforward the stage saw Nell Gwynn no more. She had stipulated that £500 a year should be settled on her. This Charles refused; but the influence she obtained over him was so great that, within four years, she had received £60,000. Subsequently, she was placed on the Excise as a pensioner for £6,000 a year, and for £3,000 more for the expenses of each of her two sons :—Charles Beauclerc, born in her house in Lincoln's Inn Fields, in May, 1670, and James, born in the following year, at her house in Pall Mall. The latter died in 1680. The elder, who had Otway for his tutor, was created Earl of Burford in 1676, and Duke of St. Albans in 1684.* The present ducal family of St. Albans is descended from him.

The fetters of Court etiquette—never very heavy in the reign of the second Charles—sat lightly enough upon the wayward and audacious Nelly. She rattled out her small oaths; she exchanged brisk repartees with whomsoever was bold enough to encounter her sharp and ready wit; and when her royal master sank into one of his graver moods,

". . . . . would still be jocund,
And chuck the royal chin of Charles the Second."

On one occasion, Bowman, the actor, then a young man, famous for his fine voice, had been engaged to take part in a concert at her house, and the King, with the Duke of York and two or three courtiers, were present. At the close of the performance Charles expressed himself highly pleased. "Then, sir," said Nell Gwynn, "to show you don't speak like a courtier, I hope you will make the performers a handsome present." The King said he had no money about him, and asked the Duke if he had any. "I believe, sir," said the Duke, "not above a guinea or two." Then, with her delightful laugh, Nell turned to the people about her, and boldly adopting the King's favourite oath, "Od's fish!" she cried, "What company have I got into!"

The grave Evelyn relates that, accompanying the King

---

* Madam Ellen, as she was called after her instalment as the King's mistress, secured her son's advancement to a title by a characteristic device. One day, when the King was in her apartments, the boy was amusing himself in some childish game. " Come here," she cried, " you little bastard ! " The King reproving her for using an epithet which, if justifiable, was certainly offensive, " Indeed," she replied, " I am very sorry, but I have no other name to give him, poor boy ! " Charles took the hint, and gave him a name and a title.

during one of his daily constitutional walks in the Park, in 1671, he could not but overhear "a very familiar discourse" between his Majesty and the "impudent comedian." She was looking out of her garden, on a terrace at the top of a wall, while the King stood on the green walk beneath. No wonder Evelyn was scandalized at what he saw and heard. This house stood on the south side of Pall Mall; it was given by the King to Nell Gwynn on a long lease. The story runs, that on her discovering it to be only a lease under the Crown she returned him the lease and conveyance, saying she had always "conveyed free" under the Crown, and always would; and would not accept it till it was conveyed free to her by an Act of Parliament, made on and for that purpose. It was afterwards in the possession of the famous physician Heberden; and, until recently, was occupied by the Society for the Propagation of the Gospel in Foreign Parts. It is now numbered 79. She had previously lived on the other side of Pall Mall, in a house on the left-hand of St. James's Square, the site of which is occupied by the present Army and Navy Club. She had also a house by the river-side, two miles out of town, built, it is said, by the architect of Chelsea Hospital, and later known as Sandford Manor House. The tradition is that the King's Road received its name from the King's frequent visits to this spot. At Windsor she resided in Burford House, in which she was succeeded by the Princess Anne. Her name is also associated with Lauderdale House, Highgate (now a convalescent branch of St. Bartholomew's Hospital); where, according to a popular myth, she received Charles's recognition of her infant, afterwards Duke of St. Alban's, by holding it out of a window, and threatening to let it fall unless he gave it a title.

When Charles II. visited Winchester in the spring of 1681, to superintend the erection of a stately palace which he had projected, he was accompanied by Nell Gwynn, and desiring to lodge her close to his own apartments at the Deanery, he demanded her admittance to the adjoining prebendal residence of the illustrious Ken. With all the courage of a truly virtuous mind the future Bishop refused the royal request. "Not for his kingdom!" was the uncompromising answer; and Charles had the good sense to admire his chaplain's conscientiousness.

Nor did Nell Gwynn take offence. To do her justice, she made no hypocritical pretence of virtue, but candidly acknowledged her dishonourable position. In February, 1680, when she visited the Duke's Theatre, in Lincoln's Inn Fields, a person in the pit loudly applied to her the coarse name which the language of the streets bestows upon lewd women. She heard it with a laugh; but with mistaken chivalry it was resented by Thomas Herbert, afterwards Earl of Pembroke,—perhaps because he had married the younger sister of another of the King's favourites, Louise de la Querouaille. A commotion ensued. Some of the audience sided with Nelly's champion, others with her assailant. Swords were drawn, and a few scratches exchanged, before the unseemly quarrel could be subdued. She was one day driving through the streets of Oxford, when the populace, mistaking her for the French harlot, the Duchess of Portsmouth, who was, of course, a Roman Catholic, began to hurl at her the foulest epithets in their vocabulary. Nell put her head out of the coach window. "Good people," she said, with that charming laugh of hers, which nobody could resist, "you are mistaken; I am the Protestant w—e!"

The rivalry between Nell and the infamous Duchess of Portsmouth was open and avowed, and a curious picture of it is drawn in one of her letters by Madame de Sevigné. "The Duchess of Portsmouth," she writes, "has not failed in anything she proposed to herself. She desired to be mistress to the King, and so she is; he lodges with her almost every night, in the face of the Court; she has had a son, who has been acknowledged, and presented with a couple of duchies. She accumulates wealth, and makes herself feared and respected by as many as she can. But she did not anticipate that she should find in her way a young actress, on whom the King dotes; and from whom she finds it impossible to withdraw him. He divides his time, his care, and his health between the two. The actress is not less haughty than the Duchess; she insults her, she makes grimaces at her, she attacks her: she frequently steals the King from her, and boasts whenever he gives her the preference. She is young, indiscreet, confident, wild, and of an agreeable humour. She sings, she dances, and she acts with a good grace. She has a son by the King, and hopes to have him acknowledged. For she reasons thus: 'This Duchess pretends to be a person of quality; she affirms that she is related to the best families in France, and whenever any person of distinction dies, she puts herself in mourning.* If she

---

* It was the custom of Mademoiselle de la Querouaille to put on mourning at the death of any member of the French aristocracy, on the pretence that she was related to all the great families of France. A French prince dying about the same time as the Cham of Tartary, Mademoiselle put on mourning, and so did Nelly, who, when asked for whom she wore sable, laughingly replied, " Oh, for the Cham of Tartary, who was quite as nearly related to me as the Prince de —— was to Mademoiselle de Querouaille."

be a lady of such quality, why does she lower herself to be a courtesan? She ought to die with shame. As for me, it is my profession; I pretend to nothing better. The King entertains me, and I am constant to him at present. He has a son by me; I profess that he ought to acknowledge him; and I am well assured that he will, for he loves me as well as he loves the Duchess.'"

The popular affection for Nell Gwynn was probably due in no small degree to the popular hatred of the Duchess of Portsmouth. The latter was a foreigner and a Papist; the former was English-born and a Protestant. These facts are duly insisted upon in a pasquinade, entitled, "A Pleasant Battle between Two Lap-dogs of the Utopian Court," which Mr. Jesse quotes. Part of the argument is, he says, as follows:—

> "The English lap-dog here does first begin
> The vindication of his lady, Gwynn:
> The other, much more Frenchified, alas,
> Shows what his lady is, not what she was."

The two curs, Tutty (Nell Gwynn's) and Snap-Short (the Duchess of Portsmouth's), discuss with much freedom the qualities of their respective mistresses, who, in the middle of the contention, enter the room, and themselves take up the cudgels:—

"DUCHESS OF PORTSMOUTH.—Pray, Madam, give my dog fair play; I protest you hinder him with your petticoats; he cannot fasten. Madam, fair play is fair play.

"MADAM GWYNN.—Truly, Madam, I thought I knew as well what belonged to dog-fighting as your ladyship: but since you pretend to instruct me in your French dog-play, pray, Madam, stand a little farther; as you respect your own flesh, for my little dog is mettle to the back, and smells a Popish Miss at a far greater distance: pray,

Madam, take warning, for you stand on dangerous ground. Haloo, haloo, haloo : ha brave Tutty, ha brave Snap-Short ! A guinea on Tutty,—two to one on Tutty: done, quoth Monsieur ; begar, begar, we have lost near tousand pound.

> "Tutty it seems beat Snap-short, and the bell
> Tutty bears home in victory : farewell !" *

Against Nell Gwynn's many vices, her immorality, her gambling habits, her wild extravagance,* her love of strange oaths, we may set that one great virtue of Charity, which covers, as we know, a multitude of sins. She was generous by nature, and no case of distress came to her knowledge but her hand was immediately open. The story that she persuaded Charles to build Chelsea Hospital may be apocryphal ; but at all events it shows the popular conviction of her goodness of heart. Poor men of genius found in her a liberal benefactress, as Dryden and Butler, Otway and Nathaniel Lee were ready to acknowledge.

Nell Gwynn died at her house in Pall Mall in November, 1687. She was only thirty-eight years of age. It is noticeable that most of the frail beauties and dashing cavaliers of the Merry Monarch's saturnalian reign passed from the scene while still comparatively young. The reason is not far to seek : they lived at high-pressure. To borrow a phrase from the sporting world, the pace was too fast, and they exhausted their stock of vitality in an endless round of intrigue, revelry, and dissipation. The immediate cause of Nell Gwynn's death was apoplexy. She lingered for some weeks after the first attack, and gave many tokens of her sorrow for the failings and follies

---

* This may be forgiven, perhaps, to one who rose from indigence to the enjoyment of almost unlimited wealth.

in which she had wasted her feverish life. "Her repentance in her last hours," says Cibber, "I have been unquestionably informed appeared in all the contrite symptoms of a Christian sincerity."

She was buried in the church of St. Martin's-in-the-Fields, and Dr. Tenison, the vicar, preached a funeral sermon in which he warmly and frankly praised her kindness of heart and her charities, and bore testimony to the sincerity of her earnestness and the peace of her last hours. This discourse was brought to the notice of Queen Mary, at a later period, in the hope it would injure the Doctor's chances of perferment. But with characteristic good sense the Queen replied :—"I have heard as much; it is a sign that the poor unfortunate woman died penitent; for if I can read a man's heart through his looks, had she not made a pious and Christian end, the Doctor would never have been induced to speak well of her."

Of the birth or antecedents of Mrs. Hughes the historians of the stage say nothing. She first came before the public in 1663, after the opening of the theatre in Drury Lane, and was the first female representative (it is said) of Desdemona. Less by her artistic than by her personal gifts she charmed the town. When the Court was at Tunbridge Wells in 1668, drinking the waters, raffling for toys, lace, or gloves, jesting with the country girls in the market, and at evening assembling on the bowling-green, where those who liked could dance "upon a turf more soft and smooth than the finest carpet in the world," the Queen sent for the players, and among them came Mistress Hughes, with such a splendour of loveliness that she took captive the grave and reserved Prince Rupert. Abandoning his laboratory, with its alembics, crucibles, and forges, he laid siege to the proud beauty, and renounced his "chemical speculations" for the more critical study of a woman's varying moods. "The impertinent gipsy," says Count Hamilton, with his usual indifference to the claims of virtue, "chose to be attacked in form, and proudly refusing money, that in the end, she might sell her favours at a dearer rate, she caused the poor Prince to act a part so unnatural, that he no longer appeared like the same person. The King was greatly pleased with that event, for which great rejoicings were made at Tunbridge—'what a strange condition of society this one fact reveals!'—but nobody was bold enough to make it the subject of satire, though the same constraint was not observed respecting the follies of other personages."

The Prince was supposed to have been preceded in her goodwill by Sir Charles Sedley. Pepys, who had had the privilege of saluting her with a kiss in the green-room at Drury Lane in May, 1668, describes her as "the pretty woman called Pegg, that was Sir Charles Sidley's mistress . . a mighty pretty woman, and seems, but is not, modest." But the curse of lewdness then rested upon the stage, and scarcely man or woman escaped it.

Margaret Hughes was settled by her princely "protector" in the house at Hammersmith, built by Sir Nicholas Crispe, which, in 1683, the Prince purchased from his nephew, and presented to her. She resided in it for ten years, and then sold it to one Timothy Lanney, "a scarlet dyer."* She had one daughter by the Prince, Ruperta, who became the wife of General Howe.

* In 1748 it was purchased by Bubb Dodington, and in 1792 by the Margrave of Brandenburg-Anspach, who named it "Brandenburg House." In 1820 it was tenanted by Queen Caroline, wife of George IV.

Among the most prominent figures in Pepys' picture-gallery is the pretty, sweet-voiced, lively, and clever Mistress Knipp (or Knep), for whom our immortal diarist had evidently a strong partiality. As an actress she excelled in the parts of fine ladies, ladies' maids, and milk maids; she dressed with taste, acted with intelligence, and sang with natural skill and feeling. Her delivery of a prologue was always a feat of elocution. Mrs. Knipp was unfortunate in her husband, a horse-jockey, who ill-treated and even beat her; but she seems never to have forgotten her duty as a wife, though Mrs. Pepys called her "a wench," and disapproved very strongly of her husband's attentions to the fascinating actress. Her career on the stage extended from 1664 to 1678, during which period she acted sixteen different characters.

The first reference to her in Pepys is under the date "December 6th, 1665," when he was spending some merry hours at the house of his friends, Mr. and Mrs. Pierce. "The best company for music I ever was in in my life," he says, "and wish I could live and die in it, both for musique and the face of Mrs. Pierce, and my wife, and Knipp, who is pretty enough, but the most excellent, mad-humoured thing, and sings the noblest that ever I heard in my life."

On the following day the same company met at Pepys' house:—"Most excellent musique we had in abundance, and a good supper, dancing, and a pleasant scene of Mrs. Knipp's rising sick from table, but whispered me it was for some hard word or other her husband gave her just now when she laughed, and was more merry than ordinary. But we got her in humour again, and mighty merry." She seems to have been of an April nature; alternating between smiles and tears.

Thenceforward the name of Mrs. Knipp turns up constantly in the wonderful Diary. One day at Lord Brouncker's he meets his "dear Mrs. Knipp," and sings with her, and hears her sing, admiring particularly her little Scotch song of "Barbara Allen." Next day he receives a letter from her to which she has subscribed "Barbary Allen" as her name; and he sends an answer to it, signing himself "Dapper Dicky." On another occasion comes Mrs. Knipp to speak with him privately, "complaining how like a devil her husband treats her"—a strange confidence for a wife to repose in the ears of her husband's friend!

A curious illustration of the manners of the time comes out in the entry for January 18th, 1666:—"To Captain Cocke's, where Mrs. Williams was, and Mrs. Knipp. I was not heartily merry, though a glass of wine did a little cheer me. After dinner to the office [at the Admiralty]. Anon comes to me thither my Lord Brouncker, Mrs. Williams, and Mrs. Knipp. I brought down my wife in her night-gown, she not being indeed very well, to the office to them. My wife and I anon and Mercer, by coach, to Pierce's, when mighty merry, and sing and dance with great pleasure; and I danced, who never did in company in my life." This was at a time when the Plague was gathering up its last harvest of victims in the Metropolis, "the deaths being now but 79" (in the week) says Pepys.

We pass on to February 23rd:—"Comes Mrs. Knipp to see my wife, and I spent all the night talking with this baggage, and teaching her my song of 'Beauty, retire,' which she sings and makes go most rarely, and a very fine song it seems to be. She also entertained me with repeating many of her own and others' parts of the playhouse, which she do most excellently; and tells me the whole practices of the play-house and players, and is in every respect most excellent company."

Mrs. Knipp, indeed, can no more be kept out of Mr. Pepys's written confidences, than "the head of King Charles I." out of the speeches of Mr. Dick. On the 20th, Mrs. Knipp dines with Mr. and Mrs. Pepys, and mighty pleasant company she is, so that the careful Pepys actually gives his wife 20s. "to lay out on Knipp." She is the fortunate recipient of six pairs of gloves on Valentine's Day. On the 9th of March he and Mrs. Pierce and the charming actress set out to dine at Chelsea, but are frightened back by a report that the inn there was "shut up of the plague." On the 9th of May he accompanies them to Cornhill; on his return finds his wife "mightily vexed at his being abroad with other women" (as she had some right to be), so that when they were gone she called them names, which offended Mr. Pepys' sense of propriety. On the 6th of August we have further evidence of Mrs. Pepys' not unreasonable displeasure:—
"After dinner, in comes Mrs. Knipp, and I sat and talked with her. . . I very pleasant to her; but perceive my wife hath no great pleasure in her being here. However, we talked and sang, and were very pleasant. By and by comes Mr. Pierce and his wife. . . Knipp and I sang, and then I offered to carry them home, and to take my wife with me, but she would not go; so I with them leaving my wife in a very ill humour. However, I would not be removed from my civility to them, but sent for a coach,

and went with them; and in our way, Knipp saying that she came out of doors without a dinner to us, I took them to Old Fish Street, to the very house and woman where I kept my wedding dinner, where I never was since, and then I did give them a jole of salmon, and what else was to be had. And here we talked of the ill-humour of my wife, which I did excuse as much as I could, and they seemed to admit of it, but did both confess they wondered at it. . . . I set them both at home, Knipp at her house, her husband being at the door; and glad she was to be found to have stayed out so long with me and Mrs. Pierce, and none else. Home, and then find my wife mightily out of order, and reproaching Mrs. Pierce and Knipp as wenches, and I know not what. But I did give her no words to offend her, and quietly let all pass."

Mrs. Knipp does not reappear in the Diary until October 25th, when Pepys notes that he met her at Mrs. Williams's, and "was glad to see the jade." His wife's "ill-humour," no doubt, had something to do with her long absence. We may assume, however, that by this time Mrs. Pepys had got over it, since she accompanied Knipp and Mr. and Mrs. Pierce to the new playhouse at Whitehall. In November Mr Pepys goes to "Knipp's lodgings, whom I find," he says, "not ready to go home with me, and then staid reading of Waller's verses while she finished dressing, her husband being by. Her lodging very mean, and the condition she lives in; yet makes a show without doors, God bless us!"

One of the saddest stories in Count Grammont's "Memoirs"—a book which, from the moralist's point of view, is full of melancholy stories—is that of which Mrs. Davenport, the "Roxalana" of Sir William Davenant's "Siege of Rhodes" was the heroine. Count Hamilton tells it with more feeling than he exhibits on any other occasion:—

"The Earl of Oxford (Aubrey de Vere, 20th Earl, and the last of his house who held the title) fell in love with a handsome, graceful actress belonging to the Duke's Theatre, who performed to perfection, particularly the part of Roxana, in a very fashionable new play, inasmuch that she ever after retained that name : this creature being both very virtuous, and very modest, or, if you please, wonderfully obstinate, proudly rejected his addresses and presents. This resistance influenced his passion ; he had recourse to invectives, and even to spells ; but all in vain. This disappointment had such effect upon him that he could neither eat nor drink ; this did not signify to him ; but his passion at length became so violent that he could neither play nor smoke. In this extremity love had recourse to Hymen : the Earl of Oxford, one of the first peers of the realm, is, you know, a very handsome man ; he is of the order of the Garter, which greatly adds to an air naturally noble. In short, from his outward appearance, you would suppose he was really possessed of some sense ; but as soon as ever you hear him speak you are perfectly convinced of the contrary. This passionate lover presented her with a promise of marriage, in due form, signed with his own hand ; she would not, however, rely upon this ; but the next day she thought there could be no danger, when she and himself came to her lodgings, attended by a clergyman, and another man for a witness : the marriage was accordingly solemnized with all due ceremonies in the presence of one of her fellow-players, who attended as a witness on her part. You will suppose, perhaps, that the new countess had nothing to do but to appear at court according to her rank, and to display the Earl's arms upon her carriage. This was far from being the case. When examination was made concerning the marriage it was found to be a mere deception: it appeared that the pretended priest was one of my Earl's trumpeters, and the witness his kettle-drummer. The parson and his companion never appeared after the ceremony was over; and as for the other witness, they endeavoured to persuade her that the Sultana Roxana might have supposed, in some part or other of a play, that she was really married. It was all to no purpose that the poor creature claimed the protection of the laws of God and man, both which were violated and abused, as well as herself, by this infamous imposition; in vain did she throw herself at the King's feet to demand justice; she had only to rise up again without redress; and happy might she think herself to receive an annuity of one thousand crowns, and to resume the name of Roxana instead of Countess of Oxford."

It seems, however, to have been through the King's interposition that "Lord Oxford's Miss," as Evelyn calls her, obtained her annuity (£300). In due time she recovered her spirits, and Pepys records that at the play he saw "the old Roxalan in the chief box, in a velvet gown, as the fashion is, and very handsome, at which I was glad."

Mary Davis, or Davies, reported to be the natural daughter of Charles Howard, second Earl of Berkshire, though some authorities claim for her a more honourable origin as the lawful daughter of a blacksmith, appeared at the Duke's Theatre early in 1667, and by her good looks, graceful dancing, and fine voice soon (and by no means reluctantly) attracted the attention of the King, whose conquest she completed by her admirable singing—in the character of Celania, in "The Mad Shepherdess"—of the old song, "My lodging is on the cold ground." We will hope that Pepys romances when he declares that her own father acted the part of Pandar. The King caused a house to be furnished for her in Suffolk Street, and presented her with a ring worth £700. Pepys chanced, on one occasion, to be passing through the street as the King's mistress was stepping into her coach, and a "mighty fine coach" it was, he says.

The rise of this new favourite, who presumed not a little upon her scandalous prosperity, was very unwelcome at Court. When she was to dance a jig in the presence of the enamoured sovereign, the Queen, we are told, retired hastily, as if unwilling to be publicly insulted. The imperious Duchess of Cleveland was unable to conceal her indignation. On the authority of one of the ladies of the Court, Pepys relates that during some private theatricals at Whitehall the King's eyes were fixed so constantly on the charming Moll that the angry Duchess was "in the sulks" during the whole of the play. On another occasion, when Pepys was at the theatre, the King, throughout the evening, kept his gaze at a particular box, where shone the temporary loadstar of his fickle affections. The Duchess of Cleveland lifted her eyes to discover the object of the King's demonstrative regard, and when she perceived who it was, broke out into such a passion that "she looked like fire."

Of the later history of Mary Davis nothing is known. She had a daughter by the King in 1673, who received the name of Mary Tudor, and in 1687 married the second Earl of Derwentwater. Their son was the brave and chivalrous young nobleman who lost his head for his share in the Rebellion of 1715. Thus, the grandson of Charles II. became the victim of his loyalty to the royal house with which he was himself by blood connected. Before his death the Duke of Richmond, son of Charles II. by Louise de la Querouaille, was requested to present to the Lords a memorial on behalf of the young Earl, his kinsman. He presented the memorial, but with astounding inhumanity expressed his earnest hope that their lordships would not suffer themselves to be influenced by it.

About the time that Moll Davis left the stage a bright particular star rose upon its horizon in the person of Mrs. Elizabeth Barry, the original "Belvidera" of Otway's "Venice Preserved," and the "Zara" of Congreve's "Mourning Bride."

Elizabeth Barry was the daughter of Robert Barry, a loyal barrister, who, in the Civil War, raised a regiment for the King, and was rewarded with the rank of Colonel. He fell into great poverty during the Protectorate, and left his daughter (who was born in 1658) nothing but his honourable name. She found a friend in Sir William Davenant, who, struck by her beauty and vivacity, sought to train her for the stage, but failed to awaken the dormant talent. Thrice she was rejected by the managers as possessing none of the qualifications of an actress. Such however, was not the opinion of Rochester, who lodged her in his house in Lincoln's Inn Fields, and with infinite skill and patience educated her for her profession. He made her repeat every sentence of her author until she fully understood its meaning, and could render it with suitable expression. The management of the voice, the employment of appropriate gesture, the assumption of graceful attitudes; he neglected nothing which could render her proficiency indisputable; and to accustom her to the stage he superintended thirty rehearsals, twelve of which were "dress rehearsals" of each of the characters she was to represent. In all these pains he was actuated by his love of the charming young actress, who, to judge from his letters, exercised a considerable influence over him to the very end of his career.

About 1671 she appeared on the stage, but failed to captivate the fancy of her audience, until she enacted Isabella, the Hungarian Queen, in "Mustapha," Lord Brooke's once-famous tragedy. Thenceforward her progress was sure, if slow; and, in 1680, she placed herself at the head of her profession by her brilliant performance of Monimia, in Otway's tragedy of "The Orphan; or, The Unhappy Marriage." This was the nineteenth of her original characters; but the first with which she succeeded in really identifying herself. In 1682, all London flocked to see her Belvidera in Otway's finest drama, and to be moved to tears by the intensity of her pathos. Her genius was so true and profound that she could take the skeleton-character of the dramatist, and endue it with flesh and blood—a task she performed for Cassandra in Dryden's bombastic tragedy of "Cleomenes" (1692). "Mrs. Barry," says the poet in his preface, "always excellent, has in this tragedy excelled herself, and gained a reputation beyond any woman I have ever seen in the theatre." "In characters of greatness," says Colley Cibber, "Mrs. Barry had a presence of elevated dignity;

her mien and motion superb, and gracefully majestic; her voice full, clear, and strong; so that no violence of passion could be too much for her; and when distress or tenderness possessed her, she subsided into the most affecting melody and softness. In the art of exciting pity, she had a power beyond all the actresses I have yet seen, or what your imagination can conceive. In scenes of anger, defiance, or resentment, while she was impetuous and terrible, she poured out the sentiment with an enchanting harmony; and it was this particular excellence for which Dryden made her the above-recited compliment, upon her acting Cassandra in his Cleomenes. She was the first person whose merit was distinguished by the indulgence of having an annual benefit play, which was granted to her alone in King James's time, and which did not become common to others till the division of this company, after the death of King William and Queen Mary."

Another of her finest impersonations was Isabella in Southern's drama of "The Fatal Marriage" (1694). In 1697 she gave fresh proof of her versatility by enacting the two opposite characters of Lady Brute in Vanburgh's "Provoked Wife" and Zara in Congreve's "Mourning Bride." In 1703 she enacted Calista in Rowe's tragedy of "The Fair Penitent" (founded on "The Fatal Dowry" of Massinger); and in 1705, Clarissa, in Sir John Vanburgh's comedy of "The Confederacy." About three years later, ill-health compelled her to retire from the stage; her last new character of importance being Phœdra, in Edmund Smith's tragedy of that name (1708). She returned, however, for one night, in the following year, to play with Mrs. Bracegirdle; and she performed Mrs. Frail, in Congreve's "Love for Love," on the occasion of Betterton's benefit. Her last years were spent at Acton in the enjoyment of the wealth she had gained by her genius and preserved by her prudence; and she died of fever,* "greatly respected,"—in her case no mere form of words—on the 7th of November, 1713. She lies buried in Acton churchyard.

Two of her speeches, or phrases, which always commanded the applause of her admiring audiences, have been handed down to us: "Ah, poor Castalio!" in Otway's "Orphan," and "What mean my grieving subjects?" in Banks's "Unhappy Favourite." In the latter play she represented Queen Elizabeth, and with so much dignity that Mary of Modena, the wife of James II., as a mark of her approbation, presented her with the dress she had worn upon her marriage.

The charm of Mrs. Barry's beauty lay in its expression. Her eyes and forehead were fine, but it was "the mind, the music breathing o'er the face" that rivetted the gaze of the beholder. Her rich dark hair, drawn back from her brow, revealed its gracious curve. Her mouth was mobile and full of expression, though, according to Tony Aston, it opened a little too much on the right side. She was not below the average height, and her figure was plump and well-made.

Her powers were seen to the best advantage in tragedy; but her comic characters were distinguished by their freedom and vivacity. "In comedy," says Tony Aston, "she was alert, easy, and genteel, pleasant in her face and action, filling the stage with variety of gesture."

---

* Cibber says that during her delirium, she dropped into blank verse, saying—in remembrance, apparently, of Queen Anne's creation, in 1711, of twelve peers at once!—

"Ah, ah! and so they make us lords by dozens."

She yielded so entirely to the emotions she was called upon to depict, that in stage dialogues she often turned pale or flushed red, as varying passions prompted.

In Nathaniel Lee's "Rival Queens; or, The Death of Alexander the Great," she, on one occasion, played Roxana to Mrs. Boutell's Statira. A dispute arose between the ladies as to the wearing of a certain veil, which the latter affirmed to belong to her part; and the stage-manager decided in her favour. Both actresses went upon the stage with their passions strongly excited, and probably the wrath and jealousy with which the dramatist endows the rival queens were never more faithfully represented. When, in the gardens of Semiramis, Roxana seizes her hated enemy, and a final struggle takes place, Mrs. Barry exclaiming, "Die, sorceress, die! and all my wrongs die with thee!" drove her keen dagger right through Statira's steel-bound stays. A slight wound was the result; and a considerable commotion. When the matter came to be investigated, Mrs. Barry protested that she had been carried away by the excitement of the scene; but there were not wanting censorious tongues to declare that she enjoyed the punishment she had inflicted on a rival.

To dwell on the record of Mrs. Barry's frailties would be humiliating and unprofitable. Like most of the actresses of her time, she lived a life of unbridled indulgence, which the contemporary wits of the coffee-houses knew how to paint in the darkest colours. She had a daughter by Sir George Etherege, who died before her mother. Tom Brown censures her avarice; others speak of her as cold and heartless; but the woman to whom poor Otway addressed the six pathetic letters preserved in his published works could not have been without some singular charm.

As Mrs. Betterton does not figure in the *Chroniques Scandaleuses* of the Merry Monarch's reign, we know but little of her history; but for thirty years she was on the stage, and all that time she ranked amongst its greatest ornaments. As Miss Saunderson she won the heart and hand of the great actor, Thomas Betterton; and it is on record that she played Ophelia to his Hamlet, during the period of his courtship, and that the audience dwelt with particular interest on their dramatic love-passages, knowing that the two were shortly to be united in wedlock. Their married life was without a cloud; as their professional careers were without a failure. So profound was Mrs. Betterton's love for her noble husband, that at his death, in 1710, she lost her reason, and survived him only eighteen months.

Pepys always refers to this charming actress as Ianthe, from the part she played in Davenant's "Siege of Rhodes." His numerous allusions evidence the esteem in which she was held by the public. It was due to her artistic merits as well as to her unblemished private character that she was chosen, in 1674, to instruct the Princesses Mary and Anne in elocution. Afterwards, she was engaged to teach the Princess Anne the part of Semandra in Lee's noisy tragedy of "Mithridates." When Betterton died, Queen Anne settled on his widow a pension of £500 a year.

Cibber says—" She was so great a mistress of Nature, that even Mrs. Barry, who acted Lady Macbeth after her, could not in that part, with all her superior strength and melody of voice, throw out those quick and careless strokes of terror, from the disorder of a guilty mind, which the other gave us, with a facility in her manner that rendered them at once tremendous and delightful."

In November, 1685, when the United Company, comprising the "best talent" both of Davenant and Killigrew's old companies, opened their season at Drury Lane Theatre, among the leading ladies, and second only to Mrs. Barry, were Mrs. Mountfort, and Mrs. Bracegirdle.

Mrs. Mountfort was the soul of comedy; and in Cibber's admirable portrait-gallery he devotes to this charming actress one of his most finished sketches. She was mistress, he says, of more variety of humour than he had ever known in any one actress. "This variety," he continues, "was attended with an equal vivacity, which made her excellent in characters extremely difficult. As she was naturally a pleasant mimic, she had the skill to make that talent useful on the stage. When the elocution is round, distinct, voluble, and various, as Mrs. Mountfort's was, the mimic there is a great assistance to the actor. Nothing, though ever so barren, if within the bounds of nature, could be flat in her hands. She gave many brightening touches to characters but coldly written, and often made an author vain of his work, that, in itself, had but little merit. She was so fond of humour, in what part soever to be found, that she would make no scruple of defacing her fair face to come heartily into it, for when she was eminent in several desirable characters of wit and humour, in higher life, she would be in as much fancy, when descending into the antiquated Abigail of Fletcher, as when triumphing in all the airs and vain graces of a fine lady; a merit that few actors care for. In a play of D'Urfey's now forgotten, called 'The Western Lass,' which part she acted, she transformed her whole being—body, shape, voice, language, look and features—into almost another animal, with a strong Devonshire dialect, a broad laughing voice, a poking head, round shoulders, an unconceiving eye, and the most bedizening dawdy dress that ever covered the untrained limbs of a Joan trot. To have seen her here, you would have thought it impossible that the same could ever have been removed to, what was as easy to her, the gay, the lively, and the desirable. Nor was her humour limited to her sex, for while her shape permitted, she was a more adroit, pretty fellow than is usually seen upon the stage. Her easy air, action, mien, and gesture, quite changed from the coif to the cocked-hat and cavalier in fashion. People were so fond of seeing her a man that when the part of Bayes, in 'The Rehearsal,' had for some time lain dormant, she was desired to take it up, which I have seen her act with all the true coxcomly spirit and humour that the sufficiency of the character required.

"But what found most employment for her whole various excellence at once was the part of Melantha, in 'Marriage á la Mode.'* Melantha is as finished an impertinent as ever fluttered in a drawing-room, and seems to contain the most complete system of female foppery that could possibly be crowded into the tortured form of a fine lady. The language, dress, motion, manners, soul, and body, are in a continual hurry to be something more than is necessary or commendable. The first ridiculous airs that break from her are upon a gallant, never seen before, who delivers her a letter from her father, recommending him to her good graces as an honourable lover. Here, now, one would think that she might naturally show a little of the sex's decent reserve, though never so

* Dryden's comedy, produced in 1672.

slightly covered. No, sir! not a tittle of it! Modesty is the virtue of a poor-souled country gentlewoman. She is too much a Court lady to be under so vulgar a confusion. She reads the letter, therefore, with a careless, dropping lip, and an erected brow, humming it hastily over, as if she were impatient to out go her father's commands, by making a complete conquest of him at once; and that the letter might not embarrass her attack, crack! she crumbles it at once into her palm, and pours upon him her whole artillery of airs, eyes, and motion. Down goes her dainty, diving body to the ground, as if she were sinking under the conscious load of her own attractions; then launches into a flood of fine language and compliment, still playing her chest forward in fifty falls and risings, like a swan upon waving water; and, to complete her impertinence, she is so rapidly fond of her own wit that she will not give her lover leave to praise it. Silent assenting bows, and vain endeavours to speak, are all the share of the conversation he is admitted to, which at last he is relieved from, by her engagement to half a score visits, which she *swims* from him to make, with a promise to return in a twinkling."

She made her *début* on the stage as Miss Percival, and enacted the character of Nell in "The Devil to Pay." After her marriage to William Mountfort, her best characters were Melantha, already spoken of, and Belinda in Congreve's "Old Bachelor." Mountfort, a comedian of brilliant merit, who played the airy, graceful, ardent lover as to the manner born, was slain by Captain Hill in 1692; and his widow soon afterwards married the actor Verbruggen. She died in 1703.

Mrs. Bracegirdle, like Mrs. Mountfort, belongs to the stage of Charles II.'s reign only as a *débutante*. Her fame was won in later years. Yet our sketches will hardly be complete if they do not include this admirable actress, who, unlike most of her contemporaries, was also a virtuous woman. She was the ornament of the stage and the delight of the public from 1680 to 1707, when she gave way to the rising star of Mrs. Oldfield. "Never," says Cibber, "was any woman in such general favour of the spectators. . . . She was the darling of the theatre; for it will be no extravagant thing to say, scarce an audience saw her that were less than half of them lovers, without a suspected favourite among them; and though she may be said to have been the universal passion, and under the highest temptations, her constancy in resisting them served but to increase her admirers. It was even the fashion among the gay and young to have a taste or *tendre* for Mrs. Bracegirdle." It was the fashion, also, among the old. One day the Earl of Burlington sent her a present of some fine old china. She told the servant he had made a mistake; that it was true the letter was for her, but the china was for his lady, to whom she bade him carry it. "Lord!" exclaims Walpole, "the Countess was so full of gratitude when her husband came home to dinner." Lord Lovelace was another of her suitors, and as unsuccessful as the rest. To the number and variety of the love-tokens poured in upon her Dryden alludes, in one of his epilogues written for her:—

> "I have had to-day a dozen billets-doux
> From fops, and wits, and cits, and Bow Street beaux:
> Some from Whitehall, but from the Temple more:
> A Covent Garden porter brought me four."

Congreve also entered the lists, and there is no doubt

his addresses were welcome to her; but she could not be induced to forfeit her self-respect. This he himself admits in verses which we confess we are almost ashamed to quote :—

> " Pious Belinda goes to prayers
> Whene'er I ask the favour,
> Yet the tender fool's in tears
> When she thinks I'd leave her.
> Would I were free from this restraint,
> Or else had power to win her;
> Would she could make of me a saint,
> Or I of her a sinner."

One Captain Richard Hill, a dissolute man about town, fell so violently in love with her person—he could not appreciate her mind—that he resolved to carry her off by force, and persuaded Lord Mohun, who was as wild and wicked as himself, to assist. Ascertaining that, with her mother and brother, she was to sup one evening at the house of a friend, Mr. Page, in Prince's Street, Drury Lane, they hired six soldiers for the deed of violence, and posted them near Mr. Page's house. It was the 9th of December, 1692, and about ten at night, as she left Mr. Page's, the ruffians pounced upon her, but she screamed so loudly, and her brother and friend made so gallant a resistance, that the attempt failed. An excited crowd assembled, and Lord Mohun and Hill thought it prudent to undertake to escort her to her residence in Howard Street, Strand. Close at hand lived Mountfort, the actor, and Mrs. Bracegirdle, overhearing Captain Hill indulging in violent threats against him—from an absurd suspicion that he was a favoured rival—sent to Mrs. Mountfort to warn her husband, who was gone home, to be on his guard. The brilliant young cavalier, nothing alarmed, came round into Howard Street and saluted

Lord Mohun; at the same moment Hill stepped up behind, struck him on the head, and, before he could draw in his defence, ran his sword through Mountfort's body. Captain Hill fled to the Continent; but Lord Mohun was tried by his peers for the murder, and acquitted by three-score against fourteen. He afterwards fell in the fatal duel with the Duke of Hamilton.

Mrs. Bracegirdle retired from the stage in 1707, but lived in the enjoyment of an inconsiderable fortune, the centre of a wide circle of wits and men of letters, until 1748.

THE POETS.

Milton.
Herrick.
Marvell.
Cowley.
Waller.
Sir W. Davenant.
Earl of Dorset.
Earl of Roscommon.
Earl of Rochester.

Sheffield, Duke of Buckinghamshire.
Sir C. Sedley.
Sir John Denham.
Thomas Stanley.
Sir W. Killigrew.
Anne Killigrew.
Samuel Butler.
John Dryden.

CHAPTER III.

THE POETS.

MILTON—HERRICK—MARVELL—COWLEY—WALLER—SIR W. DAVENANT—EARL OF DORSET—EARL OF ROSCOMMON—EARL OF ROCHESTER—SHEFFIELD, DUKE OF BUCKINGHAMSHIRE—SIR C. SEDLEY—SIR JOHN DENHAM—THOMAS STANLEY—SIR W. KILLIGREW—ANNE KILLIGREW—SAMUEL BUTLER—JOHN DRYDEN.

AT the Restoration Milton was in his fifty-second year, and one of the most conspicuous men, not in England only, but in Europe. As yet, it is true, he had not shown the world the full measure and range of his power as a poet, and the scholars of Europe knew little or nothing of English poetry; but they honoured him as a controversialist who had crossed swords successfully with one of the doughtiest of Continental combatants. In his encounter with Salmasius, he had, by common consent, brought that champion of absolute monarchy to his knees. After reading the "Defensio pro-Populo Anglicano," in which, with almost an excess of strength, he replied to the "Defensio Regia," the apology for Charles I., Queen Christina, of Sweden, had frankly told Salmasius that he was beaten. Whereupon Salmasius, who had enjoyed so much of the Queen's favour that she had been wont to light his fire with her own hands when she indulged with him in confidential morning walks, declared that the Swedish climate disagreed with him, and returned to France. "Who is this Milton?" asked Henisius, the Dutchman, of Isaac Voss. The latter replied, " I have learned all about Milton from my uncle, Junius, who is familiar with him. He tells me that he serves the Parliament in foreign affairs; is skilled in many languages; is not, indeed, of noble, but, as they say, of gentle birth; kindly, affable, and endowed with many other virtues." Who is this Milton? If the question had been put to his countrymen they might have informed the querist that he was the second—ranking Oliver Cromwell as the first—great Englishman of his time; a man with a powerful genius and a singular loftiness and purity of thought; a courageous, resolute, and eloquent champion of civil and religious liberty; a master of English prose, which he wrote with a stateliness that reflected the dignity of his character; a poet of rare gifts and accomplishments, who, before all other English singers, had proved himself conscious of the nobleness and sacredness of the poet's mission.

Good and great work Milton had already done; but his best and greatest work belongs to the reign of Charles II., and is the distinguishing glory of that reign. The "Paradise Lost" is one of the world's half-dozen immortal poems—like "The Iliad," and "The Æneid," and the "Divina Commedia"—and the age and the country which produced it have necessarily something to be proud of. If we have little else to thank the Restoration for, we have to thank it, I believe, for our great

English epic. But for the obscurity and privacy to which it relegated Milton, he might never have enjoyed the leisure, or the self-concentration, without which its composition would have been impossible. He was thirty-two when he conceived the idea; but he found no time to attempt its realization during the stirring periods of the Civil War and the Protectorate. For Milton was not only a poet, but a man of action. There was nothing of the recluse about him; he did not live for poetry alone, like Wordsworth. His strong, deep sympathies with the cause of human liberty and human hope impelled him to take an active part in the struggle, and for twenty years, from 1641 to 1660, he gave to public affairs the resources of his intellectual strength and opulence. With the exception of a few sonnets, his muse, meanwhile, was silent. Those graceful Italian pastorals, " L'Allegro " and " Il Penseroso," were written while he lingered in his earlier manhood among the orchard blooms of Horton. The "Comus," which so admirably illustrates the grave purity of his mind, and the beautiful monody of " Lycidas," belong to the year 1637. In 1639, the death of his friend Diodati drew from him his "Epitaphium Damoris," and thereafter he devoted his genius to the service of his country. His wonderful intellectual activity knew no pause of weariness; it embraced the whole field of conflict: Church Discipline, Divorce, the Freedom of the Press, Education, Civil Government—on all these various themes he had much to say, to which it was good for his countrymen to listen, and he said it with such a strenuousness and vehemence that they durst not close their ears.

As to his prose style, writers differ. "Is he truly a

prose writer?" says Taine, and he adds:—"Entangled dialectics, a heavy and awkward mind"—who but a Frenchman would have used these epithets?—"fanatical and furious rusticity, an epic grandeur of sustained and superabundant images, the blast and the recklessness of implacable and all-powerful passion, the sublimity of religious and logical exaltation: we do not recognize in these features a man born to explain, pursuade, and prove." No; it was not Milton's business to explain or persuade; he crushed. Like a shock of cavalry, he charged the errors and sophisms of his time, and they went down before him. How could he stop to explain or persuade, when his opponents were the minions of Prelacy and Absolutism, the deadly foes of Freedom? You might as well have asked Cromwell's Ironsides to halt on the field of Naseby, and reason with Rupert and his cavaliers. Milton's prose is the prose of a poet. It is rich in images and illustrations; it abounds in harmonious cadences; it frequently lapses into a measured rhythm. No doubt it is sometimes rugged and sometimes exuberant; but this ruggedness is due to his intense earnestness, and this exuberance to the marvellous wealth of his resources. He has no call to be thrifty like lesser men; and so the great river of his eloquence rolls on with copious force, carrying with it both gold and mud.

Is is in the "Areopagitica," that noble plea for the liberty of the press—which so completely achieved its object that in England, at least, no serious effort has since been made to curb the free expression of free thought—we see Milton's eloquence in its fullest majesty. The title is borrowed from the "Areopagitic" oration of Isocrates; but nothing more. Between the calm gracefulness of the Greek orator and the splendid fervour of the English author there is not the slightest similarity. The "Areopagitica" is warm with Milton's heart-blood. It kindles with the fire of enthusiasm from the first line to the last. The trumpet-strain never falters; the well-poised wings never droop or weary in their lofty flight. Whoever would know of what our English language is capable, to what heights it can reach, into how grand an organ-music it can swell, let him read the "Areopagitica." "Though all the winds of doctrine," says Milton, "were let loose to play upon the earth, so Truth be in the field, we do injuriously by licensing and prohibiting to misdoubt her strength. Let her and Falsehood grapple; whoever knew Truth put to the worse in a free and open encounter? Her confuting is the best and surest suppressing. He who hears what praying there is for light and clearer knowledge to be sent down among us, would think of other matters to be constituted beyond the discipline of Geneva, framed and fabrict already to our hands. Yet when the new light which we beg for shines in upon us, there be who envy, and oppose, if it come not first in at their casements. What a collusion is this, whereas we are exhorted by the wise man to use diligence, *to seek for wisdom as for hidden treasures* early and late, that another order shall enjoin us to know nothing but by statute. When a man hath been labouring the hardest labour in the deep mines of knowledge, hath furnished out his findings in all their equipage, drawn forth his reasons as it were a battle ranged, scattered and defeated all objections in his way, calls out his adversary into the plain, offers him the advantage of wind and sun if he please, only that he may try the matter by dint of argument, for his opponents then to skulk, to lay ambushments, to keep a narrow bridge of licensing where the challenger should pass, though it be valour enough in soldiership, is but weakness and cowardice in the wars of Truth. For who knows not that Truth is strong next to the Almighty; she needs no policies, no stratagems, no licensings to make her victorious; these are the shifts and defences that Error uses against her power."

Here is a fine passage which none but a poet could have written:—

"Truth, indeed, came once into the world with her Divine Master, and was a perfect shape, most glorious to look on; but when He ascended, and His Apostles after Him were laid asleep, then straight arose a wicked race of deceivers, who, as that story goes of the Egyptian Typhon with his conspirators, how they dealt with the good Osiris, took the virgin Truth, hewed her lovely form into a thousand pieces, and scattered them to the four winds. From that time ever since, the sad friends of Truth, such as durst appear, imitating the careful search that Isis made for the mangled body of Osiris, went up and down gathering up limb by limb still as they could find them. We have not yet found them all, lords and commons, nor ever shall do, till her Master's second coming; He shall bring together every joint and member, and shall mould them into an immortal pattern of loveliness and perfection."

And this almost lyrical outburst in praise of Books:—

"Books are not absolutely dead things, but do contain a progeny of life in them to be as active as that soul was whose progeny they are; nay, they do preserve as in a vial the purest efficacy and extraction of that living intellect that bred them. I know they are as lively, and as vigorously productive, as those fabulous dragon's teeth; and being sown up and down, may chance to spring up armed men. And, yet, on the other hand, unless wariness be used, as good almost kill a man as kill a good book: who kills a man kills a reasonable creature, God's image ; but he who destroys a good book, kills reason itself, kills the image of God, as it were, in the eye. Many a man lives a burden to the earth; but a good book is the precious life-blood of a master spirit, embalmed and treasured up on purpose to a life beyond life."

The "Areopagitica" was written in 1644. Early in 1649 its author was appointed Latin Secretary to the Council of State; a post he continued to hold under Cromwell, assisted, after his blindness in 1654, by Andrew Marvell. Milton's form of blindness was that now known as *amaurosis*, formerly called, from an altogether erroneous supposition of its cause, *gutta serena* ("drop serene"). The fine clear brown eyes remained unimpaired, but the nerve of sight was irreparably injured, partly through excessive application, and partly through a gouty habit of body. In his domestic life Milton had not been wholly happy ; from his first wife, Mary Powell, he had been divorced, separated by the wrongdoing of her family, and after her death, he married Catherine Woodcock, who was taken from him in a year at the birth of her first child. His sonnet "on his deceased wife" is an undying evidence of the love he bore her. One night after her death he had dreamed of her as coming to him with veiled face. . . .

> "And such as yet once more I trust to have
> Full sight of her in heaven without restraint—
> Came, vested all in white, pure as her mind:
>   Her face was veiled, yet to my fancied sight,
> Love, sweetness, goodness, in her person shined
>   So clear, as in no face with more delight;
> But, oh, as to embrace me she inclined,
>   I waked, she fled, and day brought back my night."

At the Restoration Milton, though he knew himself to be obnoxious to the new Court, showed no sign of timidity, and made no attempt to escape its vengeance. He retired, with that quiet dignity which characterised all the actions of his life, to a friend's house in Bartholomew Close; and looked on unmoved, while a Parliament of Cavaliers and fanatical Royalists voted his prosecution, and ordered that his "Eikonoclastes" and his "Defensio Populi Anglicani" should be burnt by the hands of the common hangman. What powerful influence was exerted on his behalf is uncertain; some authorities give the credit to his friend and assistant, Andrew Marvell, who had been elected to Hull: others, to Sir William Davenant, who thus repaid an obligation he had incurred to the poet; but, at all events, he was fortunate enough not to be placed among the exceptions to the Act of Indemnity and Oblivion passed on the 29th of August. He was arrested; but the House of Commons ordered his release on the 15th December, and he was so confident in his security that he ventured to appeal against the excessive fees charged in connection with his brief imprisonment. For about a year he lived in Holborn, near Red Lion Square. Thence, in 1662, he removed to Jewin Street, Aldersgate, and afterwards to a small house in Artillery Walk, near Bunhill Fields, his residence for the remainder of his life. While in Jewin Street he took to himself, by the advice of Dr. Paget, his physician, a third wife; Elizabeth, daughter of Sir Edward Minshull, of Cheshire, a distant kinswoman of the doctor's. She devoted herself to her husband's happiness; but his three daughters, of whom Anne, the eldest, was sixteen—Mary, the second fifteen—and Deborah, the youngest, ten, did not relish the rule of a young step-mother. On the whole, however, his household, during his latter years, was peaceful and well-ordered. The method of his daily life was simplicity itself: he rose at four in the summer, and at five in the winter; heard a chapter of the Hebrew Bible, and was left to meditate until seven. After breakfast some one read to him, and he dictated to his amanuensis until noon. One hour, from twelve to one, was reserved for exercise, either walking or in a swing. He dined at one, and occupied himself with books, music, and composition until six. Two hours were given to conversation with his friends; and, as might be supposed, he was a fine talker. He supped at eight, smoked a pipe, and retired to bed at nine.

Among his readers was young Thomas Ellwood, the Quaker. Burning with a great desire for knowledge, he came up to London, shortly after the Restoration, and through a friend made the acquaintance of Dr. Paget, who, in 1662, introduced the young man (he was then twenty-three) to the blind poet. His reception was very favourable; and he was invited to visit Milton at home, whenever he wished, "and to read to him what books he should appoint," which was all that Ellwood desired. He tells us that Milton taught him the foreign pronunciation of Latin, and perceiving with what earnest desire he pursued learning, gave him not only all the encouragement but all the help he could. "For, having a curious ear, he understood by my tone," says Ellwood, "when I understood what I read, and when I did not; and accordingly would stop me, examine me, and open the most difficult passages."

In 1665, when all who could hastened to escape from the plague-stricken city, young Ellwood, at Milton's request, hired for him "a pretty box"—a plain, half-timbered, gable-fronted cottage*—at Chalfont St. Giles. When the poet took up his residence there, Ellwood, under a new and stringent law against the Quakers and their meetings, had been thrown into Aylesbury prison; but as soon as he was released, he paid Milton a visit. "After some common discourses had passed between us," writes Ellwood, "he called for a manuscript of his, which, being brought, he delivered to me, bidding me take it home with me and read it at my leisure, and when I had done so return it to him with my judgment thereupon. When I came home and had set myself to read it, I found it was that excellent poem, which he entitled *Paradise Lost*. After I had, with the best attention, read it through, I made him another visit, and returned him his book, with the acknowledgment of the favour he had done me in communicating it to me. He asked me how I liked it, and what I thought of it, which I modestly but freely told him; and, after some further discourse about it, I pleasantly said to him, 'Thou hast said much here of *Paradise Lost*, but what hast thou to say of *Paradise Found?*' He made me no answer, but sat some time in a muse; then broke off that discourse and fell upon another subject. After the sickness was over and the city well cleansed and

---

* The cottage is still in excellent preservation. It stands on the right, near the end of the village; and its little low parlour is said to be the room in which Milton dictated his "Paradise Regained."

become safely habitable again, he returned thither. And when afterwards I went to wait on him there (which I seldom failed of doing whenever my occasions drew me to London), he showed me his second poem, called *Paradise Regained*, and in a pleasant tone said to me, 'This is owing to you; for you put it into my head by the question you put to me at Chalfont, which before I had not thought of.'" Milton, however, probably felt that a sequel was needed in order to emphasize and define more precisely the plan of Christ in the Divine scheme of redemption.

"Paradise Lost" was completed before the end of 1665; "Paradise Regained" (though not published until 1671) probably in the course of the following year, or early in the spring of 1667. Milton's first great epic found a publisher in Samuel Simmons, who bought the copyright for £15; £5 paid down, £5 to be paid on the sale of 1,300 copies out of a first edition of 1,500, and £5 more on the sale of 1,300 out of a second edition of 1,500 copies. Milton lived to receive a second five pounds, and to his widow were paid £8 for her remaining interest in the copyright. The poem, divided at first into only ten books, was handsomely printed in a small quarto volume, which was sold for 3s. It had neither preface, notes, nor "arguments" prefixed to the different books (1667). A license for publication was not obtained without some difficulty, the licencer (the Rev. Thomas Tomkyns, chaplain to the Archbishop of Canterbury) stumbling at a supposed political allusion in the following well-known passage:—

> "As when the sun, now risen,
> Looks through the horizontal misty air,
> Shorn of his beams; or, from behind the moon,
> In dim eclipse disastrous twilight sheds
> On half the nations, and with fear of change
> Perplexes monarchs."

At length, however, it was published, and the English people soon showed their sense of the inestimable value of this new addition to their literature. Thirteen hundred copies were sold in two years, and in eleven years the sale reached three thousand copies; not a bad sale for a religious epic at a time when readers were limited to the affluent classes, and the popular taste had been corrupted by the introduction of French models and the influence of a dissolute and luxurious Court.

To criticise " Paradise Lost " would be work as supererogatory as analysing the sun. It is universally accepted as the great English epic, which no other has yet threatened in its pride of place. It is part of the inheritance of every Englishman, like Magna Charta and the Bill of Rights. No doubt it has its defects; it is prolix and even wearisome in some of its passages; its theology is narrow; its conceptions of Heaven and Hell are necessarily materialistic;* but what are these when compared with those essential qualities of grandeur of thought and diction of loftiness of purpose, to which it owes its immortality? But in Mr. Mark Pattison's monograph (in the "English Men of Letters" series), and in Professor Masson's comprehensive biography, the reader will find elaborate estimates which answer almost every question that can arise in connection with its study; and he may advantageously compare Macaulay's and Dr. Channing's

---

* Milton was conscious of this defect, which was forced upon him by the structure of his poem, and endeavours to explain it away, or apologise for it, in the words he puts into the mouth of Raphael:—
" What surmounts the reach
Of human sense, I shall delineate so
By likening spiritual to corporal forms
As may express them best : though what if earth
Be but the shadow of Heaven, and things therein
Each to other like, more than on earth is thought ? "

well-known essays. His attention will of course be directed to such matters as the extent of Milton's obligations to Cœdmon and Vondel, which scarcely affect more than the framework of the poem; the obvious traces of Spenser, and in a less degree of Marlowe, in the versification and treatment; the characteristics of Milton's blank verse, its processional pomp, its complex harmonies, its majestic rhythm; the rich variety of the allusions and images; the effect of his Calvinistic theology on the development of his subject; his felicitous choice of epithets; his incidental descriptions of natural scenery; and, finally, the relation of the poem to the religious thought of the age. It is specially interesting to compare it with Spenser's "Faery Queen,"* which presents one side or aspect of the difficult problem of which "Paradise Lost" presents the other. Thus, if we take it to be Spenser's primary object to indicate the aspiration of man's soul towards its God, it is not less the purpose of Milton to

"Assert eternal Providence,
And justify the ways of God to man;"

while the minds of both are fascinated by the constant struggle which prevails in the soul and in the world between the antagonistic principles of Good and Evil.

"Paradise Lost" and "Paradise Regained" should be taken together as one great continuous allegorical epic, which divides naturally into four parts, and each part into four books. The first part, Books i. to iv., describes the origin and progress of the war between Good and Evil, the fall of Evil into Hell, and the renewal of the struggle upon

---

* In the preface to his "Fables," Dryden remarks that Milton is the poetical son of Spenser. "Milton has confessed to me," he adds, "that Spenser was his original."

earth with Man's soul as the prize of the victor. The second part, Books v. to viii., forms an intermezzo, in which, through the narrative of the Archangel Raphael, we learn the order of the events that preceded the creation of Man. In the third part, Books ix. to xii., the story of the great conflict is resumed, with Man's fall, its immediate consequences, and the Archangel Michael's forecast of the way in which they will eventually be retrieved. Lastly, the fourth part ("Paradise Regained") brings us to the realisation of the grand Archangelic vision in Christ's victory over the Power of Evil. On "the highest pinnacle" of the glorious Temple of Jerusalem, which shone afar

"Like a mount
Of alabaster top't with golden spires,"

Divine Good, in the person of Jesus Christ, wins the last battle in that tremendous war which, ages agone, had begun in "heaven's wide champaign." Celestial choirs break forth into strains of victory :—

"Now Thou hast avenged
Supplanted Adam, and, by vanquishing
Temptation, hast regained lost Paradise,
And frustrated the conquest fraudulent."

"Samson Agonistes"* was published in the same year (1671) as "Paradise Regained." It is a choral drama, after the Greek model, but in a severe style, and is instinct with the poet's strong individuality. In its stately verse the main aim and work of his life found their final expression. For twenty years he had championed the sacred cause of civil and religious freedom, and to the superficial observer the battle had gone against him; the banner was torn down, and the hands which had held it

* Samson is taken by the poet as the type of Puritanism, which, though fallen, had nevertheless defeated the enemies of God.

aloft would do so no more. But the poet is, by virtue of his office, a seer, and Milton foresaw that the principles he had advocated would ultimately prevail; just as the blind and aged Samson—Samson Agonistes, the wrestler—triumphed over the Philistines. And the drama ends with a noble song of content and faith, which fitly closed Milton's work as a poet:—

> "So virtue, given for lost,
> Depressed, and overthrown, as seemed,
> Like that self-begotten bird
> In the Arabian woods imbost,
> That no second knows nor third,
> And lay erewhile a holocaust,
> From out her ashy womb now teemed,
> Revives, reflourishes, then vigorous most
> When most unactive deemed;
> And, though her body die, her fame survives
> A secular bird ages of lives."

And again:—

> "All is best, though we oft doubt
> What the unsearchable dispose
> Of highest Wisdom brings about,
> And ever best found in the close.
> Oft He seems to hide His face,
> But unexpectedly returns,
> And to His faithful champion hath in place
> Bore witness gloriously."

Milton's last years were years of peace. He bore with calmness the pains of the disease (gout) which he had inherited, and to the worst ills of Poverty happily he was never exposed. Retaining to the last his faculties unclouded, he passed away without pain on Sunday, the 8th of November, 1674.*

Just three weeks before (October 15th) the grave had closed over a poet of very different mould, Robert Her-

---

* The best commentary on Milton's life is to be found in his own words:—
"He who would not be frustrate of his hope to write well hereafter of laudable things, ought himself to be *a true poem.*"

rick, the author of "The Hesperides." In life and in character a greater contrast could hardly be found than Herrick, the gay lyrist of English Epicureanism, whose philosophy was summed up in the Horatian "carpe diem," whose life was animated by no elevated purpose—consecrated by no patriotic or philanthropic work, to the great Puritan poet, with his deep sense of duty, his intense religious conviction, and his lofty zeal for the welfare of his country. Herrick was born in Cheapside, London, in 1591. In his youth he made the acquaintance of Ben Jonson, and sat with him at "those lyric feasts" which he afterwards commemorated. He studied at Cambridge—unfortunately for himself took holy orders, thereby missing his vocation—and was presented by Charles I., in 1629 to the vicarage of Dean Prior, in Devonshire. Poor Herrick! His tastes, his gifts, and his accomplishments fitted him to shine among the wits and beaux of London society, and he was relegated to the companionship of Devonshire boors. He did his best to be cheerful in these adverse circumstances; and amused his superabundant leisure by singing the daintiest, gracefullest songs imaginable to imaginary Julias, Silvias, Corinnas, by writing in fluent but vigorous verse about country customs and rural peculiarities, while he drank ample draughts of generous liquor, or taught his pet pig to drink, out of a tankard, or chatted airily with his faithful servant Prue. In 1648 he was expelled from his vicarage, and he returned to London, where he published his lyrics, epigrams, and miscellanies, under the title of "Hesperides"—so called, of course, because written in the West of England. In the previous year he had given to the world some soberer strains, his "Noble Numbers; or, Pious

Pieces;" but in these his genius is seen to less advantage.

During the Puritan period Herrick lived at Westminster, on the alms of the wealthier Royalists, and I cannot suppose that this chapter of his life was a happy, and it was certainly not an honourable, one. After the Restoration he returned to his Devonshire vicarage, and probably with the burden of gathering years upon him, knew better how to appreciate its quiet. He was in his 84th year when he died.

As Herrick wrote nothing in his later life, we may be thought to have erred in placing him among the poets of Charles the Second's reign; but his lyrics breathe the true spirit of the Restoration. They were much more in harmony with the time, when king and courtiers gave up everything to pleasure, than at the date of their publication, when the country was divided into two hostile camps, and the minds of men were informed with a deep earnestness and a strenuous ardour of which the poet of "The Hesperides" was wholly incapable. However this may be, Herrick, as a lyrist, has few equals among our English poets. The English language becomes plastic as clay in his ingenious hands, and assumes the most graceful and fantastic forms. Rhymes come at his bidding; and felicities of expression of the most artistic character seem to spring up spontaneously. No doubt he polished his verses with the utmost care, but he had the art to conceal art, and perhaps none of our poets is more successful in producing the impression that he sings, like the birds, because he cannot help singing. He lifts up his voice among the flowers and the green leaves with notes as sweet and natural as those of the mavis.

An accent of melancholy sometimes finds its way into Herrick's bright, gay verse; but it is the melancholy of Paganism. It is the pleasure-seeker's sorrow as he sees the dregs in the wine-cup; as he observes the shortening of the days and the fading of the flowers. "Let us be merry," he cries with something of forced merriment, "for to-morrow we die." It is not that he recognizes the vanity and triviality of his pleasures; but that they must so soon come to an end. It is this thought which interrupts his hilarious song with a sudden cadence of pain. He weeps to see the daffodils haste away so soon; because they remind him of the mortality of human affairs, and the brief span of human existence.

> "We have short time to stay as you;
> We have as short a spring;
> As quick a growth to meet decay
> As you or anything:
> We die,
> As your hours do; and dry
> Away
> Like to the summer's rain,
> Or as the pearls of morning-dew,
> Ne'er to be found again."

We have here no hint of a brighter future, no suggestions of immortality; it is the old Pagan creed, and it sits unbecomingly on the English priest.

As might be expected, there is no earnestness in Herrick's religious poetry. I do not say that it is intentionally insincere, but he does not put his heart into his song; and it has happily been said that he sings to the old heathen tunes. "Even at his prayers, his spirit is mundane and not filled with heavenly things." He carries his gay jocular temper into the sanctuary; in his "Dirge of Jepthah's Daughter" he introduces the strangest, the most alien allusions to seventeenth century customs as far removed as possible from his subject. He is most at home, however, when singing of his real or ideal mistresses, of bright eyes and sweet flowers, of wassail-bowls and morris-dances, of all that is bright and luxuriant in rural life, of country wakes and races, of the may-pole and the harvest-field; and when dealing with such themes his verse is always vigorous, always musical, and always picturesque,, though, unfortunately, not always decent. "I sing," he says:—

> "I sing of brooks, of blossoms, birds, and bowers,
> Of April, May, of June, and July flowers;
> I sing of May-poles, hock-carts, wassails, wakes,
> Of bridegrooms, brides, and of their bridal cakes.
> I write of Youth, of Love; and have access
> By those, to sing of cleanly wantonness;
> I sing of dews, of rains, and, piece by piece,
> Of balm, of oil, of spice, and ambergris.
> I sing of times trans-shifting; and I write
> How roses first came red, and lilies white.
> I write of groves, of twilights, and I sing
> The court of Mab, and of the Fairy King.
> I write of Hell; I sing, and ever shall
> Of Heaven, and hope to have it after all."

Herrick is a poet for the summer-time, for golden noons and warm, sweet twilights, when our "bosom's lord" sits lightly on its throne, and we are disposed for awhile to listen to the strains of careless lyres and to watch the free dances of rustic maids.

Four years after Milton, died his collaborateur and friend, Andrew Marvell (1624-1678), who, in the Civil War period, had laboured both in prose and poetry to advance the cause of the Parliament and discredit that of the Crown. Though bred in the atmosphere of Puritanism,

Marvell, however, was not a Puritan; and though he assailed the absolutism of Charles I., he was not a Republican. He served Cromwell as Milton's assistant;* and after the Restoration, as a member of Parliament, would have given his support to the King's ministry, had the King's policy been honest and constitutional. He was as inflexible and as incorruptible as a Roman patriot. Everybody knows the story—how Charles II. once sent to him Danby, the Lord Treasurer, to offer him in return for his advocacy a place at Court and a thousand pounds. The member for Hull was poor, but he could not be induced to stain the whiteness of his soul by accepting a bribe; his only answer to the King's agent was to call his servant to bear witness that for three successive days he had dined on a shoulder of mutton.

As a poet Marvell has grace and fancy, wit and learning; he has some descriptive power and much earnestness of feeling; but he is very unequal, and his wit sometimes degenerates into an idle ingenuity. In his "Britannia and Raleigh" he struck upon that vein of grave, ironical banter which was afterwards worked to such effect by Swift and Junius. He is seen at his best in "The Garden," which, of its kind, is perfect; in "The Bermudas," and "The Horatian Ode on Cromwell's

---

* In 1650 Marvell became tutor to Mary, the daughter of Sir Thomas Fairfax, the general of the Parliament; and it was probably through this engagement that he became personally known to Milton, who, in 1659, recommended him to Bradshaw as Assistant-Secretary to the Council of State—speaking of him as a man of good family, well versed in French and Italian, Spanish and Dutch, a good scholar in Greek and Latin, and a man of so much capacity and so many accomplishments that, if he had had any feeling of jealousy or rivalry, he might have been slow to introduce him as a coadjutor. It was not until Cromwell's Protectorate that Marvell received his appointment.

Return from Ireland." This last contains the well-known picture of Charles I. on the scaffold:

> "While round the armèd bands
> Did clap their bloody hands:
> He nothing common did, or mean,
> Upon that memorable scene,
> But with his keener eye
> The axe's edge did try ;
> Nor called the gods, with vulgar spite,
> To vindicate his helpless right,
> But bowed his comely head
> Down, as upon a bed."

Some good, strong lines occur in his poem upon Milton's "Paradise Lost," which has a special interest as having been written by one of the poet's friends and intimate associates. "That majesty," he says,

> "That majesty which through thy work doth reign
> Draws the devout, deterring the profane;
> And things divine thou treat'st of in such state
> As them preserves, and thee, inviolate.
> At once delight and horror on us seize,
> Thou sing'st with so much gravity and ease,
> And above human flight dost soar aloft
> With plume so strong, so equal, and so soft:
> The bird named from that paradise you sing
> So never flags, but always keeps on wing.
> Where could'st thou words of such a compass find?
> Whence furnish such a vast expanse of mind?
> Just Heaven thee, like Tiresias, to requite,
> Rewards with prophecy thy loss of sight."

In the year that witnessed the publication of "Paradise Lost,"—Dryden's "Annus Mirabilis,"—died Abraham Cowley, whose later life had been spent among the pleasant groves of Chertsey, and within hearing of the murmurous waters of the Thames. Born in 1618, he was the posthumous son of a London stationer. His mother did her best to get him a careful and comprehensive education; and from Spenser's works, which lay constantly in her parlour, a cherished companion, the boy drank in his first poetical inspiration. While at Westminster School he wrote a pastoral comedy, called "Love's Riddle;" and in 1633 appeared his "Poetical Blossoms," with a portrait of the author at the age of thirteen. This juvenile volume contained "The Tragical History of Pyramus and Thisbe," written when he was ten, and "Constantia and Philetus," written when he was thirteen years old.* From 1636 to 1643 he was a student at Trinity College, Cambridge; and when expelled on account of his royalist sympathies, he entered St. John's, Oxford, and wrote satirical verse against the Puritans. Afterwards he accompanied Queen Henrietta Maria to Paris, where he acted as her Secretary, and conducted

* In this volume we find "The Wish," of which, in mature years, he spoke as verses "of which I should hardly now be ashamed." Few boys of thirteen have written with so much gravity, clear judgment, and dignified expression. We quote two or three stanzas, embodying "wishes" which he lived to realize:—

"This only grant me, that my means may lie
Too low for envy, for contempt too high.
   Some honour I would have
Not from great deeds, but good alone.
The unknown are better than ill known;
   Rumour can ope the grave.
Acquaintance I would have, but whose 't depends
Not on the number, but the choice of friends.

Books should, not business, entertain the light,
And sleep, as undisturbed as death, the night.
   My house a cottage, more
Than palace, and should fitting be,
For all my use, not luxury.
   My garden painted o'er
With nature's hand, not art's; and pleasures yield,
Horace might envy in his Sabine field.

Thus would I double my life's fading space,
For he that runs it well, twice runs his race.
   And in this true delight,
These unbought sports, this happy state,
I would not fear nor wish my fate,
   But boldly say each night,
To-morrow let my sun his beams display,
Or in clouds hide them; I have lived to-day."

the correspondence that passed between her and the King.

He remained in France until 1656. Returning to England he resided there under surveillance until the death of Cromwell, and published the first folio edition of his Works. He was made an M.D. of Oxford, and began to take up the study of botany, under the impulse of the new love of scientific pursuits which was springing up in England. On the death of Cromwell, apprehensive probably of civil commotion, he rejoined his friends in France; but at the Restoration came back, and took up his abode, first at Barnes, and afterwards at Chertsey. Notwithstanding his well-proven loyalty, the time treated him with neglect; and he owed the means of livelihood to the munificence of Lord St. Albans and the Duke of Buckingham.* His comedy, "The Cutter of Coleman Street," had painted with a good deal of freedom the dissolute joviality of the Cavaliers; and he had given offence by an ode in honour of Brutus.

When involved in the work and anxiety of the world, Cowley had breathed many an aspiration for the joys of rural Solitude; yet it is certain that in his retirement at Chertsey he was not altogether happy. Surrey, he soon discovered, was not Arcadian; and the Restoration had not brought back the Golden Age. There was as little innocence in Chertsey as in London; his tenants would not pay their rents, and his neighbours turned their cattle every night to pasture freely in his meadows. If Pope may be credited, his death came of an ignominious cause:—" It was occasioned," says the poet, " by

---

* Through their influence he obtained a lease of some lands belonging to the Queen, worth about £300 per annum.

a mean accident while his great friend Dean Sprat was with him on a visit. They had been together to see a neighbour of Cowley's, who, according to the fashion of those times, made them too welcome. They did not set out for their walk home till it was too late, and had drunk so deep that they lay out in the fields all night. This gave Cowley the fever that carried him off"—on the 28th of July, 1667. His remains were carried by water to Westminster, and interred with much pomp in the Abbey.

In the folio edition of his "Works" we find them arranged in five divisions: 1, "Miscellanies," including "Anacreontiques;" 2, "The Mistress," a collection of love poems; 3, "The Davideis," an heroic poem of the troubles of David; 4, "Pindarique Odes," to which were afterwards added, 5, "Verses on Various Occasions;" and 6, "Several Discourses by way of Essays in Verse and Prose." Taken as a whole, the poems are dreary reading; for Cowley, like Wordsworth, thought that whatever he had written must needs be worth preserving; and, therefore, one has to plod wearily through a great stretch of desert to reach an oasis where the leaves are green and the birds sing. In the "Miscellanies" there is much that is mean, much that is forced, but there is also much that is very good—as the fine monody on William Hervey and the elegy on Crashaw. The former will bear comparison with Matthew Arnold's "Thyrsis;" the latter contains some weighty lines, familiar to every lover of English Poetry. As, for instance, the couplet:—

> "His faith, perhaps, in some nice tenets might
> Be wrong; his life, I'm sure, was in the right."

And the exquisite compliment :—

> "Poet and Saint ! to thee alone are given
> The two most sacred names of earth and heaven,
> The hard and rarest union which can be
> Next that of godhead with humanity."

Of the Love Poems we may say with Johnson that they are "such as might have been written for penance by a hermit, or for hire by a philosophical rhymer who had only heard of another sex." He did not "look into his own heart and write" (as Sidney bids the poet do), but composed his amatory lyrics as exercises in verse— as part of the obligation which rested on every man who sought admission to the poetic brotherhood. "Poets," he says, "are scarce thought Freemen of the Company without paying some duties and obliging themselves to be true to Love." One can easily understand what will be the result when a man writes love poems in this spirit! They abound with frigid and unpleasant conceits; far-fetched images; the misapplied ingenuities of a vexatious pedantry. What they do *not* contain is a spark of true passion—a flash of real and genuine feeling. It is in the "Pindarique Odes" I think that Cowley is seen at his best; for by common consent "The Davideis" has long ago been given over to oblivion; and in the "Ode to Mrs. Hobbs" and the "Ode on the Royal Society" he writes with an elevation, a fervour, and even a simplicity which constrain us to cry—*O si sic omnia!* In some of his less ambitious efforts he is also seen to great advantage, and they help us to understand the influence he exercised over his contemporaries. Cowley, in fact, is just one of those poets who shine most in our Anthologies, where their gold is presented without their dross. In his wide poetical garden weeds are profusely mingled with flowers; but of these flowers there are enough to make up a posy which, for bloom and colour, shall please the most fastidious. In our Anthologies we can forget the metaphysics, the artificialities, the "conceits," and the "mixed wit" which Johnson and Addison have so severely and justly condemned; those grave pervading errors which have heaped the dust of forgetfulness on the poetry of a man who possessed not a few of the essential qualities of a true poet. Cowley was unfortunate in his age; he came too late, and too soon. The prodigal strength and exuberant vigour of the Elizabethans were almost exhausted, and as yet the fine taste and critical judgment of Dryden and Pope had not begun to assert their influence. How well he could write when he threw off his self-imposed fetters may be seen in those verses on Solitude which we extract from his admirable "Discourses by way of Essays," in which ripe thought and calm, clear judgment are expressed in a manly and dignified prose:—

> "Hail, old patrician trees, so great and good!
> Hail, ye plebeian underwood!
>   Where the poetic birds rejoice,
> And for their quiet nests and plenteous food,
>   Pay with their grateful voice.
>
> Hail, the poor muse's richest manor seat!
>   Ye country houses and retreat,
>   Which all the happy gods so love,
> That for you oft they quit their bright and great
>   Metropolis above.
>
> Here Nature does a house for me erect,
>   Nature the wisest architect,
>   Who those fond artists does despise
> That can the fair and living trees neglect,
>   Yet the dead timber prize.

> Here let me careless and unthoughtful lying,
>   Hear the soft winds above me flying,
>   With all their wanton boughs dispute,
> And the more tuneful birds to both replying,
>   Nor be myself too mute. . . .
>
> Ah, wretched, and too solitary he
>   Who loves not his own company!
>   He'll feel the weight of 't many a day
> Unless he call in sin or vanity
>   To help to bear 't away.
>
> O solitude, first state of human-kind!
>   Which blest remained till man did find
>   Even his own helper's company.
> As soon as two (alas!) together joined,
>   The serpent made up three. . .
>
> Thou the faint beams of reason's scattered light,
>   Dost like a burning-glass unite,
>   Dost multiply the feeble heat,
> And fortify the strength, till thou dost bright
>   And noble fires beget.
>
> Whilst this hard truth I teach, methinks I see
>   The monster London laugh at me,
>   I should at thee too, foolish city,
> If it were fit to laugh at misery,
>   But thy estate I pity.
>
> Let but thy wicked men from out thee go,
>   And all the fools that crowd thee so,
>   Even thou who dost thy millions boast,
> A village less than Islington will grow,
>   A solitude almost."

One of the fairest spots in Kent is that Penshurst which the poets have endowed with a lasting fame; and few of the old Kentish manor-houses are better worth a visit than Penshurst Place, the Home of the Sidneys. If the reader should obtain admission to it, he will, of course, direct his particular attention to the Gallery, which contains some good specimens of the great masters, and a few portraits of historical interest. Among the latter he will observe two of Lady Dorothea Sidney, daughter of the Earl of Leicester. One, by Vandyke, represents her in her lovely youth, attired as a shepherdess, with long golden curls crowning the virgin beauty of her brow. The other, by Hoskins, shows her in her married womanhood, when she seems to have lost none of her personal attractions. This noble lady, in 1639, married the Earl of Sunderland; but in English literature she is known by the name of Saccharissa ("the sweetest"), given to her in his polished verses by her poet-lover, Edmund Waller. An avenue of beeches at Penshurst is still called "Saccharissa's Walk."

Edmund Waller occupies a niche among our English poets, not so much on account of his lyrical praises of this old-world beauty, as on account of his share in the development of our versification. Dryden, in the dedication to his drama of "The Rival Ladies," speaking of rhyme, observes that "the excellence and dignity of it were never fully known till Mr. Waller taught it; he first made writing easily an art: first showed us to conclude the sense most commonly in distichs, which in the verse of those before him runs on for so many lines together that the reader is out of breath to overtake it." Elijah Fenton also speaks of him as the

"Maker and model of melodious verse;"

and this exaggerated praise was repeated by Voltaire, who affirmed that he had created the art of liquid numbers. The French wit might be forgiven for not knowing much of our earlier literature; but Dryden and Fenton ought to have known—and, indeed, Dryden *did* know—that melodious verse and excellent rhyme had been written long before Waller wrote. The share of credit really due to him is that he introduced the French fashion of writing couplets; those heroic distichs which Denham and Dryden adopted, and Pope, Johnson, Goldsmith, and others, down to Byron, esteemed so highly.

Waller's principal merit is the polish of his verses. They are sweet, accurate, and fluent; but never glow with passion or break into lyrical music. There is such an uniform elegance about them that they cloy and weary the reader, who longs with a singular impatience for some interruption to this elaborate monotony. Even in his love-songs there is not the slightest warmth—no evidence of manly feeling—no sign and token of the trustfulness and fervour and tenderness of love. Waller's suit was unsuccessful; but it does not seem that he felt very deeply the disappointment to his hopes. The truth is, that he thought a great deal more of himself than of the lady, and while he sang was chiefly anxious about the figure he should make in the eyes of posterity. Would Saccharissa do for him what Laura had done for Petrarch? That was what he really cared about; in his case the last thing to be feared was a broken heart. Perhaps the Lady Dorothy saw this as clearly as we see it; and it may account for her dismissal of the sweet singer and insincere lover.

Waller's poetical work is easily summed up: besides his love-songs, he wrote a long epical poem on the Summer's Islands;* a vigorous "Panegyric upon Oliver Cromwell;" some feeble stanzas on the "Death of the late usurper, O.C.;" and, towards the close of his career, six dreary cantos "Of Divine Life." He is now best remembered by his graceful lyric, "Go, lovely Rose;"

---

* Evidently in Byron's mind when he wrote "The Island."

his pathetic couplets on " Old Age and Death ; " and his pretty conceit about the Girdle :—

> " A narrow compass, and yet there
> Dwelt all that's good, and all that's fair;
> Give me but what this ribbon bound,
> Take all the rest the sun goes round."

It is a characteristic of his good and passionless verse that it was always the same, in old age as in early manhood; drawing ingenious moralities from a fading rose, or celebrating " His Majesty's Escape at St. Andrew's ; " never rising to any heights of eloquence or power, and never sinking below a certain level of graceful execution.

Edmund Waller was born at Coleshill, in Warwickshire, on the third of March, 1605—the year in which Sir William Davenant was born. His father died in his infancy, and left him an income of £3,500 a year, equal to about £10,000 or £11,000 at the present value of money. His mother was John Hampden's sister—a relationship of which any Englishman might be proud. He was educated at Eton and Cambridge, and at the age of seventeen the precocious young man entered Parliament as member for Agmondesham. He was scarcely twenty-five when he married a city heiress, who, dying within a twelvemonth, left him richer than before ; and the wealthy young gallant, already of some repute as a poet, began his suit to Lady Dorothy Sidney. He pelted her with love-verses for some years, but she proved obdurate, and, in 1639, bestowed her hand on the Earl of Sunderland. It is said that, meeting her in later life, when Time had dealt hardly with her, he replied to her inquiry when he would again write such verses upon her, " When you are as young, madam, and as handsome as then you were." But no gentleman would have made such a reply, and, with all his faults, Waller was a gentleman. Returned to Parliament in 1640, he took at first the popular side, owing, probably, to the influence of his uncle Hampden, and was foremost in the opposition to the ship-money tax; but he veered round to the Royalists as events hurried on the Civil War. For his share in a plot to surprise the London train bands and let in the royal troops, in 1643, he narrowly escaped the scaffold; but his abject entreaties saved his life, and he was let off with a fine of £10,000 and a year's imprisonment.* On his release, he crossed over to France, and lived at Rouen with a good deal of splendour.

After some years he returned to England, and made his peace with Cromwell, by whose majestic character he seems to have been strongly impressed. His "Panegyric on Oliver Cromwell" contains some of his best writing. With easy morality he prepared a congratulatory address to Charles II., which was so inferior in poetical merit that the *débonnair* monarch rallied him on the disparity. "Poets, sir," answered Waller, with felicitous impertinence, " succeed better in fiction than in truth." He sat in several Parliaments after the Restoration, and Bishop Burnet tells us that he was the delight of the House of Commons. For his loyal subservience he was rewarded with the Provostship of Eton. At the accession of James II., he was elected representative for a Cornish borough; and his keen political sagacity soon predicted the issue to which the new King's arbitrary measures would bring

---

* "He had much ado to save his life," says Aubrey, "and in order to do it sold his estate in Bedfordshire, about £1,300 per annum, to Dr. Wright, for £10,000 (much under value), which was procured in twenty-four hours' time, or else he had been hanged. With this money he bribed the House, which was the first time a House of Commons was ever bribed." The money really went to pay the fine.

him. "He will be left," he said, "like a whale upon the strand." About this time he purchased a small property at Coleshill, his native place, saying, "He was fain to die like the stag, where he was raised." But he was not fated to realise his wish. An attack of dropsy carried him off at Beaconsfield, on the 21st of October, 1682; and he was buried in the churchyard, where the ashes of Edmund Burke also rest.

One of his later literary acts was the mutilation of Beaumont and Fletcher's "Maid's Tragedy." The performance of this fine play was prohibited after the Restoration, its moral—that

> "On lustful Kings
> Unlooked-for sudden deaths from heaven are sent"—

being necessarily disagreeable to the royal protector of Mrs. Barbara Palmer, Mistress Eleanor Gwynn, Louise de la Querouailles, and others. Waller rehabilitated it in Charles's favour by contriving a new act, in which the wronged Melantius rejoices in the gracious condescension of the licentious King of Rhodes who offers him "satisfaction" in a duel:—

> "The royal sword thus drawn, has cured a wound
> For which no other salve would have been found,
> Your brother now in arms ourselves we boast,
> A satisfaction for a sister lost.
> The blood of Kings exposed, washes a stain
> Cleaner than thousands of the vulgar slain."

The new ending required a new moral, and here it is:—

> "Long may he reign that is so far above
> All vice, all passion but excess of love."

"Excess of love"—a nice euphemism, truly, for vulgar lust! The conscience of Mr. Edmund Waller must have thrilled with satisfaction as he wrote these charming lines.

Let us get rid of this nauseous remembrance by repeating the one perfect—or almost perfect—lyric which will keep Waller's name alive in future ages:—

> " Go, lovely Rose,
> Tell her that wastes her time and me,
> That now she knows
> When I resemble her to thee
> How sweet and fair she seems to be.
>
> Tell her that's young,
> And shuns to have her graces spied,
> That hadst thou sprung
> In deserts where no men abide,
> Thou must have uncommended died.
>
> Small is the worth
> Of beauty from the light retired;
> Bid her come forth,
> Suffer herself to be desired,
> And not blush so to be admired.
>
> Then die, that she
> The common fate of all things rare
> May read in thee,
> How small a part of time they share
> Who are so wondrous sweet and fair."

In none other of his poems has Waller touched such a chord of truth and virtue. In none other are his cadences so new and fresh, and yet so sweet—sweet with almost a Shakespearian sweetness. The song is one of those which set themselves naturally, as it were, to music. You set an air to the words perforce as you repeat them. One can forgive Waller a good deal for this lustrous and exquisitely wrought gem.

In all Sir William Davenant's ponderous folio collection of masques, tragedies, operas, heroic poems, and what not, I can find nothing to equal Waller's claim to immortality. The dust of oblivion rests upon them. The life-blood of genius was wanting, and so they decayed rapidly, and the world put them out of sight, as dead things that were not worthy even of decent interment. Yet his epic poem of "Gondibert" (published in 1651) had its admirers in its day—a very short one—and Waller and Cowley would predict for it an enduring renown. And that its author had a large command of sonorous rhetorical verse and no small amount of technical skill, we are constrained to admit. He was a man of ingenuity, scholarship, and patience; but he was no poet. The dry bones were there; but he could not put into them the breath of life.

"Gondibert" is an epic of chivalry, in which the story carries an inner significance, being designed to recommend and illustrate the study of Nature, and to deduce therefrom certain philosophical conclusions. It is written in two-syllabled lines, and in quatrains; a metrical form* afterwards adopted by Dryden in his "Annus Mirabilis." Davenant, in his preface, explains his use of it on the ground "that it would be more pleasant to the reader, in a work of length, to give this respite or pause between every stanza (having endeavoured that each should contain a period) than to run him out of breath with continued couplets. Nor doth alternate rhyme by any lowliness of cadence make the sound less heroick, but rather adapt it to a plain and stately composing of musick; and the the brevity of the stanza renders it less subtle to the composer and more easy to the singer, which in *stilo recitativo*, where the story is long, is chiefly requisite." And he goes on to express the astounding hope that the cantos of his poem—of this dreary, monotonous, semi-philosophical essay in rhyme, which has neither dramatic incident nor lyrical break—would be sung at

---

* Davenant borrowed it from Sir John Davies's "Nosce teipsum."

village feasts! Heaven help the villagers who had the misfortune to join the audience! They could escape being reduced to utter imbecility only by falling into a heavy sleep.

The argument, briefly told, is this:—

Aribert the Lombard is prince of Verona. His beautiful daughter, Rhodalind, who is his heiress, is sought in marriage by two renowned warriors, Prince Oswald, who is a man of great worldly ambition, and Duke Gondibert, whose aims and aspirations are loftier. While engaged in the chase, Gondibert falls into an ambush laid by Oswald; in the duel which ensues, he is wounded, but Oswald is slain. The wounded Gondibert is carried to the house of the philosopher Astragon, which is in itself an allegory, with its garden labelled "Nature's Nursery," and its "Nature's Office, and its Library," "The Monument of Vanished Minds," and its threefold Temple, dedicated to "Days of Praise, of Prayer, and Penitence." Here he is tenderly nursed by Astragon's daughter, Birtha, who seems intended as a type of Nature, and soon learns to love her. He applies to Astragon to sanction his suit, and, in doing so, gives an account of his aim and purpose, which shows that Davenant was not incapable of serious and elevated thought. He desires to bring the world under the rule of a single monarchy, not to gratify a mean ambition, but in order to secure the happiness of the peoples, and inaugurate a reign of peace. This object accomplished he would then abandon himself to the study of Nature in company with Birtha:—

> "Here all reward of conquest I would find;
> Leave shining thrones for Birtha in a shade;
> With Nature's quiet wonders fill my mind,
> And praise her most because she Birtha made."

There are some fine lines scattered through this ponderous poem, and its general tone is grave and earnest; but apart from its want of interest and the monotony of its versification, the entire absence of human passion and feeling will account for the neglect it has experienced. We give a specimen or two of the poet's happier flights:—

"And now the weary world's great medicine, Sleep.
  This learnèd host dispensed to every guest,
Which shuts those wounds where injured lovers weep,
  And flies oppressors to relieve the opprest.

It loves the cottage and from Court abstains,
  It stills the seaman though the storm be high,
Frees the grieved captive in his closest chains,
  Stops Want's loud mouth, and blinds the treacherous spy."

The description of the Virgin Birtha is not without a certain poetical grace:—

"Her beauty princes durst not hope to use,
  Unless, like poets, for their morning theme;
And her mind's beauty they would rather choose,
  Which did the light in beauty's lanthorn seem.

She ne'er saw courts, yet courts could have undone
  With untaught looks and an unpractised heart;
Her arts, the most prepared could never shun,
  For Nature spread them in the scorn of Art.

She never had in busy cities been,
  Ne'er warmed with hopes, nor e'er allayed with fears;
Not seeing punishment, could guess no sin;
  And sin not seeing, ne'er had use of tears.

But here her father's precepts gave her skill,
  Which with incessant business filled the hours;
In spring she gathered blossoms for the still;
  In autumn, berries; and in summer, flowers.

And as kind Nature, with calm diligence,
  Her own free virtue silently employs,
Whilst she, unheard, does ripening growth dispense
  So were her virtues busy without noise."

The following would make a fit inscription for a Library:—

> "Where, when they thought they saw in well-sought books,
> Th' assembled souls of all that Men held wise,
> It bred such awful reverence in their looks,
> As if they saw the buried writers rise."

Sir William Davenant (or D'Avenant, as he preferred to write it) was the son of an Oxford vintner, and born in February 1605. An apocryphal story, told to Pope by Betterton the player, makes him the natural son of Shakespeare, who, it is said, on his journeys between London and Stratford-on-Avon, was accustomed to lodge at the Crown Tavern, kept by the elder Davenant. The poet, we are told, was proud of the supposed relationship. He always professed a great admiration for Shakespeare, and one of the earliest essays of his boyish muse was an Ode to his memory. Receiving his education at the Oxford Grammar School, he was afterwards sent to Lincoln College, but left without taking a degree. He became page to the Duchess of Richmond, and next was in the service of Sir Philip Sidney's friend, Fulke Greville, Lord Brooke. After his father's death, in 1628, he took to writing for the stage. His first composition was a tragedy, "Albovine, King of the Lombards" (1629), and this was followed by two plays, "The Cruel Brother" and "The Just Italian," which are condemned by their very titles. In 1634 he wrote a masque, for Queen Henrietta Maria and her ladies, entitled "The Temple of Love." The following year witnessed the production of a volume of poetry, containing his Shakespearian Ode and a poem in heroic couplets, entitled "Madagascar," which celebrated the exploits at sea of Prince Rupert. He was so much esteemed at Court for his poetical invention that, in 1637, on the death of Ben Jonson, he was appointed poet-laureate; and, two years later, was made director of the King and Queen's company of actors at the Cockpit in Drury Lane. His royalist sympathies led to his apprehension and imprisonment when the Civil War broke out; but he effected his escape to France.

When Queen Henrietta despatched to the Earl of Newcastle a supply of military *matériel*, Davenant returned to England, was made the Earl's Lieutenant-General of the Ordnance, and for his courage and conduct at the siege of Gloucester and in the field, received, in 1643, the honour of knighthood. The successes of the Puritans decided him to seek refuge in France, and while living with Lord Jermyn, in the Louvre, began his "heroic poem" of "Gondibert," sending the manuscript to Hobbes ("of Malmesbury") as he wrote it. His restless spirit soon wearying of inaction, he resolved to found a settlement in the loyal colony of Virginia; but the ship in which he had embarked was captured by one of the Parliament's men-of-war, and he was lodged in prison at Cowes Castle, in the Isle of Wight.* There he continued his poetical *magnum opus*, of which Waller sang in complimentary phrase:—

> "Here no bold tales of gods or monsters swell,
> But human passions such as with us dwell;
> Man is thy theme, his virtue or his rage,
> Drawn to the life in each elaborate page."

* Aubrey's version of the incident is as follows:—"He laid an ingenious design to carry a certain number of artificers, chiefly weavers, from France to Virginia, and by Mary, the queen mother's means, he got favour from the King of France to go into the prison and pick and choose; so when the poor wretches understood what his design was they cried, *uno ore*, 'Tous tisserans' (We are all weavers). Well, he took thirty-six, as I remember, and not more, and shipped them; and as he was on his voyage to Virginia he and his weavers were all taken by the ships then belonging to the Parliament of England. The French slaves, I suppose, they sold, but Sir William was brought prisoner to England. Whether he was at first a prisoner at Carisbrooke Castle, in the Isle of Wight, or at the Tower of London, I have forgotten. He was a prisoner at both."

He carried it down to the middle of the third book, and as he intended to have five books answering to the five acts of a play, with cantos answering to scenes, he had consequently finished one-half. He therefore drew up a postscript, in which he says: "I am here arrived at the middle of the third book. But it is high time to strike sail and cast anchor, though I have run but half my course, when at the helm I here am threatened with Death, who, though he can visit us but once, seems troublesome, and even in the innocent may beget such a gravity as diverts the music of verse." Davenant was removed to the Tower, but through the influence, as some say, of two Aldermen of York, whom he had once obliged, or, as others say, of Milton, to whom he afterwards repaid the service in kind, he escaped the punishment of high treason, and though kept in prison for two years, was treated with great indulgence.

On his release the indefatigable wit planned the establishment of a theatre, and in spite of a world of difficulties, succeeded in opening Rutland House, Charterhouse Yard, on the 21st of May, 1656, for what he called "operas," in which he combined (as the elder Disraeli puts it) "the music of Italy and the scenery of France." There he produced, with scenic effects, illustrative music, songs, and choruses, the first part of his "Siege of Rhodes."

After the Restoration he obtained the management of the Duke of York's company of players (which included the famous Betterton), acting first at the theatre in Portugal Row, Lincoln's Inn Fields, and aferwards in Dorset Gardens. A clause in his patent sanctioned a great innovation :—" Whereas the women's parts in plays have hitherto been acted by men in the habits of women, at which some have taken offence, we do permit and give leave for the time to come that all women's parts be acted by women on the stage." For his new company Davenant remodelled his " Siege of Rhodes," and also produced a second part, in which, instead of blank verse for the dialogue, he adopted the French use of rhymed couplets.

"In the 'Siege of Rhodes,'" says Morley, " Davenant held by the extension of that theory of Hobbes's to contending nations as well as to contending men of the same country, which he had made the ground of Gondibut's ambition to subdue the world. His life was too much given to low pleasures, and he was called upon to entertain the frivolous. If Davenant could have felt with Milton that he who would excel in poetry should be himself a poem, his genius had wings to bear him higher than he ever reached. Among the musical love-passions of 'The Siege of Rhodes' he was still aiming at some embodiment of his thought that the nations of Christendom failed in their work for want of unity. They let the Turks occupy Rhodes because they could not join for succour. In his dedication of the published play to the Earl of Clarendon, Davenant (referring with humour to 'the great images represented in tragedy by Monsieur Corneille') says : 'In this poem I have revived the remembrance of that desolation which was permitted by Christian princes, when they favoured the ambition of such as defended the diversity of religions (begot by the factions of learning) in Germany; whilst those who would never admit learning into their empire (lest it should meddle with religion, and intangle it with controversy) did make

Rhodes defenceless; which was the only fortified academy in Christendom where divinity and arms were equally professed.' "

Davenant's latest literary efforts were in an unfortunate direction—the adaptation of Shakespeare to the taste of the Court of Charles II. In these efforts he displayed not only a corrupt task, but a singular want of the dramatic instinct. He died at the age of 63, on the 7th of April, 1668.

In another chapter we have had something to say of the cause of Charles Sackville, Earl of Dorset. Among the poets he claims notice as one of the earliest of our writers of society verse; and probably no English Anthologies will ever fail to include those bright, brisk stanzas, beginning :—

> "To all you Ladies now at land
> We men at sea indite ;
> But first would have you understand
> How hard it is to write:
> The Muses now, and Neptune, too,
> We must implore to write to you."

The fame they enjoyed well deserved their absolute and genuine excellence ; but probably owes something to the alleged romantic circumstances of their composition. They are entitled a " Song written at Sea, in the First Dutch War, 1665, the Night before an Engagement," the engagement being supposed to be the bloody battle off the coast of Suffolk, fought, on the 3rd June, between the English fleet, under the Duke of York, and the Dutch under Opdam. But from the diary of Pepys it is evident that they were written six months before this great sea fight, and their connection with it was an invention of the poet Prior. As a matter of fact, the fifth stanza disposes of the "night before the battle" theory:—

> "Should foggy Opdam chance to know
> Our sad and dismal story,
> The Dutch would scorn so weak a foe,
> And quit their fort at Goree,
> For what resistance can they find
> From men who've left their hearts behind?"

The Earl's literary performance was not equal to his literary promise. He had a fine taste, much skill in composition, and abundant leisure; but he accomplished little. A few satires, more remarkable for violence than vigour, and a few graceful songs, are all that bear his name. When Prior asserts that, "there is a lustre in his verses like that of the sun in Claude Lorraine's landscapes," his language is that of a friend, not of a critic. All that can truly be said of them is that neither in polish nor point are they deficient. A characteristic specimen of Lord Dorset's verse, and of the kind of verse that pleased his contemporaries, is found in the following song:—

> "Dorinda's sparkling wit and eyes
> United cast too fierce a light,
> Which blazes high, but quickly dies,
> Pains not the heart, but hurts the sight.
>
> Love is a calmer, gentler joy,
> Smooth are his looks, and soft his pace;
> Her Cupid is a blackguard boy,
> That runs his link full in your face."

Lord Dorset was a generous patron of literature, and literary men, who, by the way, have never fared so well in England as during the latter half of the seventeenth and the first half of the eighteenth centuries. He assisted almost all the poets of his time, from Waller to Pope, and counted among his intimates and friends "glorious John" and "Matt Prior." His clear judgment recognised the trenchant wit and profuse power of Butler's "Hudibras," which he helped to make popular at Court. He loved to gather round him a brilliant circle of men of letters at Knowle, his seat near Sevenoaks, where Shadwell wrote his best comedy. A pleasant story is told of one of their symposia, whereat it had been agreed that each person present should write an impromptu, and that Dryden should decide which was the best. While the others were laboriously cudgelling their brains, Dorset penned only a line or two, and threw his paper towards the judge, who, on reading it, easily obtained the assent of the company to his decision in its favour. For it ran thus:—" I promise to pay Mr. John Dryden, or order, £500 on demand. DORSET." This was a golden impromptu, about the merits of which there could be no mistake.

Pope speaks of this accomplished nobleman as "the grace of courts, the muses' pride;"* and Horace Walpole says, " he was the first gentleman in the voluptuous court of Charles II., and in the gloomy one of King William. He had as much wit as his first master, or his contemporaries Buckingham and Rochester, without the King's want of feeling, the duke's want of principle, or the earl's want of thought."

When Dorset became William III.'s Lord Chamberlain in 1689, one of the first acts which official duty imposed upon him was peculiarly painful to a man of his generous sympathies, a man so loyal to his humblest friends. Dryden could no longer remain poet-laureate. He was not only a Papist, but an apostate, and the country would not have him among the subjects of their Majesties.

* " Blest courtier, who could King and country please,
   Yet sacred keep his friendship and his ease."

"He had aggravated the guilt of his apostasy by calumniating and ridiculing the Church which he had deserted. He had, it was facetiously said, treated her as the Pagan persecutors of old treated her children. He had dressed her up in the skin of a wild beast; and then baited her for the public amusement." Accordingly, he was deprived of his place; but the bounty of Dorset bestowed on him a pension equal in amount to the salary which he had lost.*

It must be owned that the aristocracy of seventeenth century England was, whatever its faults, an aristocracy of culture; its members loved literature with a generous affection, cherished men of letters with a fervour which had no humiliation in it, and themselves wooed the Muse with ardour and not wholly without success.† Among these noble poets I own to a particular respect for Wentworth Dillon, Earl of Roscommon, upon whom Pope has bestowed no common eulogium:—

> "In all Charles's days
> Roscommon only boasts unspotted lays."

His judgment was sound and clear, his taste accurate, and he wrote with ease and smoothness, if not with any degree of fervour or with any of the passion of genius. The nephew and godson of the great Earl of Strafford, he

---

* An ill-natured allusion to Dryden's reception of this beneficence occurs in Blackmore's ponderous " Prince Arthur ":—

> "Sakil's high roof, the Muses' palace, rung
> With endless airs, and endless songs he sung.
> To bless good Sakil Laurus would be first;
> But Sakil's prince and Sakil's God he curst.
> Sakil without distinction threw his bread,
> Dispised the flatterer, but the poet fed."

" Sakil " of course is Sackville; and " Laurus " Dryden,—either in allusion to the lost Laureateship, or as a translation of his celebrated nickname *Bayes.*

† So Lord Mulgrave wrote:
"Without his song no fop is to be found,"—but all the singers were not fops.

was born in 1633. At the age of ten, while receiving his education at the Protestant College at Caen, he succeeded to his father's title. He remained abroad and travelled in Italy till the Restoration, when he was made captain of the company of Gentlemen Pensioners, and afterwards Master of the Horse to the Duchess of York. The evil influence of the Court led him to a temporary indulgence at the gaming-table; but his sound sense prevailed. He married, and devoted his leisure to literary pursuits. On the Continent he had acquired a taste for French poems;* and he studied with much devotion Boileau's "L'Art Poetique," in which the canons of a frigid criticism are applied to the poet's inspired work. In conjunction with Dryden, he meditated a scheme for establishing in England an Academy like that which in France has exercised a considerable influence over the world of letters. In 1681 he published an "Essay on Translated Verse," which may be held to entitle him to the name of "the English Boileau;" and in 1684 he put his principles into practice in a translation of Horace's "Art of Poetry." He translated also a part of Guarini's "Pastor Fido," Virgil's Sixth Eclogue, one or two Odes of Horace, and the old Latin hymn, "Dies Iræ." The national unrest due to the arbitrary measures of James II. inspired him with apprehensions of civil war, and he prepared to retire to Rome saying it was best to sit near the chimney when the chamber smoked. But an attack of gout prevented his departure, and he died in London on the 17th of January, 1685, while still in the prime of manhood. "At

---

* Yet was he not at all narrow in his poetical sympathies ; he was one of the first English critics to do justice to the sublimity of Milton. We may infer that though he wished to introduce Academic exactness, it was not at the expense of any of the essential characteristics of the English genius.

the moment in which he expired," says Johnson, "he uttered with an energy of voice that expressed the most fervent devotion, two lines of his own version of 'Dies Iræ' : —

'My God, my Father, and my Friend,
Do not forsake me in my end!'"

That he could write with force and terseness the following extract will show :—

"On sure foundations let your fabric rise,
And with attractive majesty surprise;
Not by affected, meretricious arts,
But strict harmonious symmetry of parts,
While through the whole insensibly must pass,
With vital heat to animate the mass;
A pure, an active, an auspicious flame,
And bright as heaven, from where the blessing came;
But few, few spirits, pre-ordained by fate,
The race of gods, have reached that envied height;
No rebel Titan's sacrilegious crime,
By heaping hills on hills, can thither climb.
The grizzly ferryman of hell denied
Æneas entrance, till he knew his guide;
How justly then will impious mortals fall,
When pride would soar to heaven without a call?
Pride, of all others the most dangerous fault,
Proceeds from want of sense or want of thought."

It is something of surprise to find a writer in Charles II.'s reign putting forward a plea on behalf of decency :—

"Immodest words admit of no defence,
For want of decency is want of sense.
What moderate fops would rake the park or stews,
Who among troops of faultless nymphs may choose?
Variety of such is to be found;
Take then a subject proper to expound,
But moral, great, and worth a poet's voice;
For most of sense despise a trivial choice:
And such applause it must expect to meet,
As would some painter busy in a street
To copy bulls and bears, and every sign
That calls the staring sots to musty wine."

Another poet-peer who claims our notice is John Wilmot, Earl of Rochester, who, in his saner moments and happier moods, could sing with a grace and sweetness not surpassed by any of his intimate contemporaries. Had those moods and moments been more frequent and of longer duration he must have attained a high place among English poets of the second rank. Oh, the pity of it that a man of such fine endowments should have yielded them up to the devils of lust and intemperance! What can be more tender or delightful than the following "swallow-flight of song?" It wants the peculiar quaintness of the Elizabethans, but has a charm of its own which it is impossible to resist:—

> " My dear Mistress has a heart
>   Soft as those kind looks she gave me;
> When, with love's resistless art,
>   And her eyes, she did enslave me;
> But her constancy's so weak,
>   She's so wild and apt to wander,
> That my jealous heart would break
>   Should we live one day asunder.
>
> Melting joys about her move,
>   Killing pleasures. wounding blisses,
> She can dress her eyes in love,
>   And her lips can arm with kisses;
> Angels listen when she speaks,
>   She's my delight, all mankind's wonder,
> But my jealous heart would break
>   Should we live one day asunder."

This is one of those songs which sing themselves. In the following we note the unusual strain of pathos:—

> " Absent from thee I languish still,
>   Then ask me not, when I return?
> The straying fool 'twill plainly kill
>   To wish all day, all night to mourn.
>
> Dear, from thine arms thou let me fly,
>   That my fantastic mind may prove
> The torments it deserves to try,
>   That tear my fixed heart from my love

> When, wearied with a world of woe,
>   To thy safe bosom I retire,
> Where love and peace and honour grow,
>   May I contented there expire.
>
> Lest once more wandering from that heaven,
>   I false on some base heart unblest,
> Faithless to thee, false, unforgiven,
>   And lose my everlasting rest."

"With Rochester," says Mr. Gosse, "the power of writing songs died in England until the age of Blake and Burns. He was the last of the Cavalier lyrists, and in some respects the best. In the qualities that a song demands, simplicity, brevity, pathos and tenderness, he arrives nearer to pure excellence than any one between Carew and Burns. His style is without adornment, and, save in this one matter of song-writing, he is weighed down by the dryness and inefficiency of his age. But by the side of Sedley or of Congreve he seems as fresh as by the side of Dryden he seems light and flowing, turning his trill of song brightly and sweetly, with the consummate artlessness of true art. Occasionally, he is surprisingly like Donne in the quaint force and ingenuity of his images. But the fact is that the muse of Rochester resembles nothing so much as a beautiful child which has wantonly rolled itself in the mud, and which has grown so dirty that the ordinary wayfarer would rather pass it hurriedly by, than do justice to its native charms."

Rochester's satires are not deficient in vigour and keenness; but their filthiness renders them unquotable. I have no fancy for wading through a sewer on the chance of picking up a piece of silver. His poem on "Nothing" is ingenious; and some happy characterisation is to be found in the "Trial of the Poets for the Bays," a satirical poem after the manner of Suckling's "Session of the

Poets." The writers brought on the stage are—Dryden, Etherege, Wycherley, Shadwell, Settle, Otway, Mrs. Behn, Tom D'Urfey, and Betterton—to the last of whom the bays are ironically given. Rochester also wrote, or, more correctly speaking, travestied from Fletcher, the tragedy of "Valentinian."

Yet another poet pen flourished in these days of aristocratic culture, John Sheffield, Earl of Mulgrave, Marquis of Normanby, and Duke of Buckinghamshire (to name at once his three stages in the peerage), who outlived most of his contemporaries, and died at the age of seventy in the reign of George I. He was born in 1649. At the age of seventeen, he volunteered to serve at sea against the Dutch. "He passed six weeks on board," says Macaulay, " diverting himself, as well as he could, in the society of some young libertines of rank, and then returned home to take the command of a troop of horse. After this he was never on the water till 1672, when he again joined the fleet, and was almost immediately appointed captain of a ship of 84 guns [the *Royal Catherine*], reputed the finest in the navy. He was then twenty-three years old, and had not, in the whole course of his life, been three months afloat. As soon as he came back from sea he was made Colonel of a regiment of foot. This," adds the historian, " is a specimen of the manner in which naval commands of the highest importance were then given; and a very favourable specimen; for Mulgrave, though he wanted experience, wanted neither parts nor courage."

To gain some knowledge of war, he entered the French service, and made a campaign under Turenne, in which his bravery was conspicuous. He afterwards commanded the forces defending Tangier against the Moors, and during the expedition (1680) wrote his poem of "The Vision," characterised by Johnson as a licentious poem, with little power of invention or propriety of sentiment. He became a member of the Privy Council of James II., who appointed him governor of Hull and Lord Chamberlain; and he proved his loyalty by giving the king much sound and sensible advice, which the king never followed. He acquiesced in the Revolution of 1688, though at first he refused office under the new Government. It is to his honour that he signed the protest of some of the peers against the Bill, in 1693, for instituting a censorship of the Press; and in the same session he opposed, with all the force of his eloquence, the Bill for the regulation of Trials in cases of High Treason. Though created Marquis of Normanby, with a pension of £3,000 a year, he maintained his independence; and among the opponents of the harsh and arbitrary measure known as Sir John Fenwick's Attainder Bill none was more perseveringly active. On the accession of Queen Anne, whose lover he had at one time been, he was distinguished with special favour, made Lord of the Privy Seal, and created Duke of Buckinghamshire. He was president of council, and one of the Lords Justices in Great Britain; but when George I. succeeded to the throne, he threw himself into active opposition to the Court. His death took place on the 24th of February, 1720. He was interred in Westminster Abbey, where his epitaph, written by himself, unblushingly proclaims that he lived and died a sceptic.

His Tory politics will account for the strain of bitterness that runs through Macaulay's character of this able statesman: " Mulgrave wrote verses which scarcely ever rose above absolute mediocrity; but as he was a man of high note in the political and fashionable world, these verses found admirers. Time dissolved the charm, but, unfortunately for him, not until his lines had acquired a prescriptive right to a place in all collections of the works of English poets. To this day, accordingly, his insipid essays in rhyme and his paltry songs to Amoretta and Gloriana are reprinted in company with Comus and Alexander's Feast. The consequence is that our generation knows Mulgrave chiefly as a poetaster, and despised him as such. In truth, however, he was, by the acknowledgment of those who neither loved nor esteemed him, a man distinguished by fine parts, and in parliamentary eloquence inferior to scarcely any orator of his time. His moral character was entitled to no respect. He was a libertine without that openness of heart and hand which sometimes makes libertinism amiable, and a haughty aristocrat without that elevation of sentiment which sometimes makes aristocratical haughtiness respectable. The satirists of the age nicknamed him Lord Allpride, and pronounced it strange that a man who had so exalted a sense of his dignity should be so hard and niggardly in all pecuniary dealings."

I venture to think more highly than does the brilliant historian of the Duke's literary qualifications. He writes with vigour and perspicuity, and his canons of criticism are just and sensible. His two principal works are—an "Essay on Satire," published in 1675, and his "Essay on Poetry,"—the latter a kind of *Ars Poetica*, published anonymously in 1682, and enlarged and revised, with some touches by Pope, in 1691. It is written in the heroic couplet, and was warmly commended by Pope and

Roscommon and Dryden. Not a few of its lines have become familiar quotations, as, for example:—

> "Fancy is but the feather of the pen;
> Reason is that substantial, useful part
> Which gains the head; while t'other wins the heart."
>
> "Of all those arts in which the wise excel,
> Nature's chief master-piece is writing well."
>
> "True wit is everlasting like the sun,
> Which, though sometimes behind a cloud retired,
> Breaks out again, and is by all admired."
>
> "Read Homer once, and you can read no more,
> For all books else appear so mean, so poor,
> Verse will seem prose; but still persist to read,
> And Homer will be all the books you need."

Like Rochester, Mulgrave indulged in a squib against contemporary poets and poetasters. In 1719, on the appointment of Eusden to the post of poet laureate, he published the satire of "The Election of a Laureate," in which he introduced Blackmore, Congreve, Lansdowne, Bishop Atterbury, Philips, Gay, Cibber, D'Urfey, Prior, and Pope. It concludes thus:—

> "At last in rushed Eusden, and cried, 'Who shall have it,
> But I, the true laureat, to whom the King gave it?'
> Apollo begged pardon, and granted his claim,
> But vowed, though, till then he'd ne'er heard of his name."

Mulgrave had the good sense and the good taste to rank Shakespeare and John Fletcher before all other English dramatists; but in later life his good sense and good taste deserted him, partly through the influence of French criticism, and partly perhaps through the strength of his political prejudices, and he undertook a revision of Shakespeare's "Julius Cæsar." A believer in the gospel of the unities, he was shocked by the boldness with which Shakespeare treats time and place, and proceeded to reconstruct Shakespeare's great historical drama on the

model of a French tragedy. The result was seen in *two*
plays instead of one, "Julius Cæsar" and "Marcus
Brutus," each ending with a denunciation of the Roman
hero's act of tyrannicide. The audacious adapter ventured
even to meddle with Shakespeare's language, and translated the fine, terse, and pregnant line, "The good is oft
interred with their bones," into "The good is often buried
in their graves"—an alteration which throws a startling
light on the noble author's want of true poetical perception.

Among the crowd of aristocratic poets whom the
Restoration warmed into activity one of the most refined
and graceful was Sir Charles Sedley, the friend of Dorset
and Roscommon and Dryden, and the "Lisideius" of
Dryden's "Essay of Dramatic Poesie." He was born at
Aylesford, in Kent, in 1639. His mother was Elizabeth,
daughter of Sir Henry Saville, the learned provost of
Eton, whose talents and love of scholarship she seems
to have inherited.* At the age of seventeen, young
Sedley, already distinguished by his intellectual gifts,
entered Wadham College, Oxford, but left the University
without taking a degree, and went abroad. He returned
to England at the Restoration, and about 1667 found
his way to Court, where the grace of his address and
the charm of his conversation soon made him "the
observed of all observers." With the King he was a
great favourite, and among the beauties and wits that
assembled in the gay circle at Whitehall no one was

---

* Compare Waller's epitaph:—

"Here lies the learned Saville's heir,
So early wise, and lasting fair,
That none, except her years they told,
Thought her a child, or thought her old."

more popular. Shadwell says of him that he would speak more wit at a supper than all his adversaries could have written in a year. Pepys tells us that to sit near him at the theatre, and hear his comments on a new play, was an intellectual treat. It was gracefully said by the King that "Nature had given him a patent to be Apollo's Viceroy."

His love-verses are bright, vivacious, and graceful. They are free from the indelicate expressions which offend us as those of Suckling or Rochester, but it cannot be pretended that they are purer in sentiment. His muse is attired in the garb of a courtezan, but the courtezan is a Lais or a Phryne, and not a common street-walker. Whether she is less dangerous may well be doubted. The sober Evelyn couples him with Etherege:—

> "But gentle Etherege and Sedley's Muse
> Warm the coy maid, and melting love infuse."

And to this evil power of stimulating the imagination, while assuming a mask of decency, Rochester alludes:—

> "For songs and verses, mannerly obscene,
> That can stir nature up by springs unseen;
> And, without forcing blushes, warm the queen—
> Sedley has that prevailing, gentle art,
> That can, with a resistless charm, impart
> The loosest wishes to the chastest heart;
> Raise such a conflict, kindle such a fire
> Between declining virtue and desire;
> Till the poor vanquished maid dissolves away
> In dreams all night, and sighs and tears all day."

This fascinating sweetness is designated by Buckingham "Sedley's witchcraft," though it would seem to have been more apparent to his contemporaries than it is to the critics of a soberer day. That he could, at will, write with elegance and yet without offending the most fastidious taste, I readily admit. Take the following song as a specimen :—

> "Ah, Chloris, that I now could sit
>   As unconcerned as when
> Your infant beauty could beget
>   No pleasure, nor no pain!
>
> When I the dawn used to admire
>   And praised the coming day;
> I little thought the growing fire
>   Must take my rest away.
>
> Your charms in harmless childhood lay,
>   Like metals in the mine,
> Age from no face took more away
>   Than youth concealed in thine.
>
> But as your charms insensibly
>   To their perfection prest,
> Fond love as unperceived did fly,
>   And in my bosom rest,
>
> My passion with your beauty grew,
>   And Cupid at my heart,
> Still as his mother favoured you,
>   Threw a new flaming dart.
>
> Each gloried in their wanton part:
>   To make a lover, he
> Employed the utmost of his art,
>   To make a beauty she.
>
> Though now I slowly bend to love,
>   Uncertain of my fate,
> If your fair self my chains approve,
>   I shall my freedom hate.
>
> Lovers, like dying men, may well
>   At first disordered be,
> Since none alive can truly tell
>   What future they must see."

The opening lines of another of his songs have received the merit-mark of universal approbation, and to this day are quoted :—

> "Love still has something of the sea
>   From whence his mother rose."

Sir Charles Sedley's plays are now known only to the

scholar, and though they contain some witty passages and a felicitous sketch or two of character-painting, they are not worthy of deliverance from the oblivion into which they have fallen. Their construction is irregular, and they are deficient in dramatic interest. The tragedy of "Antony and Cleopatra" was produced at the Duke's Theatre in 1667; his comedy (the best of his dramatic works) of "The Mulberry Garden," at Drury Lane, in 1668; and "Bellamira; or, The Mistress," at the King's House in 1687. We are told that "while this play was acting, the roof of the play-house fell down; but very few were hurt, except the author, whose merry friend, Sir Fleetwood Shepherd, told him that there was so much fire in the play, that it blew up the poet, house, and all. Sir Charles answered, 'No; the play was so heavy it brought down the house, and buried the poet in his own rubbish.'" Sedley also wrote the tragedy of "Beauty the Conqueror," and two other dramas have, but on no good grounds, been ascribed to him.

This brilliant wit and easy courtier was guilty on one occasion of a profligacy so vile that one is inclined to attribute it to mental aberration. He presented himself, after "a wild revel," perfectly naked in the balcony of the Cock Tavern, in Bow Street, and harangued the crowd of porters and orange-girls in such profane and indecent language that they resented it with volleys of stones, and compelled him and his companions (among whom, unhappily, was Buckhurst, afterwards Earl of Dorset) to retire. For this shameful exploit they were brought before the Court of Common Pleas, and heavily fined, Sir Charles Sedley's penalty being not less than £500. The Lord Chief Justice, Sir Robert Hyde, sarcastically inquired of the dissolute wit if he had ever read "The Complete Gentleman?"* "I believe," he replied, unabashed, "I have read more books than your lordship." It is said that Sir Charles and his companions engaged Killigrew and another courtier to intercede with the King for a reduction of the penalty; but, contrary to the proverb, honour does not always prevail among such men, they obtained a grant of the money for themselves, and extorted it to the last farthing.

Another of Sedley's indefensible pranks is related by Oldys :—" There was a great resemblance," he says, " in the shape and features, between him and Kynaston the actor, who once got some laced clothes made exactly after a suit Sir Charles wore, who therefore got him well caned. Sir Charles's emissary pretending to take Kynaston for Sir Charles, quarrelled with him in St. James's Park, and beat him as Sir Charles. When some of his friends, in pity to the man, reproved Sir Charles for it, he told them that they misplaced their pity, and that it was himself they should bestow it on; that Kynaston's bones would not suffer as much as his reputation; for all the town believed it was him that was thrashed, and suffered such a public disgrace."

It seems to be generally agreed that, after his mad orgie at the Cock Tavern, Sedley adopted a more serious mode of life, and began to take an active interest in public affairs. As member for Romney, in Kent, he took a frequent part in the debates in the House of Commons, and by his eloquence and vivacity obtained a considerable influence. During the reign of James II. he distinguished

---

* Henry Peacham's book, published in 1622, of which a new edition had appeared in 1661.

himself by his vigorous opposition to the measures of the Court. It is true that in this opposition he was influenced, perhaps, as much by personal feelings as by regard for the public interest. Profligate as he was, or had been, he could not as a father witness without shame and indignation the illicit connection which James, when Duke of York, had formed with his daughter, the notorious Catherine Sedley.* And when he was asked the reason of his bitter antipathy to a king who had loaded him with favours, he replied, "I hate ingratitude; and, therefore, as the king has made *my* daughter a Countess, I will endeavour to make *his* daughter a Queen."

On his accession to the throne, James was reluctantly induced, by the advice of his confessors and the remonstrances of his queen,† to dissolve the connection; though he had just shown the strength of his affection by creating

---

* Catherine Sedley was distinguished by her wit and accomplishments, but possessed no personal charms, except two brilliant eyes. Her countenance was haggard, and her form lean. Charles II., though he admired her intellectual gifts, laughed at her want of comeliness, and declared that the priests must have recommended her to his brother by way of penance. She was too clever a woman not to know and own her ugliness, and affirmed that she could not understand the secret of James's passion for her. "It cannot be my beauty," she said, "for he must see that I have none; and it cannot be my wit, for he has not enough to know that I have any." Like many plain women, she was fond of sumptuous dress, and Lord Dorset has somewhat coarsely satirised the weakness which led her to appear in public places, in all the gorgeousness of Brussels lace, diamonds, and paint:—

> "Tell me, Dorinda, why so gay,
> Why such embroidery, fringe, and lace?
> Can any dresses find a way
> To stop the approaches of decay,
> And mend a ruined face? . . . .
>
> So have I seen in larder dark
> Of veal a lucid loin,
> Replete with many a brilliant spark,
> (As wise philosophers remark)
> At once both stink and shine."

† The intrigues of which she was the author are described at length by Macaulay. See also Evelyn's Diary, under date January 19, 1686; Bishop Barnet's History of His Own Time, i, 682; and Rousby's Memoirs.

her (1686) Baroness of Darlington and Countess of Dorchester for life. She afterwards became the wife of Sir David Colyear, first Earl of Portmore. She died at Bath in 1717.

In the Parliaments of King William and Queen Mary, Sir Charles was generally on the side of the Opposition; and in the session of 1690 made one of his best speeches in condemnation of the large sums expended on salaries and pensions. Macaulay refers to it as proving, what his poems and plays might make us doubt, that his contemporaries were not mistaken in considering him as a man of parts and vivacity. Gradually, as he advanced in years, he withdrew from the political arena; and the public had almost forgotten him at the time of his death, which took place at Haverstock Hill* on the 20th of August, 1701. A complete edition of his works, including love songs, translations from martial and other classic writers, prologues and epilogues, plays and speeches, was published in the following year by his friend and kinsman, Captain Ayloff, who observes that "he (Sir Charles) was a man of the first class of wit and gallantry; his friendship was courted by everybody; and nobody went out of his company but pleased and improved; Time added but very little to Nature, and he was everything that an English gentleman could be." That his powers were considerable no one can reasonably doubt. It is to be regretted that he did not make a worthier use of them.

The last of the aristocratic poets whom we shall notice

---

* Steele for awhile (1712) resided at this house. He writes to Pope:—
"I am at a solitude, a house between Hampstead and London, wherein Sir Charles Sedley died. This circumstance set me a-thinking and ruminating upon the employments in which men of wit exercise themselves." The house was pulled down in 1869, and its site is now occupied by Steele Terrace.

is Sir John Denham, whose " chief claim to immortality," according to a recent critic, rests on the fine lines in his poem of "Cooper's Hill," descriptive of the Thames :—

> " O could I flow like thee, and make thy stream
> My great example, as it is my theme ;
> Though deep yet clear, though gentle yet not dull,
> Strong without rage, without o'er flowing full."

But these are not the only good lines in a poem, which had at all events the merit of being the first of its kind (for Ben Jonson's "Penshurst" cannot fairly be considered of the same category), which Dryden, with exuberant praise, declares "for the majesty of its style is, and ever will be, the exact standard of good writing." The allusion to St. Paul's (not Wren's Cathedral, but its predecessor) is worth quotation :—

> " That sacred pile, so vast, so high,
> That whether 'tis a part of earth or sky
> Uncertain seems, and may be thought a proud
> Aspiring mountain or descending cloud."

The following couplet seems to have suggested a passage in Dr. Johnson's "London" :—

> " Under his proud survey the city lies,
> And like a mist beneath a hill doth rise,
> Whose state and wealth, the business and the crowd,
> Seems at this distance but a darker cloud,
> And is to him who rightly things esteems
> No other in effect but what it seems,
> When, with like haste, though several ways, they run,
> Some to undo, and some to be undone ;
> While luxury and wealth, like war and peace,
> Are each the other's ruin and increase ;
> As rivers lost in seas some secret vain
> Thence reconveys, then to be lost again.
> O happiness of sweet retired content !
> To be at once secure and innocent ! "

And surely the impartial critic will own that in these

lines—on the reformation and the sharp contrast between Monasticism and Puritanism—strength and smoothness are not unhappily combined :—

> "No crime so bold but would be understood
> A real, or at least a seeming good,
> Who fears not to do ill, yet fears the name,
> And, free from conscience, is a slave to fame.
> Thus he the Church at once protects and spoils :
> But princes' swords are sharper than their styles.
> And thus to th' ages past he makes amends,
> Their charity destroys, their faith defends.
> Then did religion in a lazy cell,
> In empty, airy contemplation dwell ;
> And like the block unmoved lay ; but ours,
> As much too active, like the stork devours.
> Is there no temperate region can be known
> Betwixt their frigid and our temperate zone ?
> Could we not wake from that lethargic dream,
> But to be restless in a worse extreme ?
> And for that lethargy was there no cure
> But to be cast into a calenture ?
> Can knowledge have no abound, but must advance
> So far, to make us wish for ignorance,
> And rather in the dark to grope our way
> Than, led by a false guide, to err by day ! "

"Cooper's Hill" was written in 1640 and published in 1643.* It is a poem of nearly four hundred lines, written

* "The epithet, *majestic* Denham, conferred by Pope, conveys rather too much ; but Cooper's Hill is no ordinary poem. It is nearly the first instance of vigorous and rhythmical couplets, for Denham is incomparably less feeble than Browne, and less prosaic than Beaumont. Close in thought, and nervous in language like Davies, he is less hard and less monotonous; his cadences are animated and various, perhaps a little beyond the regularity that metre demands ; they have been the guide to the finer ear of Dryden. Those who cannot endure the philosophic poetry, must ever be dissatisfied with Cooper's Hill : no personification, no ardent words, few metaphors beyond the common use of speech, nothing that warms, or melts, or fascinates the heart. It is rare to find lines of eminent beauty in Denham ; and equally so to be struck by any one as feeble or low. His language is always well-chosen and perspicuous, free from those strange terms of expression, frequent in our older poets, where the reader is apt to suspect some error of the press, so irreconcilable do they seem with grammar or meaning. The expletive *do*, which the best of his predecessors use freely, seldom occurs in Denham ; and he has in other respects brushed away the rust of languid and ineffective redundancies which have obstructed the popularity of men with more native genius than himself." — Hallam, "Literature of Europe," iii., 254, 255.

in the heroic couplet, and embodies the reflections suggested to a thoughtful observer by the various scenes which are visible from the summit of its author's "Mount Parnassus."* These include a long reach of the winding Thames, the towers of Windsor Castle, St. Paul's Cathedral, and the field of Runnymede. The freshness of the subject,† and the fluent strength of the versification, secured for this poem an immediate popularity. Dryden pronounced it "the exact standard of good writing." "This poem," says Johnson, "had such reputation as to excite the common artifice by which envy degrades excellence. A report was spread that the performance was not his own, but that he had bought it of a vicar for forty pounds." Pope, in his poem of "Windsor Forest," which "Cooper's Hill" suggested, affirms that —

> "On Cooper's Hill eternal wreaths shall grow
> While lasts the mountain, or while Thames shall flow;"

while Somerville, in "The Chase," calls upon us to tread with respectful awe —

> "Windsor's green glades ; where Denham, tuneful bard,
> Charmed once the list'ning Dryads with his song,
> Sublimely sweet."

By a natural law of reaction the excessive praise of one generation is succeeded by the extreme depreciation of another. Southey writes of Denham with great frigidity:

---

* Cooper's Hill lies about half-a-mile to the north-west of Egham, where the poet's father had built for himself a house—(now the Vicarage)—"in which his son Sir John (though he had better seats) took most delight." The spot from which the poet made his survey is traditionally said to be now comprised within the grounds of Kingswood Lodge ; a seat marks the site.

† Johnson praises Denham as "the author of a species of composition that may be denominated local poetry, of which the fundamental subject is some particular landscape, to be poetically described, with the addition of such embellishments as may be supplied by historical retrospection or incidental meditation."

—"That Sir John Denham began a reformation in our verse, is one of the most groundless assertions that ever obtained belief in literature. More thought and more skill had been exercised before his time in the construction of English metre than he ever bestowed on the subject, and by men of far greater attainments and far higher powers. To improve, indeed, either upon the versification or the diction of our great writers, was impossible; it was impossible to exceed them in the knowledge or in the practice of their art, but it was easy to avoid the more obvious faults of inferior authors: and in this way he succeeded, just so far as not to be included in

'The mob of gentlemen who wrote with ease;'

nor consigned to oblivion with the 'persons of quality' who contributed their vapid effusions to the miscellanies of those days. His proper place is among those of his contemporaries and successors who called themselves wits, and have since been entitled wits by the courtesy of England." I venture to claim for him a higher position. Surely some hearty praise may be given to a writer who virtually introduced into our poetical literature a new kind of composition, and one peculiarly adapted to the tastes and sympathies of Englishmen? Surely some hearty praise is justly due to a writer who had so strong a relish for the beauties of landscape, and was so keenly alive to the pastoral sentiment. And though he did not begin " a reformation in our verse," he certainly showed how the heroic couplet might be written with vigour while not losing in ease.

Denham's other works include an " Essay on Gaming;" and a translation of the second book of "The Æneid." In 1641, his feeble tragedy of " The Sophy " was produced at a private house in Blackfriars with so much success that Waller said "he broke out like the Irish rebellion, some ten thousand strong, when nobody was aware, or in the least suspected it." The best thing in it is a Song to Morpheus, in the fifth Act, which is graceful and pleasing:—

> "Morpheus, the humble god, that dwells
> In cottages and smoky cells,
> Hates gilded roofs and beds of down;
> And, though he fears no prince's frown,
> Flies from the circle of a crown.
>
> Come, I say, thou powerful god,
> And thy leaden charming rod,
> Dipt in the Lethean lake,
> O'er his wakeful temples shake,
> Lest he should sleep and never wake.
>
> Nature, alas! why art thou so
> Obliged to thy greatest foe?
> Sleep, that is thy best repast,
> Yet of Death it bears a taste,
> And both are the same thing at last."

In a satirical poem, written at a much later date, in imitation of Suckling's "Session of the Poets," occurs a caustic allusion to Denham's tragedy and poem:

> "Then in came Denham, that limping old bard,
> Whose fame on The Sophy and Cooper's Hill stands;
> And brought many stationers, who swore very hard,
> That nothing sold better, except 'twere his lands."

Denham also wrote "An Elegy on Abraham Cowley," which is full of grace, and contains a happy reference to the great Elizabethan poets and their immortal predecessors:—

> "Old Chaucer, like the morning star,*
> To us discovers day from far.
> His light those mists and clouds dissolved
> Which our dark nation long involved.

* Borrowed by Tennyson in his "Dream of Fair Women," where he speaks of Chaucer as "the morning star of song."

> Next (like Aurora) Spenser rose,
> Whose purple blush the day foreshows;
> The other three with his own fires
> Phœbus, the poet's god, inspires:
> By Shakespeare's, Jonson's, Fletcher's lines
> Our stage's lustre Rome's outshines."

Denham also wrote a translation of "Cato Major," and a metrical version of the Psalms.

We turn from the poems to the poet. Sir John Denham was the son of Sir John Denham, Chief Baron of the Exchequer in Ireland, who married the daughter of the Irish baron of Mellofont, Sir Garret More. He was born in Dublin in 1615. When he was two years old, his father was made Baron of the English Exchequer, and the family removed to England. In 1631, young Denham was entered a gentleman commoner of Trinity College, Oxford, where "he was looked upon," says Wood, "as a slow, dreaming young man, and more addicted to gaming than study; they (his companions) could never imagine he could ever enrich the world with the issue of his brain, as he afterwards did." After taking his degree he entered Lincoln's Inn, where the dice-box divided his attention with the desk. "He was much rooked by gamesters, and fell acquainted with that unsanctified crew to his ruin." Wood relates that at this time, his father, receiving certain intimation of the follies which enfeebled Denham's life, addressed to him a letter of strong but affectionate remonstrance; and that the son, with unworthy duplicity, composed and printed an "Essay against Gaming," which, being forwarded to the Chief Baron, completely lulled his suspicions. The anecdote seems hardly credible; an astute and veteran lawyer would hardly be deceived by so simple an artifice. Aubrey relates another story, which seems to have greater pretensions to authenticity. Denham, he says, was generally temperate in drinking; but "one time, when he was a student of Lincoln's Inn, having been away at the tavern with his comrades, late at night a frolic came into his head, to get a plasterer's brush and a pot of ink, and blot out all the signs between Temple Bar and Charing Cross, which made a strange confusion the next day, as it was in June time; but it happened that they were discovered, and it cost him and them some moneys. This," adds Aubrey, "I had from R. Estcourt, Esquire, who carried the ink-pot."

The death of his father soon afterwards placed him in enjoyment of a considerable fortune, which enabled him to make a conspicuous figure among the wits and gentlemen of the Court. The success of his tragedy of "The Sophy" increased his reputation; upon which a seal was set by the publication of "Cooper's Hill." In the civil troubles which then convulsed the land, Denham espoused the loyal cause with grave enthusiasm, and was entrusted with several missions of delicacy and importance. In 1648 (it is said) he conveyed the young Duke of York to France, when he shared the seclusion of the royal family. In 1650, the exiled king sent him on an embassy to the King of Poland; and in 1652 appointed him Surveyor of His Majesty's Buildings—an office which, at that time, was equally without emoluments and without duties. Returning to England at the Restoration, he received both honours and rewards, and made one of the brilliant circle which Charles II. loved to assemble round him. Unfortunately he was weak enough to be beguiled by the charms of the fair Miss Brooke, whose beauty had attracted the attention of the Duke of York. As soon as she had secured a position by becoming Lady Denham,* she scrupled not to encourage the suit of her royal lover, who, according to Pepys, followed her up and down the presence chamber "like a dog." Writing in 1667, he says:—"The Duke of York is wholly given up to his new mistress, my Lady Denham; going at noon-day with all his gentlemen to visit her in Scotland Yard; she declaring she will not be his mistress, as Mrs. Price, to go up and down the Privy Stairs."

His beautiful wife's infidelity seems to have afflicted Sir John Denham with mental disorder. "He became crazed for a time," says old Anthony Wood, "and so, consequently, contemptible among vain fops." Aubrey says:—"This madness first appeared when he went from London to see the famous free-stone quarries in Portland, in Dorset. When he came within a mile of it, he turned back to London again, and would not see it. He went to Hounslow, and demanded rents of lands he had sold many years before; but it pleased God that he was cured of this distemper, and wrote excellent verses, particularly on the death of Abraham Cowley, afterwards." From a letter preserved among the correspondence of Sir William Temple, we gather that his insanity was of a very mild form (1667): "Poor Sir John Denham is fallen to the ladies also. He is at many of the meetings, at dinners talks more than ever he did, and is extremely pleased with those that seem willing to hear him, and from that obligation exceedingly praises the Duchess of Monmouth and my Lady Cavendish: if he had not the name of being mad, I believe in most companies he would be thought

---

* Miss Brooke was his second wife; his first was a Miss Cotton, of Gloucestershire, by whom he had issue one son and two daughters.

wittier than ever he was. He seems to have few extravagances besides that *of telling stories of himself, which he is always inclined too.*" Heavens! if a man is to be declared insane, because he tells stories of himself, our asylums would cease to have room for their inmates.

At this date Denham was a widower, having lost his lovely wife on the 7th of January, 1667. The report spread abroad that she had been poisoned, and as he was supposed to have sacrificed her to his jealousy, " the populace of his neighbourhood threatened to tear him in pieces " as soon as he ventured abroad. The suspicion is improbable, however, and her death was more likely due to the ignorance of the physicians of the age. Sir John recovered his faculties towards the close of the year, wrote the Elegy on Cowley, and a few months afterwards closed his chequered career—dying at Whitehall, in March, 1668. A resting-place was provided for him in Westminster Abbey, near the graves of the two poets whom he had warmly admired, Chaucer and Cowley.

In 1678, the year in which Andrew Marvell died—ten years after the death of Denham—the grave closed over the ashes of a thoughtful poet and a ripe scholar, Thomas Stanley. He was born at Cumberlow, in Herts, in 1625, and was the son of Sir Thomas Stanley, the author of several poems, who was knighted by Charles I. The younger Stanley had the advantage of being educated by Fairfax, the accomplished translator of Tasso, and attained a wide and profound knowledge of Latin and Greek, French and Italian. At Cambridge his reputation for scholarship stood very high, and he carried off the degree of M.A. when only in his seventeenth year (1641). After a tour on the Continent he returned to England,

and in the Middle Temple, London, settled down to the pursuit of his legal and literary studies, apparently undisturbed by the din of civil war, or by the great political changes which were giving a new direction to English history. That they did not greatly affect the social fabric, however, is evident from the fact that, only a few weeks after the execution of Charles I., Stanley published a volume of poems, as one might do in the most ordinary times. In 1655 he issued the first part of his great "History of Philosophy, containing the Lives, Opinions, Actions, and Discoveries of the Philosophers of every Sect," which was completed in 1660. "It is, in a great measure, confined to biography, and comprehends no name later than Carucales. Most is derived from Diogenes Laertius; but an analysis of the Platonic philosophy is given from Alcinous, and the author has compiled one of the Peripatetic system from Aristotle himself. The doctrine of the Stoics is also elaborately deduced from various sources. Stanley, on the whole, brought a good deal from an almost untrodden field; but he is merely an historian, and never a critic of philosopy." * Latin translations of it were published at Amsterdam, in 1690, and at Leipzig, in 1711.

Stanley raised still higher the fame of English scholarship by his celebrated edition of Æschylus, with Latin translations and copious notes in 1663. That he owed a great deal to Casaubon, Dorat, and Scaliger may be admitted, without making any substantial deduction from the credit due to him for patient and persevering erudition. His Æschylus must always remain "a great monument of critical learning."

* Hallam, "Literature of Europe," iv., 63.

Stanley died in London, April 12th, 1678, at the comparatively early age of 53.

As a poet Stanley had nothing in common with his immediate contemporaries. He belonged to what Johnson has designated (not very happily) the Metaphysical School, the School of Crashaw and Donne, though his scholarly taste enabled him to avoid the extravagant conceits and far-fetched ingenuities on which his predecessors so often made shipwreck. An innate refinement led him also to avoid the indelicacy which disfigures so much of the poetry of the age. His translations are, perhaps, even better than his original poems; they are singularly graceful, while conveying, with happy fidelity, the spirit of the originals. But it is of his own work that we shall give a brief specimen. One could wish there had been more of it, for it is always finished in execution, and admirable in tone.

" CELIA, *singing.*
Roses in breathing forth their scent,
Or stars their borrowed ornament,
Nymphs in the watery sphere that move,
Or angels in their orbs above,
The wingèd chariot of the light,
Or the slow silent wheels of night,
The shade which from the swifter sun
Doth in a circular motion run,
Or souls that their eternal rest do keep,
Make far less [more ?] noise than Colin's breath in sleep.

But if the Angel which inspires
This subtle flame with active fires,
Should mould this breath to words, and those
Into a harmony dispose,
The music of this heavenly sphere
Would steal each soul out at the ear,
And into plants and stones infuse
A life that Cherubim would choose,
And with new powers invest the laws of fate,
Kill those that live, and dead things animate."

We may add that in 1657 Stanley published the "Psalterium Carolinum; the Devotions of his Sacred Majestie in his Solitude and Sufferings, rendered into verse."

An elder brother of Thomas Killigrew—the wit and dramatist, and unofficial jester to Charles II.—Sir William Killigrew (born in 1605) dabbled freely in verse, some specimens of which are embedded in the dulness of his "Artless Midnight Thoughts of a Gentleman at Court, who for many years built of sand, which every blast of cross fortune has defaced; but now he has laid new foundations on the Rock of his Salvation" (1693). Unfortunately the "Artless Thoughts" were built on sand. They are upwards of two hundred and thirty in number, but not one is worth preservation. Killigrew was a brave Cavalier and a loyal servant of the Crown; he held the post of Vice-Chamberlain to the Queen for two-and-twenty years; but he was neither poet, philosopher, nor dramatist. He wrote five plays—"The Siege of Urbin," "Selindra," "Pandora,"* and "Love and Friendship"—published in 1666, in which there is none of the wit that, it is said, his conversation displayed—and "The Imperial Tragedy," published in 1669. Sir William lived to a ripe old age, dying in the early part of 1693, when he had just attained his eighty-ninth year.

Sir William's niece, Anne Killigrew, daughter of his youngest brother, Dr. Henry Killigrew (author of "The Conspiracy,") maintained the reputation of the family for

---

* This was cast, at first, in the form of a tragedy; but as the authorities of the theatre did not want tragedies, its author obligingly converted it into a comedy. Sir Robert Stapylton says of Sir William's plays that they contained

. . . . plots well laid,
The language pure and every sentence weighed!

literary gifts and accomplishments. Dryden has celebrated her genius for painting and poetry in one of the finest of his odes; and she deserves to be remembered with gratitude if only for having inspired this noble lyric effusion. Allowing for the genial extravagances of a poet's imagination, there must still have been rare merit in the young artist of whom Dryden could say:—

> "Art she had none, yet wanted none,
> For nature did that want supply,
> So rich in treasure of her own,
> She might our boasted stores defy:
> Such noble vigour did her verse adorn,
> That it seemed borrowed where 'twas only born."

Anthony Wood affirms that "she was a Grace for beauty, and a Muse for wit; and gave the earliest discoveries of a great genius, which, being improved by a polite education, she became eminent in the arts of poetry and painting." These engaging and eminent accomplishments, says Betham, were the least of her perfections, for "she crowned all with an exemplary piety and unblemished virtue."

She painted several historical compositions, some pieces of still life, and portraits of the Duke and Duchess of York. But the promise of her genius never ripened into performances; she was carried off by small-pox, on the 16th of June, 1685, in her twenty-fifth year. Her "Poems," in a thin quarto, were published in 1686.

Hallam ranks Oldham as a satirist "next to Dryden;" he characterises him as "spirited and pointed," but thinks his versification "too negligent" and his subjects "temporary." It is his good fortune, however, that he preceded Dryden, so that no one can diminish his merits by accusing him of imitation. For ourselves, the chief interest of his poetry lies in its indications of what he might have become if his genius had had time to mature. With longer experience, riper thought, and calmer judgment he would have been the English Juvenal. As it is, the strength and strenuousness of his verse compel our admiration; but we can hardly forgive the occasional grossness of his language and the unmeasured fury of his invective, to say nothing of his defects of execution. To these defects Dryden, who greatly valued his young predecessor, and praised him with the fullest generosity, alludes, when he admits that, had his brief career been prolonged,

> "Years might (what Nature gives the young)
> Have taught the numbers of thy native tongue."

We who know how Keats and Shelley wrote while "young," can hardly accept this kindly excuse; nor Dryden's other plea, that

> "Satire needs not those, and wit will shine
> Through the harsh cadence of a rugged line."

The full splendour of the diamond is not brought out until it has been polished.

Oldham was never feeble. Even in his Translations, or rather, Imitations from Horace, Juvenal, and Boileau, his manly vigour and force and frankness are very noticeable.

The following quotation affords not only a good specimen of his style, but an interesting illustration of the social position of a domestic chaplain in the days of Charles II. :—

> "Some think themselves exalted to the sky,
> If they light in some noble family,
> Diet, a horse, and thirty pounds a year,
> Besides the advantage of his lordship's ear,
> The credit of the business, and the state,
> Are things that in a youngster's sense sound great.
> Little the inexperienced wretch does know
> What slavery he oft must undergo,

Who, though in silken scarf and cassock drest,
Wears but a gayer livery at best.
When dinner calls, the implement must wait,
With holy words to consecrate the meat,
But hold it for a favour seldom known,
If he be deigned the honour to sit down—
Soon as the tarts appear, Sir Crape, withdraw!
Those dainties are not for a spiritual maw.
Observe your distance, and be sure to stand
Hard by the cistern with your cap in hand;
There for diversion you may pick your teeth,
Till the kind voider* comes for your relief.

For mere board wages such their freedom sell,
Slaves to an hour, and vassals to a bell;
And if the enjoyment of one day be stole,
They are but prisoners out on parole:
Always the marks of slavery remain,
And they, though loose, still drag about their chains.
And where's the mighty prospect after all,
A chaplainship served up, and seven years' thrall?
The menial thing, perhaps, for a reward
Is to some slender benefice perferred,
With this proviso bound: that he must wed
My lady's antiquated waiting-maid
In dressing only skilled, and marmalade."†

John Oldham, the author of this forcible satire, was born at Shipton, in Gloucestershire, on the 9th of August, 1653. He received from his father, a non-conforming clergyman, the elements of a sound education, and was afterwards sent to Tilbury Grammar School, whence, with credit, he proceeded to Edmund Hall, Oxford. His natural ability was soon made manifest, and he acquired a local reputation as a writer of good English verse and a proficient in Latin scholarship. In 1674 he took his degree of B.A., and in the same year was engaged as a master at Whitgift Hospital, Croydon, where he remained for three years, wrote his "Satires against the

* The basket containing the broken victuals left over from dinner.
† Lord Macaulay has largely availed himself of this passage in his description of the condition of the clergy at the Restoration.

Jesuits," and was discovered by Rochester, Dorset, and Sir Charles Sedley, who introduced him to the Earl of Kingston, and procured him a tutorship in the family of Sir Edward Thurlow, at Reigate. He seems to have quickly wearied of this engagement; nor did he much longer hold a similar appointment in the house of Dr. Lower, a famous London physician, who advised him to study medicine (1681). After a brief experience of the life of a man of pleasure, he retired to the Earl of Kingston's mansion, with the view, it is said, of preparing for holy orders, and accepting a chaplaincy in his patron's family—though one would think that such a position would have been eminently distasteful to his proud and independent spirit. He escaped the trial, however, by his early death, which took place from small-pox, at the Earl's seat, Holme Pierpoint, on December 8, 1683.

One of the most celebrated names in the poetical literature of the reign of Charles II. is that of Samuel Butler, though we suspect that his great work, "Hudibras," is, like "The Fairy Queen," more talked about than read. We could take large odds that the number of readers who have actually gone through its nine cantos from beginning to end is infinitesimally small. People pick up their knowledge of this poem from the extracts which appear in all our Anthologies, and it must be owned that in this way they get at the poet's best, and are led to form a higher estimate of his genius than would be the case if they had to wade through all his diffusiveness and the multiplicity of minute details which his ingenious fancy crowds one upon another.

"Hudibras" is a work of wonderful wit, singular learning, and felicitous versification, but not to our thinking a great poem. We should even be inclined to say that it is not a poem at all. It is an elaborate satire, thrown into a clever metrical form; but there is nothing of that dramatic fervour, or glow of imagination, or depth of passion which we look for in true poetry. The imagery is always grotesque; the sentiment generally trivial and mean. There is wit enough, and to spare; there is a good deal of shrewd reflection and acute knowledge of men and things; there are terse epigrammatic couplets which the memory readily seizes and appropriates; there are felicitous rhymes which in themselves have a rare element of humour—as for instance,

> " And pulpit, drum ecclesiastic,
> Was beat with fist, instead of a stick "—

but this is all. No doubt this is enough to prove Butler's genius; only it does not make him a poet, in the sense in which Spenser, and Keats, and Wordsworth are poets.

"Hudibras," as everybody knows, is a parody of "Don Quixote," in which the satire, bitter always and sometimes savage, is directed against Puritanism, or, rather, against Butler's conception of it. The nobler side of Puritanism, its heroic courage, its sublime faith, he either could not or would not see; and, therefore, his satire to some extent fails, because it is directed against an unreality. So far as it was levelled at externals, at the fanatical legislation of the Puritans, and their affectations of dress and language, it was effective, but then it was also of only temporary influence. None but those portions have lived which are applicable to folly and fanaticism everywhere and at all times. And here it may be observed that many of the attributes with which the satirist invests his Puritan Knight were by no means peculiar to the Puritans.

Hypocrisy, and pretension, and bigotry belong to no one sect or faction. In Butler's own party were to be found men to whom the following passage was at least as appropriate as to any of his opponents :—

> " For rhetoric, he could not ope
> His mouth but out there flew a trope ;
> And when he happened to break off
> I' th' middle of his speech, or cough,
> H' had hard words, ready to show why,
> And tell what rules he did it by :
> Else, when with greatest art he spoke,
> You'd think he talked like other folk ;
> For all a rhetorician's rules
> Teach nothing but to name his tools."

This want of veracity is conspicuous throughout Butler's work, and renders it a burlesque as well as a satire. It is pitched throughout in too low a key; and the exaggeration is so gross and so obvious that we are inclined to sympathize with the objects of it. A man in a pillory is contemptible only so long as his persecutors refrain from making a martyr of him.

Another defect is Butler's discursiveness. His stores of learning were so vast that they supplied his ingenious fancy with material for the prodigal decoration of any point it touched upon ; and when once his fancy was let loose, it ran away with him. He luxuriated in his own profuseness; he could not rest until he had said everything that could be said: and the thought never occurred to him that what did not weary himself might very probably weary his readers. Thus, he has to describe the breeches of his hero, and it takes him more than forty lines to do it in. At first the description is exquisitely comic, and we are delighted with the happy conceits which follow one another so quickly ; but after a while the fun grows forced and tedious, and we begin to wonder when the writer will make an end of it.* We see that he is writing for his own entertainment, and not for ours :—

> "His breeches were of ragged woollen,
> And had been at the siege of Bullen;
> To old King Harry so well known,
> Some writers held they were his own;
> Though they were lined with many a piece
> Of ammunition, bread and cheese,
> And fat black puddings, *proper food*
> *For warriors that delight in blood*;
> For, as we said, he always chose
> To carry victual in his hose,
> That often tempted rats and mice
> The ammunition to surprise;
> And when he put a hand but in
> The one or t'other magazine,
> They stoutly on defence on't stood,
> And from the wounded foe drew blood."

Had the poet ceased here all would have been well, but he continues with merciless amplitude to pile conceit upon conceit, until we feel that Ben Jonson's criticism of Shakespeare would more justly be applied to our much-offending author, "that sometimes it was necessary he should be stopped: *Sufflaminandus erat,* as Augustus said of Halerius." He goes on at full gallop, thus:—

> "And till th' were stormed and beaten out,
> Ne'er left the fortified redoubt;
> And though knights-errant, as some think,
> Of old, did neither eat nor drink,
> Because when through deserts vast,
> And regions desolate they passed,
> When belly-timber above ground,
> Or under, was not to be found,
> Unless they grazed, there's not one word
> Of their provision on record;
> Which made some confidently write
> They had no stomachs but to fight.

---

* The wildest of all criticisms is surely Prior's. He praises Butler for what Butler never understood :—

> "Yet he, consummate master, knew
> When to recede and when pursue."

> 'Tis false for Arthur wore in hall
> Round table like a farthingal;
> On which, with shirt pulled out behind,
> And eke before, his good knights dined;
> Though 'twas no table some suppose,
> But a huge pair of round trunk-hose,
> In which he carried as much meat
> As he and all the knights could eat;
> When laying by their swords and truncheons,
> They took their breakfasts on their nuncheons."

There is scarcely any plot or definite action* in "Hudibras," and the incidents are few; though some are diverting enough, such as the attack of the knight and his squire on the bear and the fiddle, and their imprisonment in the stocks. The want of continuity helps as much as the diffusiveness to make it wearisome. As it stands, the story extends in time over three days. From the initial line, "When civil dudgeon first grew high," it is clear that Butler intended its action to bear date with the Civil Wars; but, after two days and nights are completed, he suddenly passes, in the third part, to Oliver Cromwell's death, and then, in the last canto, turns again to his hero. The thin stream of narrative with which he begun has by this time disappeared. Even the original intention of the poem seems to have been changed, and the satire against the Puritans concludes with an attack on Charles II. and his mistresses. For these reasons "Hudibras" remains a poem which all admire and few read, and the few who read do so " by fits and starts," a continuous perusal of it being almost impossible.

Butler is one of the most allusive, because he is one of the most learned of writers. What Burton's " Anatomy of Melancholy " is in our prose literature, " Hudibras " is

---

* Nash, however, distinguishes four principal actions, or episodes.—The victory of Hudibras over Cruodero—Trulla's victory over Hudibras—Hudibras' victory over Sidrophel—and the Widow's repulse of Hudibras.

in our poetical. To enjoy it thoroughly one needs a knowledge almost as wide and deep as its author's. "There is always an undercurrent of satiric allusion," says a critic, "beneath the main stream of his satire. The juggling of astrology, the besetting folly of alchymy, the transfusion of blood, the sympathetic medicines, the learned trifling of experimental philosophers, the knavery of fortune-tellers, and the folly of their dupes, the marvellous relations of travellers, the subtleties of the school-divines, the freaks of fashion, the fantastic extravagancies of lovers, the affectations of piety, and the absurdities of romance, are interwoven with his subject, and soften down and relieve his dark delineation of fanatical violence and perfidy."

Of wise saws and modern instances "Hudibras" is full to overflowing. No writer has ever shown more readiness in compressing "the wisdom of the many" into a terse couplet or two, as easily remembered as a proverb or a popular apophthegm or a nursery rhyme. Many of his "good things" have become part and parcel of our daily discourse, and we speak Butler, as Molière's Jourdain spoke prose, without knowing it. His works are sufficiently accessible to render unnecessary on our part any attempt to exhibit by quotation their general characters; but of the felicity with which their witty author condensed a thought or an image into a sentence, and pointed it by a couple or so of felicitous rhymes, we shall make bold to furnish some illustrations.

Here is a graceful simile:—

"True as the dial to the sun,
Although it be not shined upon."

We agree with Leigh Hunt that the following is as elegant as anything in Lovelace or Waller:—

> ".. What security's too strong
> To guard that gentle heart from wrong,
> That to its friend is glad to pass
> Itself away, and all it has,
> And like an anchorite, gives over
> This world, for the heaven of a lover?"

There is an exceptional elevation (for Butler) in the following:—

> "Like Indian widows, gone to bed
> In flaming curtains to the dead."

An "exquisite and never-to-be-sufficiently repeated couplet":—

> "Compound for sins they are inclin'd to,
> By damning those they have no mind to."

And now for some wise thoughts:—

> "Doubtless the pleasure is as great
> Of being cheated as to cheat;
> As lookers-on feel most delight
> That least perceive a juggler's sleight;
> And still the less they understand,
> The more they admire his sleight-of-hand."

> "For what in worth is anything,
> But so much money as 'twill bring."

> "He that is valiant and dares fight,
> Though drubbed can lose no honour by 't.
> Honour's a lease for lives to come,
> And cannot be extended from
> The legal tenant: 'Tis a chattel
> Not to be forfeited in battle.
> If he that in the field is slain
> Be in the bed of honour lain,
> He that is beaten may be said
> To lie in honour's truckle-bed.
> For as we see the eclipsèd sun
> By mortals is more gazed upon
> Than when, adorned with all his light,
> He shines in serene sky most bright,
> So valour in a low estate
> Is most admired and wondered at."

The following miscellaneous thoughts are partly from "Hudibras" and partly from Butler's "Remains":—

"In Rome no temple was so low
  As that of Honour, built to show
  How humble Honour ought to be,
  Though there 'twas all authority."

"Money that, like the swords of Kings,
  Is the last reason of all things."

"Ay me! what perils do environ
  The man that meddles with cold iron?"

"'Tis not restraint or liberty
  That makes men prisoners or free,
  But perturbations that possess
  The mind, or equanimities.
  The whole world was not half so wide
  To Alexander when he cried
  Because he had but one to subdue,
  As was a paltry narrow tub to
  Diogenes, who is not said
  (For aught that ever I could read)
  To whine, put finger i' th' eye, and sob
  Because he had ne'er another tub."

"Fools are known by looking wise,
  As men tell woodcocks by their eyes."

"All smatterers are more brisk and pert
  Than those that understand an art;
  As little sparkles shine more bright
  Than glowing coals that give them light."

"Great conquerors greater glory gain
  By foes in triumph led than slain."

"As at the approach of winter, all
  The leaves of great trees are to fall,
  And leave then naked, to engage
  With storms and tempest when they rage,
  While humbler plants are forced to wear
  Their fresh green liveries all the year;
  So when their glorious season's gone
  With great men, and hard times come on,
  The greatest calamities oppress
  The greatest still, and spare the less."

"Valour's a mousetrap, wit a gin,
  That women oft are taken in."

"Night is the sabbath of mankind
To rest the body and the mind."

"Opinion governs all mankind,
Like the blind's leading of the blind."

"Wedlock without love, some say,
Is like a lock without a key."

"As if artillery and edge-tools
Were th' only engines to save souls!"

"Those that fly may fight again,
Which he can never do that's slain." *

"He that complies against his will
Is of his own opinion still."

"In the hurry of a fray
'Tis hard to keep out of harm's way."

"In all the trade of war no feat
Is nobler than a brave retreat,
For those that run away and fly
Take plan at least of the enemy."

We select a few of Butler's humorous and happy rhyme endings:—

"A true beard's like a batter'd ensign;
That's bravest which there are most rents in."

"Convened at midnight in outhouses,
To appoint new rising rendezvouses."

"Doctor epidemic,
Stored with deletery med'cins,
Which whosoever took is dead since,"

"Wholesale critics, that in coffee-
Houses cry down all philosophy."

"To th' emperor Caligula,
That triumphed o'er the British sea,†

---

* In the "Apophthegms" of Erasmus, translated by Udall, 1542, we read:—

"That same man that runnith awaie
Maie again fight another daie."

Butler was imitated by Goldsmith in his "Art of Poetry on a New Plan"—

"He who fights and runs away
May live to fight another day;
But he who is in battle slain
Can never rise and fight again."

† Pronounced *say*.

> Took crabs and oysters prisoners,
> And lobsters 'stead of cuirassiers:
> Engaged his legions in fierce bustles
> With periwinkles, prawns, and mussels,
> And led his troops, with furious gallops,
> To charge whole regiments of scallops."

> " Madame, I do as is my duty,
> Honour the shadow of your shoe-tie."

> " Anti-christian assemblies
> To mischief bent as far's in them lies."

> "That proud dame
> Used him so like a base rascallion,
> That old Pyg—what d' you call him—malion,
> That cut his mistress out of stone,
> Had not so hard a hearted one."

> "' O Heaven !' quoth she, ' can that be true?
> I do begin to fear 'tis you ;
> Not by your individual whiskers,
> But by your dialect and discourse.'"

Samuel Butler, the author of "Hudibras," was born at Strensham, in Worcestershire, in 1612. About almost every main incident in his life the authorities differ, and they differ also in their descriptions of his father's position; for while Anthony Wood says his father was comparatively wealthy, others assert that he was simply a yeoman of poor estate, and that it was with difficulty he provided his son with such education as the Worcester Grammar School afforded. As to the future poet, it is equally uncertain whether he went from school to Oxford University or to Cambridge, or whether he went to either. While still in his early manhood he obtained an appointment as clerk to Mr. Jefferys, of Earl's Coombe, in Worcestershire, an eminent justice of the peace; and here he turned his leisure to advantage in the study of books, and the cultivation of music and painting. He was next at Wrest, in Bedfordshire, the seat of the Countess of Kent, where he enjoyed the use of a good library and the conversation of the learned Selden. Afterwards we find him in the family of Sir Samuel Luke, a Presbyterian Colonel and one of Cromwell's officers, " scout master for Bedfordshire, and governor of Newport Pagnell." We must suppose the treatment he received at the hands of his patron was harsh and ungenerous, or we shall be unable to excuse the want of gratitude and good faith which led him to caricature Sir Samuel in the person of Sir Hudibras.* And that Sir Samuel was the original seems by no means doubtful from the following allusion:

> " 'Tis sung there is a valiant Mamaluke
> In foreign land ycleped . . . ."

when the rhyme obviously requires that the blank should be filled up with the Colonel's name.†

At the Restoration Butler was made secretary to the Earl of Carberry, Lord President of Wales, and also steward of Ludlow Castle. About the same time he married—Mrs. Hubert, a widow of means, says one biographer,—a widow, says another, who had lost her fortune by injudicious investments. In 1662, at the age of fifty, he rose into sudden reputation by the publication of the first part of his colossal satire, which, as we learn from Pepys, was the admiration of the King and his courtiers. The

---

* The name was borrowed from Spenser: — "Sir Hudibras, a hardy man" ("Fairy Queen," ver. 2, i., 17.) Sidrophel, the astrologer, was meant for Lilly.

† The elder Disraeli, in his "Curiosities of Literature," in an elaborate paper endeavours to vindicate Butler from the accusation of ingratitude in having caricatured his patron, Sir Samuel Luke. His vindication seems to us worth nothing, if it be agreed that Luke was really the original, as most persons believe, of Butler's hero. But it is only justice to state that the editors of "The Grub Street Journal" (January 1730) assert that the actual prototype was "a Devonshire man, Colonel Rolle," and that the name "Hudibras" is derived from "Hugh de Bras," the old tutelar saint of Devonshire. The assertion would be easier to credit if those who made it had given us some particulars both of the Devonshire Colonel and the Devonshire saint!

second part followed in 1663; the third in 1678. Butler had to be content with fame. If he needed, and anticipated, a more solid recompense he was disappointed. The story that Charles presented him with a purse of three hundred guineas rests on no authentic foundation; and though Clarendon, it is said, gave him reason to hope for perferment he never received it. Anthony Wood asserts, but the other authorities deny, that the Duke of Buckingham, when Chancellor of Cambridge, appointed him as his secretary, and on all occasions treated him with liberality and kindness. But if this be untrue, there seems reason to believe that the following anecdote is not less untrue:

"Mr. Wycherley had always laid hold of any opportunity which offered of representing to the Duke of Buckingham how well Mr. Butler had deserved of the royal family by writing his inimitable Hudibras, and that it was a reproach to the Court that a person of his loyalty and wit should suffer in obscurity, and under the wants he did. The Duke always seemed to hearken to him with attention enough, and after some time undertook to recommend his pretensions to his Majesty. Mr. Wycherley, in hopes to keep him steady to his word, obtained of his Grace to name a day, when he might introduce that modest and unfortunate poet to his new patron. At last an appointment was made, and the place of meeting was agreed to be the Roebuck. Mr. Butler and his friend attended accordingly; the Duke joined them, but as the devil would have it, the door of the room where they sat was open, and his Grace, who had seated himself near it, observing a pimp of his acquaintance (the creature too was a knight) trip by with a brace of ladies, immediately quitted his engagement to follow another kind of business, at which he was more ready than to do good office to those of desert, though no one was better qualified than he, both in regard to his fortune and understanding, to protect them; and from that time to the day of his death, poor Butler never found the least effect of his promise."

This is a good story; but, with Johnson, we disbelieve its authencity.

That Butler did not meet with the generous support and recognition to which his genius, and his services to the cause of the Royalists, entitled him, is evident enough from the complaints of Oldham and Dryden, which could never have been so publicly and generally made if there had been no warranty for them. Oldham writes with honest indignation:—

> "On Butler, who can think without just rage,
> The glory and the scandal of the age?
> Fair stood his hopes, when first he came to town,
> Met everywhere with welcomes of renown.
> Courted and loved by all, with wonder read,
> And promises of princely favour fed.
> But what reward for all had he at last,
> After a life in dull expectance past?
> The wretch, at summing up his misspent days,
> Found nothing left but poverty and praise.
> Of all his gains by verse he could not save
> Enough to purchase flannel and a grave.
> Reduced to want, he in due time fell sick,
> Was fain to die, and be interred on tick,
> And well might bless the fever that was sent
> To rid him hence, and his worse fate prevent."
>
> *(Satire against Poetry).*

And Dryden:

> " Unpitied Hudibras, your champion friend,
> Has shown how far your charities extend.
> This lasting verse shall on his tomb be read,
> ' He shamed you living, and upbraids you dead!' "

But Butler himself had already protested, in his "Hudibras at Court" (in the " Remains ") against the royal ingratitude :—

> "Now after all, was it not hard
> That he should meet with no reward,
> That fitted out this knight and squire,
> This monarch did so much admire."

It may be that the obscurity in which the poet was suffered to remain originated in the faults of his character. Aubrey speaks of him as choleric, and of a severe and sound judgment; adding, with keen knowledge of human nature, "satirical wits disoblige whom they converse with, and consequently make themselves many enemies and few friends." Such, he says, was Butler's case.

In this " mist of obscurity "—the phrase is Johnson's— died Samuel Butler, on the 25th of September, 1680; and at the expense of his friends was buried in St. Paul's Churchyard, Covent Garden, the honour of a public funeral in Westminster Abbey having been refused. About forty years afterwards, Alderman Barber erected in the Abbey a monument to his memory, on which is engraved an elaborate laudatory inscription in Latin, which in pithiness and force is much surpassed by the epitaph ascribed to John Dennis :—

> "Near this place lies interred
> The body of Mr. Samuel Butler,
> Author of Hudibras.
> He was a whole species of poet in one,
> Admirable in a manner
> In which no one else has been tolerable:
> A manner which began and ended with him,
> In which he knew no guide,
> And has found no followers."

The tardiness of this tribute to the poet elicited some epigrammatic lines from Samuel Wesley :—

> "While Butler, needy wretch, was yet alive,
>   No generous patron would a dinner give;
>   See him, when starved to death and turned to dust,
>   Presented with a monumental bust.
>   The poet's fate is here in emblem shown,
>   He asked for bread, and he received a stone."

Besides his immortal "Hudibras," Butler was the author of a couple of pamphlets, a satirical Ode on the exploits of the famous highwayman, "Claude Duval," and various poems and prose writings included in his "Remains," of which we may notice as the most important, "The Elephant in the Moon;" "A Satire upon the Royal Society;" "A Satire upon the Imperfection and Abuse of Human Learning;" and "A Panegyric upon Sir John Denham's Recovery from his Madness." His "Description of Holland," with its richly humorous exaggeration, is well known.

A COUPLE OF COURTIERS.

The Earl of Rochester.   The Duke of Buckingham.

CHAPTER IV.

A COUPLE OF COURTIERS.

THE EARL OF ROCHESTER.   THE DUKE OF BUCKINGHAM.

John Wilmot, Earl of Rochester.

THE most brilliant figure of a brilliant Court—a man of unquestionable ability, but of the most shameless profligacy—wit, poet, dramatist, politician—gifted with rare personal graces and a wonderful charm of manner, yet perverting his fine endowments to the worst purposes—John Wilmot, Earl of Rochester, has, in the most literal sense of Johnson's hackneyed lines, left a name to point a moral, if not exactly to adorn a tale. It would seem as if at his birth those powers in whose hands rest the distribution of the good things of nature had lavished upon him all except that one which is indispensable to their right use, the heavenly gift of virtue. With all his talents, with all his opportunities of rank and fortune, his was a wrecked life—a life misspent, and, therefore, unenjoyed—and the only part of it to be contemplated with satisfaction are the hours of contrition and reflection which he spent with the shadow of death upon him.

John Wilmot, Earl of Rochester, was born at Ditchley, in Oxfordshire, on the 10th of April, 1647. His father was Henry, Lord Wilmot, a brave and loyal Cavalier, who attended Charles II. during his wanderings after the battle of Worcester, and was rewarded for his faithful service with the Earldom of Rochester. His son and only surviving child received his early education at the Grammar School of Burford, whence he was removed to Wadham College, Oxford, in 1659. His intellectual powers were quickly conspicuous; he attained with facility a wide knowledge of the classics; wrote verses with fluency; and spoke epigrams with careless profusion. In 1661, at the age of fourteen, he was admitted to the degree of M.A., and the Chancellor of the University, Lord Clarendon, distinguished him from other candidates by kissing him in the Continental fashion. He made the customary "grand tour" of France and Italy, and, returning to England in 1665, became at once a splendid figure at Charles's splendid Court. His wit, his handsome person, his graceful address, made him the observed of all observers. Charles admitted him to his intimacy, conferring on him the appointment of a Gentleman of the Bedchamber and Controller of Woodstock Park; and soon in that dissolute scene the young Earl was gayest among the gay.

There were times in the wayward career of this remarkable man when he seems to have struggled against himself—to have been conscious of his powers, and made desultory efforts to direct them to a worthy purpose. Thus, in the winter of 1665, he joined, as a volunteer, the Earl of Sandwich's expedition against the Dutch, whose East India fleet took refuge in Bergen harbour, and were there attacked by Sandwich with desperate resolution. Rochester served on board *The Revenge*, was in the thick of the action, and under a tremendous fire preserved his usual air of careless gallantry. In the following year he was present at the great battle of the 3rd of June, and was sent by Sir Edward Sprague with a message to one of his captains in the heat of the engagement, going and returning in an open boat, under a storm of shot, as coolly as if he had been sauntering in the Mall. The stern experience of war exercised for a time a salutary influence on his conduct. He avoided the gay gallants with whom he had plunged into dissipation, and lived with a temperance and a discretion which led his friends to hope he might yet justify their high opinions.

He was already married. In his early manhood he chose for his wife one Elizabeth Mallet, the daughter of John Mallet, Esquire, of Enmore, in Somersetshire, a young lady of considerable personal charms, with a fortune valued at £2,500 a year.* The match was favoured by Charles II., who deigned to recommend his favourite to the lady's attention; nor does there seem to have been any insuperable obstacle to its successful conclusion. Yet, with the perverseness which distinguished him, Rochester resolved to carry her off by force. As the lady was returning home one evening, after supping with Mrs. Frances Stewart, her coach was surrounded by a number of armed men, afoot and on horseback, who violently hurried her into another, drawn by six horses, and drove off rapidly towards Uxbridge, where Rochester was awaiting his intended bride. But the alarm having been given, and a hot pursuit undertaken, the abducted heiress was restored, and Rochester, by the

---

* This is the "melancholy heiress" (*la triste héritière*) of Count Hamilton; so called, I suppose, as the wife of Rochester.

King's order, committed to the Tower. Eventually, however, he was pardoned both by his King and by Miss Mallet, and their marriage soon afterwards took place.* Nor does it seem, on the whole—in spite of his infidelities and numerous absences—to have been an unhappy one Rochester's letters afford convincing proof, as we shall see, that he could be an affectionate husband and a tender father; his better nature revealing itself in the pure atmosphere of Home.

After the temporary reformation to which I have alluded Rochester broke out into the wildest escapades. His fantastic freaks were the amusement, as his epigrams were the terror, of the Court. He mimicked the Lord Chancellor in the King's presence; he played audacious tricks on the ladies who fluttered, butterfly-like, in the sunshine of royal smiles; he quarrelled with the courtiers, and, as in his quarrel with Lord Mulgrave (afterwards Duke of Buckinghamshire), bore himself in such a manner as to show that his once brilliant courage had been impaired by the excesses which were ruining his constitution. "He gave himself up," says Bishop Burnet, "to all sorts of extravagance, and to the wildest frolics that

* Pepys gives the following account of this boyish escapade (Rochester was then in his 18th year):—" May 28, 1665. To my Lady Sandwich's, where, to my shame, I had not been a great while. There, upon my telling her a story of my Lord of Rochester's running away on Friday night last with Mrs. Mallett, the great beauty and fortune of the North, who had supped at Whitehall with Mrs. Stewart, and was going home to her lodgings with her grandfather, my Lord Hally, by coach; and was at Charing Cross seized on by both horse and footmen, and forcibly taken from him, and put into a coach with six horses, and two women provided to receive her, and carried away. Upon immediate pursuit, my Lord of Rochester (for whom the King had spoke to the lady often, but with no success) was taken at Uxbridge; but the lady is not yet heard of, and the King mighty angry, and the Lord sent to the Tower. Hereupon my lady did confess to me, as a great secret, her being concerned in this story. For if this match breaks between my Lord Rochester and her, then, by the consent of all her friends, my Lord Hinchingbroke (Lord Sandwich's son and heir) stands fair, and is invited for her."

wanton wit could devise. He would have gone about the streets as a beggar, and made love as a porter. He set up a stage as an Italian mountebank. He was for some years always drunk; and was ever doing some mischief. The King loved his company, for the diversion it afforded, better than his person; and there was no love lost between them. He took his revenges in many libels. He found out a footman that knew all the Court; and he furnished him with a red coat and a musket, as a sentinel, and kept him all the winter long, every night, at the doors of such ladies as he believed might be in intrigues. In the Court, a sentinel is little minded, and is believed to be posted by a captain of the guards to hinder a combat; so this man saw who walked about and visited at forbidden hours. By this means Lord Rochester made many discoveries; and when he was well furnished with materials, he used to retire into the country for a month or two to write libels. Once, being drunk, he intended to give the King a libel he had writ on some ladies, but, by mistake, he gave him one written on himself. He fell into an ill habit of body, and, in set fits of sickness, he had deep remorses, for he was guilty both of much impiety and of great immoralities. But as he recovered, he threw these off, and turned again to his former ill courses."

"He set up a stage as an Italian mountebank." This was one of Rochester's most extraordinary exploits. He had been banished from Court for one of his bitter lampoons, but growing weary of rural retirement, and feeling sure that the King would soon recall him, he ventured up to London. Here he took lodgings among the rich merchants and leading tradesmen; changed his dress and assumed a fictitious name; and, having a wonderful facility in adapting himself to all classes and persons, he soon wormed his way into the good graces of some of the wealthy aldermen and the favour of their stately ladies. He was invited to all their feasts and assemblies, and while, in the company of the husbands, he declaimed against the faults and mistakes of Government, he joined their wives in railing against the profligacy of the Court ladies, and in inveighing against the King's mistresses. He agreed with them that the cost of all these extravagances fell upon the industrious poor; that the city beauties were not inferior to those of the other end of the town, although, in the city, a sober husband was contented with one wife; and, finally, he protested that he wondered Whitehall was not yet consumed by fire from heaven, since such rakes as Rochester, Killigrew, and Sidney were suffered there. In this way he endeared himself to the cits, and made himself welcome at their clubs, until the restless gallant grew weary of the endless round of banquets.

But, instead of approaching the Court, he retired into one of the obscurest corners of the City, where, changing again his name and dress, he caused bills to be distributed, announcing—" The recent arrival of a famous German doctor, who, by long study and extensive practice, had discovered wonderful secrets and infallible remedies." Of this curious document we give such passages as are consistent with a regard for decency :—

" To all gentlemen, ladies, and others, whether of city, town, or country, Alexander Bendo wisheth all health and prosperity.

" Whereas this famed metropolis of England (and were the endeavours of its worthy inhabitants equal to their power, merit, and virtue, I should not stick to denounce it in a short time, the metropolis of the whole world); whereas, I say, this city (as most great ones are) has ever been infested with a numerous company of such, whose arrogant confidence, backed with their ignorance, has enabled them to impose on the people, either by premeditated cheats, or at best, the palpable, dull, and empty mistakes of their self-deluded imagination in physic, chymical and Galenic; in astrology, physiognomy, palmistry, mathematics, alchymy, and even, in government itself, the last of which I will not propose to discourse of, or meddle at all in, since it in no way belongs to my trade or vocation, as the rest do; which (thanks to my God) I find much more safe, I think equally honest, and therefore more profitable.

"But as to all the former, they have been so erroneously practised by many unlearned wretches, whom poverty and neediness, for the most part (if not the restless itch of deceiving), has forced to struggle and wander in unknown parts, that even the professions themselves, though originally the products of the most learned and wise men's laborious studies and experience, and by them left a wealthy and glorious inheritance for ages to come, seem, by this bastard race of quacks and cheats, to have been run out of all wisdom, learning, perspicuousness, and truth, with which they were so plentifully stocked; and now run into a repute of mere mists, imaginations, errors, and deceits, such as, in the management of these idle professors, indeed they were.

"You will therefore, I hope, gentlemen, ladies, and others, deem it but just that I, who for some years have with all faithfulness and assiduity courted these arts, and received such signal favours from them, that they have admitted me to the happy and full enjoyment of themselves, and trusted me with their greatest secrets, should with an earnestness and concern more than ordinary, take their parts against those impudent fops, whose saucy, impertinent addresses and pretensions have brought such a scandal upon their most immaculate honours and reputations.

"Besides, I hope you will not think I could be so impudent, that if I had intended any such foul play myself, I would have given you so fair warning by my severe observations upon others. 'Qui alterum incusant probri, ipsum se intueri oportet.' However, gentlemen, in a world like this, where virtue is so exactly counterfeited and hypocrisy so generally taken notice of, that every one, armed with suspicion, stands upon his guard against it, it will be very hard, for a stranger especially, to escape censure. All I shall say for myself on this score is this:—if I appear to any one like a counterfeit, even for the sake of that, chiefly, ought I to be construed a true man. Who is the counterfeit's example? His original; and that, which he employs his industry and pains to imitate and copy; is it therefore my fault, if the cheat by his wits and endeavours makes himself so like me, that consequently I cannot avoid resembling him? Consider, pray, the valiant and the coward, the wealthy merchant and the bankrupt, the politician and the fool; they are the same in many things, and differ but in *one* alone.

"The valiant man holds up his head, looks confidently round about him, wears a sword, courts a lord's wife, and owns it; so does the coward: *one* only point of honour excepted, and that is courage, which (like false metal, *one* only trial can discover) makes the distinction.

"The bankrupt walks the exchange, buys bargains, draws bills, and accepts them with the richest, whilst paper and credit are current coin: that which makes the difference is real cash; a great defect indeed, and yet but *one*, and *that* the last found out, and still, till then, the least perceived.

"Now for the politician:—he is a grave, deliberating, close, prying man: pray, are there not grave, deliberating, close, prying fools?

"If then the difference betwixt all these (though infinite in effect) be so nice in all appearance, will you expect it should be otherwise betwixt the false physician, astrologer, etc., and the true? The first calls himself learned doctor, sends forth his bills, gives physic and counsel, tells and foretels; the other is bound to do just as much: it is only your experience must distinguish betwixt them; to which I willingly submit myself. I will only say something to the honour of the MOUNTEBANK, in case you discover me to be one.

"Reflect a little what kind of creature it is:—he is one then, who is fain to supply some higher ability he pretends to with craft; he draws great companies to him by undertaking strange things, which can never be effected. The politician (by his example no doubt) finding how the people are taken with spurious miraculous impossibilities, plays the same game; protests, declares, promises I know not what things, which he is sure can never be brought about. The people believe, are deluded, and pleased; the expectation of a future good, which shall never befal them, draws their eyes off *a* present evil. Thus are they kept and established in subjection, peace, and obedience; *he* in greatness, wealth, and power. So you see the politician is, and must be a *mountebank* in State affairs; and the *mountebank* no doubt, if he thrives, is an arrant politician in physic. But that I may not prove too tedious, I will proceed faithfully to inform you, what are the things in which I pretend chiefly, at this time, to serve my country.

"First, I will (by the leave of God) perfectly cure that *labes Britannica, or grand English disease, the scurvy:* and that with such ease to my patient, that he shall not be sensible of the least inconvenience, whilst I steal his distemper from him. I know there are many who treat this disease with mercury, antimony, spirits, and salts, being dangerous remedies; in which I shall meddle very little, and with great caution; but by more secure, gentle, and less fallible medicines, together with the observation of some few rules in diet, perfectly cure the patient, having freed him from all the symptoms, as looseness of the teeth, scorbutic spots, want of appetite, pains and lassitude in the limbs and joints, especially the legs. And to say true, there are few distempers in this nation that are not, or at least proceed out originally from the scurvy; which, were it well rooted out (as I make no question to do it from all those who shall come into my hands), there would not be heard of so many gouts, aches, dropsies, and consumptions; nay, even those thick and slimy humours, which generate stones in the kidneys and bladder, are for the most part offsprings of the *scurvy*. It would prove tedious to set down all its malignant race; but those who address themselves here, shall be still informed by me of the nature of their distempers, and the grounds I proceed upon to their cure: so will all reasonable people be satisfied that I treat them with care, honesty, and understanding; for I am not of their opinion, who endeavour to render their vocations rather mysterious than useful and satisfactory.

"I will not here make a catalogue of diseases and distempers; it behoves a physician, I am sure, to understand them all; but if any one come to me (as I think there are very few that have escaped my practice) I shall not be ashamed to own to my patient, when I find myself to seek; and, at least, he shall be secure with me from having experiments tried upon him; a privilege he can never hope to enjoy, either in the hands of the grand doctors of the court and Tower, or in those of the lesser quacks and mountebanks.

"It is thought fit, that I assure you of great secrecy, as well as cure, in diseases, where it is requisite; whether venereal or others; as some peculiar to women, the greensickness, weaknesses, inflammations, or obstructions in the stomach, reins, liver, spleen, &c.; for I would put no word in my bill that bears any unclean sound; it is enough that I make myself understood. I have seen physician's bills as bawdy as *Aretine's Dialogues*, which no man, that walks warily before God, can approve of. . . .

"I have, likewise, got the knowledge of a great secret to cure barrenness. . . Cures of this kind I have done signal and many. . . .

"As to astrological predictions, physiognomy, divination by dreams, and otherwise (palmistry I have no faith in, because there can be no reason alleged for it), my own experience has convinced me more of their considerable effects and marvellous operations, chiefly in the direction of future proceedings, to the avoiding of dangers that threaten, and laying hold of advantages that might offer themselves; I say, my own practice has convinced me, more than all the sage and wise writings extant, of those matters; for I might say this of myself (did it not look like ostentation), that I have very seldom failed in my predictions, and often been very serviceable in my advice. How far I am capable in this way, I am sure is not fit to be delivered in print: those who have no opinion of the truth of this art, will not, I suppose, come to me about it; such as have, I make no question of giving them ample satisfaction.

"Nor will I be ashamed to set down here my willingness to practise rare secrets (though somewhat collateral to my profession), for the help, conservation, and augmentation of beauty and comeliness; a thing created at first by God, chiefly for the glory of His own name, and then for the better establishment of mutual love between man and woman; for when God had bestowed on man the power of strength and wisdom, and thereby rendered woman liable to the subjection of his absolute will, it seemed but requisite that she should be endued likewise, in recompense, with some quality that might beget in him admiration of her, and so enforce his tenderness and love.

"The knowledge of these secrets I gathered in my travels abroad (where I have spent my time ever since I was fifteen years old, to this my nine and twentieth year) in France and Italy. Those that have travelled in Italy will tell you what a miracle art does there assist nature in the preservation of beauty; how women of forty bear the same countenance with those of fifteen; ages are no ways distinguished by faces; whereas, here in England, look a horse in the mouth, and a woman in the face, you presently know both their ages to a year. I will, therefore, give you such remedies that, without destroying your complexion (as most of your paints and daubings do) shall render them perfectly fair; clearing and preserving them from all spots, freckles, heats, pimples, and marks of the small-pox, or any other accidental ones, so the face be not seamed or scarred.

"I will also cleanse and preserve your *teeth* white and round as pearls, fastening them that are loose; your gums shall be kept entire, as red as coral; your lips of the same colour, and soft as you could wish your lawful kisses.

"I will likewise administer that which shall cure the worst of breaths, provided the lungs be not totally perished and imposthumated; as also certain and infallible remedies for those whose breaths are yet untainted; so that nothing but either a very long sickness, or old age itself, shall ever be able to spoil them.

"I will, besides (if it be desired) *take away* from their fatness, who have over much, and *add* flesh to those that want it, without the least detriment to their constitutions.

"Now, should Galen himself look out of his grave, and tell me these were troubles below the profession of a physician, I would boldy answer him, that I take more glory in preserving God's image in its unblemished beauty, upon one good face, than I should do in patching up all the decayed carcases in the world.

"They that will do me the favour to come to me, shall be sure, from three of the clock in the afternoon till eight at night, at my lodgings in Tower Street, next door to the sign of the Black Swan, at a goldsmith's house, to find

"Their humble servant,

"ALEXANDER BENDO."

The fame of Alexander Bendo soon spread to the west-end of the town, and the maids of honour sent their servants to wait upon him, and secretly put to the test his supposed wonderful powers. His knowledge of the inner life of the Court, and of its scandals and intrigues, enabled him to answer their questions in a way that caused either alarm or diversion, according to circumstances. The curiosity of Miss Jennings, afterwards Duchess of Tyrconnel, and Miss Price, two of the most daring of the court sirens, was so moved that they ventured on the hazardous enterprise of visiting the new magician in person. Disguised as orange-girls they drove thither in a hackney-coach, but when within half a street of the desired goal attracted the attention of the infamous Brouncker—"a pestilent rogue," says Pepys, "an atheist, that would have sold his King and country for sixpence almost, so corrupt and wicked a rogue he is by all men's report"—and, to escape his insolent addresses, abandoned their design. "While they were under these alarms," says Count Hamilton, "their coachman was engaged in a squabble with some blackguard boys, who had gathered round his coach in order to steal the oranges; from words they came to blows: the two nymphs saw the commencement of the fray as they were returning to the coach, after having abandoned the design of going to the fortune-teller's. Their coachman being a man of spirit, it was with great difficulty they could persuade him to leave their oranges to the mob, that they might get off without any further disturbance: having thus regained their hack, after a thousand frights, and after having received an abundant share of the most low and infamous abuse applied to them during the fracas, they at length reached St. James's, vowing never more to go after fortune-tellers, through so many dangers, terrors, and alarms, as they had lately undergone."

Rochester was soon afterwards recalled to Court, where he resumed his old course of profligate folly. In his lucid intervals he read a good deal, and it seems that he was specially partial to the study of history. He did not refrain from his ironical comments on his Sovereign's infirmities. Charles was very fond of repeating the story of his adventures in Scotland and Paris, and this he did with such frequency that Rochester said, severely, "He wondered that a man with so good a memory as to repeat the same story without losing the least circumstance, yet could not remember that he had told it to the same person the very day before." Still sharper was the well-known epigram which penetrated even through the King's easy indifference:—

> "Here lies our sovereign lord the King,
> Whose word no man relies on;
> He never said a foolish thing,
> And never did a wise one."

The sting of this terse satire lay, no doubt, in its truth. Charles, we are told, never forgave it.

Like Lord Lytton's Gabriel Varney, Rochester possessed a constitution which alcoholic excess could not directly affect. It was a dangerous organisation, and, perhaps, the ruin of his life was partly owing to this physical gift. "He was unhappily made for drunkenness," says Bishop Burnet, "for he had drunk all his friends dead, and was able to subdue two or three sets of drunkards one after another: so it scarce ever appeared that he was disordered after the greatest drinking: an hour or two of sleep carried all off entirely, that no sign of them remained. He would go about business without any uneasiness, or discovering heat either in body or mind." But a terrible Nemesis dogged the profligate's footsteps. "After he had killed all his friends, he fell at last into such weakness of stomach, that he had perpetual cholic when he was not within, and full of strong liquor, of which he was frequently seized, so that he was always either sick or drunk."

He was not yet thirty when his constitution suddenly gave way, and the brilliant wit found himself overtaken by a premature old age. Feeble and weary, dissatisfied with himself, conscious of the manner in which he had abused his powers, he began to turn his mind to serious thoughts, and with remorse for the past mingled uncertainty as to the future. Might not that religion be true which he had so constantly ridiculed? And if so, then, indeed, he had cause to tremble! About this time he made the acquaintance of Bishop Burnet, and held with him many earnest conversations on those great truths which concern the eternal destiny of man. The Bishop has left a record of these conversations, which it is impossible to read without the liveliest interest. Rochester was not at once converted; but it does not appear that he ever had been a confirmed atheist, and his disbelief was that of the head rather than that of the heart.

In the spring of 1680, Rochester retired to his country seat at Woodstock, and in the fresh country air recovered some small portion of his former health. But the exertion of a long journey on horseback into Somersetshire proved too much for his enfeebled frame, and he returned to Woodstock with the shadow of death upon him.

Suffering acutely from a troubled conscience, he sought the advice of Mr. Parsons, his mother's chaplain; he was also attended by the Bishop of Oxford, Dr. Marshall, rector of Lincoln, and Dr. Pierce, President of Magdalen. One day, while Mr. Parsons was reading to the invalid that 53rd chapter of Isaiah, which has ever been expressibly dear to the Christian, a sudden light seemed to break upon his mind, and the darkness of unfaith in which he had hitherto been involved was swept aside. He was not only convinced by the argument which Mr. Parsons founded upon it, but by a Divine power which moved him so effectually that thenceforward he believed as firmly in his Saviour as if, like Thomas, he had seen the wounded side, and the prints of the nails in the hands and feet. The sincerity and completeness of his conversion appear in the letter which, at this time, he wrote to Dr. Pierce :—

"My indisposition renders my intellectuals almost as feeble as my person, but considering the candour and extreme charity your natural mildness hath always shown me, I am assured at once of a favourable construction of my present lines, which can but faintly express the sorrowful character of an humble and afflicted mind: and also those great comforts your inexhaustible goodness, learning, and piety, plenteously afford to the drooping spirits of poor sinners, so that I may truly say,— Holy man! to you I owe what consolation I enjoy, in urging God's mercies against despair, and holding me up under the weight of those high and mountainous sins, my wicked and ungovernable life hath heaped upon me. If God shall be pleased to spare me a little longer here, I have unalterably resolved to become a new man; to wash out the stains of my lewd courses with my tears, and weep over the profane and unhallowed abominations of my former doings; that the world may see how I loath sin, and abhor the very remembrance of those tainted and unclean joys I once delighted in; these being, as the Apostle tells us, the things whereof I am now ashamed; or, if it be His great pleasure now to put a period to my days, that He will accept my last gasp, that the smoke of my death-bed offering may not be unsavoury to His nostrils, and drive me like Cain from His presence.

"Pray for me, dear Doctor, and all you that forget not God, pray for me fervently. Take heaven by force, and let me enter with you in disguise; for I dare not appear before the dread majesty of that Holy One I have so often offended. Warn all my friends and companions to a true and sincere repentance to-day, while it is called to-day, before the evil day come and they be no more. Let them know that sin is like the Angel's book in the Revelations, it is sweet in the mouth, but bitter in the belly. Let them know that God will not be mocked; that He is an holy God, and will be served in holiness and purity, that requires the whole man and the early man: bid them make haste, for the night cometh when no man can work. Oh that they were wise, that they would consider this, and not with me, with wretched me, delay it until their latter end. Pray, dear sir, continually pray for your poor friend,

"ROCHESTER."

A narrative exists in the British Museum of a visit paid to the dying Earl by one of his boon companions, who seems to have been ignorant of his illness:—

"When Wilmot, Earl of Rochester, lay on his death-bed, Mr. Fanshawe * came to visit him, with an intention to stay about a week with him. Mr. Fanshawe, sitting by the bedside, perceived his lordship praying to God through Jesus Christ, and acquainted Dr. Radcliffe, who attended my Lord Rochester in this illness, and was then in the house, with what he had heard; and told him, that my lord was certainly delirious, for to his knowledge, he said, he believed neither in God nor in Jesus Christ. The doctor, who had often heard him pray in the same manner, proposed to Mr. Fanshawe to go up to his lordship to be further satisfied touching this affair. When they came to his room, the doctor told my lord what Mr. Fanshawe said, upon which his lordship addressed himself to Mr. Fanshawe, to this effect: ' Sir, it is true you and I have been very bad and profane together, and then I was of the opinion you mention. But now I am quite of another mind, and happy am I that I am so. I am very sensible how miserable I was whilst of another opinion. Sir, you may assure yourself that there is a Judge and future state;' and so entered into a very handsome discourse concerning the Last Judgment, future state, &c., and concluded with a serious and pathetic exhortation to Mr. Fanshawe, to enter into another course of life; adding that he (Mr. F.) knew him to be his friend; that he never was more so than at this time: and, ' Sir,' said he, ' to use a Scripture expression, I am not mad, but speak the words of truth and soberness.' Upon this Mr. Fanshawe trembled, and went immediately a-foot to Woodstock, and there hired a horse to Oxford, and thence took coach to London."

---

* Probably Mr. William Fanshawe, who married Mary, one of Charles II.'s daughters by Mary Walters.

Bishop Burnet was a welcome visitor to the bedside of the dying Earl, who told him, at intervals, for he was in too feeble a condition to hold any prolonged speech, of the remorse with which he looked back upon his misspent life and its wasted opportunities,—of his deep contrition for having so offended his Maker and dishonoured his Redeemer,—and of the longing with which he turned to his God and crucified Saviour. He hoped to obtain the Divine mercy, for he knew and felt that he had sincerely repented; and after the storm and stress in which his mind had been tossed for weeks, he now enjoyed a heavenly calm. At one time he asked Burnet what he thought of the efficacy of a death-bed repentance. At another, he declared that, as for himself, he freely forgave all who had done him wrong; he bore ill will to no man, he had made arrangements for the payment of his debts, and suffered pain with cheerfulness. He was content to live or die, as God pleased; and though it was a foolish thing for a man to pretend to choose whether he would live or die, yet, so far as wishes went, he was fain to die and be at rest. He knew that he could never again recover his health so far that life would leave any comfort for him; and while he was confident he should be happy if he died, he feared that if he lived he might relapse. To his friends he sent affectionate messages, reminding them of the uncertain tenure of life, and enjoining them to publish to the world any circumstances connected with his own life and death which might possibly prove of benefit to others. It was his prayer, he said, that as by his life he had inflicted injury upon religion, he might at least do it some service by his death.

At the Bishop's hands he received the bread and wine

of the Holy Eucharist, his wife, for whom he expressed the most tender affection, participating with him. His children were brought to his bedside; he took leave of them lovingly, and bestowed upon them his solemn blessing. He sent, too, for all his servants, and while they surrounded his bed, declared to them in strong and simple words his regret for his dissolute life and pernicious opinions. At last, the slow decay came to an end; the flickering lamp of life went out; and this man of brilliant parts and rare gifts expired, in the thirty-third year of his age, on the 26th of July, 1680. He was interred by the side of his father in the north aisle of Spilsbury Church, Oxfordshire.

By his Countess, Rochester left four children; Charles, the third Earl, who died on the 12th of November, 1686, and with whom the title became extinct; Anne, whose second husband was Francis, the son of Fulke Greville, Lord Broke; Elizabeth, afterwards wife of Edward Montague, Earl of Sandwich; and Mallet, who married John Vaughan, first Viscount Lisburne.

M. Taine's portrait of Rochester is painted in the darkest colours. Byron allows his Corsair "*one* virtue" as a set-off against his "thousand crimes," but Taine deals less mercifully with the dissolute Earl. Here is his incisive sketch:—

"His manners were those of a lawless and wretched mountebank; his delight was to haunt the stews, to debauch women, to write filthy songs and lewd pamphlets; he spent his time between gossipping with the maids of honour, broils with men of letters, the receiving of insults, the giving of blows. By way of playing the gallant he eloped with his wife before he married her. Out of a spirit of bravado, he declined fighting a duel, and gained the name of a coward. For five years together he was said to be drunk. The spirit within him failing of a worthy outlet, plunged him into adventures more befitting a clown. Once with the Duke of Buckingham he rented an inn on the Newmarket road, and turned innkeeper, supplying the husbands with drink and defiling their wives. He introduced himself, disguised as an old woman, into the house of a miser, robbed him of his wife, and passed her on to Buckingham. The husband hanged himself; they made very merry over the affair. At another time he disguised himself as a chairman, then as a beggar, and paid court to the gutter-girls. He ended by turning a quack astrologer, and vendor of drugs for procuring abortion, in the suburbs. It was the licentiousness of a fervid imagination, which fouled itself as another would have adorned it, which forced its way into lewdness and folly as another would have done into sense and beauty."

All this may be, and, indeed, is true; but on the other side it is only fair to remember that this profligate wit was capable of generous actions, and had the grace, in his soberer moments, to be ashamed of the life he led, and of the waste of powers of which he was guilty. There is this excuse—we do not put it forward as altogether satisfactory—to be made for Rochester and his roistering companions; that with superabundant vitality, and all the energy and ripe vigour of their race, they had absolutely no fitting field of action open to them. Beyond the seas no such outlets for a spirit of adventure were open then as are open now; no great war braced up their manhood, and awakened their loftier impulses. Parliamentary life offered no generous and elevating career; no healthy public opinion held in check their riotous and exuberant animalism. So they went into the streets and the stews, and there exhausted the gifts and graces which, under happier circumstances, might have done so much for their country and themselves. They were unfortunate in the age into which they were born. A century earlier, and they would have shone among the daring spirits who adorned the times of great Elizabeth. A century later, and their pulses would have been stirred by that inspiration of freedom and humanity which breathed a new life into the dry bones of the European nations. As it was, they came into an atmosphere of corruption and luxurious apathy, and sensual indulgence, the evil influence of which not even a Sidney or a Russell could wholly escape. We may and must condemn them, and yet something of pity may rightly mingle with our anger.

On the literary work of Rochester we are not prepared to say that M. Taine's criticism is wholly just. He makes no attempt to separate the golden grain from the worthless chaff, while he evidently accepts as Rochester's very much which belongs to other and even filthier writers.

"We cannot copy," he says, "even the titles of his poems; they were written only for the haunts of vice. Stendhal said that love is like a dried-up bough cast into a mine; the crystals cover it, spread out into filigree work, and end by converting the worthless stick into a sparkling tuft of the purest diamonds. Rochester begins by depriving love of all its adornment, and to make sure of grasping it, converts it into a stick. Every refined sentiment, every fancy; the enchantment, the serene, sublime glow which transforms in a moment this wretched world of ours; the illusion which, uniting all the powers of our being, shows as perfection in a finite creature, and eternal bliss in a transient emotion, all has vanished; there remain but satiated appetites and palled senses. The worst of it is, that he writes without spirit, and methodically enough. He has no natural ardour, no picturesque sensuality; his satires prove him a disciple of Boileau. Nothing is more disgusting than obscenity in cold blood. We can endure the obscene works of Giulio Romano, and his Venetian voluptuousness, because in them genius sets off sensuality, and the loveliness of the splendid coloured draperies transforms an orgie into a work of art.* We pardon Rabelais, when we have entered into the deep current of manly joy and vigour, with which his feasts abound. We can hold our nose and have done with it, while we follow with admiration, and even sympathy, the torrent of ideas and fancies which flows through his mire. But to see a man trying to be elegant and remaining obscene, endeavouring to paint the sentiments of a navvy in the language of a man of the world, who tries to find a suitable metaphor for every kind of filth, who plays the blackguard studiously and deliberately, who, excused neither by genuine feeling, nor the glow of fancy, nor knowledge, nor genius, degrades a good style of writing to such work; it is like a rascal who sets himself to sully a set of gems in a gutter. The

---

* But Giulio Romano, and the writers who write as Romano painted, are infinitely more dangerous than Rochester. Evelyn saw that the insinuated sensuality of "gentle Etherege" and Sedley was more corrupting than Rochester's open lewdness. As for Rabelais, he descends into depths into which even Rochester would hardly have followed him.

end of all is but disgust and illness. While La Fontaine continues to the last day capable of tenderness and happiness, this man at the age of thirty insults the weaker sex with spiteful malignity:—

> ' When she is young, she whores herself for sport;
> And when she's old, she bawds for her support.
> She is a snare, a shamble, and a stews;
> Her meat and sauce she does for lechery choose,
> And does in laziness delight the more,
> Because by that she is provoked to whore.
> Ungrateful, treacherous, enviously inclined,
> Wild beasts are tamed, floods easier far confined,
> Than is her stubborn and rebellious mind . . .
> Her temper so extravagant we find,
> She hates, or is impertinently kind.
> Would she be grave, she then looks like a devil,
> And like a fool or whore, when she be civil. . . .
> Contentious, wicked, and not fit to trust,
> And covetous to spend it on her lust.'

What a confession is such a judgment! what an abstract of life! You see the roisterer stupified at the end of his career, dried up like a mummy, eaten away by ulcers. Amid the choruses, the crude satires, the remembrance of plans miscarried, the sullied enjoyments which are heaped up in his wearied brain as in a sink, the fear of damnation is persecuting; he dies a devotee at the age of thirty-three."

That Rochester's coarse lines embody a libel on woman we readily admit, but Rochester drew from the women he was acquainted with—the shameless harlots, the abandoned adulteresses, who made Charles's Court hideous. See them in the pages of Hamilton and Pepys,* and you feel that the wonder is, not that Rochester wrote of

---

* One specimen will suffice:—" Here," says Pepys, " I first understood by their talk the meaning of company that were lately called Ballers; Harris telling how it was by a meeting of some young blades, where he was among them, and my Lady Burnet and her ladies; and *their dancing naked*, and all the roguish things in the world."

them with such savage cynicism, but that he did not rather curse them as the cause of his indecency. How different might have been his life and death had he but had the good fortune to fall under the purifying influence of some woman worthy of the name! if he had lived among the Violas and Imogens of Shakespeare instead of among the Lucys and Lady Dapperwits of Wycherley!

Rochester was unquestionably a man of versatile genius, who, with wider culture and more knowledge of men and manners, might have added something considerable to his country's literature. As it was, he expended himself, when at his best and sanest, upon trifles. He had no earnest ambition, no lofty purpose; he took no serious view of life; it was enough for him if he pleased a mistress with a dainty love-song or stung a rival with an epigram. Yet his natural vigour and strength were such that epigram and love-song had almost always in them a true poetic touch. Unhappily his writings are stained by the lewdness which then permeated the social life of the English upper classes, and the wit and fancy which were capable of really noble work were degraded to the level of the bagnio. But we must again remind the reader that a large proportion of the coarse and indelicate verses ascribed to Rochester were not written by him, and that the only authentic edition of his works is that which was published in 1691.

When he chose he could write with a grace, a playfulness, and a rhythmical flow worthy of all praise. For instance, the freshness, the tender exaggeration, the simple sweetness of the following song must be felt by every reader, and especially by the reader who is still in the flush of his first true passion :—

> "My dear Mistress has a heart
>   Soft as those kind looks she gave me
> When, with love's resistless art,
>   And her eyes she did enslave me;
> But her constancy's so weak,
>   She's so wild and apt to wander,
> That my jealous heart would break
>   Should we live one day asunder.
>
> Melting joys about her move,
>   Killing pleasures, wounding blisses,
> She can dress her eyes in love,
>   And her lips can arm with kisses;
> Angels listen when she speaks,
>   She's my delight, all mankind's wonder,
> But my jealous heart would break,
>   Should we live one day asunder."

He manages double-syllable endings with happy facility. Can anything be more fluent and graceful than this?—

> "When on those lovely looks I gaze,
>   To see a wretch pursuing,
> In raptures of a blest amaze,
>   His pleasing happy ruin,
> 'Tis not for pity that I move;
>   His fate is too aspiring,
> Whose heart, broke with a load of love,
>   Dies wishing and admiring.
>
> But if this murder you'd forego,
>   Your slave from death removing,
> Let me your art of charming know,
>   Or you learn mine of loving;
> But whether life or death betide,
>   In love 'tis equal measure,
> The victor lives with empty pride,
>   The vanquished dies with pleasure."

In his lyric on "The Bowl" there is evidence of a facile fancy, while the versification is perfect in its musical flow and exquisite choice of words:—

THE BOWL.

> "Contrive me, Vulcan, such a cup
>   As Nestor used of old,
> Show all thy skill to trim it up,
>   Damask it round with gold.

> Make it so large that, filled with sack
>   Up to the swelling brim,
> Vast toasts on that delicious lake,
>   Like ships at sea, may swim.
>
> Engrave not battle on his cheek,
>   With war I've nought to do,
> I'm none of those that took Maestrick,
>   Nor Yarmouth leaguer knew.
>
> Let it no name of planets tell,
>   Fixed stars or constellations,
> For I am no Sir Sindrophel,
>   Nor none of his relations.
>
> But carve thereon a spreading vine;
>   Then add two lovely boys:
> Their limbs in amorous folds entwine,
>   The types of future joys.
>
> Cupid and Bacchus my saints are,
>   May Drink and Love still reign,
> With wine I wash away my care,
>   And then to love again."

One more specimen of his powers as a lyrist, which we take as foisted by him upon Fletcher's tragedy of "Valentinian." A comparison of it with Fletcher's own lyrics will illustrate the singular change in the spirit and form of English poetry which had been effected in half a century *:—

Nymph.

> "Injurious charmer of my vanquished heart,
>   Canst thou feel love, and yet no pity know?
> Since of myself from thee I cannot part,
>   Invent some gentle way to let me go;
>   For what with joy thou didst obtain,
>   And I with more did give,
>   In time will make thee false and vain,
>   And me unfit to live."

---

* Fletcher died in 1625—twenty-two years before Rochester's birth, and fifty-five before his death.

Shepherd.

"Frail angel, that wouldst leave a heart forlorn,
  With vain pretence Falsehood therein might lie,
Seek not to cast wild shadows o'er your scorn,
  You cannot sooner change than I can die;
    To tedious life I'll never fall,
    Thrown from thy dear-loved breast!
  He merits not to live at all
    Who cares to live unblest."

"With Rochester," says Mr. Gosse, "the power of writing songs died in England until the age of Blake and Burns. He was the last of the Cavalier lyrists, and in some respects the best. In the qualities that a song demands, simplicity, brevity, pathos, and tenderness, he arrives nearer to pure excellence than any one between Carew and Burns. His style is without adornment, and, save in this one matter of song-writing, he is weighed down by the dryness and insufficiency of his age. But by the side of Sedley or of Congreve he seems as fresh as by the side of Dryden he seems light and flowing, turning his trill of song brightly and sweetly, with the consummate artlessness of true art."

His satires are vigorous enough, but so stained with licentiousness that we cannot quote from them. We note, however, a terse and telling allusion to Charles II. as

"A merry monarch, scandalous and poor."

Modern readers will hardly agree with Johnson that the poem "On Nothing" (suggested, perhaps, by the French poet, Passerat's, "Nihil") is "the strongest effort of his muse;" but it contains some ingenious quips and quiddities:—

"Nothing! thou elder brother even to shade,
  Thou hadst a being ere the world was made,
  And, well fixed, art alone of ending not afraid. . . .

> Nothing, who dwell'st with fools in grave disguise,
> For whom they reverend shapes and forms devise,
> Lawn sleeves, and furs, and gowns, when they like thee look wise.
>
> French truth, Dutch prowess, British policy,
> Hibernian learning, Scotch civility,
> Spaniards' dispatch, Danes' wit, are mainly seen in thee."

Rochester's prose style was excellent. His letters are among the best in the language; they are written with so much clearness, pertinency, force, and such happy terms of expression. Here is one addressed to a reckless man of pleasure, like himself, Sir Henry Saville:—

"Whether Love, Wine, or Wisdom, which rule you by turns, have the present ascendant, I cannot pretend to determine at this distance; but Good Nature, which waits about you with more diligence than Godfrey himself, is my security that you are not unmindful of your former friends. To be from you, and forgotten by you at once, is a misfortune I never was criminal enough to merit, since to the black and fair countesses I villanously betrayed the daily addresses of your divided heart. You forgave that upon the first bottle, and upon the second, on my conscience, would have renounced the whole sex. Oh! that second bottle, Henry, is the sincerest, wisest, and most impartial downright friend we have; tells us truth of ourselves, and forces us to speak truth of others; banishes flattery from our tongues and distrust from our hearts; sets us above the mean policy of court prudence, which makes us lie to one another all day, for fear of being betrayed by others at night. And before God I believe the arrantest villain breathing is honest as long as that bottle lives, and few of that tribe dare venture upon him, at least among the courtiers and statesmen. I have seriously considered one thing, that of the three businesses of this age—women, politics, and drinking, the last is the only exercise at which you and I have not proved ourselves arrant fumblers. If you have the vanity to think otherwise, when we meet next, let us appeal to friends of both sexes, and, as they shall determine, live and die mere drunkards or entire lovers: for, as we mingle the matter, it is hard to say which is the most tiresome creature, the loving drunkard or the drunken lover."

"Bath, the 22nd of June."

But his letters to his wife possess an additional charm; the charm of an affectionate nature. They are tender, playful, and loving. It is impossible to read them without forming a strong impression that their writer had in him the germs of abundant good, and, under happier social conditions, or had his life been fortunately inspired by some noble motive, would have done justice to his rich endowments of mind and person. He was the victim, so far as any man can be, who, after all, has, to a certain extent, his fate in his own hands, of circumstances. It was his misfortune, while young, to be thrown into the midst of a dissolute Court, and to be entangled in a web of temptation from which he never succeeded in extricating himself. His very virtues and engaging qualities—his wit, his high-bred manners, his fascinating conversation, his generosity—helped him on to his ruin. But no severer condemnation of the profligate society cherished by Charles II. can be found, or is needed, than that which is supplied by the wrecked life and dishonoured name of Rochester.

Of his letters to his wife, who, be it said, was fully worthy of them, we give some specimens:—

"Wife,

"I am very glad to hear news from you, and I think it very good when I hear you are well; pray be pleased to send me word what you are apt to be pleased with, that I may show you how good a husband I can be; I would not have you so formal as to judge of the kindness of a letter by the length of it, but believe of everything that it is as you would have it.

"'Tis not an easy thing to be entirely happy; but to be kind is very easy, and that is the greatest measure of happiness. I say not this to put you in mind of being kind to me; you have practised that so long, that I have a joyful confidence you will never forget it; but to show that I myself have a sense of what the methods of my life seemed so utterly to contradict, I must not be too wise about my own follies, or else this letter had been a book dedicated to you, and published to the world. It will be more pertinent to tell you, that very shortly the King goes to Newmarket, and then I shall wait on you at Adderbury; in the meantime, think of anything you would have me do, and I shall thank you for the occasion of pleasing you.

"Mr. Morgan I have sent on this errand, because he plays the rogue here in town so extremely, that he is not to be endured; pray, if he behaves himself so at Adderbury, send me word, and let him stay till I send for him. Pray, let Ned come up to town; I have a little business with him, and he shall be back in a week.

"Wonder not that I have not written to you all this while, for it was hard for me to know what to write upon several accounts; but in this I will only desire you not to be too much amazed at the thoughts my mother has of you, since, being mere imaginations, they will as easily vanish, as they were groundlessly created; for my own part, I will make it my endeavour they may. What you desired of me in your other letter, shall punctually be performed. You must, I think, obey my mother in her commands to wait on her at Aylesbury, as I told you in my last letter. I am very dull at this time, and therefore think it pity in this humour to testify myself to you any further. Only, dear wife, I am your humble servant,

"ROCHESTER."

There is a pleasant lively humour in the following:—

"From our tub at Mrs. Forward's, this 18th of Oct.

"WIFE,

"We are now in bed, so that we are not in a condition of writing either according to thy merit or our desert. We therefore do command thy benign acceptance of these our letters, in what way soever by us inscribed or not directed, willing thee therewithal to assure our sole daughter and her issue female, the Lady Anne Tart, of our best respects. This with your care and diligence, in the execution of our firmans, is at present the utmost of our will and pleasure.

"I went away like a rascal without taking leave, dear wife. It is an unpolished way of proceeding, which a modest man ought to be ashamed of. I have left you a prey to your own imaginations amongst my relations, the worst of damnations. But there will come an hour of deliverance, till when, may my mother be merciful unto you. The small share I could spare you out of my pocket

I have sent as a debt to Mrs. Rouse: within a week or ten days I return you more.

"Pray write as often as you have leisure to your

"ROCHESTER."

In the next specimen a little soreness is evident:—

"MY WIFE,

"The difficulties of pleasing your Ladyship do increase so fast upon me, and are grown so numerous, that, to a man less resolved than myself never to give it over, it would appear a madness ever to attempt it more. But through your frailties mine ought not to multiply. You may therefore secure yourself that it will not be easy for you to put me out of my constant resolutions to satisfy you in all I can. I confess there is nothing will so much contribute to my assistance in this as your dealing freely with me; for since you have thought it a wise thing to trust me less and have reserves, it has been out of my power to make the best of my proceedings effectual to what I intended them. At a distance, I am likeliest to learn your mind, for you have not a very obliging way of delivering it by word of mouth; if, therefore, you will let me know the particulars in which I may be useful to you, I will show my readiness as to my own part; and if I fail of the success I wish, it shall not be the fault of your humble servant,

"ROCHESTER."

His letters to his son are not less admirable:—

"I hope, Charles, when you receive this, and know that I have sent this gentleman to be your tutor, you will be very glad to see I take such care of you, and be very grateful, which is best shown in being obedient and diligent.

You are now grown big enough to be a man, if you can be wise enough; for the way to be truly wise is to serve God, learn your book, and observe the instructions of your parents first, and next your tutor, to whom I have entirely resigned you for this seven years, and according as you employ that time, you are to be happy or unhappy for ever; but I have so good an opinion of you, that I am glad to think you will never deceive me; dear child, learn your book and be obedient, and you shall see what a father I will be to you. You shall want no pleasure while you are good, and that you may be so are my constant prayers.

"ROCHESTER."

"Charles, I take it very kindly that you write me, though seldom, and wish heartily you would behave yourself so as that I might show how much I love you without being ashamed. Obedience to your grandmother, and those who instruct you in good things, is the way to make you happy here and for ever. Avoid idleness, scorn lying, and God will bless you.

"ROCHESTER."

Such was this brilliant man of fashion, in his happier and worthier moods, and under the purifying influence of the sweet Home affections.*

---

* Dr. Johnson, "Lives of the Poets," *sub voce*; " Poems by Earl of Rochester," ed. 1691; "Some Passages in the Life and Death of John, Earl of Rochester," by Gilbert Burnet, Bishop of Salisbury (1680); Pepys' " Diary;" Evelyn, " Diary;" etc., etc.

George Villiers, Duke of Buckingham.

The pseudo-romance attaching to the career of this splendid but wayward noble has given him a remarkable place in our literature. It has been his strange fortune to have had his memory preserved by the genius of Dryden, Pope, and Scott. It cannot be said that the portraits they have drawn present him in flattering colours, but they have seized the popular imagination, so that it may well be doubted whether George Villiers, Duke of Buckingham, is not the best known of all the figures that played their parts in the tragi-comedy of Charles the Second's reign. Before we attempt a sketch of his life we shall bring together these skilfully elaborated " characters " of the brilliant Duke, together with some other notices, showing the light in which historians have agreed to regard him.

Everybody knows that he is the Zimri of Dryden's " Absalom and Achitophel," and in that fine satire no other portrait is drawn with more care or point. It has all the terseness of an epigram; its compact and vigorous couplets *make* themselves remembered; and their irresistible force leaves us no time to doubt their truth:—

> "Some of their chiefs were princes of the land;
> In the first rank of these did Zimri stand:
> A man so various, that he seemed to be
> Not one, but all mankind's epitome:
> Stiff in opinions, always in the wrong;
> Was everything by starts, and nothing long;
> But, in the course of one revolving moon,
> Was chymist, fiddler, statesman, and buffoon:
> Then all for women, painting, rhyming, drinking,
> Besides ten thousand freaks that died in thinking.
> Blest madman, who could every hour employ
> With something new to wish or to enjoy!
> Railing and praising were his usual themes;
> And both, to show his judgment, in extremes:

> So over-violent, or over-civil,
> That every man with him was God or Devil.
> In squandering wealth was his peculiar art:
> Nothing went unrewarded but desert.
> Beggared by fools, whom still he found too late;
> He had his jest, and they had his estate.
> He laughed himself from court; then sought relief
> By forming parties, but could ne'er be brief:
> For, spite of him, the weight of business fell
> On Absalom and wise Achitophel: *
> Thus, wicked but in will, of means bereft,
> He left not faction, but of that was left."

Not less finished is Pope's antithetical description of the mean and obscure death of the once brilliant Duke:—

> "In the worst inn's worst room, with mat half-hung,
> The floors of plaster, and the walls of dung,
> On once a flock-bed, but repaired with straw,
> With tape-tied curtains, never meant to draw,
> The George and Garter dangling from that bed
> Where tawdry yellow strove with dirty red,
> Great Villiers lies—alas! how changed from him,
> That life of pleasure and that soul of whim!
> Gallant and gay, in Clieveden's proud alcove,
> The bower of wanton Shrewsbury and love;
> Or just as gay at council, in a ring
> Of mimic statesmen and their merry King.
> No wit to flatter, left of all his store!
> No fool to laugh at, which he valued more—
> There, victor of his health, of fortune, friends,
> And fame, this lord of useless thousands ends!"

Says Horace Walpole, speaking of the Duke:—"His portrait has been drawn by four masterly hands: Burnet has hewn it out with his rough chisel—Count Hamilton touched it with that slight delicacy that finishes while it seems but to sketch—Dryden catched the living likeness—Pope completed the historical resemblance." He has also attempted it himself:—"When this extraordinary man," he says, "with the figure and genius of Alcibiades, could

---

* "Absalom:" the Duke of Monmouth. "Achitophel:" the Earl of Shaftesbury.

equally charm the presbyterian Fairfax and the dissolute Charles; when he alike ridiculed that witty King and his solemn Chancellor; when he plotted the ruin of his country with a cabal of bad ministers, or, equally unprincipled, supported its cause with bad patriots, one laments that such parts should have been devoid of any virtue. But when Alcibiades turns chemist; when he is a real bubble and a visionary miser; when ambition is but a frolic; when the worst designs are for the foolishest ends, contempt extinguishes all reflections on his character."

Bishop Burnet describes him as "a man of noble presence. He had a great liveliness of wit, and a peculiar faculty of turning all things into ridicule, with bold figures, and natural descriptions. He had no sort of literature, only he was drawn into chemistry; and for some years he thought he was very near the finding of the philosopher's stone, which had the effect that attends on all such men as he was, when they are drawn in to lay out for it. He had no principles of religion, virtue, or friendship; pleasure, frolic, or extravagant diversion was all that he laid to heart. He was true to nothing; for he was not true to himself. He had no steadiness nor conduct; he could keep no secret, nor execute any design without spoiling it. He could never fix his thoughts, nor govern his estate, though then the greatest in England. He was bred about the King, and for many years he had a great ascendant over him; but he spake of him to all persons with that contempt, that at last he drew a lasting disgrace upon himself. And he at length ruined both body and mind, fortune and reputation equally. The madness of vice appeared in his person in very eminent instances; since at last he became contemptible and poor, sickly, and sunk in his parts, as well as in all other respects; so that his conversation was as much avoided as ever it had been courted."

In still blacker colours the unfortunate Duke is painted by Butler, the author of "Hudibras," who thus revenged himself upon a man he hated:—"The Duke of Bucks," he says, "is one that has studied the whole body of vice. His parts are disproportionate to the whole; and, like a monster, he has more of some, and less of others, than he should have. He has pulled down all that nature raised in him, and built himself up again after a model of his own. He has dammed up all those lights that nature made into the noblest prospects of the world, and opened other little blind loop-holes backward, by turning day into night, and night into day. His appetite to his pleasures is diseased and crazy, like the pica in a woman, that longs to eat that which was never made for food, or a girl in the green sickness, that eats chalk and mortar. Perpetual surfeits of pleasure have filled his mind with bad and vicious humours (as well as his body with a nursery of diseases), which makes him affect new and extravagant ways, as being sick and tired with the old. Continual wine, women, and music put false values upon things, which, by custom, become habitual, and debauch his understanding so, that he retains no right notion nor sense of things. And as the same dose of the same physic has no operation on those that are much used to it; so his pleasures require a larger proportion of excess and variety, to render him sensible of them. He rises, eats, and goes to bed by the Julian account, long after all others that go by the new style, and keeps the same hours with owls and the antipodes. He is a great observer of the Tartar customs, and never eats till the Great Cham, having dined, makes proclamation that all the world may go to dinner. He does not dwell in his house, but haunts it like an evil spirit, that walks all night, to disturb the family, and never appears by day. He lives perpetually benighted, runs out of his life, and loses his time as men do their ways in the dark: and as blind men are led by their dogs, so is he goverened by some mean servant or other, that relates to his pleasures. He is as inconstant as the moon which he lives under; and although he does nothing but advise with his pillers all day, he is as great a stranger to himself as he is to the rest of the world. His mind entertains all things very freely that come and go, but, like guests and strangers, they are not welcome if they stay long. This lays him open to all cheats, quacks, and impostors, who apply to every particular humour while it lasts, and afterwards vanish. Thus, with St. Paul, though in a different sense, he dies daily, and only lives in the night. He deforms nature, while he intends to adorn her, like Indians that hang jewels in their lips and noses. His ears are perpetually drilled with a fiddlestick. He endures pleasures with less patience than other men do their pains." *

In his "Memoirs of Count Grammont," Count Hamilton, whose touch is exact and incisive, light as it appears, in his scandalous chronicle of Frances Stewart, says :—" The Duke of Buckingham formed the design of governing her in order to ingratiate himself with the King; God knows what a governor he would have been, and what a head he was possessed of, to guide another; however, he was the properest man in the world to

* Butler, " Posthumous Works," ii., 72,

insinuate himself with Miss Stewart," who was very childish in her behaviour and amusements, and delighted in building houses of cards, "as playful children do." She had, however, a passion for music, and had some taste for singing. Now, according to Hamilton, the Duke " who built the finest towers of cards imaginable, had an agreeable voice : she had no aversion to scandal ; and the Duke was both the father and the mother of scandal; he made songs, and invented old women's stories with which she was delighted; but his particular talent consisted in turning into ridicule whatever was ridiculous in other people, and in taking them off, even in their presence, without their perceiving it. In short, he could act all parts with so much grace and pleasantry, that it was difficult to do without him, when he had a mind to make himself agreeable. . . He was extremely handsome, and still thought himself much more so than he really was. Although he had a great deal of discernment, yet his vanity made him mistake some civilities as intended for his person, which were bestowed only on his wit and drollery."

The master-hand of Scott has portrayed the splendidly wayward Duke with wonderful power and fidelity in his romance of "Peveril of the Peak." The reader will remember the scene in which the pretended Mauritanian sorceress addresses the Duke with so much boldness. " What are you ? " she says. " Nay, frown not; for you must hear the truth for once. Nature has done its part, and made a fair outside, and courtly education hath added its share. You are noble, it is the accident of birth—handsome, it is the caprice of nature—generous, because to give is more easy than to refuse—well-apparelled, it is to the credit of your tailor—well-natured in the main, because you have youth and health—brave, because to be otherwise were to be degraded—and witty, because you cannot help it. . . . I have neither allowed you a heart nor a head. . . . Nay, never redden as you would fly at me. I say not but nature may have given you both; but folly has confounded the one, and selfishness perverted the other."

With these estimates before us of his complex character, we proceed to sketch the career of George Villiers, Duke of Buckingham.

George Villiers, son of the first Duke of Buckingham of that family, was born at Wallingford House, St. James's Park, on the 30th of January, 1627. His mother was Lady Catherine Manners, and the daughter and heiress of the wealthy Earl of Rutland. Thus, while to his father he owed the proudest title of any subject in England, he was indebted to his mother for the greatest estate. He was only a year and a half old when his father fell beneath the knife of Felton, and public wrongs were avenged by individual enmity. His younger brother, Lord Francis Villiers, was a posthumous child. The two brothers were educated with the children of Charles I., and at an early age entered Trinity College, Cambridge. But the outbreak of the Civil War kindled their loyal and chivalrous sympathies; and, suddenly abandoning their studies, they left the University and repaired to the royal camp, just before the attack upon Lichfield. For this imprudent exhibition of fidelity they were punished by the confiscation of their estates; which, however, the Parliament very soon returned them in generous recognition of the fact that they were young and inexperienced. They were then sent to travel abroad, under the care of their tutor, a Mr. Aylesbury, and the young Duke dazzled the nobles of France and Italy by the splendid state which he maintained. Their chief stay was made at Florence and at Rome, where the Duke studied mathematics under Abraham Woodhead, the Roman Catholic controversialist. When, at a later period, Woodhead was ejected from his fellowship in University College, Oxford, by the influence of the dominant faction, his former pupil generously lodged him at York House.

The two brothers returned to England in 1648, when the Civil War was in its last throes. Though the King's cause was hopeless, they gallantly joined the small force assembled by Lord Holland, who appointed the Duke his master of the horse. Closely pressed by the Commonwealth soldiers, under Colonel Rich, the little band of cavaliers fell back towards Kingston in Surrey; but at Nonsuch, near Ewell, were overtaken and defeated (July 7th). This was the last stroke struck on behalf of Charles I. Lord Holland was taken prisoner; Lord Francis Villiers slain, while, with his back to a tree, and refusing quarter, he fought against overwhelming numbers. On this elm (says Aubrey), which was cut down in 1680, was carved an ill-shaped V for Villiers, in memory of the brave young noble.*

---

* Two different versions of the circumstances of his death are on record. Brian Fairfax, in his "Memoirs of the Duke of Buckingham" (p. 17), says:—"My Lord Francis, at the head of his troop, having his horse slain under him, got to an *oak* tree in the highway about two miles from Kingston, where he stood with his back against it, defending himself, scorning to ask quarter, and they barbarously refusing to give it; till with nine wounds in his beautiful face and body, he was slain. The oak tree is his monument, and has the two first letters of his name, F. V., cut in it to this day." On the other hand, Ludlow, in his "Memoirs" (i. 256), tells a more scandalous story:—"The Lord Francis, presuming perhaps that his beauty would have charmed the soldiers, as it had done Mrs. Kirke, for whom he had made a splendid entertainment the night before he left the

Meanwhile, the Duke made his way towards St. Neot's, attended by Tobias Rustat;* but the house in which he took refuge was presently surrounded by the enemy, and perceiving that only in a desperate measure lay any means of safety, he dashed through the leaguer, sword in hand, and effected his escape. By way of London he gained the sea coast, and embarking in a fishing-boat, joined Prince Charles, who, with a small squadron, was cruising in the Downs. The Parliament called upon him to surrender within forty days; but he gallantly adhered to the royal cause, and was accordingly deprived of his vast estates. This, we must own, was a trial of loyalty which few young men of twenty would have been able to withstand, and that there was something noble in the Duke's nature we may fairly argue from his loyalty under such harsh conditions.

Something was saved for the young Duke out of the wreck of his fortunes. An old servant, one John Trailman, who had been allowed to remain at York House, succeeded, by the exercise of great pains and ingenuity, in forwarding to him at Antwerp the valuable collection of pictures formed by the first Duke during his travels in Italy. By the sale of these pictures Buckingham supported himself while in exile.

When the Scots invited Charles II. to take possession of his Northern Kingdom, Buckingham was the only Englishman of quality they permitted to accompany him; and many lively stories are told of the ridicule which, in

town, and made her a present of plate to the value of a thousand pounds stayed behind his company, when unseasonably daring the troopers, and refusing to take quarter, he was killed, and after his death there was found upon him some of the hair of Mrs. Kirke sewed in a piece of ribbon that hung next his skin."

* Afterwards groom of the bedchamber to Charles II.

private, he and the young monarch lavished on the sour faces, canting language, and rigid tenets of the Covenanters. At Worcester Field he fought bravely by the King's side (September 3, 1656); and after the battle was lost, accompanied him in his flight as far as Boscobel House. There he parted from him; and, with Lords Derby and Lauderdale, went northward, in the hope of overtaking General Lesley, with the main body of the Scottish horse. After dispersing a small body of the Commonwealth troops under Colonel Blundel, they were encountered, near Newport, by Colonel Lilburn's regiment, and the two Earls were taken prisoners. Buckingham, and half-a-dozen other Cavaliers, abandoning their horses, crept along the lanes and fields to a wood at Blowe Park, where the Duke, having placed his George (given him by Queen Henrietta Maria) in safe custody, exchanged clothes with a labourer, and was conveyed by Nicholas Matthews, a carpenter, to Bilstrop, in Nottinghamshire. There he was hospitably entertained by a "hearty cavalier" named Hawley, and after rest and refreshment, proceeded to his kinswoman, Lady Villiers, at Brooksby, in Lincolnshire. Finally, after enduring many hardships, he reached London in safety.

The strain of waywardness in his nature which did so much to neutralise the value of his gifts of mind and person here first showed itself. It might have been thought that, at the very head-quarters of his enemies, he would have lived in privacy and chosen some obscure retreat; but, if a gossiping chronicler of the times may be credited, he attired himself as a mountebank, and played his antics in the most public places. "He caused himself to be made a Jack Pudding's coat, a little hat with a fox's tail in it, and adorned with cock's feathers. Sometimes he appeared in a wizard's mask; sometimes he had his face bedaubed with flour, sometimes with lamp-black, as the fancy took him. He had a stage erected at Charing Cross, where he was attended by violins and puppet-players. Every day he produced ballads of his own composition upon what passed in town, wherein he himself often had a share. These he sung before several thousands of spectators, who every day came to see and hear him. He also sold mithridate and his galbanum plaister in this great city, in the midst of his enemies, whilst we were obliged to fly, and to conceal ourselves in some hole or other." It is impossible that Buckingham's proceedings can have been unknown to the authorities; but the Commonwealth Government were probably content to ignore the freaks of a young man of twenty-three, so long as he abstained from political intrigues.

Growing weary of this amusement, Buckingham suddenly left London, and hastened to cross over to France. Incapable of rest or repose, he joined the French army as a volunteer, and won distinction by his gallantry at the sieges of Arras and Valenciennes.

About this time Parliament conferred on Sir Thomas Fairfax a large portion of the Buckingham estates, some of which, however, the Puritan general had the grace to restore to the Duchess. Then to the excitable imagination of the young Duke occurred an idea worthy of a Don Quixote or any of the heroes of the old chivalry. He proposed to himself to recover his patrimonial inheritance by the simple process of wedding Mary Fairfax, the General's only daughter and heiress. To be sure, as a preliminary it was needful to see and be seen; which was no easy matter in the case of an exile. And further, if the young lady's consent were obtained, the sanction of the father was indispensable, and that this would be forthcoming was by no means a certain result. But to triumph over difficulties was Buckingham's great delight, and at length, in the summer of 1657, he boldly crossed over to England, and appeared before Fairfax as a suitor for his daughter's hand. The young lady was charmed, no doubt, by the romance of the adventure, and speedily won by the graceful manners and lively conversation of her handsome gallant. Nor was her father averse to the match. He was somewhat troubled in conscience by the possession of the confiscated estates, which would thus return to their legitimate owner in a natural and facile manner; and as he was himself of aristocratic descent, he was by no means unwilling that his daughter should occupy the highest position in the English nobility. The marriage accordingly took place on the 7th of September, 1657, at Fairfax's seat of New Appleton, near York. Cromwell, when he heard of it, committed Buckingham to the Tower, and refused his release when petitioned for it by Fairfax. The following is the purport of the reply to the General's memorial:—

"AT THE COUNCIL AT WHITEHALL.
"Tuesday, 17th November, 1657.

"His Highness having communicated to the Council that the Lord Fairfax made address to him, with some desires on behalf of the Duke of Buckingham: Ordered, that the resolves and Act of Parliament, in the case of the said Duke, be communicated to the Lord Fairfax, as the grounds of the Council's proceedings touching the said

Duke; and that there be withal signified to the Lord Fairfax, the Council's civil respects to his lordship's own person. That the Earl of Mulgrave, the Lord Deputy Fleetwood, and the Lord Strickland, be desired to deliver a message from the Council to the Lord Fairfax, to the effect aforesaid.

"HENRY SCOBELL, Clerk of the Council."

On the accession of Richard Cromwell, in 1658, the Duke was removed to Windsor Castle, and allowed to enjoy the company of the poet Cowley, whose acquaintance he had made while a student at Cambridge. Early in the following year he obtained his release, through the influence of his powerful friends. In the *Mercurius Politicus* for February 21st, 1658-9, is the following entry :—

"The humble petition of George Duke of Buckingham was this day read. Resolved, That George Duke of Buckingham, now prisoner at Windsor Castle, upon his engagement upon his honour at the bar of this House, and upon the engagement of Lord Fairfax, in twenty thousand pounds, that the said Duke shall peaceably demean himself for the future, and shall not join with, or abet, or have any correspondence with, any of the enemies of the Lord Protector, and of this Commonwealth, in any of the parts beyond the sea, or within this Commonwealth, shall be discharged of his imprisonment and restraint; and that the Governor of Windsor Castle be required to bring the said Duke of Buckingham to the bar of this House on Wednesday next, to engage his honour accordingly. Ordered, that the security of twenty thousand pounds to be given by the Lord Fairfax, on the behalf of the Duke of Buckingham, be taken in the name of his Highness the Lord Protector."

After his release the young Duke retired to his father-in-law's seat at New Appleton, where, with his wonderful faculty for adapting himself to the most novel conditions, he lived the quiet and orderly life of a country squire of the old school, and gained the esteem of Fairfax by his Puritanical professions. This was a happy time for the Duchess, who was afterwards to suffer so much from his gross infidelities. It was her misfortune that nature had not fitted her to retain the affections of her volatile husband. Her person was far from prepossessing—she is spoken of as " lean, brown, and little "—while she had neither the fascination of manner nor the vivacity of conversation in which the absence of physical attractions is forgotten. All that can be said of her—and it is no mean praise—is that she was pure and amiable; but purity and amiability were not the womanly qualities most admired by George, Duke of Buckingham.

At the Restoration Buckingham recovered his estates, and was appointed a member of the Privy Council, as well as Master of the Horse, a Lord of the Bedchamber, and Lord Lieutenant of Yorkshire. At once he plunged into the career of profligacy and pleasure by which his name is best remembered. For shining in a Court like Charles II's., he possessed every qualification. High birth, rank, and abundant wealth; a handsome countenance and well-knit figure; while the charm of his address was irresistible, and no one excelled him in pointing an epigram or turning a compliment. He moved with an easy elegance, which drew all eyes upon him as he sauntered into the presence chamber or aired his graces in the Mall. " No man," says Madame Dunois, " was ever handsomer, or more nicely made; and there was such an attraction in his conversation that he pleased more by his wit than even by his person. His words subdued every heart; he seemed borne for gallantry and magnificence, and in both respects surpassed all the lords of the English Court."

Buckingham's pursuits were as various as his talents. He dabbled in alchemy, and amused himself with the vain dream of discovering the philosopher's stone; he scribbled with careless fluency lampoons and love-songs; he lavished large sums of money in building—an amusement as fascinating and as dangerous as gambling, in which he also indulged; he patronised poets and made love to frail beauties; he led the fashion in gay and gorgeous costumes; and at Court he was foremost in every intrigue and the moving spirit in every startling exploit. In this way he contrived to get rid of his vast income, until to meet his expenditure he was compelled to mortgage his estates, and borrow money at usurious rates from the Jews. Of the buffoonery with which he at times condescended to divert the king an instance will suffice. On one occasion he entered the royal presence attired as the Lord Chancellor—whom he hated—mimicking his stately gait and his habit of puffing out his cheeks; a pair of bellows hanging before him for the purse, while Colonel Titus, as mace-bearer, preceded him with a fire-shovel on his shoulders. The imitation was so perfect that the spectators were convulsed with laughter.

It would not be interesting, and assuredly it would be far from profitable, to dwell upon the amours of this volatile man of pleasure. He was by no means the most profligate of Charles's profligate Court, but one of his engagements was attended with consequences which has given it a sinister importance. Among the beautiful women of the time a foremost place was held by Anna Maria, Countess of Shrewsbury, whose name had already figured in many a *chronique scandaleuse* before she became the mistress of Buckingham. As both parties were notorious for their fickleness, it was generally believed that the intrigue would be of brief duration; nevertheless it lasted for years, and it may be doubted whether the frail Countess was not the only woman for whom Buckingham felt a real attachment.

"The Duke of Buckingham and Lady Shrewsbury," says Hamilton, "remained for a long period both happy and contented: never before had her constancy been of so long a duration; nor had he ever been so submissive and respectful a lover. This continued until Lord Shrewsbury, who never before had shown the least uneasiness at his lady's misconduct, now chose to resent it: true, it was public enough, but less dishonourable to her than any of her former intrigues. Poor Lord Shrewsbury, too polite a man to make any reproaches to his wife, was resolved to have redress for his injured honour. He accordingly challenged the Duke of Buckingham; and the Duke of Buckingham, as a reparation for his honour, having killed him upon the spot, remained a peaceable possessor of this famous Helen" (January 16th, 1667).*

* Pepys has the following entry in his Diary, January 17th, 1667:—"Much discourse of the duel yesterday between the Duke of Buckingham, Holmes, and one Jenkins on one side, and my Lord of Shrewsbury, Sir John Talbot, and one Bernard Howard, on the other side; and all about my Lady Shrewsbury, who is at this time, and hath for a great while been, a mistress to the Duke of Buckingham. And so her husband challenged him, and they met yesterday in a close near Barn Elms, and there fought; and my Lord Shrewsbury is run through the body, from the right breast through the shoulder; and Sir John Talbot all along up one of his arms; and Jenkins killed upon the place, and the rest all in a little measure wounded. This will make the world think that the King hath good counsellors about him, when the Duke of Buckingham, the greatest man about him, is a fellow of no more sobriety than to fight about a mistress. And this may prove a very bad accident to the Duke of Buckingham, but that my Lady Castlemaine do

Lord Shrewsbury was not killed on the spot, but, having been run through the body from the right breast to the shoulder, died of the wound on the 16th of March. The affair is tragical enough in this brief statement of it, and supplies a moral which anyone may read; but we may possibly dismiss as invented embellishments the stories that the shameless woman for whom so much blood was shed held the Duke's horse during the combat, attired as a page, and that afterwards the Duke passed the night with her in his bloody shirt. For the credit of human nature let us hope that these horrible circumstances are not true. Without them the narrative is dark enough, and fills the mind with wonder that the chief characters who figure in it were not overwhelmed with the anger and detestation of society. Parliament, it is true, took some slight notice of the double adultery and murder, faintly remembering the maxim that "Noblesse oblige." Buckingham was called to the bar of the House of Peers for " scandalously living with Lady Shrewsbury as man and wife, he being a married man ; and for having killed my Lord Shrewsbury, after he had debauched his wife ;" but it does not appear that any public censure was pronounced upon him.

Two months after the death of her husband, the Duke installed the Countess in his own house. For the first time in her married life the Duchess found courage to

rule all at this time as much as ever she did, and she will, it is believed, keep all matters well with the Duke of Buckingham : though this is a time that the King will be very backward, I suppose, to appear in such a business. And it is pretty to hear how the King had some notion of this challenge a week or two ago, and did give it to my Lord General to confine the Duke, or take security that he should not do any such thing as fight: and the general trusted to the King that he, sending for him, would do it ; and the King trusted to the general. And it is said that my Lord Shrewsbury's case is to be feared, that he may die too ; and that may make it much worse for the Duke of Buckingham : and I shall not be much sorry for it, that we may have some sober man come in his room to assist in the Government."

protest against the dishonour done her, and angrily protested that it was impossible she could live under the same roof with her husband's paramour. "So I thought, Madam," said the Duke, coldly, "and have therefore ordered your coach to convey you to your father." It has been stated that the Duke was married to the Countess by his chaplain, Dr. Sprat; but as the illegal act would have placed him in the power of his enemies, we may dismiss the tale as without foundation. He had a son by the Countess, to whom the King was weak enough and shameless enough to stand godfather. Buckingham bestowed on him his second title of Earl of Coventry; but the child died at an early age.

There can be no question that the Countess, by her wit and beauty, exercised over the fickle Duke a very considerable influence. The French Ambassador thought it worth his while to secure her good offices for political purposes, and it is on record that he presented her with a gratuity of 10,000 livres. A pension was afterwards settled upon her by the French Court, and she then undertook that "she would make Buckingham comply with King Charles in all things."

That he was capable of better things, and, if he had concentrated his powers, could have done some worthy work in English literature, was shown by his amazingly clever burlesque of "The Rehearsal," produced at the King's Theatre in 1671. Its merits are very great: it is original in design, is witty, decent, well written, and skilfully constructed. Its vigorous protest against the extravagance and lewdness of the Caroline drama was urgently needed, for Dryden and Sir Robert Howard had flooded the stage with nonsensical and indecent rant.

It was in just ridicule of this hyperbolical absurdity that Buckingham wrote his "Rehearsal,"* produced at the Theatre Royal on 7th of December, 1671. Its success was immediate, " the very popularity of the plays ridiculed aiding," as Sir Walter Scott has remarked, "the effect of the satire, since everybody had in their recollection the originals of the passages parodied;" and the heroic drama eventually sank under the effectual blows levelled at it by the satirist.

"The Rehearsal" is, of course, in five acts, but it has no plot; the characters come and go without any interdependence upon each other's actions. These characters are Bayes,† Johnson, and Smith; the Two Kings of Brentford (an allusion, perhaps, to Charles II. and his brother, the Duke); Prince Prettyman, Prince Volscius; Gentleman Usher; Physician; Drawcansir (to rhyme with Dryden's Almanzor); General and Lieutenant-General; Cordelia, Tom Thimble, Fisherman, Sun, Thunder, Players, Soldiers, Two Heralds, Four Cardinals, Mayor, Judges, Sergeants-at-Arms; Amaryllis, Cloris, Parthenope, Pallas, Lightning, Morn, Earth. The scene is laid at Brentford, and the first act opens with a dialogue between Smith, a countryman, and Johnson, a citizen, upon plays. To them enters Bayes, who presently informs them that the last rehearsal of a new play of his is fixed for that very morning, and invites them to attend. They are well pleased to do so, and thenceforth Bayes, throughout the piece, acts as a kind of Chorus, explaining

---

* In conjunction, it is said, with Martin Clifford, Master of the Charter House, Dr. Sprat, Butler, and others.

† At first Sir Richard Howard, under the name of Bilboa, was the hero. Then Davenant was substituted, and as he was poet laureate, Bayes was substituted for Bilboa. Finally, Dryden, as the chief author of heroic plays, was selected as the object of ridicule.

everything that takes place on the stage. There is a little joke about Amarillis: as she wears armour, Bayes will call her Armarillis, and then he proceeds:—

"Look you, sir, the chief hinge of the play, upon which the whole plot moves and turns, and that causes the variety of all the several accidents, which, you know, are the thing in Nature that make up the grand refinement of a play, is, that I suppose two Kings to be of the same place: as, for example, at Brentford; for I love to write familiarly. Now the people having the same relations to 'em both, the same affections, the same duty, the same obedience, and all that; are divided among themselves in point of devoir and interest, how to behave themselves equally between 'em: these Kings differing sometimes in particular; though, in the main, they agree (I know not whether I make myself well understood).

John.—I did not observe you, sir; pray say that again.

Bayes.—Why, look you, sir (nay, I beseech, you be a little curious in taking notice of this; or else you'll never understand my notion of the thing); the people being embarrassed by their equal ties to both, and the Sovereigns concerned in a reciprocal regard, as well to their own interest, as the good of the people, make a certain kind of a—you understand me—upon which, there do arise several disputes, turmoils, heart-burnings, and all that— In fine, you'll apprehend it better when you see it.

[*Exit to call the Players.*

Smith.—I find the author will be very much obliged to the players, if they can make any sense out of this.

Enter BAYES.

Now, gentlemen, I would fain ask your opinion of one thing. I have made a prologue and an epilogue, which may both serve for either; that is, the prologue for the epilogue, or the epilogue for the prologue* (do you mark?); nay, they may both serve too, I'gad, for any other play as well as this.

Smith.—Very well; that's indeed artificial.

Bayes.—And I would fain ask your judgments, now, which of them would do best for the prologue? For, you must know there is, in nature, but two ways of making very good prologues: the one is by civility, by insinuation, good language, and all that, to—a—in a manner, steal your plaudit from the courtesy of the auditors; the other, by making use of some certain personal things, which may keep a hawk upon such censuring persons, as cannot otherwise, I'gad, in nature, be hindered from being too free with their tongues. To which end, my first prologue is, that I come out in a long black veil, and a great huge hangman behind me, with a furred cap, and his sword drawn; and there tell 'em plainly, that if out of good nature they will not like my play, I'gad, I'll e'en kneel down, and he shall cut my head off. Whereupon they all clapping—a—

* An allusion to the two Prologues to the "Maiden Queen."

Smith.—Ay, but suppose they don't.

Bayes.—Suppose! Sir, you may suppose what you please, I have nothing to do with your suppose, sir; nor am at all mortified at it; not at all, sir; I'gad, not one jot, sir. Suppose quoth a!—ha, ha, ha!   [*Walks away.*"

The dialogue then turns on the various devices contrived for securing the applause of an audience; and with the introduction of Thunder and Lightning to speak the Prologue, the first act ends. A lively parody occurs in this part of the scene :—

"*Bayes.*—I have made too, one of the most delicate dainty similes in the whole world, I'gad, if I knew but how to apply it.

Smith.—Let's hear it, I pray you.

Bayes.—'Tis an allusion to Love.

    So Boar and Sow, when any storm is nigh,
    Snuff up, and smell it gath'ring in the sky:
    Boar beckons Sow to trot in chestnut groves,
    And there consummate their unfinished loves.
    Pensive in mud they wallow all alone,
    And snort and gruntle to each other's moan."*

The second act introduces the Gentleman Usher and Physician of the two Kings, who converse in whispers—a hit at Davenant's "Play-house to be Let" and at "The Amorous Prince"—on matters of State, and then go off, without having in any way advanced the action. The two Kings enter, hand-in-hand—"speak French to show their breeding"—and quickly exeunt. Prince Prettyman next appears :—

"*Prince.*—How strange a captive am I grown of late!
    Shall I accuse my love, or blame my fate?
    My love, I cannot; that is too divine:
    And against fate what mortal dares repine?

---

* Of Dryden's "Conquest of Granada," part ii., a. i., s. 2.:—

    "So two kind turtles, when a storm is nigh,
    Look up, and see it gathering in the sky.
    Each call his mate to shelter in the groves,
    Leaving in murmurs their unfinished loves.
    Perched on some drooping branch they sit alone,
    And coo, and hearken to each other's moan."

Enter CLORIS.

But here she comes.
Since 'tis some blazing Count, is it not? [*Lies down.*
Bayes.—Blazing Count! mark that. I'gad, very fine.
Pret.—But I am so surprised with sleep, I cannot speak the rest.
[*Sleeps.**

Bayes.—Does not that, now, surprise you, to fall asleep just in the nick? His spirits exhale with the heat of his passion, and all that, and swop falls asleep, as you see. Now here she must make a *simile*.

Bayes.—But she's surprised.† That's a general rule: you must ever make a simile when you are surprised; 'tis the new way of writing.

Cloris.—As some tall Pine which we on Etna find
    I have stood the rage of many a boisterous wind,
    Feeling without, that flames within do play,
    Which would consume his root and sap away;
    He spreads his wasted arms unto the skies,
    Silently grieves, all pale, repines and dies:
    So, shrouded up, your bright eye disappears.
    Break forth, bright scorching sun, and dry my tears. [*Exit.*

Bayes.—I am afraid, gentlemen, this scene has made you sad; for I must confess, when I writ it, I wept myself.

Smith.—No, truly, sir, my spirits are almost exhaled too, and I am likelier to fall asleep.

PRINCE PRETTYMAN *starts up, and says*—
Pret.—It is resolved. [*Exit.*

Smith.—Mr. Bayes, may one be so bold as to ask you a question, now, and you not be angry?

Bayes.—O Lord, sir, you may ask me what you please. I vow to gad, you do me a great deal of honour: you do not know me, if you say that, sir.

Smith.—Then, pray, sir, what is it that this Prince here has resolved in his sleep?

Bayes.—Why, I must confess, that question is well enough asked, for one that is not acquainted with this our way of writing. But you must know, sir, that, to out-do all my fellow-writers, whereas they keep their *intrigs* secret till the very last scene before the dance; I now, sir, do you mark me?—a—

Smith.—Begin the play, and end it, without ever opening the plot at all?

Bayes.—I do so, that's the very plain truth on't: ha, ha, ha; I do, I'gad. If they cannot find it out themselves, e'en let 'em alone for Bayes, I warrant you. But here now, is a scene of business: pray observe it; for I daresay you'll think it no unwise discourse this, nor ill-argued."

In this scene of business, the Gentleman Usher and

---

* In ridicule of an incident in Sir W. Berkeley's "The Lost Lady."
† Dryden's "Indian Emperor," a. iv., s. 4.

Physician seat themselves on the thrones of the Two Kings, and then march out, flourishing their swords. Smith naturally asks, "how they came to depose the Kings so easily?" but expresses himself satisfied when Bayes replies, that "they long had a design to do it before; but never could put it in practice till now; and, to tell you true," he adds, "that's one reason why I made 'em whisper so at first."

At the end of the scene Mr. Bayes accidentally injures his nose—an allusion to Sir William Davenant's damaged feature—so that in Act iii. he appears with a paper on it. Prince Prettyman enters with Tom Thimble, and the two are made to caricature Dryden's comic writing in "The Wild Gallant." The second scene brings on the two Usurpers, to whom Cordelia brings news from Prince Volscius; and afterwards enters Amarillis, " with a book in her hand." By a mysterious turn of fate, Prince Prettyman is revealed as a fisherman's son—

"A secret, great as is the world,
In which I, like the Soul, am tossed and hurled"—

and having disclosed this secret, goes out, in order that Prince Volscius, Cloris, Amarillis, and Harry "with a riding cloak and boots" (in ridicule of James Steward's "English Musician") may enter; with Parthenope afterwards. While Prince Volscius is pulling on his boots, to join his army at Kightsbridge, he sees Parthenope, and falls in love with her.

VOLSCIUS *sits down.*
"How has my passion made me Cupid's scoff!
This hasty boot is on, the other off,
And sullen lies, with amorous design
To quit loud fame, and make that Beauty mine.
My legs, the emblem of my various thought,
Show to what sad distraction I am brought.

Sometimes, with stubborn Honour, like this boot,
My mind is guarded, and resolved to do't:
Sometimes, again, that very mind, by Love
Disarmed, like this other Leg does prove.

Johnson.—What pains Mr. Bayes takes to act this speech himself! *

Smith.—Aye, the fool, I see, is mightily transported with it.

Volscius.—Shall I to Honour or to Love give way?
Go on, cries Honour; tender Love says, nay:
Honour, aloud, commands, pluck both boots on;
But softer Love does whisper, put on none.
What shall I do? what conduct shall I find
To lead me through this twilight of my mind?
For as bright Day with black approach of Night
Contending, makes a doubtful puzzling light;
So does my Honour and my Love together
Puzzle me so, I can resolve for neither.

[*Exit with one boot on, and the other off.*

Johnson.—By my troth, sir, this is as difficult a combat as ever I saw, and as equal; for 'tis determined on neither side.

Bayes.—Ay, is't not, I'gad,† ha? For, to go off hip hop, hip hop, upon this occasion, is a thousand times better than any conclusion in the world, I'gad. But, sirs, you cannot make any judgment of this Play, because we are come but to the end of the second Act. Come, the Dame."

The fourth act opens with the usual conversation between the dramatist and his visitors, in which Buckingham takes occasion to ridicule the absurd custom then in vogue of writing plays in several parts—as, for instance, Davenant's "Siege of Rhodes,"—making Bayes say—" Whereas every one makes five acts to one play, what do me I but make five plays to one plot; by which means the auditors have every day a new thing. And then, upon Saturday, to make a close of all, (for I ever begin upon a Monday), I make you, sir, a sixth play that sums up the whole matter to 'em, and all that, for fear they should have forgot it." He has also a satiric allusion to the horrors accumulated in Dryden's "Conquest of Granada."

---

* An allusion to Dryden's bad mode of reading.
† A favourite expletive with Dryden.

"*Bayes.*—I make a male person to be in love with a female.

Smith.—Do you mean that, Mr. Bayes, for a new thing?

Bayes.—Yes, sir, as I have ordered it. You shall hear. He having passionately loved her through my five whole plays, finding at last that she consents to his love, just after that his mother had appeared to him like a ghost, he kills himself. That's one way. The other is, that she coming at last to love him, with as violent a passion as he loved her, she kills herself."

A funeral now comes upon the stage, with the two Usurpers and attendants.

"*King Usher.*—Set down the Funeral Pile, and let our grief
Receive, from its embraces, some relief.

King Physician.—Was't not unjust to ravish hence her breath,
And, in life's stead, to leave us nought but death?
The world discovers now its emptiness,
And, by her loss, demonstrates we have less.

Bayes.—Is not that good language now? is not that elevate? It's my *non ultra*, I'gad. You must know they were both in love with her.

Smith.—With her? with whom?

Bayes.—Why, this is Lardella's funeral.

Smith.—Lardella! I, who is she?

Bayes.—Why, sir, the sister of Drawcansir. A lady that was drowned at sea, and had a wave for her winding-sheet.*

King Usher.—Lardella, O Lardella, from above,
Behold the tragic issue of our love.
Pity us, sinking under grief and pain,
For thy being cast away upon the main.

Bayes.—Look you now, you see I told you true.

Smith.—Aye, sir, and I thank you for it, very kindly.

Bayes.—Ay, I'gad, but you will not have patience; honest Mr. —a— you will not have patience.

Johnson.—Pray, Mr. Bayes, who is that Drawcansir?†

Bayes.—Why, sir, a fierce hero, that frights his mistress, snubs up kings, baffles armies, and does what he will without regard to good manners, justice, or numbers.

Mr. Bayes then snatches from the coffin a copy of verses

---

* So in "The Conquest of Granada":—
"For my winding sheet, a wave
I had; and all the ocean for my grave."

† Almanzor, in the same play. "I have found a hero," says Dryden, in his Dedication; "I confess, not absolutely perfect; but of an excessive and over boiling courage. Both Homer and Tasso are my precedents. Both the Greek and the Italian poet had well considered that a tame hero who never transgresses the bounds of moral virtue, would shine but dimly in an epic poem."

which Lardella composed, just as she was dying, with the view that it should be pinned upon her coffin, and so read by one of the Usurpers, who was her cousin. Bayes is at much pains to explain that Lardella, in this paper, makes love " like a Humble Bee." The whole passage is in close and exquisite parody of Dryden's " Tyrannic Love," Act iii, s. 1.

    " Since death my earthly part will thus remove,
    I'll come a Humble Bee to your chaste love.
    With silent wings, I'll follow you, dear couz;
    Or else, before you, in the sunbeams buz.
    And when to melancholy groves you come,
    An airy ghost, you'll know me by my Hum;
    For sound, being air, a ghost does well become.

[Dryden:—My earthly part . . .
    Which is my tyrant's right, death will remove,
    I'll come all soul and spirit to your love.
    With silent steps I'll follow you all day;
    Or else before you, in the sunbeams, play.
    I'll lead you thence to melancholy groves,
    And there repeat the scenes of our past loves.]

    At night, into your bosom I will creep,
    And Buz but softly if you chance to sleep:
    Yet, in your dreams, I will pass sweeping by,
    And then, both Hum and Buz before your eye.

[Dryden:—At night I will within your curtains peep;
    With empty arms embrace you while you sleep.
    In gentle dreams I often will be by;
    And sweep along before your closing eye.]

    Your bed of love from dangers I will free;
    But most from love of any future Bee.
    And when, with pity, your heart-strings shall crack,
    With empty arms I'll bear you on my back,
    Then at your birth of immortality,
    Like any winged archer hence I'll fly,
    And teach you your first flutt'ring in the sky.

[Dryden:—All dangers from your bed I will remove;
    But guard it most from any future love.
    And when, at last, in pity, you will die,
    I'll watch your birth of immortality:
    Then, turtle-like, I'll to my mate repair;
    And teach you your first flight in open air.]"

The two Usurpers are about to kill themselves on Lardella's tomb, when Pallas enters; forbids the sacrifice; informs them that Lardella lives; and that from these funeral obsequies shall arise a nuptial banquet. The coffin opens and discovers the promised banquet. While the two Usurpers are partaking of it, enters Drawcansir:—

"*King Physician.*—What man is this that dares disturb our feast?
Draw.—He that dares drink, and for that drink dares die,
  And knowing this, dares yet drink on, am I.*
Johnson.—That is as much as to say, that though he would rather die than not drink, yet he would fain drink for all that too.
Bayes.—Right; that's the conceipt on't.
Johnson.—'Tis a marvellous good one; I swear.
King Usher.—Sir, if you please, we should be glad to know
  How long you here will stay, how soon you'll go.
Bayes.—Is not that now like a well-bred person, I'gad? So modest, so gent!
Smith.—Oh, very like.
Draw.—You shall not know how long I here will stay;
  But you shall know I'll take my bowls away.†
  [*Snatches the bowls out of the King's hands, and drinks 'em off.*
Smith.—But, Mr. Bayes, is that (too) modest and gent?
Bayes.—No, I'gad, Sir, but its great.
King Usher.—Though, Brother, this grum stranger be a clown,
  He'll leave us, sure, a little to gulp down.
Draw.—Whoe'er to gulp one drop of this dares think,
  I'll stare away his very power to drink.
  [*The two Kings sneak off the Stage with their Attendants.*
I drink, I huff, I strut, look big and stare;
And all this I can do, because I dare." ‡

The next persons involved in this amazing mystery, which reminds us of Pope's famous line—" a mighty maze,

---

* Dryden, "Conquest of Granada":—
 Almahide.—" My Light will sure discover those who talk;
  Who dares to interrupt my private walk?
 Almanzor—He who dares love; and for that love must die,
  And knowing this, dares yet love on, am I."
† " I will out now, if thou would'st beg me, stay:
 But I will take my Almahide away."
   Dryden, "Conquest of Granada," pt. i, a. v.
‡ *Almanzor.*—Spite of myself I'll stay, fight, love, despair,
 And I can do all this, because I dare.
   "Conquest of Granada," part ii., a. ii.

yet not without a plan "—are the two princes, Prettyman and Volscius. Bayes explains that, according to another new conceit, he makes them fall out because they are *not* in love with the same woman. The dialogue between them is carried on in sonorous "heroic couplets," because, says Bayes, "the subject is too great for prose," and he interrupts at almost every line to express his admiration of his own work. "Oh, I'gad," he says, "that strikes me . . . Now the Rant's a coming . . . Ah, Godsookers, that's well writ! . . . Well, gentlemen, this is that I never yet saw any one write but myself. . . Here's true spirit and flame all through, I'gad." And amid this self-laudation the curtain drops.

Act the fifth opens with the usual introductory words on the part of Bayes. "Now, gentlemen," he says, "I will be bold to say, I'll show you the greatest scene that ever England saw: I mean not for words, for those I do not value; but for state, show, and magnificence." It is to surpass the great scene in *Henry VIII.*, for instead of ten bishops, he brings in four cardinals. Here is the stage direction:—"The curtain is drawn up, and the two Usurping Kings appear in State, with the four Cardinals, Prince Prettyman, Prince Volscius, Amarillis, Cloris, Parthenope, &c., before them Heralds and Serjeants at Arms with Maces." The two Princes contend who shall speak first, each wishing the other to take precedence, but at last they give priority to Amarillis. Just as she is on the point of addressing the company, "soft music" is heard, and the two right kings of Brentford descend in the clouds, singing, in white garments, with three fiddlers sitting before them in green. At this unexpected sight the two Usurpers steal away; and the two rightful monarchs join in a duet, which as well as "the descent in clouds," is parodied from Dryden's "Tyrannic Love." We print the original and the travesty side by side that the spirit and fun of the latter may be better appreciated :—

From "The Rehearsal."	*From* "Tyrannic Love."
"1 *King*.—Haste, brother King, we are sent from above.	"*Nakar*.—Hark, my Damilear, we are called below.
2 *King*.—Let us move, let us move: Move to remove the Fate Of Brentford's long united State.	*Damilear*.—Let us go, let us go! Go to relieve the care Of longing lovers in despair!
1 *King*.—Tara, tara, tara, full East and by South;	*Nakar*.—Merry, merry, merry, we sail from the East.
2 *King*.—We sail with thunder in our mouth, In scorching noon-day, whilst the traveller strays, Busy, busy, busy, busy, we hustle along. Mounted upon warm Phœbus his rays, Through the heavenly throng, Haste to those Who will feast us, at night, with a pig's pretty toes.	Half tippled at a rainbow feast.
	Damil.—In the bright moonshine while winds whistle loud, Tivy, tivy, tivy, we mount and we fly, All racking along in a downy white cloud; And lest our leap from the sky should prove too far, We slide on the back of a new-falling star.
1 *King*.—And we'll fall with our pate In an ollio of hate.	*Nakar*.—And drop from above In a jelly of love!
2 *King*.—But now supper's done, the servitors try, Like soldiers, to storm a whole half-moon pie.	*Damil*.—But now the sun's down, and the elements red, The spirits of fire against us make head!
1 *King*.—They gather, they gather hot custard in spoons, Alas, I must leave these half-moons, And repair to my trusty dragoons.	*Nakar*.—They muster, they muster, like gnats in the air, Alas! I must have thee, my fair, And to my light horsemen repair.

2 *King.*—O stay, for you need not
as yet go astray;
The tide, like a friend,
has brought ships in
our way,
And on their high ropes
we will play.
Like maggots in filbirds,
we'll snug in our shell;
We'll frisk in our shell,
We'll frisk in our shell,
And farewell.

1 *King.*—But the ladies have all
inclination to dance,
And the green frogs
croak out a corants of
France.

2 *King.*—Now, mortals, that hear
How we tilt and career,
With wonder will fear,
The want of such things
as shall never appear.

1 *King.*—Stay you to fulfil what
the gods have decreed;

2 *King.*—Then call me to help you,
if there shall be need.

1 *King.*—So firmly resolved is a
true Brentford King
To save the distressed
and help to 'em bring,
That ore a full pot of good
ale you can swallow,
He's here with a whoop,
and gone with a hollow."

Damil.—O stay, for you need not
to fear 'em to-night;
The wind is for us, and
blows full in their
sight:
And o'er the wide ocean
we fight!
Like leaves in the
autumn our foes will
fall down;
And hiss in the water—
Both.—And hiss in the water
and drown!
Nakar.—But their men lie
securely entrenched
in a cloud:
And a trumpeter hor-
net to battle sounds
loud.

Damil.—Now mortals that spy
How we tilt in the sky
With wonder will
gaze;
And fear such events
as will ne'er come to
pass!

Nakar.—Stay you to perform
what the man will
have done.

Damil.—Then call me again
when the battle is
won.

Both.—So ready and quick is a
spirit of air
To pity the lover and
succour the fair,
That, silent and swift,
the little soft god
Is here with a wish, and
is gone with a nod."

The two Kings descend from the cloud and occupy their thrones after this flow of lyrical nonsense. Says King No. 1, "Come now, to serious counsel we'll advance." The 2nd King replies, "I do agree; but first, let's have a dance." The dance is interrupted by the entrance of two Heralds, who announce that

> "The Enemy's at the door, and in disguise,
> Desires a word with both your Majesties:
> Having, from Knightsbridge, hither march'd by stealth."

King No. 2 bids them attend a while, and "drink our health." With two guineas in their pockets—"we have not seen so much the Lord knows when"—the two Heralds retire, and Amarillis resumes her address. It is immediately interrupted by the appearance of a soldier with his sword drawn, who warns the two Kings to save their royal persons, the army having quarrelled among themselves. Here Bayes explains that to avoid indecorum and tediousness he sums up "his whole battle in the representation of two persons only." "I make 'em both come out in armour, *cap-a-pee*, with their swords drawn, and hung, with a scarlet ribbon at their wrists (which, you know, represents fighting enough) each of 'em holding a lute in his hand." "How, sir," says Smith, "instead of a buckler?" "O lord, O lord! instead of a buckler? Pray, sir, do you ask no more questions. I make 'em, sir, play the battle in recitative." [A parody on "The Siege of Rhodes."] "Just at the very same instant that one sings, the other, sir, recovers you his sword, and puts himself in a warlike posture: so that you have at once your ear entertained with music, and good language, and your eye satisfied with the garb and accoutrements of war."

> "*Enter, at several doors, the* GENERAL *and* LIEUTENANT-GENERAL *armed* '*cap-a-pee,*' *with each of them a lute in his hand, and his sword drawn, and hung, with a scarlet ribbon at his wrist.*
> *Lieut.-Gen.*—Villain, thou liest.
> *Gen.*—Arm, arm, Gonzalvo, arm; what No
> The lie no flesh can brook, I trow.

Lieut.-Gen.—Advance, from Acton, with the Musqueteers.
Gen.—Draw down the Chelsea cuirassiers.
Lieut.-Gen.—The band you boast of, Chelsea cuirassiers,
　　　　Shall, in my Putney pikes, now meet their peers.
Gen.—Chiswickians, aged, and renowned in fight,
　　　Join with the Hammersmith brigade.
Lieut.-Gen.—You'll find my Mortlake boys will do their right,
　　　　Unless by Fulham numbers over-laid.
Gen.—Let the left wing of Twick'nam foot advance,
　　　And line that eastern hedge.
Lieut.-Gen.—The horse I raised in Petty France
　　　　Shall try their chance,
　　　　And scour the meadows over-grown with sedge.
Gen.—Stand: give the word.
Lieut.-Gen.—Bright Sword.
Gen.—That may be thine,
　　　But 'tis not mine.
Lieut.-Gen.—Give fire, give fire, at once give fire,
　　　　And let those recreant troops perceive mine ire.
Gen.—Pursue, pursue; they fly
　　　That first did give the lie.
　　　　　　　　　　　　　　　　　　[*Exeunt.*"

But every battle must come to an end. And how does Bayes effect this? "By an eclipse, which, let me tell you, is a kind of fancy that was yet never so much as thought of, but by myself, and one person more, that shall be nameless."

"*Enter the* LIEUTENANT-GENERAL.
What midnight darkness does invade the day,
And snatch the victor from his conquered prey?
Is the sun weary of his bloody sight,
And winks upon us with his eye of light?
'Tis an Eclipse. This was unkind, O Moon,
To clap between me and the Sun so soon,
Foolish Eclipse! thou this in vain hast done;
My brighter honour had eclipsed the sun,
But now behold eclipses two in one. [*Exit.*"

Bayes goes on to explain his "conceit" for representing an eclipse, the first hint of which, he says, was derived from the dialogue between Phœbus and Aurora in [Sir R. Stapylton's comedy of] "The Slighted Maid":—

"*Bayes.*—You have heard, I suppose, that your eclipse of the Moon is nothing else but an interposition of the Earth between the Sun and Moon: as likewise your eclipse of the Sun is caused by an interlocution of the Moon betwixt the Earth and Sun?

Smith.—I have heard so, indeed.

Bayes.—Well, Sir; what do me I but make the Earth, Sun, and Moon, come out upon the Stage, and dance the Hey * hum? And, of necessity, by the very nature of this dance, the Earth must be sometimes between the Sun and the Moon, and the Moon between the Earth and the Sun; and there you have both your Eclipses. That is new, I'gad, ha?

Johnson.—That must needs be very fine, truly.

Bayes.—Yes, there is some fancy in it. And then, Sir, that there may be something in it of a joke, I make the Moon sell the Earth a bargain. Come, come out, Eclipse, to the tune of *Tom Tyler.*

Enter LUNA.

Luna.—*Orbis,* O *Orbis,*
  Come to me, thou little rogue *Orbis.*

Enter the EARTH,

Orbis.—What calls *Terra-firma* pray?
Luna.—*Luna,* that ne'er shines by day.
Orbis.—What means *Luna* in a veil?
Luna.—Luna means to show her tail.†

Enter SOL.

Sol.—Fie, sister, fie; thou mak'st me muse,
  Derry, derry down.
 To see thee, Orb, abuse
Luna.—I hope his anger 'twill not move;
  Since I did it out of love.
 Hey down, derry down.
Orb.—When shall I thy true love know,
  Thou pretty, pretty Moon?
Luna.—To-morrow soon, ere it be noon,
  On Mount Vesuvius.
 Sol.—Then I will shine.

---

* Hey, or Hay: a dance borrowed from the French. In Sir John Davies's poem of "The Orchestra" we read:—
 "He taught them rounds and winding hays to tread."

† In Sir R. Stapylton's "Slighted Maid" we read:—
 "*Phœb.*—Who calls the world's great light?
  Aur.—Aurora, that abhors the night.
 Phœb.—Why does Aurora, from her cloud,
  To drowsy Phœbus cry so loud?"

Orb.—And I will be fine.

Luna.—And we will drink nothing but Lipary wine.*

Omnes.—And we, &c., &c.

Bayes.—So, now, vanish Eclipse, and enter t'other Battle, and fight. Here now, if I am not mistaken, you will see fighting enough.

> [*A battle is fought between foot and great Hobby-horses. At last,* DRAWCANSIR *comes in, and kills 'em all on both sides. All this while the battle is fighting,* BAYES *is telling them when to shout, and shouts with 'em.*

Drawc.—Others may boast a single man to kill;
> But I, the blood of thousands, daily spill.
> Let petty Kings the names of Parties know:
> Where'er I come, I slay both friend and foe.
> The swiftest horseman my swift rage controls,
> And from their bodies drives their trembling souls.
> If they had wings, and to the gods could fly,
> I would pursue, and beat 'em through the sky:
> And make proud Jove, with all his thunder, see
> This single arm more dreadful is than he. [*Exit.*

Bayes.—There's a brave fellow for you now, Sirs. I have read of your Hector, your Achilles, and a hundred more; but I defy all your histories, and your romances too, I gad, to show me one such conqueror as this Drawcansir.

Johnson.—I swear, I think you may.

Smith.—But, Mr. Bayes, how shall all these dead men go off? for I see none alive to help 'em.

Bayes.—Go off! why, as they came on; upon their legs; how should they go off? Why, do you think the people do not know they are not dead? He is mighty ignorant, poor man; your friend here is very silly, Mr. Johnson, I'gad he is. Come, Sir, I'll show you go off. Rise, Sirs, and go about your business. There's go off for you. Hark you, Mr. Ivory.† Gentlemen, I'll be with you presently. [*Exit.*

Johnson.—Will you so? Then we'll be gone.

Smith.—I, prithee let's go, that we may preserve our hearing. One battle more would take mine quite away. [*Exeunt.*

Enter BAYES *and* PLAYERS.

Bayes.—Where are the gentlemen?

1 *Player.*—They are gone, Sir.

Bayes.—Gone! 'Sdeath, this last Act is best of all. I'll go fetch 'em again. [*Exit.*

3 *Player.*—Stay, here's a foul piece of paper of his. Let's see what 'tis.

---

* " What can make our figures so fine?
Drink, drink, Wine Lippari-wine."—SIR R. STAPYLTON.

† " Abraham Ivory had formerly been a considerable actor of women's parts; but afterwards stupified himself so far with drinking strong waters, that, before the first acting of this farce, he was fit for nothing but to go of errands; for which, and mere charity, the Company allowed him a weekly salary.'—*From* " The Key to the Rehearsal," 1704.

[*Reads.*]

The Argument of the Fifth Act.—Cloris, at length, being sensible of Prince Prettyman's passion, consents to marry him; but, just as they are going to Church, Prince Prettyman meeting, by chance, with old Joan the Chandler's widow, and remembering it was she that brought him acquainted with Cloris, out of a high point of honour, breaks off his match with Cloris, and marries old Joan. Upon which, Cloris, in despair, drowns herself: and Prince Prettyman, discontentedly, walks by the river side.

1 *Player.*—Pox on't, this will never do: tis just like the rest. Come, let's be gone. [*Exeunt.*

Enter BAYES.

Bayes.—A plague on 'em both for me, they have made me sweat to run after 'em. A couple of senseless rascals, that had rather go to dinner * than see this play out, with a pox to 'em. What comfort has a man to write for such dull rogues? Come, Mr. —a— Where are you, Sir? come away quick, quick.

Enter PLAYERS *again.*

Players.—Sir, they are gone to dinner.

Bayes.—Yes, I know the Gentlemen are gone; but I ask for the Players.

Players.—Why an't please your worship, Sir, the Players are gone to dinner too.

Bayes.—How? are the Players gone to Dinner? 'Tis impossible: the Players gone to dinner! I'gad, if they are, I'll make 'em know what it is to injure a person that does 'em the honour to write for 'em, and all that. A company of proud, conceited, humorous, cross-grained persons, and all that. I'gad, I'll make 'em the most contemptible, despicable, inconsiderable persons, and all that, in the whole world for this trick. I'gad, I'll be revenged on 'em, I'll sell this play to the other House.

Player.—Nay, good Sir, don't take away the Book; you'll disappoint the Town, that comes to see it acted here, this afternoon.

Bayes.—That's all one. I must reserve this comfort to myself, my Book and I will go together, we will not part, indeed, Sir. The Town! why, what care I for the Town? I'gad, the Town has used me as scurvily as the Players have done: but I'll be revenged on them too: I will both Lampoon and print 'em too, I'gad. Since they will not admit of my Plays, they shall know what a satirist I am. And so farewell to this Stage for ever, I'gad. [*Exit.*

1 *Player.*—What shall we do now?

2 *Player.*—Come then, let's set up Bills for another Play: We shall lose nothing by this, I warrant you.

1 *Player.*—I am of your opinion. But, before we go, let's see Haynes and Shirley practice the last Dance; for that may serve for another Play.

2 *Player.*—I'll call 'em: I think they are in the tyring-room.

The Dance done.

1 *Player.*—Come, come; let's go away to dinner. [*Exeunt* OMNES."

* The fashionable time of dining, when this play was written, was twelve o'clock. "The Rehearsal" is, therefore, supposed to take place in the morning.

"The Rehearsal" is Buckingham's chief literary work; but he was also the author of a farce entitled "The Battle of Sedgmoore," which possesses no claim on the attention of posterity, and he adapted from Beaumont and Fletcher the comedy of "The Chances." His unquestionable talent is seen to some advantage in the religious tracts which he wrote in his maturer years. In these he argues with considerable vigour for entire freedom of conscience as the surest safeguard for the principles of the Reformation; and seeks to demonstrate the truth of the Christian religion by ingenious logical conclusions.*

Buckingham's political career is a part of the history of his time, and cannot, therefore, be examined in these pages. He carried into it his characteristic levity; but had he combined with his brilliant parts a steady resolution and a calm judgment, with reticence of speech and tenacity of purpose, he might surely have taken a foremost place among English statesmen. Unfortunately he touched nothing which his wayward temper did not mar, and he took up politics not as a serious business, but as a gamester's speculation, not with any regard for the interests of his country, but either as a means of increasing his personal influence or gratifying his spirit of adventure. In 1666 we find him intriguing against Clarendon, and playing with projects which verged close upon the borders of treason. Though detected, and deprived of all his commissions, in the following year he again basked in the sunshine of the royal favour. After discharging with some success an embassy to the French Court, he was gratified by the downfall of Clarendon, and took the lead in the council of Ministers to which was applied the famous epithet of "The Cabal" from the

* "Discourse upon Reasonableness of Men's having a Religion."

initials of its principal members, Clifford, Arlington, Buckingham, Ashley, Lauderdale. In 1672 he was again sent on an embassy to Louis XIV., who was then at Utrecht. Landing at the Hague, he had an interview with the Princess of Orange. Eulogizing with his usual fluent eloquence the admirable qualities of the Dutch, he referred to the deep interest which England felt in the prosperity of the Commonwealth. "We do not use Holland like a mistress," he said, "we love her as a wife." "Aye, in truth," replied the Princess, "I believe you love us as you love your own."

On the death of Charles II., Buckingham retired from Court and from public life, and spent the brief remainder of his wasted years on his Yorkshire estate. He died on the 16th of April, 1688, after a three days' illness. Having over-heated himself while hunting, he sat down on the wet grass, and the result was a violent inflammation which his enfeebled constitution was unable to withstand. His last breath was not drawn, as Pope represents, "in the worst inn's worst room," but in the house of one of his own tenants at Kirby-Moorside; and the Earl of Arran, Lord Fairfax, and others, stood by his death-bed. He professed himself at the last a member of the Church of England, and received the Sacrament, according to the Anglican rite, "with all the decency imaginable." His body, having been embalmed, was removed to Westminster Abbey. The principal authority for the private life of the Duke is Brian Fairfax. In almost all the histories and correspondence of his time, he necessarily figures; and his character has been drawn by Bishop Burnet, Warburton, Butler, Walpole, Macaulay, Scott, Count Hamilton, Dryden, and Pope. A brief but interesting memoir occurs in Mr. J. Heneage Jesse's "England under the Stuarts."

THE PROSE WRITERS.

Bishop Jeremy Taylor.
Dr. Robert South.
Dr. Isaac Barrow.
Bishop Beveridge.
Dr. Ralph Cudworth.
Benjamin Whichcote.
John Bunyan.
Thomas Hobbes.
Abraham Cowley.
Izaak Walton.
John Dryden.
Sir William Temple.
Thomas Rymer.
Dr. Henry More.
Valentine Greatrakes.
Dr. Theophilus Gale.
James Harrington.
Sir Robert Filmer.
Bishop Cumberland.

Bishop Wilkins.
Bishop Sprat.
Earl of Clarendon.
Bishop Burnet.
Anthony à Wood.
Sir William Dugdale.
Elias Ashmole.
Archbishop Leighton.
Bishop Ken.
Richard Baxter.
George Fox.
William Penn.
Sir Roger L'Estrange.
Robert Boyle.
John Ray.
Thomas Sydenham.
Sir Isaac Newton.
Sir Thomas Browne.

CHAPTER V.

THE PROSE WRITERS OF THE RESTORATION.

BISHOP JEREMY TAYLOR—DR. ROBERT SOUTH—DR. ISAAC BARROW—BISHOP BEVERIDGE—DR. RALPH CUDWORTH—BENJAMIN WHICHCOTE—JOHN BUNYAN—THOMAS HOBBES—ABRAHAM COWLEY—IZAAK WALTON—JOHN DRYDEN—SIR WILLIAM TEMPLE—THOMAS RYMER—DR. HENRY MORE—VALENTINE GREATRAKES—DR. THEOPHILUS GALE—JAMES HARRINGTON—SIR ROBERT FILMER—BISHOP CUMBERLAND—BISHOP WILKINS—BISHOP SPRAT—EARL OF CLARENDON—BISHOP BURNET—ANTHONY À WOOD—SIR WILLIAM DUGDALE—ELIAS ASHMOLE—ARCHBISHOP LEIGHTON—BISHOP KEN—RICHARD BAXTER—GEORGE FOX—WILLIAM PENN—SIR ROGER L'ESTRANGE—ROBERT BOYLE—JOHN RAY—THOMAS SYDENHAM—SIR ISAAC NEWTON—SIR THOMAS BROWNE.

CHARLES II. had been seven years on the throne when Jeremy Taylor died. Chronologically, therefore, we may claim the English Chrysostom as one of the Prose Writers of the Restoration; but, with a single exception, his great works had all been written in the reign of Charles I., or during the Commonwealth, and in style they are related to those of the Elizabethan rather than to those of the Caroline school. The exception is his great treatise on casuistical divinity, the "Ductor Dubitantium" on which he himself based his hopes of fame. This was issued in the year of the Restoration; and in the same year he published his tractate on the Lord's Supper, entitled, "The Worthy Communicant," and received his episcopal preferment. His sermon, "Via Intelligentiæ," was published in 1662. Also, the three sermons which he dedicated to the Duchess of Ormond; and the "Dissuasive from Popery," which he wrote at the request of the Irish Bishops. On the strength of these post-Restoration publications, we include the great bishop in our list of "Worthies," thankful that the lustre of his name lights up the dark pages of Charles's reign.

Jeremy Taylor, who, by the consent of all, ranks as the greatest orator the English Church has produced, was the son of a Cambridge barber, or barber-surgeon, and first saw the light in his father's house about the 13th of August, 1613. He came of a reputable family, which for generations had held lands in Gloucestershire, but had been reduced to honourable poverty after the martyrdom of Dr. Rowland Taylor,* the courageous and learned rector of Hadleigh, by the confiscation of his estates.

The barber, or barber-surgeon, had education enough to be able to ground his son, as the son informs us, "in grammar and the mathematics." At the early age of three he had begun to attend Parse's Grammar School, then recently founded; and it was probably some indications of more than ordinary capacity which led his father to enter him, when only thirteen years of age, at Caius College, in the University of his native town, as a "poor scholar." It is pleasant to remember that he was the contemporary of John Milton, who entered Christ's College in 1625, and it is not an unreasonable conjecture that sympathy of tastes and intellectual power united in friendly relations the future author of "Holy Living and Dying" and the future poet of the "Paradise Lost." "Though in after life," remarks Prebendary Humphreys, "a wide gulf was interposed between the poet and the divine, the one becoming secretary to the Protector, the other chaplain to the King, at this

* In the third year of Queen Mary."

time they might be friendly opponents in the dreary exercises of the schools; they might well be companions in lighter and more congenial studies; they might go up to the house of God together; they might be compared for their poetical temperament, for their love of ancient learning, for the beauty of their souls, and for their outward comeliness." During his University career Taylor must also have heard of George Herbert, the "sweet singer" of "The Temple;" nor is it unlikely that he was familiar with the name of Oliver Cromwell, then an undergraduate of Sidney Sussex College.

The course of study then in vogue at Cambridge was not adapted to develop Taylor's imaginative faculties. His Alma Mater did not nourish him with satisfying food; she was still teaching that old scholastic philosophy which Bacon censured for its "unprofitable subtlety and curiosity," while Millar characterised its "ragged notions and brabblements" as "an asinine feast of sow-thistles and brambles." Duns Scotus and Avicenna still perplexed their students with intricate speculations and vain hypotheses. To a genius so subtle as Taylor's it was easy, perhaps, to detect some grains of gold even in sandy wastes of Ockham, Lauretus, and Suarez; but we can fancy with what delight he turned from this disappointing pursuit to the study of the great masters of the Greek and Roman literature.

In 1631 Taylor took his Bachelor's degree, and soon afterwards was elected to a Fellowship. Before proceeding to his degree of M.A. he received holy orders, though, like the illustrious Usher, he wanted two years of the canonical age of twenty-three. He quickly became celebrated for his pulpit eloquence; but his future career seems to have been decided by one of those opportunities which always occur to men capable of making use of them. At the request of a college friend he preached for him in St. Paul's Cathedral; where by his "florid and youthful beauty, his sweet and pleasant air, and his sublime and learned discourses," he at once secured the attention of the public. They took him, says Bishop Rust, for some young angel, newly descended from the visions of glory. The repute of his great excellence as a preacher soon spread to Lambeth; and Archbishop Laud, who, whatever his faults and failings, was always quick in the detection and recognition of merit, summoned him to preach before him. The singular promise of the brilliant young genius he at once acknowledged; and thinking it more to the advantage of the world that such mighty parts should be afforded better opportunities of study and improvement than a course of constant preaching would allow of, he secured for him the nomination to a fellowship of All Souls, Oxford—a distinction of no ordinary kind, which carried with it, moreover, a considerable income. During his residence at Oxford the sweet courtesy of his manners and the wide range of his powers made him the object of general esteem and admiration (1635-7). In 1637, Bishop Juxon, at the instigation of the Primate, promoted the splendid young divine to the rectory of Uppingham, in Rutlandshire. In the following year, he was selected to preach at St. Mary's, in that famous pulpit since occupied by so many illustrious men; and in connection with the sermon which he preached on that occasion old Anthony à Wood tells a strange story of Taylor's intended secession to the Roman Church, affirming that the Vice-Chancellor interpolated certain passages in the sermon with the view of inducing the Romanists to reject his advances. As if Taylor would have adopted such interpolations! The whole fabrication was suggested probably by Taylor's intimacy with the learned Franciscan, À Sancta Clara, the queen's chaplain. In Jeremy Taylor's writings ample evidence exists of his strong repudiation of the erroneous doctrines of Rome; and that he did not favour the Roman discipline was demonstrated by his marriage, on the 27th of May, 1639, to Phœbe Landisdale. By this lady he had three sons, one of whom, William, died in May, 1642, and was soon afterwards followed to the grave by his mother.

At Uppingham, Jeremy Taylor spent five years in peaceful seclusion, until the storm and stress of civil war broke over the country. He must have felt very keenly the committal of his friend and patron, Archbishop Laud, to the Tower (in 1640), and he no doubt accepted it as a sign and a warning of sorrowful days darkening over the afflicted Church. He did not hesitate as to the side it was his duty to support; and when, after the final rupture between Charles and his Parliament, the King retired to Oxford, Taylor hastened thither to join him, and was appointed his domestic chaplain. It was by the royal command that he published, in 1642, his first work, "Episcopacy Asserted," in which he presents with great force and clearness the arguments in favour of the episcopal government of the Church. Charles rewarded the author with the diploma of Doctor of Divinity. His learned manifesto aroused much enthusiasm among Churchmen; being "backed and encouraged by many petitions to His Majesty, and both Houses of Parliament, not only from the two Universities whom it most concerned, but from several counties of the Kingdom."

It is uncertain whether he joined the Royal army at Nottingham; but his living at Uppingham was sequestrated in the earliest months of the Civil War; his rectory-house was plundered and despoiled; and his family expelled. In these circumstances he was free to follow the King in his various marches; and it is noticeable that he gathered a knowledge of military affairs which afterwards provided him in his sermons with numerous forcible illustrations: He accompanied the royal army to Wales in the beginning of 1664; and at the siege of Cardigan Castle was taken prisoner. With the treatment he received he had, however, no fault to find. He was speedily released; and then for some time gained a laborious livelihood as a schoolmaster at Llanvihangel Aberbythic. "In this great storm," he writes to Lord Halton, "which hath dashed the vessel of the Church all to pieces, I have been cast upon the coast of Wales, and, in a little boat, thought to have enjoyed that rest and quietness which, in England, in a greater, I could not hope for. Here I cast anchor, and thinking to ride safely, the storm followed on with so impetuous violence that it broke a cable, and I lost my anchor; and here again I was exposed to the mercy of the sea, and the gentleness of an element that could neither distinguish things nor persons. And but that He Who stilleth the raging of the sea and the noise of His waves, and the madness of His people, had provided a plank for me, I had been lost to all the opportunities of content or study. But I know not whether I have been more preserved by the courtesies of my friends, or the gentleness and mercies of a noble enemy; for 'the barbarous people showed us no little kindness; for, having kindled a fire, they received us all because of the present rain and the cold.' And now since I have come ashore, I have been gathering a few sticks to warm me; a few books to entertain my thoughts, and divert them from the perpetual meditation of my private troubles and the public dyscrasy; but those which I could obtain were so few and so impertinent, and unuseful to any great purposes, that I began to be sad upon a new stock, and full of apprehension that I should live unprofitably, and die obscurely, and be forgotten, and my bones thrown into some common charnel-house, without any name or note to distinguish me from those who only served their generation by filling the number of citizens."

It was about this time that he found a second wife in a Mistress Joanna Bridges, a lady of good means, reputed to have been an illegitimate daughter of Charles I.; and a friend in Lord Carbery, whose seat of Golden Grove was situated in the vicinity of Taylor's pleasant retreat. Another and still more valuable friend was the learned, pious, and liberal-handed John Evelyn. He continued to carry on his school, assisted by William Nicolson, afterwards Bishop of Gloucester, and William Wyatt, afterwards Prebendary of Lincoln. For the use of their scholars Taylor and Wyatt composed a "Grammar," which was published in 1647. And though he was without books, "except so many," he says, "as a man may carry on horseback," it was now that he wrote his great work, "The Liberty of Prophesying," in which he proposes to enlarge the limits of comprehension and narrow the bounds of controversy by the adoption of the Apostles' Creed as the standard and exposition of Evangelical Truth—a proposition similar, as Melissom remarks, to one put forward by Erasmus. He who traces its close-linked reasoning, observes its fertility of allusion, and warms himself in the glow and fervour of its poetical imagery, will surely join in the admiration with which Coleridge always regarded it. In itself it justifies his eulogy of its author as "the most eloquent of divines, I had almost said, of men; and if I had, Demosthenes would nod approval and Cicero express assent." Bishop Heber says:—"On a work so rich in intellect, so renowned for charity, which contending sects have rivalled each other in approving, and which was the first, perhaps, since the earliest days of Christianity, to teach those among whom differences were inevitable, the art of differing harmlessly, it would be almost impertinent to enlarge in commendation." Had he written no other book, the Christian Church, as Canon Farrar remarks, would have owed him a debt that could never be repaid. The grand cause of religious tolerance has had no mightier champion; and though his attack failed in its immediate object, it eventually succeeded in establishing religious freedom on an impregnable basis.

In plan this famous treatise is exceedingly simple. Taking the Apostles' Creed as embodying the principal articles of the Christian faith, he declares that all subsidiary dogmas are superfluous or indifferent, and not to be required of believers as indispensable to their salvation. This bold position, Taylor, with some slight misgivings when vexed by the uncompromising hostility of Irish Presbyterianism, maintained throughout his life. "I thought," he wrote in his Epistle Dedicatory, "it might not misbecome my duty and endeavours to plead for peace and charity and forgiveness and permissions mutual; although I had reason to believe that, such is the iniquity of men, and they so indisposed to receive real impresses, that I had as good plough the sands, or till the air, as persuade such doctrines which destroy men's interests, and serve no end but the great end of a happy eternity, and what is in order to it. But because the events of things are in God's disposition, and I knew them not—and because, if I had known, my good purposes would be totally as ineffectual as to others—yet my own designation and purpose would be of advantage to myself, who might, from God's mercy, expect the retribution which He is pleased to promise to all pious intendments; I resolved to encounter with all objections, and to do something to each. I should be determined by the consideration of the present distemperatures and necessities, by my own thoughts, by the questions and scruples, the sects and names, the interests and animosities, which at this day, and for some years past, have exercised and disquieted Christendom."

We have not at our command adequate space to unfold the various links of the chain of argument which he has wrought out of the purest gold, and embellished with the most precious stones. But we may venture to introduce a specimen or two of his style and method, which, we hope, will send the reader to study the original, if haply he be unacquainted with it. The essence of his reasoning, or, perhaps, we should rather say, the aim and motive of it, may be seen in the following most beautiful parable, or allegory, which comes from the Persian poet Saadi, through the medium of Grotius in his "Historia Judaica":—

"When Abraham sat at his tent door, according to his custom, waiting to entertain strangers, he espied an old man stooping and leaning on his staff, weary with age and travail, coming towards him, who was an hundred years of age. He received him kindly, washed his feet, provided supper, caused him to sit down, but observing that the old man sat and prayed not, nor begged for a blessing on his meat, he asked him why he did not worship the God of heaven. The old man told him that he worshipped the fire only, and acknowledged no other God. At which answer Abraham grew so zealously angry that he thrust the old man out of his tent, and exposed him to all the evils of the night in an unguarded condition. When the old man was gone, God called to Abraham, and asked him where the stranger was. He replied, "I thrust him away because he did not worship Thee." God answered him, "I have suffered him these hundred years, although he dishonoured Me; and couldst not thou endure him one night, when he gave thee no trouble?" Upon this, saith the story, Abraham fetched him back again, and gave him hospitable entertainment and wise instruction. "Go thou and do likewise," adds Taylor, "and thy charity will be rewarded by the God of Abraham."

That generous breadth of sympathy and that fine spirit of liberal piety which inspired our great English divine are seen in his remarks on the practice of Christian Churches towards persons who do not accept their formularies.

"In St. Paul's time," he says, "though the manner of heretics were not so loose and forward as afterwards, and all that were called heretics were clearly such and highly criminal, yet, as their crime was, so was their censure, that is, spiritual. They were first admonished, once at least, for so Irenæus, Tertullian, Cyprian, Ambrose, and Jerome, read that place of Titus iii. But since that time all men, and at that time some read it, 'after a first and second admonition,' reject a heretic. 'Rejection from the community of saints after two warnings,' that is the penalty. St. John expresses it by not 'eating with them,' not 'bidding them God speed,' but the persons against whom he decrees so severely, are such as denied Christ to be come in the flesh, direct Antichrists. And let the sentence be as high as it lists in this case, all that I observe is, that since in so damnable doctrines nothing but spiritual censure, separation from the communion of the faithful was enjoined and prescribed, we cannot pretend to an Apostolical precedent, if in matters of dispute and innocent questions, and of great uncertainty and no malignity, we shall proceed to sentence of death.

"Well, however zealous the Apostles were against heretics, yet none were by them, or their dictates, put to death. The death of Ananias and Sapphira, and the blindness of Elymas the sorcerer, amount not to this, for they were miraculous inflictions, and the first was a punishment to vow-breach and sacrilege, the second of sorcery and open contestation against the religion of Jesus Christ; neither of them concerned the case of this present question. Or if the case were the same, yet the authority is not the same; for he that inflicted these punishments was infallible, and of a power competent, but no man at this day is so. But as yet people were not converted by miracles, and preaching, and disputing, and heretics by the same means were endangered, and all men instructed, none tortured for their opinion. And this continued till Christian people were vexed by disagreeing persons, and were impatient and peevish by their own too much confidence, and the luxuriancy of a prosperous fortune; but then they would not endure persons that did dogmatize anything which might intrench upon their reputation or their interest. And it is observable that no man nor no age did ever teach the lawfulness of putting heretics to death, till they grew wanton with prosperity; but when the reputation of the governors was concerned, when the interests of men were endangered, when they had something to lose, when they had built their estimation upon the credit of disputable questions, when they began to be jealous of other men, when they overvalued themselves and their own opinions, when some persons invaded bishoprics upon pretence of new opinions, when they, as they thrive in the favour of emperors, and in the success of their disputes, solicited the temporal power to banish, to fine, to imprison, and to kill, their adversaries.

"So that the case stands thus: In the best times, among the best men, when there were fewer temporal ends to be served, when religion and the pure and simple designs of Christianity only were to be promoted, in those times and amongst such men no persecution was actual nor persuaded, nor allowed towards disagreeing persons. But as men had ends of their own and not of Christ, as they receded from their duty, and religion from its purity, as Christianity began to be compounded with interests and blended with temporal designs, so men were persecuted for their opinions."

Admirable both in thought and expression is the following :—

"As it was true of the martyrs, as often as we die, so often we are born, and the increase of their troubles was the increase of their confidence and the establishment of their persuasions; so it is in all false opinions; for that an opinion is true or false is extrinsical or accidental to the consequents and advantages it gets by being afflicted. And there is a popular pity that follows all persons in misery, and that compassion breeds likeness of affections, and that very often produces likeness of persuasion; and so much the rather because there arises a jealousy and pregnant suspicion that they who persecute an opinion are destitute of sufficient arguments to confute it, and that the hangman is the best disputant. For if those arguments which they have for their own doctrine, were a sufficient ground of confidence and persuasion, men would be more willing to use those means and arguments, which are better compliances with human understanding, which more naturally do satisfy it, which are more human and Christian, than that way which satisfies none, which destroys many, which provokes more, and which makes all men jealous. To which add, that those who die for their opinion have in all men great arguments of the heartiness of their belief, of the confidence of their persuasion, of the piety and innocency of their persons, of the purity of their intention and simplicity of purposes, that they are persons totally disinterested, and separate from design. For no interest can be so great as to be put in balance against a man's life and his soul; and he does very imprudently serve his ends, who, simply and foreknowingly, loses his life in the persuasion of them. Just as if Titus should offer to die for Sempronius upon condition he might receive twenty talents when he had done his work. It is certainly an argument of a great love, and a great confidence, and a great sincerity, and a great hope, when a man lays down his life in attestation of a proposition. 'Greater love than this hath no man, than to lay down his life,' saith our blessed Saviour. And although laying of a wager is an argument of confidence more than truth; yet laying such a wager, staking of a man's soul, and pawning his life, give a hearty testimony that the person is honest, confident, resigned, charitable, and noble. And I know not whether truth can do a person or a cause more advantages than those can do to an error. And, therefore, besides the impiety, there is great imprudence in canonizing a heretic, and consecrating an error by such means, which were better preserved as encouragements of truth and comforts to real and true martyrs. And it is not amiss to observe, that this very advantage was given by heretics, who were ready to show and boast their catalogues of martyrs; in particular the Circumcillinis did so, and the Donatists; and yet the first were heretics, the second schismatics. And it was remarkable in the scholars of Priscillian, who, as they held their master in the reputation of a saint while he was living, so, when he was dead, they held him in veneration as a martyr; they, with reverence and devotion, carried him and the bodies of his slain companions to an honourable sepulture, and counted it religion to swear by the name of Priscillian. So that the extinguishing of the person gives life and credit to his doctrine, and when he is dead, he yet speaks more effectually."

That is a fine saying of Taylor's, that God places a watery cloud in the eye, so that when the light of heaven shines on it it may produce a rainbow to be a sacrament and a memorial that God and the sons of men do not love to see a man perish. Such rainbows often shone across the clouds of Taylor's life. He experienced many seasons

of adversity, but they never failed to be lighted up by the glory of a true friendship. "When the north wind blows," he says, "and it rains sadly, none but fools sit down in it, and cry; wise people defend themselves against it with a warm garment, a good fire, and a dry roof." All these he found at Golden Grove, Lord Carberry's beautiful seat. Green woods, and the songs of birds, and the ripple of the Torvy combined their enchantments for his pleasure, and helped to stimulate his imagination. The fine metaphors and apposite similes with which he so freely ornamented his luxuriant prose were suggested to him by the broad uplands and the leafy hollows of the valley between Carmarthen and Llandovery. Conspicuous in the green landscape rose the wavy crest of Grongar Hill, which Dyer has celebrated in his pleasant pastoral poem. The picture was just such an one as Taylor, who, though he wrote in prose, was a true poet, loved to contemplate:—
"I am fallen," he writes, "into the hands of publicans and sequestrators, and they have taken all from me; what now? Let me look about me. They have left me the sun and moon, fire and water, a loving wife, and many friends to pity me, and some to relieve me; and I can still discourse, and unless I list, they have not taken away my merry countenance, and my cheerful spirit, and a good conscience; they have still left me the providence of God, and all the promises of the Gospel, and my religion, and my hopes of heaven, and my charity to them too; and still I sleep and digest, I eat and drink, I read and meditate. I can walk in my neighbour's pleasant fields, and see the variety of natural beauties, and delight in all that in which God delights—that is, in virtue and wisdom, in the whole creation, and in God Himself."

In the works which Jeremy Taylor composed at Golden Grove we trace the perceptible influence of the scenery that surrounded and delighted him. Their frequent passages of rural description are redolent with the sweet odours of poetry. Our readers will probably be familiar with his beautiful comparison of a Christian's prayer to the heavenward songful flight of a lark :—

"So have I seen a lark rising from his bed of grass, and soaring upwards, singing as he rises, and hopes to get to heaven and climb above the clouds; but the poor bird was beaten back with the loud sighings of an eastern wind, and his motion made irregular and inconstant, descending more at every breath of the tempest, than it could recover by the vibration and frequent weighing of its wings, till the little creature sat down to pant and stay till the storm was over; and then it made a prosperous flight, and did rise and sing as if it had learned music from an angel, as he passed sometimes through the air about his ministering here below. So is the prayer of a good man."

It will be seen that, as is the case with every great writer, Taylor's style is peculiarly his own, and is distinguished by a kind of stately music, like the harmonious peal of an organ. The imagery is rich and exquisite; the rhythm sustained and dignified. Here are a few specimens :—

"The love of the Divine Architect has scattered the firmament with stars, as a man sows corn in his fields."

"So have I seen a rose newly-springing from the clefts of its hood, and at first it was fair as the morning, and full with the dew of heaven as a lamb-fleece; but, when a ruder breath had forced open its virgin modesty, and dismantled its too youthful and unripe retirements, it began to put on darkness, and decline to softness and the symptoms of a sickly age; it bowed the head and broke its stalk, and at night having lost some of its leaves and all its beauty, it fell into the portion of weeds and outworn faces."

"The sun approaching towards the gates of the morning, first opening a little eye of heaven, and sending away the spirits of darkness, and giving light to a cock, and calling up the lark to matins, and by-and-bye gilding the fringes of a cloud, peeping over the eastern hills, thrusting out his golden horns like those which decked the brow of Moses, when he was forced to wear a veil, because himself had seen the face of God?"

"For so doth the humble ivy creep at the foot of the oak, and leans upon its lowest base, and begs shade and protection, and to grow under its branches, and to give and take mutual refreshment, and pay a friendly influence for a mighty patronage; and they grow and dwell together, and are the most remarkable of friends and married pairs of all the leafy nation."

It is easy, when we read such swallow-flights of poetical expression, to understand why Mason called Jeremy Taylor "the Shakespeare of English prose;" and why Mr. Lecky, with much more felicity, has compared his style to "a deeply-murmuring sea with the sunlight on it."

The love of nature which filled his soul rejoiced in "the breath of heaven, not willing to disturb the softest stalk of a violet;" in "the gentle wind shaking the leaves with a refreshment and cooling shade;" in "the rainbow, half made of the glory of light, and half of the moisture of a cloud;" and in "the fountain, swelling over the green turf." In the Divine handiwork he found a continual inspiration of praises and thanksgiving; and he was one of the very first of our writers who endeavoured to lead the soul through Creation up to Creation's God: "Let everything you see represent to your spirit the excellency and the power of God, and let your conversation with the creatures lead you unto the Creator; and so shall your actions be done more frequently with an eye to God's presence, by your often seeing Him in the glass of the creation. In the face of the sun you may see God's beauty; in the fire you may feel His heart warming; in the water His gentleness to refresh you; "it is the dew of heaven that makes your field give you bread."

In the tranquil retirement of Golden Grove Taylor's genius reached its maturity. It was there that he wrote his "Holy Living and Holy Dying," his "Life of Christ," some of his finest "Sermons," his "Treatise on the Real Presence," and the volume of devotional exercises which he affectionately entitled "The Golden Grove." And now we may pause to glance at the distinctive marks of Jeremy Taylor as a divine, a writer, a preacher, and a theologian. In all four capacities we are struck by the fulness and solidity of his thought, the breadth of his observation, the living nature of his sympathies, as well as by those minor but special characteristics, the richness of his imagery and the opulence of his diction. In all he exhibited the same well-balanced judgment, the same judicious avoidance of extremes; the moderate wisdom which sometimes induced him, after the utterance of a strong statement, to qualify it in a later work. In all, we observe the same liberal and enlightened spirit, and the same large-souled disregard of forms and formularies when set against the eternal verities. We have already commented on his style, in which "the mind, the music" that inform it compel our warmest admiration. When every deduction has been made that a cold and severe critic can claim—when we have admitted his occasional exuberance, the over-amplitude of his images, the infrequent lapse into what, to our modern taste, seems grotesque and objectionable—it still remains true that he is unquestionably one of the three or four greatest masters of English prose. His style, more animated and plastic than that of Gibbon, is more sweeping and harmonious than that of Hooker, more majestic than that of South. While Sir Thomas Browne approaches nearer to him than any other writer, he falls short of Taylor in the matter of picturesque allusiveness and poetical sensibility. To this allusiveness we have not failed to direct the reader's attention. From the accumulated treasures of reading, observation, experience, and reflection he draws without stint image and simile, metaphor and illustration. Not less conspicuous is the grandeur of his conceptions, which are those of a man living always in the pure serene air of spiritual thought. The greatest ideas were his ordinary food. He dealt with them as freely and easily as smaller minds deal with their paltry commonplaces. Pathos, terror, sublimity, tenderness—he struck each chord of the manifold lyre with even skill. He handled with equal felicity the radiant pencil of a Claude Lorraine and the powerful brush of a Salvator Rosa. He could paint scenes with the graciousness of a Spenser or the lurid power of a Dante.

We must venture on a few more quotations in illustration of this many-sidedness :—

"All the successions of time, all the changes of nature, all the varieties of light and darkness, the thousand thousands of accidents in the world, and every contingency to every man and to every creature, doth preach one funeral sermon, and calls us to look and see how the old sexton Time throws up the earth and digs a grave, where we must lay our sins or our sorrows, and sow our bodies, till they rise again in a fair or an intolerable eternity."

"When persecution hurls a man down from a large fortune to an even one, or from thence to the face of the earth, or from thence to the grave, a good man is but preparing for a crown, and the tyrant does but just knock off the fetters of the soul, the manacles of passion and desire, sensual lives and lower appetites; and if God suffers him to finish the persecution, then he can but dismantle the soul's prison, and let the soul fly to the mountains of rest. And all the intermediate evils are but like the Purian punishments: the executioner tore off their hairs, and rent their silken mantles, and discomposed their curious dressings, and lightly touched the skin; yet the offender cried out with most bitter exclamations, while his fault was expiated with a ceremony and without blood. So does God to His servants: He rends their upper garments, and strips them of their unnecessary wealth, and ties them to physic and salutary discipline; and they cry out under usages which have nothing but the outward sum and opinion of evil, not the real substance."

"The river that runs slow and creeps by the banks, and begs leave of every turf to let it pass is drawn into little hollownesses, and spends itself in smaller portions, and dies with diversion; but when it runs with vigorousness and a full stream, and breaks down every obstacle, making it even as its own brow, it stays not to be tempted by little avocations, and to creep into holes, but runs into the sea through full and useful channels. So is a man's prayer; if it moves upon the pit of an abated appetite, it wanders into the society of every trifling accident, and stays at the corners of the fancy, and talks with every object it meets, and cannot arrive at heaven; but when it is carried upon the wings of passion and strong desires, a swift motion and a hungry appetite, it passes on through all the intermediate regions of clouds, and stays not till it dwells at the foot of the Throne, where Mercy sits, and thence sends holy showers of refreshment. I deny not but some little drops will turn aside, and fall from the full channel by the weakness of the banks and hollowness of the passage; but the main course is still continued; and although the most earnest and devout persons feel and complain of some looseness of spirit and unfixed attentions, yet their love and their desire secure the main portions, and make the prayer to be strong, fervent, and effectual."

"Because friendship is that by which the world is most blessed and receives most good, it ought to be chosen among the worthiest persons, that is, amongst those that can do greatest benefit to each other; and though in equal worthiness I may choose by my eye, or ear, that is, into the consideration of the essential I may take in also the accidental and extrinsic worthinesses; yet I ought to give everyone their just value; when the internal beauties are equal, thou shalt help to weigh down the scale, and I will love a worthy friend that can delight me as well as profit me, rather than him who cannot delight me at all, and profit me no more; but yet I will not weigh the gayest of flowers, or the wings of butterflies, against wheat: but when I am to choose wheat, I may take that which looks the brightest. I had rather see thyme and roses, marjoram and July flowers (gilli-flowers), that are fair, sweet, and medicinal, than the prettiest tulips, which are good for nothing; and my sheep and kine are better servants than race-horses and greyhounds; and I shall rather furnish my study with Plutarch and Cicero, with Livy and Polybius, than with Cassandra and Ibrahim Bassa;* and if I do give an hour to these for divertisement or pleasure, yet will I dwell with those than can instruct me, and make me wise and eloquent, severe and useful to myself and others. I end this with the saying of Lalius in Cicero: 'Friendship ought not to follow utility, but utility friendship.' When I choose my friend, I will not stay till I have received a kindness; but I will choose such an one as can do me many if I need them; but I mean such kindnesses which make me wise, and which make me better; that is, I will, when I choose my friend, choose him that is the bravest, the worthiest, and the most excellent person; and then your question is soon answered. To love such a person, and to contract such friendships, is just as authorized by the principles of Christianity, as it is warranted to love wisdom and virtue, goodness and beneficence, and all the impresses of God upon the spirits of brave men."

In 1648 Taylor published "The Life of Christ; or, The Great Exemplar;" the preface to which breathes his usual liberality of view and is rendered especially valuable by its vigorous generalisations. It seeks to prove that the per-

* Two of Mademoiselle de Scuderi's interminable romances.

ceptive part of true religion, the moral law, as taught by Nature, by Moses, and our Lord, is in all its parts absolutely "reasonable;" in other words, eminently and peculiarly fitted to subserve the purpose for which man was made, of "living happily." The work itself is thoroughly practical; it elucidates the teaching of the labours and character of Christ, and applies it to the reader's benefit. Chronological order is not strictly observed; and, of course, Taylor does not anticipate the "negative criticism" which, of late years, has been applied so perseveringly to the Gospel narrative. Defects of plan are obvious, and to topics of comparative unimportance an undue space is sometimes allotted; but these and other faults are as nothing compared with the beauty and splendour of the composition as a whole, and the spiritual insight, the knowledge of the human heart, and the deep pathos which underlies particular passages.

Of the "Holy Living and Holy Dying," the most popular of Jeremy Taylor's works, and probably the most popular, as it seems to us incomparably the best, of all English devotional writings, it would be as superfluous as presumptuous to speak in praise. How many aching hearts, how many weary minds have sought and found consolation in its pages! How many consciences have they awakened—how many souls have they moved, purified, exalted! When John Wesley had read the chapter "On Purity of Intention," he was so deeply touched by it, so overcome, that he thenceforth resolved to devote his whole life to God, all his thoughts, and words, and deeds—"being thoroughly convinced that there was no medium, but that every part of life must either be a sacrifice to God or to one's self." It has been said that the "Holy Living and Dying" are the "Paradise Lost and Regained" of devotional literature, with their sublime strains softened by the singular beauty of the Christian "Allegro and Penseroso." With Keble we are ready to exclaim—" *Audiamus jam illum bene beateque vivendi ac moriendi Antistitem.*" To the depressed, the feeble, the weary—to the broken spirit and the fainting heart, as to the trusting, undoubting soul; to the eagerness of youth, the aspiration of manhood, the contentedness of old age—these consecrated pages come with a balm and a benediction; for their writer speaks as if his lips had been touched with a live coal from the altar of God. They glow with the sweet pure sunshine of heaven; in each eloquently musical period we seem to catch the echoes of angelic songs. "All images of rural delight; the rose and the lily; the lark at heaven's gate; the various incidents of sun and shade; the shadows of trees; the gilding of clouds, the murmuring of waters —whatever charms the eye, or comforts the heart, or enchants the ear, is collected in these pictures of the religious character." The rare excellence of Taylor's manual is most manifest when we compare it with the devotional treatises of the Roman Church; and the comparison is the more valuable from the way in which it brings out the sober teaching and the manly moderation of the Church of England. For with all Taylor's sweetness, there is no effeminacy; with all his strictness of discipline, no asceticism. While appealing to the heart, the soul, the conscience, he appeals also to the intellect and the understanding. He never fails to be practical and self-reliant; his earnestness is governed by good sense, and never dreams itself away in a sensuous sentimentalism. In this one sentence, which, we think, only an English Churchman, or at all events only an English Christian, could have written, you find the quintessence of Jeremy Taylor's theory of the true regimen of life:—"God hath given every man work enough to do, that there should be no room for idleness, and yet hath so ordered the world that there shall be place for devotion. He that hath the fewest businesses in the world is called upon to spend more time in the dressing of his soul; and he that has the most affairs may so order them that they shall be a service of God."

In the preface to the volume of prayers to which he gave the title of "The Golden Grove," Taylor warmly expresses his regret at the overthrow of the English Church, and his deep affection for "her sacraments so adorned and ministered," and "her circumstances of religion so useful and apt for edification." He states with much freedom his opinion of the harsh and un-Christian conduct of the Puritan preachers. At a time when Taylor stood almost alone in his advocacy of religious tolerance, his language not unnaturally excited the prejudices of the dominant party; and Taylor was arrested and thrown into prison. He was quickly released; but seems again to have offended the ruling powers, and to have been committed to Chepstow Castle, where, however, he was not uncourteously treated. He used his pen to good purpose, adding twenty-five discourses to the collection previously published, and producing his "Unum Necessarium; or, The Doctrine and Practice of Repentance, describing the Necessities and Measures of a Strict, a Holy, and a Christian Life, and rescued from Popular Errors." This theological manifesto involved him in new troubles; for by attacking the Calvinistic doctrine of Original Sin, and other related dogmas, it provoked not only the anger of the Calvinistic and Puritan preachers, but the censure of some of the Catholic divines of his own Church. The moderate Warner, Bishop of Rochester, expressed his disapproval; while the admirable Sanderson complained, even with tears, of Taylor's departure from the cautious and Scriptural teaching of the Church of England. In a strain which showed that he was no convert to the tolerant sins of the "Liberty of Prophesying," he lamented the misery of the times, so that it was not possible to suppress by authority such "perilous and unseasonable novelties." Taylor's theories, which may be traced to his dislike to the Augustinian theology, are probably much more acceptable in the present day than they were in his own. That they were not wholly consistent in themselves, however, Coleridge has shown in the "Aids to Reflection."

On his return from imprisonment, he still continued his residence in Wales, diversifying it by occasional visits to London and its neighbourhood—more particularly to Evelyn, at Sayes Court, where he met with Robert Boyle, the philosopher, the theoretical Watkins, and Berkeley, afterwards Bishop of Cloyne. In reference to one of these visits, in 1655, he writes to Evelyn:—"I did believe myself so very much bound to you for your so kind, so friendly reception of me in your *Tuscalanum*, that I had some little wonder upon me when I saw you making excuses that it was no better. Sir, I came to see you and your lady, and am highly pleased that I did so, and found all your circumstances to be an heap and union of blessings. But I have not either so great a fancy and opinion of the prettiness of your abode, or so low an opinion of your prudence and piety, as to think you can be anyways transported with them. I know the pleasure of them is gone off from their light before one month's possession; and that strangers, and seldom (*i.e.*, occasional) seers, feel the beauty of them more than you who dwell with them. I am pleased, indeed, at the order and the cleanness of all your outward things; and look upon you not only as a person, by way of thankfulness to God for His mercies and goodness to you, especially obliged to a great measure of piety, but also as one who, being freed in great degrees from secular cares and impediments, can, without excuse and alloy, wholly intend what you so passionately desire, the service of God."

We cannot wonder that such a man as Taylor drew towards him the hearts of many friends. We have seen on what terms of affectionate intercourse he lived with Richard Vaughan, Earl of Carbery. When the first Lady Carbery died, he preached her funeral sermon, and painted a portrait of her in glowing colours which, as Heber says, belongs rather to an angelic than a human character. The second Lady Carbery was the original of "the Lady" in Milton's "Comus;" she, too, bestowed on Taylor her confidence and regard. His relations to Evelyn were of the pleasantest description. Evelyn would fain have had him settle in London that he might be nearer to him; but Taylor was content with occasional visits, when he officiated to private congregations of Churchmen, and enjoyed the graceful hospitality of

Sayes Court. In 1657, Evelyn granted his friend a pension, which must have been welcome exceedingly; "since he was sorely inconvenienced by the *res angustæ domi*, and suffered much from family troubles, losing two of his sons through an attack of smallpox."

In 1658, the Earl of Conway, another of Taylor's influential friends, induced him, by enlisting Evelyn's influence, to accept a lectureship at Lisburn, or, as it was then called, Lisnagarvy, in the north of Ireland. As the stipend was small, and the duty to be shared with a Presbyterian, Taylor at first felt some reluctance; but it was overcome, and in the summer he crossed to Ireland, and settled with his family at Portmore, within about eight miles of Lisburn. There, in full view of the broad expanse of Lough Neagh, and with the silent shadows of grim mountains gathering round him, he enjoyed the seclusion so dear to a contemplative mind. "My retirement to this solitary place," he wrote to Evelyn, "hath been, I hope, of some advantage to me as to this state of religion, in which I am yet but a novice, but, by the goodness of God, I see fine things before me whither I am contending. It is a great, but a good work, and I beg of you to assist me with your prayers, and to obtain of God for me that I may arrive at the height of love and union with God, which is given to all those souls who are very dear to God." The tradition runs, that he was wont to retire for study or devotion to some of the picturesque islets which repose amid the shining waters of the lake.

In 1660, he issued, as we have already noted, his great casuistical work, the "Ductor Dubitantium," and also, "The Worthy Communicant," in which he expatiates upon the blessings to be derived from the holy receiving of the Lord's Supper, and furnishes the minister with useful directions for dealing with difficult cases of conscience. It is not without traces of the affluence and power of Taylor's earlier writings. One of the most striking passages is that in which he speaks of the Sacramental mystery as having been made intricate, like a doctrine of philosophy, and difficult by the assertion and dissolution of distinctions. "So we sometimes espy a bright cloud formed into an irregular figure; which, as it is observed by unskilful and fantastic travellers, looks like a curtain to some, and as a castle to others; some tell that they saw an army with banners, and it signifies war; but another, wiser than his fellows, says it looks like a flock of sheep, and foretells plenty; and all the while it is nothing but a shining cloud, by its own mobility and the activity of a wind cast into a contingent and artificial shape; so it is in this great mystery of our religion, in which some copy strange things which God intended not; and others see not what God hath plainly told."

To this great English divine, and greatest of English ecclesiastical orators, no higher preferment was given at the Restoration than the Bishopric of Down and Connor, to which he was nominated on the 6th of August, 1660. Shortly after, he was elected Vice-Chancellor of the University of Dublin. His consecration took place on the 27th of January, 1661, in St. Patrick's Cathedral. The sermon which he preached on the occasion won the attentive admiration of his hearers by its force of argument and brilliancy of style. "The whole ceremony was conducted without any confusion or the least clamour heard, save many prayers and blessings from the people, although the throng was great, and the windows throughout the whole passage of the procession, to and from the cathedral, filled with spectators." In the following April the adjacent diocese of Dromore was added to that of Down and Connor, in acknowledgment of the good bishop's "virtue, wisdom, and industry." He had previously been made a Privy Councillor; and in May, 1661, he was appointed to preach at the opening of the two Houses of Parliament.

His wise and energetic administration of the University of Dublin laid the foundation of that repute which it has enjoyed down to our own time. In his own diocese he displayed a similar vigour. Having found the cathedral of Dromore in a dilapidated condition, he rebuilt the choir at his own expense. He underwent no small anxiety and vexation from the Presbyterian clergy who, during the sway of the Commonwealth, had been intruded into the benefices of the Church; but the majority eventually yielded to his force of character, while the laity received him always with admiring regard. His celebrated sermon, *Via Intelligentiæ*, published in 1662, showed that his faith in his own great doctrine of toleration was still unshaken, though he seems to have arrived at the conclusion that it can hardly be applied to those who deny its validity or will not avail themselves of its operation.

Taylor's later literary labours comprised three sermons, dedicated to the Duchess of Ormond, and a "Discourse on Confirmation." He also preached the funeral sermon for Archbishop Bramhall, and published his "Dissuasive from Popery," a work, undertaken at the request of the Irish Bishops, which met with immediate and extensive success. He had projected, and was actually engaged in preparing, a treatise on the Beatitudes, when he was seized, though still in the very maturity of manhood, with what proved to be a mortal disease (1667). It has been conjectured that his health had already been affected by his grief at the misconduct of his two surviving sons, one of whom had perished in a duel, while the other had joined in the excesses of the Earl of Rochester. Symptoms of fever appeared on the 3rd of August, and ten days later, in the 55th year of his age, and the seventh of his episcopate, he passed away. His remains were interred in the choir of the cathedral church of Dromore; his name lives in the hearts of all English Churchmen who know how to appreciate the splendour of a genius devoted to God's service, and the beauty of a holy and blameless life.

"To sum up all in a few words," says Bishop Rust, " this great prelate had the good humour of a gentleman, the eloquence of an orator, the fancy of a poet, the acuteness of a schoolman, the promptness of a philosopher, the wisdom of a counsellor, and the piety of a saint."

At the Restoration the Church of England, recovering from its severe depression, seemed suddenly endowed with a new vitality, and produced a growth of eminent divines and teachers, distinguished by their intellectual vigour. Bishops Pearson, Bull, and Beveridge; Doctors South and Barrow; Baxter and Howe, who had not yet left her communion; these all came into the foremost rank in the early years of Charles II.'s reign : while a new school of eminent men arose, of whom Tillotson, Burnet, and Stillingfleet were the chief representatives—men who, in close sympathy with the bold and independent thinkers at Cambridge, became the founders of the Moderate party in the Church.

Conspicuous in this illustrious group as a rhetorician and a thinker, a scholar and a divine, was Dr. Robert South. The son of a prosperous London merchant, he was born in 1633. His early education he received at Westminster School, which was then a perfect hotbed of royalist principles of the most advanced kind. As South afterwards said, in a sermon preached to a later generation of Westomonasterians, "in the very worst of times, when it was my lot to be a member of a school untaintedly loyal, we were *really* King's soldiers, as well as called so;" and he adds that on that very day, "that eternally black and infamous day, of the King's murder, I myself heard the King publicly prayed for"—it is said, by South himself—"but an hour or two at most before his sacred head was struck off." At Christ Church, Oxford, South soon attained distinction as a scholar and a wit. His strong prejudices against Puritanism were so openly expressed that Dr. John Owen, whom Cromwell had appointed Dean of the College, rebuked him publicly as "one who sat in the seat of the scornful;" a rebuke to which South replied, with interest, in his earliest sermon on "The Professors of Godliness, but Workers of Iniquity, with their Sad Countenances and Hypocritical Groanings," preached in 1659.

At the Restoration he was immediately recognised as the great preacher of the University; and on the occasion of the issue of a Commission to expel from Oxford its Puritan professors and principles, he delivered a remarkable sermon (July 29, 1660) in favour of a learned clergy, and in severe denunciation of his opponents. He spoke with great fervour of the eloquence of Scripture, commending it for imitation to the ministers of the Church.

"Where," he said, "where do we ever find sorrow flowing in such a naturally prevailing pathos as in the Lamentations of Jeremiah? One would think that every letter was wrote with a tear, every word was the noise of a breaking heart; that the author was a man compacted of sorrows; disciplined to grief from his infancy; one who never breathed but in sighs, nor spoke but in tears and groans. So that he who said he would not read the Scripture for fear of spoiling his style, showed himself as much a blockhead as an atheist, and to have as small a gust of the elegancies of expression as of the sacredness of the matter." He adds that, "Questionless when Christ says that a Scribe must be stocked with things new and old, we must not think that He meant that he should have a hoard of old sermons (whosoever made them), with a bundle of new opinions; for this certainly would have furnished out such entertainment to his spiritual guests, as no rightly-disposed palate could ever relish."

Rewards and dignities poured in upon the brilliant and uncompromising orator. Though only 28 years of age, he was chosen Public Orator, and in this capacity congratulated Clarendon on his installation as Chancellor in a speech of rare eloquence; was made one of his chaplains, and appointed to preach before the King at Whitehall. It was during the sermon he then delivered that he was obliged, according to the Puritans, by his sudden qualms of conscience while inveighing against the Great Rebellion, to quit the pulpit. If so, his conscience was speedily quieted, for in almost all his sermons at this period he is found denouncing Cromwell and Milton, the Puritans and the Nonconformists, and this with a violence of language and an amplitude of misrepresentation which are very deplorable. He was soon afterwards appointed a Prebendary of Westminster and Canon of Christ Church, and the remainder of his long life was spent either at Westminster or Oxford, except when, in 1674, he accompanied Lawrence Hyde's embassy to Poland, to congratulate King John Sobieski on his accession.

"South," says Dean Lake, "was the great University preacher, and his subsequent career might be easily tracked by his Sermons." He, no doubt, supported Dr. Jane in the famous decree of Passive Obedience which passed Convocation on the day of the execution of Lord Russell, against "certain damnable doctrines, destructive of the sacred persons of Princes," and we may be sure that all the bitterest Acts of Parliament against the Dissenters—the two Acts of Uniformity, the Conventicle Act, the Five Mile Act, which drove 2,000 clergy out of the Church of England and imprisoned Baxter and Bunyan—received his hearty approbation. He even carried his hatred of novelties so far that, in the true old style of Oxford, he denounced the newly-formed Royal Society, of which the ancient Bishop Ward of Salisbury was the second President, in a speech, as Public Orator. It would be very curious if we could ascertain what were his relations with his old school-fellow Locke, at Christ Church, in whose expulsion he must have borne a part. He declared himself ready to put on a buff coat against Monmouth; and would take no part whatever against James II., though he did not become a Nonjuror. But he, of course, opposed every act of toleration or comprehension during the reign of William, and was a warm supporter of Sacheverel in 1706; and one of his last acts was a hearty adhesion to Lord Arran (whose brother, the

Duke of Ormond, had been just before impeached for high treason), who was elected by the Chapter to the High Stewardship of Westminster—an office still in their gift —with the words, "Heart and hand for my Lord Arran."

South died, at the age of 83, in 1716. Years had not taught him tolerance or moderation; and to the very last he breathed fiery invectives against all with whom he disagreed. To what extremes his passionate genius carried him you may see in his controversy with Sherlock on the doctrine of the Trinity. Still, with all abatements, he was a man of great intellectual power, a master of analysis and method, endowed with great gifts of expression, and possessed of a sharp and ready wit. With a little more moral enthusiasm, more self-control, and something of the poet's divine faculty of imagination, South would have taken, not the first place among English preachers, for that would still have had to be allotted to Jeremy Taylor, but, at all events, the second; which must now, we think, be given to Barrow.

Of the copiousness and fine humour of his method, and its occasional pomp of rhetoric, we have no space for illustration. But a few brief specimens of his style may be welcome to the reader :—" He who owes all his good nature to the pot and pipe, to the jollity and compliances of merry company, may possibly go to bed with a wonderful stock of good-nature overnight, but then he will sleep it all away again before the morning."

"Love is the great instrument and engine of Nature, the bond and cement of society, the spring and spirit of the universe. Love is such an affection as cannot so properly be said to be in the soul as the soul to be in that."

"The understanding arbitrated upon all the reports of sense and all the varieties of imagination, not like a drowsy judge only hearing, but directing the verdict."

"It is wonderful to consider how a command or call to be liberal, either upon a civil or religious account, all of a sudden impoverishes the rich, breaks the merchant, shuts up every private man's exchequer, and makes those men in a minute have nothing, who, at the very same instant, want nothing to spend."

"'I speak the words of soberness,' says St. Paul, 'and I preach the Gospel, not with the enticing words of man's wisdom.' This was the way of the Apostles, discoursing of things sacred. Nothing here of the fringes of the North Star; nothing of 'Nature's becoming unnatural;' nothing of 'the down of angel's wings, or the beautiful locks of cherubims;' no starched similitudes, introduced with a 'Thus have I seen a cloud rolling in its airy mansion.'* No, these were sublimities above the rise of the Apostolic spirit, for the Apostles, poor mortals! were content to take lower steps . . . and to use a dialect which only pierced the conscience, and made the hearers cry out, 'Men and brethren, what shall we do?' It tickled not the ear, but sunk into the heart; and when men came from such sermons, they never commended the preacher for his taking voice or gesture; for the fineness of such a simile, or the quaintness of such a sentence; but they spoke like men conquered by the overpowering force and evidence of the most concerning truths, much in the words of the two disciples going to Emmaus, 'Did not our hearts burn within us while He opened to us the Scriptures?'"

---

* This is an obvious allusion to Jeremy Taylor's prodigality of ornament.

In 1677, ten years after the death of Jeremy Taylor, died Dr. Isaac Barrow, Master of Trinity College, and Vice-Chancellor of the University of Cambridge, whom Charles II. is said to have described as " the best scholar in England." He demands attention here, however, not as scholar or mathematician, but as one of the most eminent of the Anglican divines and theologians, in whom are shown the best growth and fruit of the English Church. His works, as lately edited, occupy nine moderate-sized volumes; the old edition, familiar to us in our youth, was in three ponderous folios. The theological portion consists chiefly of " Sermons." Generally speaking, sermons are a very fugitive kind of literature; have as brief a life as political pamphlets—those swiftest of birds of passage—or poems "published at the request of friends" but the "discourses" of Dr. Barrow have a place among our standard classics. Charles II. said of Barrow, that he was an unfair preacher, because he exhausted every subject he touched, and left nothing for any person to say who came after him; and this exhaustiveness is, no doubt, one of his special marks. He examines the subject from every possible point of view; looks around it and about it and into it; surveys it in all its various aspects, all its lights and shades of difference and distinction. " Every sermon," says a recent critic, "is exhaustive, in the sense of being a comprehensive discussion of all the compound parts of his subject. He goes through them all, one by one, step by step, and places each in its right position. The process, it must be owned, is sometimes tedious, but it must also be allowed that the result, in the hands of a strong and laborious workman like Barrow, is vastly impressive. When the quarry is exhausted, and all the stones are in their appointed places, we have a massive and a solid edifice before us, complete from its foundations to its roof, and strongly compacted in every part." We do not think that Barrow's sermons, with all their massiveness and solidity of thought, are ever dull or tedious reading; their style is so strong, clear, exact, and decisive. It is that of a man who feels perfectly master of his theme and of himself; who knows that he has attempted nothing which he cannot easily accomplish. It lacks the splendid opulence of Taylor's richly-coloured diction, but then it exhibits a wonderful transparency; the current is strenuous and full, but you can see to the bottom of it.

As a theologian, Barrow concerns himself little about Dogma, nor does he deal with any of those subtler questions—the why, the whence, and the whither—which perplex inquiring and restless minds. He is the preacher, *par excellence*, of a practical religion, the religion of everyday life. He says himself:—" Religion consisteth not in fair profession and glorious pretences, but in real practice; not in a pretentious adherence to any sect or party, but in a sincere love of goodness and dislike of naughtiness; not in a nice orthodoxy, but in a sincere love of truth, in a hearty approbation of, and compliance with, the doctrines fundamentally good and necessary to be believed; not in harsh censuring and virulently inveighing against others, but in a carefully amending our own ways; not in a furious zeal for or against trivial circumstances, but in a conscionable practising the substantial facts of religion." This is the very essence of Barrow's teaching, the character of which is evident even in the titles of his sermons: as, for instance, "Upright Walking sure Walking," "The

Folly of Slander," "Not to Offend in Word," "Against Foolish Talking and Jesting," "Of Contentment," "Of Industry," "Of being Imitators of Christ."

Barrow was born in 1630. He was educated at the Charterhouse, and afterwards at Trinity College, Cambridge, of which he became a Fellow. He travelled extensively on the Continent from 1655 to 1659; returned to England, took holy orders, and was appointed Professor of Greek at Cambridge, and also of Geometry at Gresham College. He held the post of Lucasian Mathematical Lecturer at Cambridge until 1669, when he was succeeded by his friend and pupil, Sir Isaac Newton. Charles II. appointed him Master of Trinity, in 1672; and he was Vice-Chancellor of the University when he died, in 1677, at the early age of 47.

Bishop Beveridge was born in February, 1637, in the parish of Barrow-upon-Soar, in Leicestershire, of which parish his father was Vicar. He was a boy of twelve when Charles I. perished on the scaffold at Whitehall. His father had died some time previously; but the family seem to have had substance enough to be able to send the lad, in 1653, to Cambridge, where he entered St. John's, and came under the influence of its head, Dr. Tuckney, a distinguished Puritan and Calvinist. The influence of this able divine did not suffice to separate Beveridge from the Church of his fathers, but it modified to some extent his religious convictions. He became a hard student, and applied himself with much energy to the study of the early history of the Church, and of the languages and literature of the East. Before he was twenty he compiled a Syrian Grammar. The result of his patristic and ecclesiastical researches were given to the world in 1672 and

1679, in "The Pandectæ" and "The Canones,"—books of no small value and merit in their time, though since superseded by the labours of more fortunate scholars.

In the year following the Restoration, Beveridge was ordained deacon and priest, and instituted to the Vicarage of Ealing. Thence, in 1672, he removed to the living of St. Peter's, Cornhill, where he toiled with unabating diligence for a period of thirty years. "He applied himself," we are told, "with the utmost labour and zeal to the discharge of his ministry in several parts and offices; and so instructive was he in his discourse from the pulpit, so warm and affectionate in his private exhortations, so regular and uniform in the public worship of the Church, and in every part of his pastoral functions, and so remarkably were his labours crowned with success, that as he himself was justly styled 'the great reviver and restorer of primitive piety,' so his parish was deservedly proposed as the best model and pattern for the rest of its neighbours to copy after."

While Rector of St. Peter's, he was successively preferred Prebendary of St. Paul's (1674), Archdeacon of Colchester (1681), and Prebendary of Canterbury (1684). He carried into his archidiaconal work the same spirit of thoroughness he had infused into his parochial—personally visiting every parish, and obtaining an exact knowledge of its condition and necessities. At Canterbury his rigorous Churchmanship was somewhat unpleasantly displayed. James II. had ordered that a brief should be read for the relief of the persecuted French Protestants. Whether because he thought it illegal, which could hardly have been the case, or because, which is more probable, he did not sympathise with its purpose, he objected that it was not sanctioned by the rubrics. It was then that Tillotson epigrammatically replied—"Doctor, doctor, Charity is above rubrics!"

At the Revolution he took the oath of allegiance to William and Mary, and in 1690 was appointed one of the King's chaplains. In 1704 he was promoted to the see of St. Asaph. He died on the 5th of March, 1707, leaving behind him a hundred and fifty published sermons, distinguished by their earnest eloquence and their kind exposition of Divine truth.

To the Cambridge School of Moderate or Rational Theologians—perhaps we might more fitly call them Religious Liberals—belonged Dr. Ralph Cudworth, who was born in 1617, at Aller, in Somersetshire. In 1644 he was appointed Master of Clare Hall, Cambridge, and in the following year, Regius Professor of Hebrew. He became D.D. in 1651, and in 1654 Master of Christ's College. He died in 1688. We owe to this judicious thinker and profound scholar a vigorous refutation of Atheism, Hobbism, and other forms of scepticism, entitled, "The True Intellectual System of the Universe." The principles which he lays down are these:—First, "That all things in the world do not float without a head and governor, but that there is a God, an omnipotent, understanding Being, presiding over all." Second, "That this God being essentially good and just, there is something in its own nature immutably and eternally just and unjust, and not by arbitrary law, will, and command only." And, lastly, "That we are so far first principals or masters of our own actions as to be accountable to justice for them, or to make us guilty and blameworthy for what we do amiss, and to deserve punishment accordingly."

Another illustrious member of this School, which concerned itself more with the essentials than the accidentals of religious faith, was Benjamin Whichcote, 1610-1683, who, as Provost of King's College, strongly impressed his own mode of thought and form of belief both upon the rising generation of students and his own colleagues in the administration of the University. Principal Tulloch speaks of him, in slightly exaggerated language, as the founder of "the new school of philosophical theology," though this school is known chiefly by the works of more copious writers. "Like many eminent teachers, his personality and the general force of his mental character were obviously greater than his mental productiveness. A few volumes of his sermons are nearly all that survive of his labours to help us to understand them. Yet his sermons, comparatively neglected as they have been, are among the most thoughtful in the English language, pregnant with meaning, not only for his own, but for all time." They are comprised in four volumes, and undoubtedly deserve the reader's most careful attention; but of higher interest, we think, are the gems of crystallised thought which are known as his "Moral and Religious Aphorisms."

Tillotson, in his funeral sermon, thus draws his character:—

"A godlike temper and disposition (as he was wont to call it) was what he chiefly valued and aspired after, that universal charity and goodness which he did continually preach and practise. His conversation was exceeding kind and affable, grave and winning, prudent and profitable. He was slow to declare his judgment, and modest in delivering it. Never passionate, never peremptory—so far from imposing upon others that he was rather apt to yield. And although he had a most profound and well-poised judgment, yet he was of all men I ever knew the most patient to hear others differ from him, and the most easy to be convinced when good reason was offered; and, which is seldom seen, more apt to be favourable to another man's reason than his own. Studious and inquisitive men," he adds, " at such an age (at forty or fifty, at the utmost) have fixed and settled their judgments on most points, and, as it were, made their last understanding — supposing that they have thought, or read, or heard what can be said on all sides of things; and after that they grow positive and impatient of contradiction. But our deceased friend was so wise as to be willing to leave to the last, knowing that no man can grow wise without some change of his mind—without gaining some knowledge which he had not, or correcting some error which he had before. He had attained so perfect a mastery of his passions that for the latter and greater part of his life he was hardly ever seen to be transported with anger, and, as he was extremely careful not to provoke any man, so as not to be provoked by any; using to say, 'If I provoke a man, he is the worse for my company; and if I suffer myself to be provoked by him, I shall be the worse for his.' He was a great encourager and kind director of young divines, and one of the most candid hearers of sermons, I think, that ever was... He never spoke well of himself, nor ill of others... In a word, he had all those virtues, and in a high degree, which an excellent temper, great condescension, long care and watchfulness over himself, together with the assistance of God's grace (which he continually implored and mightily relied upon) are apt to produce. Particularly he excelled in the virtues of conversation, humanity and gentleness and humility, a prudent and peaceable and reconciling temper."

We quote a few specimens of Whichcote's aphorisms :—

"Heaven is first a temper, and then a place."

"The reason of our mind is the best instrument we have to work withal."

"There is nothing more unnatural to religion than contentions about it."

"It is not good to live in jest, since we must die in earnest."

"It is inconsistent with any kind of honesty and virtue to neglect and despise all kind of religion."

"Nothing is more specific to man than capacity of religion, and sense of God."

"We are all of us at times in a fool's paradise, more or less, as if all were our own, all as we would have it."

"Let him that is assured he errs in nothing, take upon him to condemn every man that errs in anything."

"I have always found that such preaching of others hath most commanded my heart which hath most illuminated my head."*

The Restoration brought small gain to the "inspired tinker," John Bunyan, whose influence on the religious mind of England has been infinitely greater than that of all the divines at whom we have thus briefly glanced. He was committed to prison in November, 1660, on the charge of preaching in several conventicles in the country, to the great disparagement of the government of the Church of England. For three months he lay in Bedford gaol, and at the end of that time, as he refused to conform, was re-imprisoned. Owing to his contumacy, he was left out of the general gaol-delivery which marked the coronation of Charles II. His wife made three appeals on his behalf to the Judges, pleading that she had four small children, unable to help themselves, one of whom

* Whichcote's "Aphorisms" seem to have suggested the "Guesses at Truth."

was blind, and that she and they had nothing to live upon but the charity of good people. It was in vain. " I found myself," said Bunyan, " encompassed with infirmities. The parting with my wife and poor children hath often been to me in this place as the pulling of the flesh from the bones, and that not only because I am somewhat too fond of these great mercies, but also because I should have often brought to my mind the many hardships, miseries, and wants that my poor family was like to meet with should I be taken from them, especially my poor blind child, who lay nearer my heart than all besides. Oh, the thoughts of the hardships I thought my poor blind one might go under would break my heart to pieces. 'Poor child,' thought I, 'what sorrow art thou like to have for thy portion in this world! Thou must be beaten, must beg, suffer hunger, cold, nakedness, and a thousand calamities, though I cannot now endure the wind should blow upon thee.' "

For eleven years Bunyan lay in Bedford gaol, not obtaining his release until March, 1672, when, by royal proclamation, Nonconformists were allowed to assemble for worship under their licensed ministers. His imprisonment, however, bore glorious fruit. The solitude of his dungeon was peopled by his fervid genius and all-absorbing devotion with a crowd of immortal figures, which he arranged in such a manner as to represent the successive scenes of a new and striking allegory. Transferring his visions to paper, he produced for the eternal delight and instruction of his fellows (in 1678) the first part of "The Pilgrim's Progress from this World to that which is to Come, delivered under the similitude of a Dream, wherein is discovered the Manner of his Setting Out, his Dangerous Journey, and Safe Arrival at the Desired Country." That such a book should be written, and eagerly received by the people, in the Restoration period, is a convincing proof that the national heart remained sound at the core, in spite of the baleful influences of a profligate Court.

There is a Shakespearian touch about "The Pilgrim's Progress" in the multiplicity of the characters introduced, their variety, their distinct individualisation, and the appropriateness of the language and sentiments allotted to them. No one who has read the book will ever forget the sharp portraiture and vivid presentment of Mr. Facing-both-Ways, Mr. Pliable, Mr. Worldly Wiseman, Talkative, Hopeful, and half a hundred other actors in the stirring drama. As Macaulay says, in his well-known criticism, "The mind of Bunyan was so imaginative that personifications, when he dealt with them, became men. All the forms which cross or overtake the pilgrims, giants, and hobgoblins, illfavoured ones, and shining ones, the tall, comely, swarthy Madam Bubble, with her great purse by her side, and her fingers playing with the money, the black man in the bright vesture, Mr. Worldly Wiseman and my Lord Hategood, Mr. Talkative, and Mr. Timorous, all are actually existing beings to us. We follow the travellers through their allegorical progress with interest not inferior to that with which we follow Elizabeth from Siberia to Moscow, or Jeanie Deans from Edinburgh to London. Bunyan is almost the only writer who ever gave to the abstract the interest of the concrete." But to criticise "The Pilgrim's Progress" now-a-days would be an impertinence. It has become a part of the living literature of the people, and much of it has entered into and been incorporated with their daily talk. "In the wildest parts of Scotland the Pilgrim's Progress is the delight of the peasantry. In every nursery the Pilgrim's Progress is a greater favourite than Jack the Giant-Killer. Every reader knows the straight and narrow path as well as he knows a road in which he has gone backward and forward a hundred times. This is the highest miracle of genius, that things which are not should be as though they were, that the imaginations of one mind should lessen the personal recollections of another. And this miracle the tinker has wrought. There is no ascent, no declivity, no resting-place, no turnstile, with which we are not perfectly acquainted. The wicket gate, and the desolate swamp which separates it from the City of Destruction, the long line of road, as straight as a rule can make it, the Interpreter's house and all its fine shows, the prisoner in the iron cage, the palace, at the doors of which armed men kept guard, and on the battlements of which walked persons clothed all in gold, the cross and the sepulchre, the steep hill and the pleasant arbour, the stately front of the House Beautiful by the wayside, the chained lions crouching in the porch, the low green valley of Humiliation, rich with grass and covered with flocks, all are as well known to us as the sights of our own street."

Bunyan's allegory of "The Holy War," less human than "The Pilgrim's Progress," but grander in conception, and more poetical, was published in 1682; and in 1684, the year before Charles II.'s death, appeared the second (and inferior) part of "The Pilgrim's Progress," in which is described the heavenward progress of the Pilgrim's wife and seven children. Bunyan died on the

31st of August, 1688. His autobiographical work, "Grace abounding to the Chief of Sinners," is a curiously interesting study in psychology, which must carefully be read by all who would know what manner of man John Bunyan really was.

One of the greatest literary names of the period is that of Thomas Hobbes. He was the son of a clergyman, and was born at Malmesbury, in Wiltshire, in April, 1588, the year of the Spanish Armada. His long life covered three generations, and was protracted through the reigns of Elizabeth, James I., Charles I., and Charles II.; he died on the 4th of December, 1679. It was seventy-six years since, a lad of fifteen, he had entered Magdalene Hall, Oxford. In 1608, a young man of high promise, he became tutor to the eldest son of the Earl of Devonshire, and travelled with him in France and Italy. On his return to England, with a mind enlarged and matured by experience of men and manners, he made the acquaintance of Lord Bacon, Ben Jonson, and Lord Herbert of Cherbury. In 1628 he published a translation of Thucydides, designed as a counterblast against the evils of popular government. From 1634 to 1636 he was abroad with the young Earl of Devonshire, the son of his former pupil; and from 1636 to 1641, when he retired to Paris, he was domesticated with the Devonshire family in their stately home at Chatsworth. In 1642 appeared his first great philosophical work, "Elementa Philosophica de Cive," a defence of absolutism as the best form of government. Five years later he was made tutor to the Prince of Wales, afterwards Charles II. During the Commonwealth his genius reached its ripest; and he published, in 1651, his *magnum opus*, the celebrated "Leviathan;

or, The Matter, Form, and Power of a Commonwealth, Ecclesiastical and Civil," which he caused to be transcribed on vellum for presentation to his royal pupil. He was afterwards involved in a hot controversy with Dr. John Wallis, Savilian Professor of Geometry at Oxford, who made short work of Hobbes's pretension to have squared the circle, and proved that a "great philosopher" may be a sorry mathematician. In 1675, Hobbes himself demonstrated that he may also be an indifferent poet, by publishing a dull and tedious translation of the Iliad and Odyssey into English verse. In the year of his death, the indefatigable nonagenarian gave to the world his "Behemoth; or, The History of the Civil Wars of England, and of the Counsels and Artifices by which they were carried on, from the year 1640 to the year 1660." It may be noted, in passing, that in this book Hobbes recommends to the reader the popular religious manual, which, under the title of "The Whole Duty of Man laid down in a Plain and Familiar Way," was first published in 1659. Its authorship has been attributed to a dozen different persons.

"The Leviathan" is one of those classic masterpieces which everybody admires and few people read. It is divided into four parts—1. Of Man; 2. Of a Commonwealth; 3. Of a Christian Commonwealth; 4. Of the Kingdom of Darkness. In the first part "man's nature" is defined as "the sense of his natural powers;" while his mental powers are classified as "cognitive," "imaginative," or "conceptive," and "motive." Our senses receive impressions from external objects, with which they deal by means of the cognitive faculty. According as they are produced by the senses our conceptions rise in quick succession, and we give names to them as an assistance to our memory. All knowledge is of two kinds: *original*, which we owe to memory and observation; and *science*, which is the knowledge of names and propositions derived from understanding. Both, in reality, amount to nothing more than experience; the experience which we obtain from external objects, the experience which we acquire from the proper use of names in language.

Hobbes goes on to contend that truth and a true proposition are absolutely identical, and that knowledge is the evidence of truth; while he defines conscience as a man's belief in the veracity of that which he asserts. The motive powers are, he says, those of the heart, acted upon and influenced by the impressions received through the senses. All conceptions are brain-motives originating without. When they encourage and stimulate the vital movement, they are called, and the objects producing them are called, pleasant; when they retard or depress it, they are described as painful. The former are objects of love or liking; the latter, of dislike or aversion; and every man calls that which pleases him good, and that which he dislikes evil. Absolute goodness, that is, goodness without relation or proportion, is impossible. Things can only be relatively good; even the goodness of God being His goodness to us simply as we understand and receive it.

Upon these cardinal principles or hypotheses, Hobbes erects what is known as the Selfish system of philosophy, which makes our notions of right or wrong depend upon our views of self-interest—assuming that every man's self-love is the mainspring of his thoughts, feelings, and actions. Pity is " imagination or fiction of future calamity to ourselves, proceeding from the sense of another man's calamity; that when it lighteth on such as we think have not deserved the same, the compassion is greater, because then there appeareth more probability that the same may happen to us; for the evil that happeneth to an innocent man may happen to every man. But when we see a man suffer for great crimes, which we cannot easily think will fall upon ourselves, the pity is the less. And therefore men are apt to pity those whom they love; for whom they love they think worthy of good, and therefore not worthy of calamity. Thence it is also that men pity the vices of some persons at the first sight only, out of love to their aspect. The contrary of pity is hardness of heart, proceeding either from slowness of imagination, or some extreme great opinions of their own exemption from the like calamity, or from hatred of all or most men." A similar exposition is furnished of the other passions. To love, for example, is ascribed a purely selfish motive; it is simply the desire of a certain object for our own gratification. And when we laugh, it is from a sense of our superiority to somebody.

It must be confessed that this is a mean and servile philosophy, which strikes at the root of all that is purest, brightest, best in human nature. In his work, "De Corpore Politico," Hobbes applies it to the body politic. He affirms the natural equality of men, and their right to an equal possession of all things, as distinctly as the most ardent Socialist. But he goes on to argue that, differing as they do in strength and passions—and each thinking well of himself, though detesting the same egotism when it is manifested in others—they necessarily fall into contention. In his natural liberty the state of man is a state of war, and irresistible might becomes right. Self-defence compels him to the adoption of civil institutions; and he sacrifices some of his rights in order to preserve the others. Might being right in the state of nature, one man might acquire the right of conquest over another, just as men have done over the lower animals. Conquest, or else mutual agreement, has led to the establishment of various systems of government, such as the monarchical, aristocratical, and democratical. To Hobbes the monarchical seemed to offer the most advantages, or, perhaps, it would be more correct to say, the fewest disadvantages.

The philosophy of Hobbes, with its materialistic tendencies in morals and its absolutist deductions in politics, has been attacked by numerous able controversialists, from Cudworth and Lord Shaftesbury to Bishop Butler, Lord Kaimes, and Dugald Stewart. Its unsoundness is now admitted; but all critics agree in admiring the strength and clearness with which Hobbes has developed it in his writings. Believing that these exercised an injurious influence, we do not think Hume was too severe in his condemnation of them. Their politics, he said, were fitted only to encourage tyranny; their ethics to encourage licentiousness. He adds, however, that "though an enemy to religion, Hobbes partakes nothing of the spirit of scepticism, but is as positive and dogmatical as if human reason, and his reason in particular, could obtain a thorough conviction on these subjects. Clearness and propriety of style are the chief excellences of Hobbes's writings." Let it be noted, moreover, that the philosopher's mind was essentially strong, independent, and original; that he owed nothing to any predecessor; that all his coin was stamped in his own mint. The metal was not without grievous alloy, but the die was sharply wrought and the impression clean cut. It is one of the special merits of a book like "The Leviathan" that it forces its readers to think for themselves; since we are apt to degenerate into a sleepy and languid state of mind if we read always to acquiesce and never to dispute.

That form of literary composition known as "The Essay" Bacon was the first to introduce and popularise. It was adopted in the early days of the Restoration by Abraham Cowley, the poet, whose "Essays," in style and matter, are inferior only to those of his great predecessor. Readers acquainted with Cowley's poems, and their elaborate and involved diction, overloaded with conceits, inversions, and ellipses, will certainly be surprised by the direct and forcible simplicity of his prose, which he manages with masterly ease. Among the essays we should select those on Solitude, Liberty, the Garden, and the Uncertainty of Riches, as the best.

In this connection may be mentioned Izaak Walton's charming work, "The Compleat Angler; or, Contemplative Man's Recreation," which is simply a collection of short essays on rural scenes and enjoyments, on Nature and the delights of Nature, thrown into conversational form. Deservedly, it is one of the most popular books in the language; one of those which establish themselves in a permanent place in our literature by right of their individuality. The style is exquisitely harmonious and transparent; the descriptions are not less vivid than accurate; the illustrations picturesque; the reflections spontaneous, just, and healthy; while the book is everywhere saturated with a deep, warm, unaffected love of Nature, which bubbles up in almost every sentence and brims over in every page. "What would a blind man give," he says, "to see the pleasant rivers and meadows and flowers and fountains that we have met with since we met together! I have been told that if a man that was born blind could obtain to have his sight for but only one hour during his whole life, and should at the first opening of his eyes, fix his sight upon the sun when it was in full glory, either at the rising or setting of it, he would be so transported and amazed, and so admire the glory of it, that he would not willingly turn his eyes from that first ravishing object to behold all the other various beauties this world would present to him. And this and many other like blessings *we* enjoy daily." To one in city pent, Walton's book will bring the fresh sweet odours of the hawthorn hedges, and the meek beauty of the cowslips, and the music of the murmuring stream.

For manly, vigorous, and affluent English prose, a better model could hardly be desired than that which Dryden furnishes in his "Critical Essays" and "Prefaces." It is to be remembered that Fox, the statesman, when writing his "History of England," would employ no word which Dryden had not used; and that Burke speaks of his style with warm approval. English criticism, as an act, dates from 1668, when Dryden published his "Essay on Dramatic Poesy." The sharpness of his perception and the solidity of his judgment may be seen in his "Discourse on the Original and Progress of Satire," and in his critical dissertations generally. Here is a specimen:—"I looked on Virgil as a succinct and grave majestic writer; one who weighed not only every thought, but every word and syllable; who was still aiming to crowd his name into as narrow a compass as possibly he could; for which reason he is so figurative that he requires—I may almost say—a grammar apart to construe him. His verse is everywhere sounding the very thing in your ears whose sense it bears, yet the numbers are perpetually varied to increase the delight of the reader, so that the same sounds are never repeated twice together."

In Macaulay's opinion, Sir William Temple (born in 1628) was one of those men "whom the world has agreed to praise highly without knowing much about them, and who are therefore more likely to lose than to gain by a close examination. Yet," he adds, "he is not without fair pretensions to the most honourable place among the statesmen of his time. A few of them equalled or surpassed him in talents; but they were men of no good repute for honesty. A few may be named whose patriotism was purer, nobler, and more disinterested than his; but they were men of no eminent ability. Morally, he was above Shaftesbury; intellectually, he was above Russell. . . . A temper not naturally good, but under strict command; a constant regard to decorum; a rare caution in playing that mixed game of skill and hazard, human life; a disposition to be content with small and certain winnings rather than to go on doubling the stake; these seem to us to be the most remarkable features of his character."

His diplomatic and political services belong to the province of the historian; we shall here consider him only as the man of letters. Johnson, with exaggerated praise, refers to him as "the first writer who gave cadence to English prose;" an assertion implying the greatest possible ignorance of, or want of sympathy with,

Bishop Jeremy Taylor, Sir Thomas Browne, Cowley, and Dryden. He was, however, a regular, fluent, and perspicuous writer, who adopted the fashionable essay form for the presentment of his sound and generally judicious observations on subjects which he had carefully studied. His "Essay upon the Ancient and Modern Learning," in which he took the side of the Ancients, provoked a long and bitter controversy, from an unfortunate allusion to the supposed literary merits of the Greek "Epistles of Phalaris." Bentley immediately pounced upon the mistake, proved with ease that the Epistles were a forgery, and terribly mauled Temple for his unhappy display of ignorance. Temple, to be sure, found ingenious and capable defenders in Pope, Conyers Middleton, Dr. Garth, and Swift, the last of whom came to his patron's assistance with his celebrated satire, "The Battle of the Books." But if the wits had the temporary advantage, the eventual victory, and the honour of it, were with the scholar. This famous literary quarrel, however, occurred after the Revolution.

In Dryden's preface to his best tragedy, "All for Love," he remarks, that in this play he had endeavoured to follow the practice of the Ancients, who, as Mr. Rymer has judiciously observed, are, and ought to be, our masters. Thomas Rymer, to whom this flattering allusion is made, was born about 1638; educated at Northallerton Grammar School and at Cambridge; studied law; and became a member of Gray's Inn. He was one of the first and ablest of the critics who endeavoured to restrain the exuberant genius of English literature within the trammels of the French methods; and in 1678 he published "The Tragedies of the last Age Considered and

Examined by the Practice of the Ancients, and by the Common Sense of all Ages." In this critical essay he proposes to consider and examine Shakespeare's "Othello" and "Julius Cæsar," Ben Jonson's "Catalina," and Beaumont and Fletcher's "Rollo," "King and No King," and "Maid's Tragedy;" but his remarks are really confined to the three last-named, and the spirit in which they are conceived may be inferred from the writer's crudely impertinent assertion that "our poetry of the last age" was "as rude as our architecture," and his reference to Milton's great epic as "that ' Paradise Lost' of Milton which some are pleased to call a poem." His "Short View of Tragedy," marked by equal ineptitude, appeared in 1693. Had he done no worthier work than these mistaken criticisms and a bad play ("Edgar; or, the English Monarch"), he would not be noticed here; but he rendered an important service to historical literature by the diligence and care with which he carried out the design of Montague and Lord Somers for collecting and publishing, under the title of "Fœdera, Conventiones, et cujuscunque generis Acta Publica inter Reges Angliæ et Alios Principes," the official documents relating to the transactions between England and other States. Seventeen folio volumes of this valuable work were edited by Rymer between 1703 and 1714, the year in which he died.

The English representative of Neo Platonism, Dr. Henry More, belongs to the Restoration period. He was born at Grantham, in Lincolnshire, in 1614; received his earlier education at Eton; and was thence removed to Christ's College, Cambridge, where he obtained a fellowship. Reading Plato eagerly, he followed up this line of study by devouring the so-called "New Platonists,"

Plotinus and Iamblichus, with their refined mysticisms, and the Florentine Platonists, until he completely saturated his mind with the form of religious philosophy now known as Christian Platonism. He was only twenty-eight when he published his "Ψυχῴδια Platonica; or, a Platonical Song of the Soul," in four books, which he re-issued, in 1647, with prefaces and interpretations, under the title of "Philosophical Poems." These are four in number:—1. "Psychozia;" or, "The Life of the Soul;" 2. "Psychathanasia;" or, "The Immortality of the Soul;" to which is annexed a metrical "Essay upon the Infinity of Worlds out of Platonical Principles;" 3. "Antipsychopannychia; a Confutation of the Sleep of the Soul after Death," to which is appended "The Pre-Existency of the Soul,"* and 4. "Antimonopsychia; a Confutation of the Unity of Souls," with a "Paraphrase upon Apollo's Answer concerning Plotinus his Soul departed this life."

These poems are written throughout in the Spenserian stanza, but, unfortunately, are destitute of the exquisite Spenserian imagery and music. There are occasional fine passages; but the verse is generally rugged, involved, and barren, while the meaning could hardly be got at but for the notes and interpretations supplied by More himself. His aim, however, as stated in his opening stanzas, was lofty enough:—

> "Not ladies' loves, nor knights' brave martial deeds,
> Ywrapt in rolls of live antiquities;
> But th' inward fountain, and the unseen seeds,
> From whence are these, and what so under eye
> Dost fall, or is record in memorie,

* " The fanciful theory which suggested Wordsworth's grand ode on 'The Intimations of Immortality in Childhood.' "

> *Psyche*, I'll sing. Psyche! from thee they spring.
> O life of Time and all Alterity!
> Thy life of lives instil his nectar strong,
> My soul t' inebriate while I sing Psyche's song.
>
> . . . . My task is not to try
> What's simply true. I only do engage
> Myself to make a fit discovery,
> Give some fair glimpse of Plato's hid Philosophy.
>
> What man alive that hath but common wit
> (When skilful limner seeing his intent
> Shall fairly well portray and wisely hit
> The true proportion of each lineament,
> And in right colours to the life depaint
> The fulvid eagle with her sun-bright eye),
> Would waxen wroth with inward choler brent
> Cause 'tis no buzzard or discoloured Pie?
> Why man? I meant it not: cease thy fond obloquie.
>
> So if what's consonant to Plato's school
> (Which will agree with learnèd Pythagore,
> Egyptian Trismegist, and th' antique roll
> Of Chaldee wisdom, all which Time hath tore,
> But Plato and deep Plotin do restore),
> Which is my scope, I sing out lustily:
> If any twitten me for such strange lore,
> And me all blameless brand with infamy,
> God purge that man from fault of foul malignity."

Occasionally a genuine pearl gleams among More's elaborate imitations, and we come upon a happy thought not unhappily expressed. As in the following examples:—

> "If light divine we know by divine light,
> Nor can by any other means it see,
> This ties their hands from force that have the sprite."

> "By this the sun's bright waggon 'gain ascend
> The western hill, and draw on cheerful day;
> So I full fraught with joy do homeward wend
> And fend myself with what that Nymph did say,
> And did so cunningly to me convey,
> Resolving for to teach all willing men
> Life's mystery, and quite to chase away
> Mind-mudding mist sprung from low fulsome fen,
> Praise my good will, but pardon my weak falt'ring pen."

> "I saw portrayed on this sky-coloured silk
> Two lovely lads with wings fully dispread
> Of silver plumes, their skin more white than milk,
> Their lily limbs I greatly admirèd,
> Their cheery looks and lusty livelihed:
> Athwart their snowy breast a scarf they wore
> Of a pure hue."

> "But yet, my Muse, still take a higher flight,
> Sing of Platonic faith in the first Good,
> The faith that doth our souls to God invite
> So strongly, tightly, that the rapid flood
> Of this swift-flux of things, nor with foul mud
> Can stain, nor strike us off from th' unity,
> Wherein we steadfast stand, unshaked, unmoved,
> Engrafted by a deep vitality,
> The prop and stay of things in God's benignity."

At one period of his life More deceived himself into the belief that he had had a singular vision, which, under the name of Bathynous, he afterwards described in his "Divine Dialogues." He is discussing with his companions the subject of the Divine goodness, when he informs them that in his youth he had a strange dream of "an old man with a grave countenance speaking to him in a wood." He is urged to tell his dream, and does not object:—

"You must know, then, of what an anxious and thoughtful genius I was from my very childhood, and what a deep and strong sense I had of the existence of God, and what an early conscientiousness of approving myself to Him; and how, when I had arrived to riper years of reason, and was imbued with some slender rudiments of philosophy, I was not then content to think of God in the gross only, but begun to consider His nature more distinctly, accurately, and to contemplate and compare His attributes; and how, partly from the natural sentiments of my own mind, partly from the countenance and authority of Holy Scripture, I did confidently conclude that infinite power, wisdom, and goodness were the chiefest and most comprehensive attributes of the Divine Nature, and that the sovereign of those was His goodness, the summit and power, if I may so speak, of the Divinity. In the meantime, being versed in no other natural philosophy nor metaphysics, but the vulgar, my mind was for a long time charged with inextricable puzzles and difficulties, to make the phenomena of the world and vulgar opinions of men in any tolerable way to comport or suit with these two chiefest attributes of God, His wisdom and His goodness. These meditations closed mine eyes at night; these saluted my memory at first in the morning; these accompanied my remote and solitary walks into fields and woods, sometimes so early as when most of other mortals keep their beds.

"It came to pass, therefore, that one summer morning having rose much more early than ordinary, and having worked so long in a certain wood (which I had a good while frequented) that I thought fit to rest myself on the ground, having spent my spirits partly by long motion of my body, but mainly by want of sleep, and over-anxious and solicitous thinking of such difficulties, as Hylobares [one of the interlocutors] either has already, or, as I descried at first, is likely to propose; I straightway reposed my weary limbs amongst the grass and flowers at the foot of a broad-spread and flourishing oak, where the gentle fresh morning air played in the shade on my heated temples, and with unexpressible pleasure refrigerating my blood and spirits, and the industrious bees busily humming round about me upon the dewy honeysuckles; to which nearer noise was most melodiously joined the distant singing of the cheerful birds re-echoed from all parts of the wood; these delights of nature all conspiring together, you may easily fancy, would quickly charm my weary body into a profound sleep. But my soul was then as much as ever awake, and, as it seems, did most vividly dream that I was still walking in these solitary woods with my thoughts more eagerly intent upon those usual difficulties of providence than ever. But while I was in this great anxiety and earnestness of spirit, accompanied (as frequently when I was awake) with vehement and devout suspirations and ejaculations towards God, of a sudden there appeared at a distance a very grave and venerable person walking slowly towards me. His stature was greater than ordinary. He was clothed with a loose silk garment of a purple colour, much like the Indian gowns that are now in fashion, saving that the sleeves were something longer and wider; and it was tied about him with a Levitical girdle also of purple; and he wore a pair of velvet slippers of the same colour, but upon his head a Montero of black velvet, as if he were both a traveller and an inhabitant of that place at once.

"While he was at any distance from me, I stood fearless and unmoved; only, in reverence to so venerable a personage, I put off my hat, and held it in my hand. But when he came up closer to me, the vivid full force of his eyes that shone so piercingly bright from under the shadow of his black Montero, and the whole air of his face, though joined with a wonderful deal of mildness and sweetness, did so of a sudden astonish me, that I fell into an excessive trembling, and had not been able to stand if he had not laid his hand upon my head, and spoken comfortably to me, which he did in a paternal manner, saying,—'Blessed be thou of God, my son; be of good courage, and fear not; for I am a messenger of God to thee for thy good. Thy serious aspires and breathings after the true knowledge of thy Maker and the ways of His providence (which is the most becoming employment of any rational being), have ascended into the sight of God; and I am appointed to give into thy hands the two keys of Providence, that thou mayest thereby be able to open the treasures of that wisdom thou so anxiously and yet so piously seekest after!' And where withal he put his right hand into his left sleeve, and pulled out two shining bright keys—the one silver, the other of gold, tied together with a sky-coloured ribbon of a pretty breadth—and delivered them into my hands, which I received of him, making low obeisance, and professing my thankfulness for so great a gift."

By this time, he continues, he had acquired a confidence and familiarity which enabled him to converse with the venerable figure that had appeared to him. Having received into his hands the silver key, he was instructed to observe the letters written on it, which, arranged in an intelligible order, proved to be *Claude frustras, ut luceat domus*. Then, gasping in his hand the lower part of the key, he pulled at the handle with his right, and behold, a silver tube came forth, with a scroll of thin paper—thin, but as strong as vellum, and as white as driven snow. On this scroll was drawn a representation of the motions of the planetary bodies round the sun, and of the starry hemispheres, on the principles of the Copernican system. His attention was next drawn to the motto of the golden key, which was a "treasurer of itself," namely, *Amor Dei Lux Animæ*. A golden tube with a similar scroll presented itself when the handle of the key was pressed a second time; and on this scroll was written twelve sentences, in letters of gold, to the following effect:—" Divine Goodness is commensurate with Divine Providence or Infinite; Time and Space—'the thread of time and the expansion of the universe '—proceed from a benevolent Deity; Intellectual Spirits rejoiced with God before creation; in a world of free agents, sin must be a possibility; but happiness exceeds sin and misery 'as much as the light exceeds the shadows.'" He was proceeding with his analysis of these divine sentences, when he was rudely interrupted by the braying of two asses—an unconscious touch of satire!—and the radiant vision of the grave and aged person, the keys of silver and gold, and the glorious parchment suddenly disappeared, leaving him seated at the foot of the oak, where he had fallen asleep, with an ass on each side of him!

"We confess," says Tulloch, "that we are somewhat at a loss to understand the moral of this singular interruption of his vision, the ludicrous absurdity of which strikes us at first more than anything else; unless it be intended, as he himself half hints, to signify the indifferent noisiness with which the world, and even the Church, often receive and interrupt the speculations of a higher thoughtfulness, striving to read, from the charactered scroll of nature and life, the mysteries of being. More professes that the completed vision would have been too much for him, and that he was more gratified at things happening as they did than if he had been all at once put in possession of truth—the continued search for which had been to him a repeated and prolonged pleasure.

"One of the speakers, 'a zealous but airy-minded Platonist and Cartesian, or Mechanist,' suggests that the object of the vision was not merely to attest the Copernican system of the world, but the truth of Descartes' principles. But More, in the name of Bathynous, repudiates this view on the ground that he espied in one of the sentences, or aphorisms of the golden key, which he had not time to read in full, the statement, 'That the primordials of the world are not mechanical, but spermatical, or vital, which,' he adds, 'is diametrically and fundamentally opposite to Descartes' philosophy.' He is convinced further, that, if he had had full conference with the divine sage he would have found his philosophy 'more Pythagorical, or Platonical, than Cartesian. For there was also mention of the senimal soul of the world, which some modern writers call the spirit of nature.' The aphoristic revelations, both of the silver and the golden key, gave rise to a great deal more discussion amongst the friends assembled in Caphophron's 'philosophical bower'—a delightful retreat of the 'airy-minded Platonist'—with the cool evening summer air 'fanning itself through the leaves of the harbour,' and a 'frugal collation' spread — 'a cup of wine, a dish of fruit, and a manchet.' The rest was made up with 'free discourses in philosophy.' The picture is a pleasant one, if the dialogue is sometimes tiresome; and the whole vision and description are strikingly illustrative of the dreamy ideal and enthusiasm with which the young Platonist pursued his studies and inquiries."

More's poems, as we have said, were first published in 1642. Three years before—that is, in 1639—he had taken his Master's degree, and immediately afterwards was chosen Fellow of his college. He was offered the mastership in 1654, but declined it in favour of Cudworth. In the lettered seclusion of Christ's College, this profound, if somewhat visionary, thinker lived and died. His noble friends, and he had many, begged of him to accept preferment, but he refused. "Pray not be so morose," said one of these would-be patrons; "pray be not so morose or humoursome as to refuse all things you have not known so long as Christ's College." One day his friends led him with much persuasion as far as Whitehall, in order that he might kiss the King's hand; but when he understood that the condition of his so doing was the acceptance of a bishopric, "he was not on any account to be persuaded to it."

Among More's most intimate friends was a former pupil of his, Lady Conway, and at her seat at Rugby, in Warwickshire, he spent much of his leisure. There he made the acquaintance of two remarkable men, who must not be omitted from our picture of the men of the Restoration—Baron Von Helmont and Valentine Greatrakes. The former, the son of the famous Flemish chemist and necromancer, inherited much of his father's genius, but more of his enthusiasm and wild extravagance. He devoted himself, heart and soul, to the occult studies which had such an attraction for the inquirers of his time, and lived for a while in Lady Conway's family as her physician. Greatrakes was a man of more mark. His wonderful cures were the talk of the seventeenth century; they were formally investigated by the Royal Society, and seem to have convinced men like Henry More and Judge Glanville, both of whom have specially adverted to them. Greatrakes was an Irish gentleman, who at first used his singular powers with reluctance, but becoming convinced of their efficacy tried them upon all who sought his healing aid. His mode of operation consisted merely in laying his hands upon the sick, and "stroking" them. In January, 1666, the Earl of Orrery invited him to England to attempt the cure of Lady Conway of the chronic headache from which she suffered, but he did not succeed; however, while at Rugby he healed many other persons. From Rugby he removed to Worcester, and thence to London, where he practised his strange art for many months. "At the coffee-houses and everywhere," wrote a friend ("a person of great veracity and a philosopher") to Glanville, "the great discourse now is about Mr. G., the famous Irish stroker. He undergoes curious censures here; some take him to be a conjurer, and some an impostor, but others, again, adore him as an apostle. I confess, I think the man is free from all design, of a very agreeable conversation, not addicted to any vice, nor to any sect or party; but is, I believe, a sincere Protestant. I was three weeks together with him at my Lord Conway's, and saw him (I think) lay his hands upon a thousand persons; and really there is something in it more than ordinary; but I am convinced 'tis not miraculous. I have seen pains strangely fly before his hand till he hath charmed them out of the body; dimness cleared and deafness cured by his touch; twenty persons at several times, in fits of the falling-sickness, were in two or three minutes brought to themselves, so as to tell where their pain was; and then he hath pursued it till he hath driven it out at some extreme part; running sores of the king's evil dried up, and kernels brought to a puration by his hand."

In 1666 was published "A brief account of Mr. Valentine Greatrakes, and divers of the strange cures by him performed; written by himself, in a letter to the Hon. Robert Boyle, Esq., whereunto are arranged the testimonials of several eminent and worthy persons of the chief matters of fact there related." Thereafter he passed away into oblivion.

To return to More. For thirty-five years, or from 1642 to 1687, his literary activity was immense, and he produced so large a number of pamphlets and treatises, small and great, that we have not room enough for their titles. We may mention his "Threefold Cabbala," a triple interpretation of the three first chapters of Genesis; his "Antidote against Atheism," his essay on the "Immortality of the Soul," and his treatises on the "Grand Mystery of Godliness," and the "Mystery of Iniquity." But the only attractive one, according to modern ideas, is the "Divine Dialogues," which Dr. Blair has rightly described as animated "by a variety of character and a sprightliness of conversation beyond what we commonly meet with in writings of this kind." Principal Tulloch says of them that they are upon the whole the most interesting and readable of all More's works. "The current of thought runs along smoothly, with less tendency than in any of his other writings to digressive absurdity and wearisome subdivisions; the style is here and there fresh and powerful; and there is not only some liveliness of movement in the successive conversations, but an attempt is made, as Blair implies, to impart a definite portraiture to the several speakers, and to preserve throughout their individuality and consistency. . . . The 'Divine Dialogues,' moreover, possess for the common reader the advantage of condensing his general views in philosophy and religion. In fact, most of his principles may be gathered from them."

Our English Platonist lived to a good old age. He died on the 1st of September, 1687, having numbered three-and-seventy years. For ourselves, we should say that there is much more to interest the student in his character than in his writings, which never exerted any influence on the national mind, or his theosophistical system, which we can regard only with a languid curiosity. As a man, he was well fitted to engage the attention of the psychologist. Devout mystics of his exalted type have been rare in England, the home of an eminently practical religion; and the idiosyncrasies of our race are opposed to the cultivation of an ascetic pietism. But More lived always in an atmosphere of pure devotion and serene contemplation. So great was his spiritual happiness that at times he seems to have been almost overwhelmed by it. He told a friend that he was sometimes nearly mad with pleasure; and this excitement he felt in the simplest circumstances. "Walking abroad after his studies, his sallies towards Nature would be often inexpressibly ravishing, beyond what he could convey to others."

His love of rural sights and sounds, his delight in the beauty of God's visible world, is manifested in several passages in his writings, and more particularly in his "Dialogues." He often said that he wished he could always be "sub dio"—"he could study abroad with less weariness by far to himself than within doors." His mental excitation, the rapture he felt in his own thoughts, sometimes prevailed over his judgment. He felt, to use his own words, as if his mind went faster than he almost desired, and all the while he seemed, as it were, to be in the air.

It was "this mystical glow and devotion" which distinguished his mind and character; "a certain transport and radiancy of thought which carried him beyond the common life, without raising him to any false or artificial height." His contemporaries noted that there was something "angelical" in his very air. "He seemed to be full of introversions of light, joy, benignity, and devotion at once—as if his face had been overcast with a golden shower of love and purity." The marvellous "lustre and irradiation" in his eyes and countenance were noticed even by strangers. "A divine gale," as he himself phrased it, inspired his life not less than his written utterances; but it purified while it elevated him, and he was never a victim to spiritual pride. Dr. Outram said "that he looked upon Dr. More as the holiest person upon the face of the earth." Not less conspicuous than his piety was his charity and humility. "His very chamber-door was a hospital to the needy." "When the winds were ruffling about him, he made it his utmost endeavour to keep low and humble, that he might not be driven from that anchor." It is pleasant to remember that such a man as this was the contemporary of Rochester, and Buckingham, and Sedley. He restores our pride and confidence in the higher qualities of our race, and shows that even in the reign of Charles II. the honour of England was sound at the core.

It is not within our province to explain his system, if system it can be called, of Christian theosophy, or to attempt a detailed criticism of his writings. This has been done with admirable care and success by Principal Tulloch in his "Rational Theology in England in the Seventeenth Century." We confess that *le jeu* does not seem worth *la chandelle*. There are beautiful thoughts and bright, radiant passages; but to arrive at these, the weary student has to find his way through dreary tracts of involved and barren mysticism. As Dr. Tulloch avers, More's works " do not exhibit any clear growth or system of ideas, unfolding themselves gradually, and maturing to a more comprehensive rationality. This lack of method is more or less characteristic of the school; but the multifarious character of More's writings render it more conspicuous in him than in the others. Not only so. In his later productions there is rather a decay than an increase and enrichment of the rational element. To enter into any exposition of his Cabbalistical studies — of his discovery of Cartesianism in the first chapters of Genesis, and his favourite notion of all their philosophy descending from Moses through Pythagoras and Plato; and still more to touch his prophetical reveries—the divine science which he finds in the dream of Ezekiel or the visions of the Apocalypse—would be labour thrown away, unless to illustrate the weakness of human genius, or the singular absurdities which beset the progress of knowledge, even in its most favourable stages. The supposition that all higher wisdom and speculation were derived originally from Moses and the Hebrew Scriptures, and that it was confirmatory both of the truth of Scripture and the results of philosophy to make out this traditionary connection, was widely prevalent in the seventeenth century. It was warmly supported and elaborately argued by some of its most acute and learned intellects. Both Cudworth and More profoundly believed in this connection. But this was only one of many instances of their lack of critical and historical judgment. Historical criticism, in the modern sense, was not even then dreamed of; and it is needless to consider forgotten delusions which have perished, rather with the common growth of reason than by the force of any special genius or discovery."*

A philosophical work of some learning which appeared in 1669-1675 was the "Court of the Gentiles" of the Nonconformist divine, Dr. Theophilus Gale (1628-1678), written with a view to prove that all heathen philosophy, whether barbaric or Greek, was borrowed from the Scriptures, or at least from the Jews. The first part is entitled "Of Philosophy," and traces the same leading principle by means of language; the second, "Of Philosophy;" the third, of "The Vanity of Philosophy;" and the fourth, of "Reformed Philosophy," wherein "Plato's moral and metaphysic or prime philosophy is reduced to an usual form and method." Gale has been included among the Platonic philosophers, and, indeed, he himself affirms that his philosophy bears a close resemblance to that of Plato. But he is in all respects a rigid Calvinist,

---

* "More," says Hallam, "fell not only into the mystical notions of the later Platonists, but even of the Cabalistic writers. His metaphysical philosophy was borrowed in great measure from them; and though he was in correspondence with Descartes, and enchanted with the new views that opened upon him, yet we find that he was reckoned much less of a Cartesian afterwards, and even wrote against parts of the theory. The most peculiar touch of More was the extension of spirit; acknowledging and even striving for the soul's immateriality, he still could not conceive it to be unextended. Yet it seems evident that if we give extension as well as figure, which is implied in finite extension, to the single self-conscious monad, qualities as heterogeneous to thinking as material impenetrability itself, we shall find it in vain to deny the possibility at least of the latter. Some indeed might question whether what we call matter is any real being at all, except as extension under peculiar conditions."—Hallam, "Introduction to the Literature of Europe," iv., 68.

and does not hesitate to say, " Whatever God wills is just, because He wills it ; " and again, " God willeth nothing without Himself because it is just, but it is therefore just because He willeth it. The reasons of good and evil extrinsic to the Divine essence are all dependent on the Divine will, either decurrent or legislative." This is not writing which Plato would have endorsed.

The political romance of "Oceana " was published in 1656, but its author, James Harrington, lived far into the reign of Charles II. Born in 1611, he died in 1677. He was a native of Northamptonshire, and studied at Oxford, where he came under the direction of the celebrated Chillingworth. Afterwards he travelled on the Continent for several years, and during his residence at the Hague and at Venice became a convert to the theory and practice of Republican government. While at Rome he attracted attention by his refusal, at some public ceremony, to kiss the Pope's toe ; but he afterwards excused himself to Charles I. on the ingenious plea that "having had the honour of kissing his Majesty's hand, he thought it a degradation to kiss the toe of any other monarch."

His "Oceana" is based on the lines of Sir Thomas More's " Utopia," and is designed to present the model of a commonwealth so constructed as to secure the completest freedom for every individual member of it. He maintains that all power depends upon property, and more particularly upon landed property. He would, therefore, have the balance of lands fixed by an agrarian law, and the government established on an equal agrarian basis, rising into the superstructure, or three orders—the senate, which would debate and propose ; the people, who would resolve and decide ; and the magistracy, who would execute—the said magistracy being elected by an equal rotation through the suffrage of the people given by ballot. After the Restoration Harrington's measures for the establishment of a Republican propaganda awakened the hostility of Charles II.'s government. He was arrested on a charge of treasonable practices, and thrown into prison; from which he was released on showing signs of mental derangement. Though a Republican, Harrington was not a democrat; his "Commonwealth of Oceana" is, in fact, based on the principle of a moderate aristocracy, and he himself was a great admirer of the Venetian oligarchy. "If I be worthy," he says, "to give advice to a man that would study politics, let him understand Venice; he that understands Venice right, shall go nearest to judge, notwithstanding the difference that is in every policy, right of every government in the world."

As a counterfoil to the "Oceana," we may take the "Patriarcha" of Sir Robert Filmer, published in 1680, but written in the reign of Charles I. It is an uncompromising defence and vindication of the absolute power of things; denying the right of natural government, and the power of the people to choose their own rulers; and affirming that positive laws cannot infringe or limit the natural and fatherly power of Kings. In his "Two Treatises of Government," published in 1689 and 1690, Locke demolished Sir John's feeble arguments. Algernon Sidney was also the author of a refutation, which he entitled "Discourses on Government," but they were not published until 1698. His theory is sufficiently indicated in the following passage :—" No one man or family is able to provide that which is requisite for their convenience or security, whilst every one has an equal right to everything, and none acknowledges a superior to determine the controversies that upon such occasions must continually arise, and will probably be so many and great, that mankind cannot bear them. Therefore .... there is nothing of absurdity in saying, that man cannot continue in the perpetual and entire fruition of the liberty that God hath given him. The liberty of one is thwarted by that of another; and whilst they are all equal, none will yield to any, otherwise than by a general consent. This is the ground of all just governments; for violence or fraud can create no right; and the same consent gives the power to them all, how much soever they differ from each other. Some small numbers of men, living within the precincts of one city, have, as it were, cast into a common stock the right which they had of governing themselves and children, and, by common consent, joining in one body, exercised such power over every single person as seemed beneficial to the whole; and this men call perfect democracy. Others choose rather to be governed by a select number of such as most excelled in wisdom and virtue; and this, according to the signification of the word, was called aristocracy; or when one man excelled all others, the government was put into his hands, under the name of monarchy. But the wisest, best, and far the greatest part of mankind, rejecting those simple species, did form governments mixed or composed of the three, which commonly received their respective denomination from the part that prevailed, and did deserve praise or blame as they were well or ill proportioned.

"It were a folly hereupon to say, that the liberty for which we contend is of no use to us, since we cannot endure the solitude, barbarity, weakness, want, misery, and dangers that accompany it whilst we live alone, nor can enter into a society without resigning it; for the choice of that society, and the liberty of framing it according to our own wills, for our own good, is all we seek. This remains to us while we form governments, that we ourselves are judges how far it is good for us to recede from our natural liberty; which is of so great importance, that from thence only we can know whether we are freemen or slaves; and the difference between the best government and the worst doth wholly depend on a right or every exercise of that power."

One of the most famous of the philosophical books of the Restoration period is the "De Legibus Naturæ Disquisitio Philosophica," published by Richard Cumberland, afterwards Bishop of Peterborough, in 1672. Its theory or system of ethics, which has been in vogue for nearly two centuries, differs essentially from that of the theologians, who referred all moral distinctions to Revelation; that of the Platonic philosophers, who sought them in eternal and intrinsic relations; and that of Hobbes and Spinosa, who degraded them to a matter of selfish prudence. An abstract of Cumberland's great treatise is given by the Rev. John Hunt, in his valuable "History of Religious Thought;" but in the few remarks which follow we are indebted to Hallam's analysis.

A diligent observation of all propositions which can safely be regarded as general moral laws of nature reduces them all to one, the pursuit of the common good of all rational agents, which tends to our own good as part of the whole, just as its opposite tends not only to the misery of the whole system, but to our own. At first sight, he says, this scheme may seem to want the two primary requisites of a law, a legislator and a sanction. But whatever elicits the natural assent of our minds must spring from the Author of Nature. God must necessarily be the author of every proposition proved to be true by the constitution of nature, of which He Himself is the Author. Nor is a sanction wanting in the rewards, that is, the happiness which attends the observance of the law of nature, and in the opposite efforts of its neglect; and in a lax sense, though not that of the jurists, reward as well as punishment may be included in the word sanction. But benevolence, that is, love and desire of good towards all rational beings, includes piety towards God, the greatest of them all, as well as humanity. Cumberland does not rely for support on arguments founded on revelation; and Mr. Hallam is, perhaps, quite justified in describing him as the founder of the Utilitarian school.

The "common good," and not that portion of it which belongs to the individual man, is the great end of the legislator, and of him who obeys his will. Those actions which by their natural tendency promote it may be called naturally good, more than those which tend only to the good of any one man, by how much the whole is greater than this small part. And whatever is directed in the shortest way to this end may be called right, as a right line is the shortest of all. And as the whole system of the universe, when all things are arranged so as to produce happiness, is beautiful, being aptly disposed to its end, which is the definition of beauty, so particular actions contributing to this general harmony may be called beautiful and becoming.

"Cumberland acutely remarks," says Hallam, " in

answer to the objection to the practice of virtue from the evils which fall on good men, and the success of the wicked, that no good or evil is to be considered, in this point of view, which arises from mere necessity, or external excuses, and not from our virtue or vice itself. He then shows that a regard for piety and peace, for mutual intercourse, and civil and domestic polity, tends to the happiness of everyone; and in reckoning the good consequences of virtuous behaviour we are not only to estimate the pleasure intimately connected with it, which the love of God and of good men produces, but the contingent benefits we obtain by civil society, which we promote by such conduct. And we see that in all nations there is some regard to good faith and the distribution of property, some respect to the obligation of oaths, some attachments to relations and friends. All men, therefore, acknowledge, and to a certain extent perform, those things which really tend to the common good. And though crime and violence sometimes prevail, yet these are like diseases in the body which it shakes off; or if, like them, they prove sometimes mortal to a single community, yet human society is immortal; and the conservative principles of common good have in the end far more efficacy than those which dissolve and destroy states.

"We may reckon the happiness consequent on virtue as a true sanction of natural law annexed to it by its author, and thus fulfilling the necessary conditions of its definition. And though some have laid stress on these sometimes, and deemed virtue its own reward, and gratitude to God and man its best motive, yet the consent of nations and common experience show us that the observance of the first end, which is the common good, will not be maintained without remuneration or penal consequences.

"By this single principle of common good we simplify the method of natural law, and arrange its secondary precepts in such subordination as best conduces to the general end. Hence moral rules give way in particular cases, when they come in collision with others of more extensive importance. For all ideas of right or virtue imply a relation to the system and nature of all rational beings. And the principles thus deduced as to moral conduct are generally applicable to political societies, which in their two leading institutions, the division of property and the coercive power of the magistrate, follow the steps of natural law, and adopt these rules of polity, because they perceive them to promote the common weal."

Only one of the ingenious and fanciful works of Dr. John Wilkins, Bishop of Chester, was published during the Restoration period,—namely, his "Essay towards a Real Character and a Philosophical Language," which bears the date of 1668,—the year in which he was promoted to the Episcopal Bench. Of this man of lively imagination Bishop Burnet speaks with unusual warmth: —"He was a man," he says, "of as great mind, as true a judgment, as eminent virtues, and of as good a soul as any I ever knew. Though he married Cromwell's sister, yet he made no other use of that alliance but to do good offices, and to cover the University of Oxford from the sourness of Owen and Goodwin. At Cambridge, he joined with those who studied to propagate better thoughts, to take men off from being in parties, or from narrow notions, from superstitious conceits and fierceness about opinions. He was also a great observer and promoter of experimental philosophy, which was then a new thing, and much looked after. He was naturally ambitious; but was the wisest clergyman I ever knew. He was a lover of mankind, and had a delight in doing good."

His most famous work has had many imitators; namely, "The Discovery of a New World; or a Discourse tending to prove that it is probable there may be another Habitable World in the Moon; with a discourse concerning the possibility of a Passage thither." In its lively pages he starts the proposition "that it is possible for some of our posterity to find out a conveyance to this other world, and if there be inhabitants there, to have commune with them." To the natural inquiry, how we are to ascend beyond the sphere of the earth's magnetical vigour, he answers:—" 1. It is not perhaps impossible that a man may be able to fly by the application of wings to his own body; as angels are pictured, as Mercury and Dædalus are feigned, and as hath been attempted by divers, particularly by a Turk in Constantinople, as Busbequius relates. 2. If there be such a great ruck (roc) in Madagascar as Marcus Polus, the Venetian, mentions, the feathers in whose wings are twelve feet long, which can swoop up a horse and his rider, or an elephant, as our kites do a mouse; why, then, it is but teaching one of these to carry a man, and he may ride up thither, as Ganymede does upon an eagle. 3. Or, none of these ways will serve, yet I do seriously, and upon good grounds, affirm it possible to make a flying chariot, in which a man may sit, and give such a motion into it as shall convey him through the air. And this, perhaps, might be made large enough to carry divers men at the same time, together with food for their viaticum, and commodities for traffic. It is not the bigness of anything in this kind that can hinder its motion, if the motive faculty be answerable thereunto. We see a great ship swims as well as a small cork, and an eagle flies in the air as well as a little gnat."

"This engine," he adds, "may be contrived from the same principles by which Archytas made a wooden dove, and Regiomontanus a wooden eagle."

Bishop Wilkins also wrote a defence and exposition of the Copernican system under the title of a "Discourse concerning a new Planet, tending to prove 'tis probable our Earth is one of the Planets." He died in 1672.

Dr. Thomas Sprat was another of the literary bishops of the Restoration. He was born in 1636, and died in 1713. Lord Macaulay describes him as "a very great master of our language, and possessed at once of the eloquence of the orator, the controversialist, and the historian." His birthplace was Tallaton, in Devonshire, where his father was vicar. He was educated at Wadham College, Oxford; took his degree of M.A. in 1656; and was elected to a fellowship in 1657. On the death of Oliver Cromwell he eulogised his virtues and his greatness in a Pindaric Ode; but this did not prevent him from developing into a fervent loyalist after the Restoration, and having taken holy orders, he became chaplain to the Duke of Buckingham, whom he assisted in his production of "The Rehearsal." He was afterwards made one of the King's chaplains. His close friendship with Dr. Wilkins led him to compile and publish a "History of the Royal Society," in 1667, of which he had been elected a Fellow. Ecclesiastical promotion now attended him rapidly: he became a prebend of Westminster in 1668,

Dean of Westminster and incumbent of St. Margaret's in 1683, and Bishop of Rochester in 1684. In 1685 he wrote, by command of the King, a far from impartial narrative of the Rye House Plot, under the title of "A True Account and Declaration of the Horrid Conspiracy against the late King, his present Majesty, and the present Government." But after the Revolution he had the grace, or found it convenient, to publish an apology for the injustice and misrepresentation that disfigured it. An attempt was made, in 1694, to implicate him in a conspiracy for restoring James II.; but it was easily detected, and the authors were duly punished. The Bishop died at Bromley, in Kent, on the 30th of May, 1713. He is best remembered now by his "Life of Cowley."

Among the historians of the Restoration period we must give the first place to the Earl of Clarendon.

Edward Hyde, the son of a Wiltshire gentleman of good estate, was born in 1608. For several years he pursued his studies at Oxford, with a view to taking holy orders; but the death of his two elder brothers gave a new direction to his career, and at the age of sixteen he was removed to London. There he studied law for some years, diverting his leisure meanwhile in the converse and companionship of such men as Ben Jonson, Selden, Lord Falkland, Lawes the musician, Chillingworth, Waller, and the "ever-memorable" John Hales of Eton. These he considered to have taught him more than his books; and he affirms that "he never was so proud, or thought himself so good a man, as when he was the worst man in the company." Entering the House of Commons in 1640, he gave himself up to the "fierce delights" of parliamentary strife. Not without hesitation, for his political principles were really those of a moderate Constitutionalist, he attached himself to the Royal party, and became one of Charles I.'s most trusted advisers, was nominated Chancellor of the Exchequer, and received the honour of knighthood. A couple of years were spent in retirement and lettered ease in the island of Jersey; after which, in 1648, he joined Prince Charles in Holland. Passing briefly over his embassy to Spain, we find him late in 1651 attached to the exiled Charles at Paris, as his financial minister and chief councillor, with the nominal dignity of Lord Chancellor. He was, of course, an influential agent in, and a witness of, the Restoration. He was with Charles at Canterbury in his progress to London; followed his triumphant entry into the capital; and, on the 1st of June, 1660, took his seat as Speaker of the House of Lords, and also sat on the same day in the Court of Chancery. In this year of good fortune his daughter, Anne Hyde, became the wife of the Duke of York; a marriage which made Clarendon (he received his earldom in 1661) the grandfather of two Queens of England, Mary and Anne. Though surrounded by a host of enemies and detractors, provoked partly by his haughtiness and avarice, partly by his arbitrary measures, and partly by his severe censures of the profligacy of the Court, he maintained his ground until 1665, when the King ordered him to resign the great seal. He soon afterwards retired to France, where he completed his "History of the Rebellion and Civil Wars in England." He was also the author of a finely-written "Essay on an Active and Contemplative Life, and why the One should be preferred before the Other." His Autobiography is a valuable contribution to the literature of the time. He died in 1674.

His defects as a historian are very noticeable: his style is often involved and cumbrous; he accumulates details without any lucidity of method; his prejudices and prepossessions obscure his judgment; his narrative of events is seldom clear or direct. On the other hand, his character painting is of the first order, and as a gallery of vivid and vigorous portraits his great History is almost unequalled.

It may be said of Clarendon that he treads the historical stage in the buskin of the tragedian; Bishop Burnet wears the lighter, and less dignified sock of the comedian. He writes with conversational ease: takes his reader by the button-hole, and gossips with him familiarly about the things he has seen or the men he has known. His faculty of observation is keen and exact; and what he observes he records with as much freedom as if he were committing his confidences to a private diary. Not without an inclination to credulity, and by no means exempt from strong prejudices, he seeks nevertheless to tell the truth, and is never knowingly unjust. Therefore, no one who writes of the period covered by the "History of My Own Time," can dispense with Burnet.

As a specimen of his method we subjoin some passages from his character of Charles II.:—

"He had so ill an opinion of mankind, that he thought the great art of living and governing was, to manage all things and all persons with a depth of craft and dissimulation. And in that few men in the world could put on the appearances of sincerity better than he could; under which so much artifice was usually hid, that in conclusion he could deceive none, for all were become mistrustful of him. He had great vices, but scarce any virtues to correct them. He had in him some vices that were less hurtful, which corrected his more hurtful ones. He was, during the active part of life, given up to sloth and lewdness to such a degree, that he hated business, and could not bear the engaging in anything that gave him much trouble, or put him under any constraint. And though he desired to become absolute, and to overturn both our religion and our laws, yet he would neither run the risk, nor give himself the trouble, which so great a design required.

"He had an appearance of gentleness in his outward deportment; but he seemed to have no bowels nor tenderness in his nature, and in the end of his life he became cruel. He was apt to forgive all crimes, even blood itself, yet he never forgave anything that was done against himself, after his first and general act of indemnity, which was to be reckoned as done rather upon maxims of state than inclinations of mercy.

"He delivered himself up to a most enormous course of vice, without any sort of restraint, even from the consideration of the nearest relations. The most studied extravagances that way seemed, to the very last, to be much delighted in and pursued by him. He had the art of making all people grow fond of him at first, by a softness in his whole way of conversation, as he was certainly the best bred man of the age. But when it appeared how little could be built on his promise, they were cured of the fondness that he was apt to raise in them. When he saw young men of quality, who had something more than ordinary in them, he drew them about him, and set himself to corrupt them both in religion and morality; in which he proved so unhappily successful, that he left England much changed at his death from what he had found it at his Restoration. He loved to talk on all the stories of his life to every new man that came about him. His stay in Scotland, and the share he had in the war of Paris, in carrying messages from the one side to the other, were his common topics. He went over these in a very graceful manner, but so often and so copiously, that all those who had been long accustomed to them grew weary of them; and when he entered on those stories, they usually withdrew; so that he often began them in a full audience, and before he had done, there were not above four or five persons left about him: which drew a severe jest from Wilmot Earl of Rochester. He said he wondered to see a man have so good a memory as to repeat the same story without losing the least circumstance, and yet not remember that he had told it to the same persons the very day before. This made him fond of strangers, for they hearkened to all his often-repeated stories, and went away as in a rapture at such an uncommon condescension in a king.

"His person and temper, his vices as well as his fortunes, resemble the character that we have given us of Tiberius so much, that is were easy to draw the parallel between them. Tiberius's banishment, and his coming afterwards to reign, makes the comparison in that respect come pretty near. His hating of business, and his love of pleasures; his raising of favourites, and trusting them entirely; and his pulling them down, and hating them excessively; his art of covering deep designs, particularly of revenge, with an appearance of softness, brings them so near a likeness, that I did not wonder much to observe the resemblance of their faces and persons. At Rome I saw one of the last statues made for Tiberius, after he had lost his teeth. But, bating the alteration which that made, it was so like King Charles, that Prince Borghose and Signior Dominicio, to whom it belonged, did agree with me in thinking that it looked like a statue made for him.

"Few things ever went near his heart. The Duke of Gloucester's death seemed to touch him much. But those who knew him best, thought it was because he had lost him by whom only he could have balanced the surviving brother, whom he hated, and yet embroiled all his affairs to preserve the succession to him.

" His ill-conduct in the first Dutch war, and those terrible calamities of the Plague and Fire of London, with that loss and reproach which he suffered by the insult at Chatham, made all people conclude there was a curse upon his government. His throwing the public hatred at that time upon Lord Clarendon was both unjust and ungrateful. And when his people had brought him out of all his difficulties upon his entering into the Triple Alliance, his selling that to France, and his entering on the second Dutch war with as little colour as he had for the first; his beginning it with the attempt on the Dutch Smyrna fleet, the shutting up the exchequer, and his declaration for toleration, which was a step for the introduction of popery, made such a chain of black actions, flowing from blacker designs, that it amazed those who had known all this to see with what impudent strains of flattery addresses were penned during his life, and yet more grossly after his death. His contributing so much to the raising the greatness of France, chiefly at sea, was such an error, that it could not flow from want of thought, or of true sense. Rauvigny told me he desired that all the methods the French took in the increase and conduct of their naval force might be sent him; and he said he seemed to study them with concern and zeal. He showed what errors they committed, and how they ought to be corrected, as if he had been a viceroy to France, rather than a king that ought to have watched over and prevented the progress they made, as the greatest of all the mischiefs that could happen to him or his people. They that judged the most favourably of this, thought it was done out of revenge to the Dutch, that, with the assistance of so great a fleet as France could join to his own, he might be able to destroy them. But others put a worse construction on it: and thought, that seeing he could not quite master or deceive his subjects by his own strength and management, he was willing to help forward the greatness of the French at sea, that by their assistance he might more certainly subdue his own people; according to what was generally believed to have fallen from Lord Clifford, if the King must be in a dependence, it was better to pay it to a great and generous king, than to five hundred of his own insolent subjects.

"No part of his character looked wickeder, as well as meaner, than that he, all the while that he was professing to be of the Church of England, expressing both zeal and affection to it, was yet secretly reconciled to the Church of Rome; thus mocking God, and deceiving the world with so gross a prevarication. And his not having the honesty or courage to own it at the last; his not showing any sign of the least remorse for his ill-led life, or any tenderness either for his subjects in general, or for the queen and his servants; and his recommending only his mistresses and their children to his brother's care, would have been a strange conclusion to any other's life, but was well enough suited to all the other parts of his."

To the Restoration period belonged Anthony Wood (1632-1695), the quaint, diligent, but partial author of the "Athenæ Oxoniensis," a valuable collection of memoirs of nearly all the eminent authors educated at Oxford, and of many of those educated at the sister university. Sir William Dugdale's great antiquarian work, the *Monasticon Anglicanum*, was published in the earlier years of Charles II.'s reign; and in 1672 appeared another work of antiquarian importance, Elias Ashmole's "Institution, Laws, and Memoirs of the Most Noble Order of the Garter." John Aubrey, the credulous collector of superstitions, folk-lore, ghost-stories, and the like, spent the leisure of a recluse life in gathering up the "Miscellanies" which he published in 1696. He rendered useful assistance to Dugdale and Anthony à Wood, the latter of whom repaid him by describing him, for the benefit of posterity, as "a shiftless person, roving and maggotty-headed, and sometimes little better than crazed; and being exceedingly credulous, would stuff his many letters sent to A. W. with fooleries and misinformations."

Robert Leighton was the son of a Scottish physician, Dr. Andrew Leighton, who was punished for the vehement polemics in his "Appeal to the Parliament; or, Lion's Plea against the Prelacy," by being publicly whipped, pilloried, branded, slit in the nose, and deprived of an ear—after which he lay for eleven years in the prison of the Fleet. Robert Leighton was educated at the University of Edinburgh, resided for some years at Douai, and in December, 1641, was ordained minister of Newbattle, near Edinburgh, where he composed his well-known "Commentary on the First Epistle of St. Peter." In March, 1662, he was induced to separate himself from the Presbyterian communion, and accept preferment in the Episcopal Church. For eight years he occupied the see of Dunblane—where a fine grove of trees is still pointed out as "the Bishop's Walk"—and in 1670 was appointed to the Archbishopric of Glasgow. In this high office he made a noble effort to reconcile the Presbyterian body to the ancient Church of Scotland, but his exertions were nullified by the arbitrary and cruel policy of Lauderdale and the Primate Sharp, and in sore discouragement and distress, he resigned his archbishopric. The remainder of his pure and blameless life was spent at Broadhurst in Sussex; but, being suddenly called to London, he was seized there with an illness which, in a few days, proved mortal. He died on the 25th of June, 1684, at the age of 73.

A complete edition of the works of this estimable prelate—of whom Burnet speaks as gifted with "the greatest devotion of soul, the largest compass of knowledge, the most mortified and most heavenly disposition that he ever saw in mortal"—was recently published by the Rev. William West, the Episcopalian incumbent of Nairn. Their special characteristics are their intense spirituality of tone and feeling, their large-heartedness and absolute freedom from sectarian sentiment, and their grace of style. Here is a fine thought, finely expressed:—

"Every man walketh in a vain show. His walk is nothing but an on-going in continual vanity and misery, in which man is naturally and industriously involved, adding a new stock of vanity, of his own weaving, to what he has already within, and vexation of spirit woven all along in with it. He 'walks in an image,' as the Hebrew word is; converses with things of no reality, and which have no solidity in them, and he himself has as little. He himself is a walking image in the midst of these images. They who are taken with the conceit of pictures and statues are an emblem of their own life, and of all other men's also. Life is generally nothing else to all men but a doting on images and pictures. Every man's fancy is to himself a gallery of pictures, and there he walks up and down, and considers not how vain these are, and how vain a thing he himself is."

And here is a passage which Coleridge, in his " Aids to Reflection," singles out for quotation :—" As in religion, so in the course and practice of men's lives, the stream of sin runs from one age into another, and every age makes it greater, adding somewhat to what it receives, as rivers grow in their course by the accession of brooks that fall into them; and every man when he is born, falls like a drop into the main current of corruption, and so is carried down with it, and this by reason of its strength and his own nature, which willingly dissolves into it, and runs along with it."

In this beautiful image we have, says Coleridge, "religion, the spirit; philosophy, the soul; and poetry, the body and drapery united; Plato glorified by St. Paul!"

What Leighton was to the Scottish Church, was Bishop Ken to the English Church. Both were men of devout mind and holy life, who rose above the sectarian conditions in which they had been bred, and translated their religious belief into action. Among their contemporaries they stood distinguished by the force and earnestness they threw into their Apostolic mission. They were good and great men, but great because of their goodness.

Thomas Ken, the son of a respectable attorney, was born at Little Berkhampstead, in Hertfordshire, in July, 1637. At the age of thirteen he was admitted into Winchester School, and seven years later he entered New College, Oxford, as a Probationer Fellow. Of his University life we know little, except that his fine voice and love of music led him to join a musical club that had been recently established at Oxford. In 1661, Ken took the degree of B.A., and about the same time seems to have been ordained. The respect which he had acquired by his scholarship and consistency of character was proved, in 1666, by his unanimous election to a fellowship. He thereupon returned to Winchester, where the room in which as Fellow he resided, pursued his studies, and amused his leisure by playing on his lute, is still shown to visitors.

Morley was at that time occupant of the see of Winchester, and with him resided the "Complete Angler," genial Izaak Walton, who had married Ken's sister, Anna, the Kenna of her husband's ballads. Under the episcopal roof he lived, in virtue of the friendship of many years, "a beloved and honoured guest, with mild and lighted countenance, snow-white locks, a thankful but humble heart—with piety as sincere as unostentatious—till he closed his eyes on all the 'changes and chances of this mortal life,' at ninety years of age." Through his brother-in-law, Ken was admitted to the intimacy of Bishop Morley, who quickly felt the influence of his exalted character, and, in 1669, promoted him to a prebend's stall in Winchester Cathedral. But Ken was no beneficed idler. Though not holding a pastoral charge, he laboured zealously in his Master's service.

"His most exemplary goodness and piety," we are told, "did universally exert itself; for this purpose he kept a constant course of preaching at St. John's Church in the South [a suburb of Winchester], where there was no preaching minister, and which he therefore called his *own*, and brought many Anabaptists to the Church of England; and baptized them himself."

It was at this period that Ken composed his "Manual" for the use of the Winchester Scholars; and those beautiful "Morning" and "Evening" hymns, which are the precious heritage of every English-speaking child. Not less dear to the Nonconformist than to the Anglican, they are "sung or said," day after day, in ten thousand households, in Canada—in Australia—the isles of the Pacific—on India's coral strands—as well as in the mother country. Written, originally, to be sung in the chambers of the Winchester boys, there is good reason to believe that Ken himself adapted them to that noble melody of Tallis's, with which they are indissolubly associated. Of Ken's habit of singing his Morning Hymn regularly, at daybreak, Hawkins writes:—"That neither his study might be the aggressor on his hours of instruction, nor what he judged duty prevent his improvement, he strictly accustomed himself to but one hour's sleep, which obliged him to rise at one or two o'clock in the morning, or sometimes earlier. He seemed to go to rest with no other purpose than the refreshing and enabling him with more vigour and cheerfulness to sing his Morning Hymn, as he used to do, to his lute, before he put on his clothes."

It is interesting to note that the sweet simplicity of those hymns, which in itself accounts for their enduring popularity, contrasts remarkably with the complex and artificial structure of much of Ken's later verse. They came fresh from his heart—are absolutely spontaneous in their utterance. Unadorned as are these well-known lines, what can be more touching or more impressive?—

> " All praise to Thee, my God, this night,
> For all the blessings of the light:
> Keep me, O keep me, King of Kings!
> Under Thine own Almighty wings.
>
> Forgive me, Lord, for Thy dear Son,
> The ills that I this day have done;
> That with the world, myself, and Thee
> I, ere I sleep, at peace may be."

Not a word here is superfluous; there are no ornamental epithets; language cannot be plainer, we had almost said balder; and yet the effect produced is charming. The Morning Hymn seems a jubilant expression of hopefulness and thanksgiving; the Evening Hymn fills the soul with the peace and devotion that spring from an intense faith in the loving Providence of God.

From 1669 to 1675 Ken pursued the even tenor of his way. In the latter year he broke away from his habits of seclusion, and accompanied his nephew, Izaak Walton the younger, on a Continental tour. It was the year of the Papal Jubilee; and the English Churchman had an opportunity of witnessing the Roman Court in all the splendour of its pomp and circumstance. He would often afterwards observe that he had great reason to give God thanks for his travels, since (if it were possible) he " returned rather more confirmed of the purity of the Protestant religion than before." At the close of the year he was back again in Winchester. In 1679 he took his doctor's degree, and in the same year was appointed chaplain to Charles II., who, during his frequent visits to Winchester, must have heard of his self-denial, and the golden excellence of his character. This appointment led to his being sent to Holland as the chaplain and adviser of the Princess of Orange. In this post, says Hawkins, his most prudent behaviour and strict piety gave him entire credit and high esteem with that royal lady. He contiues:—" But a consequential act of his singular zeal for the honour of his country, in behalf of a young lady, so far exasperated the Prince, that he warmly threatened to turn him from the service ; which the doctor resisting, and begging leave of the Princess (whom to his death he distinguished by the title of his mistress), warned himself from the service, till, by the entreaty of the Prince himself, he was courted to his former post and respect; and when the year expired he returned to England."

The young lady was Miss Wroth, one of the Princess's maids-of-honour, with whom Count Julienstein, half-uncle of the Prince of Orange, had fallen in love. But as he afterwards showed a disposition to behave dishonourably to the young lady, Ken constituted himself her champion, and remonstrated with him so effectively that at length he consented to marry her. The Prince was greatly offended at this marriage of so near a kinsman to an English lady, untitled and penniless, and bitterly resented Ken's chivalrous interposition.

Early in 1681 Ken returned to Winchester; and soon afterwards Charles II. visited the Cathedral city to inspect the progress made in the works of the stately palace he had projected. He was accompanied by his mistress, Nell Gwynn, and desiring to lodge her in immediate neighbourhood to his own apartments at the Deanery, he required that the adjacent prebendal residence of Ken should be allotted for her use. With virtuous indignation Ken refused compliance with the royal mandate. Give up his house to a lewd actress and courtezan? "Not for his kingdom!" Ken sternly replied; and it is to Charles's credit that he respected his chaplain's consistency and moral courage.

In 1683 Ken accompanied the Tangier expedition as Chaplain to the Admiral in command, Lord Dartmouth. When he returned to England in the early spring of 1684, he found his brother-in-law dead, and Bishop Morley dying. The good prelate did not linger long; and Mew, Bishop of Bath and Wells, was then translated to Winchester, leaving his own see vacant. The vacancy was filled up by the appointment of Ken at Charles's personal dictation:—"Odd's fish!" he exclaimed, "who shall have Bath and Wells but the little fellow who would not give poor Nelly a lodging?" This was one of the King's latest acts, and his death actually occurred before the newly made Bishop could take possession of his temporalities.

Of a promotion so unexpected, and so uncongenial to his way of thinking and his retired habits, Ken thus speaks:—

"Among the herdsmen, I a common swain,
Lived, pleased with my low cottage on the plain;
Till up, like Amos, on a sudden caught,
I to the pastoral chair was trembling brought."

In Bishop Burnet's reference to it we find a touch of ill-nature, due, perhaps, to the political and theological prejudices of the man:—"Ken," he says, "succeeded Mew in Bath and Wells; a man of an ascetic course of life, and yet of a very lively temper, but too hot and sudden. He had a very edifying way of preaching, but it was more apt to move the passions than instruct;

so that his sermons were rather beautiful than solid; yet his way in them was very taking. The King seemed fond of him; and by him and Turner the Papists hoped that great progress might be made in gaining, or at least deluding the clergy." If the Papists had any such hope, it was speedily blighted; for though Ken belonged to what is now known as the Catholic School in the Church of England, he was as hostile to Romanism as Burnet himself.

Ken was present by Charles II.'s death bed, and addressed the dying King with his usual courageous faithfulness. He refused to allow the Duchess of Portsmouth to attend in the sick man's chamber, but warmly and courageously urged upon him the duty of being reconciled to the wife he had so grossly injured by his infidelity and neglect. Burnet is compelled to admit that, in this critical time, "he spoke with a great elevation, both of thought and expression, like a man inspired. He resumed the matter often, and pronounced many ejaculations and prayers, which affected all who were present, except him that was the most concerned, who seemed to take no notice of him, and made no answers to him. He pressed the King six or seven times to take the Sacrament, but the King always declined it, saying he was very weak. A table with the elements upon it, ready to be consecrated, was brought into the room; which occasioned a report to be then spread about that he *had* received it. Ken pressed him to declare that he desired it, and that he died in the communion of the Church of England. To that he answered nothing. Ken asked him if he desired absolution of his sins? It seems the King, if he then thought at all, thought that would do him no hurt; so Ken pronounced it over him."

Charles's nomination of Ken to the see of Bath and Wells was confirmed by James II., and the Bishop, with characteristic fervour, entered at once upon the discharge of his new and important duties. He visited the poor with assiduous self-denial, traversing his diocese, on "a sorry horse," in order to make himself thoroughly acquainted with its condition; preached for every parish priest who required it of him; encouraged his clergy in good works; and, above all, set to his people a noble example of sincere and lowly piety and devotion. He devoted much care and thought to the education of the children of the poor, and encouraged the establishment of parochial schools in all the towns of his diocese. "During summer he would repair to some great parish, where he would preach, confirm, and catechize himself. In the great hall of his palace at Wells, he had always, on Sundays, twelve poor men or women to dine with him, instructing them at the same time." He delighted to maintain a dignified hospitality. "In the court of the palace at Wells there yet remain the lofty Gothic windows of that Hall, called of the Hundred Men, where public meetings were held, and the business of the county transacted. The palace was open to the judges, counsel, and noblemen and gentlemen of the county; at the head of whom appeared the mild and Apostolic host at his episcopal table. The clergy, and the neighbouring noblemen and gentlemen of the county, were at all times expected and welcome and honoured guests." To literary labour, during his episcopate, Ken did not greatly incline. His publications were few and unimportant; namely, " A Sermon preached in the Cathedral Church of Bath, on Ascension Day, May 5th, 1687;" "An Exposition of the Church Catechism; or, Practise of Divine Love;" "Directions for Prayer," printed with the former; and, "A Pastoral Letter to the Clergy of the Diocese of Bath and Wells, concerning their Behaviour during Lent."

After the collapse of the Monmouth rebellion in 1685, he extended his Christian charity to the unhappy fugitives from red Sedgmoor. His palace stood scarce a day's journey from that fatal field, and its gates were thronged with supplicants, whom he relieved with liberal hands and encouraged with prudent counsel. Considering the temper of the then Government, it was at no slight personal risk that he exercised this benevolence; but he ventured still further, and when the Earl of Faversham was hanging his prisoners in cold blood, courageously warned him that they were by law entitled to a trial, and that their execution without trial would be deemed a murder. Yet it was Ken whom the king chose as the fittest person to prepare the unfortunate Monmouth for the scaffold to which his relentless hatred had condemned him; and it was Ken, accompanied by Turner, Bishop of Ely, Drs. Tenison and Hooper, who stood by him in his death hour.

The reader needs not to be reminded that after the victory of Sedgmoor and the Bloody Assize had crushed out the rebellion, James II. felt strong enough to proceed in his design of restoring the supremacy of the Roman Church. To evade the resistance of Parliament he prorogued it, and then obtained from the judicial bench, which he had packed with his creatures, a declaration that the royal dispensation prevailed over the provisions of the Test Act. To overawe the citizens of London, who in the old days were firm guardians of the liberty of the subject, he encamped an army of thirteen thousand soldiers at Hounslow. With the view of Romanizing the government of the Church of England, he appointed seven commissioners, with the infamous Judge Jefferys at their head (1686); and their first act was to order the Bishop of London to suspend a London vicar who had preached against Popery. And when the Bishop refused, they suspended *him*. This arbitrary action of the Commissioners roused the clergy to a strenuous resistance; and anti-Roman discourses were thundered from every pulpit. Undeterred by the signs of a gathering storm, James turned to attack the Universities. The headship of Magdalen College was vacant, and in 1687 he recommended to its Fellows for election one Farmer, a man without scholarship and of evil life. The Fellows remonstrated, and when their remonstrance was ignored, elected Mr. Hough to be president. The Commissioners, in open defiance of law and custom, declared the election void; and James endeavoured to put in a second nominee, Bishop Parker, of Oxford, a servile courtier and a concealed Papist. The Fellows stoutly adhered to their own appointment. In a mood of sullen wrath James repaired to Oxford, summoned the offending Fellows before him, and sharply rebuked them for their disobedience. "I am king," he replied, "and will be obeyed! Go to your chapel this instant, and elect the bishop. Let those who refuse look to it, for they shall feel the whole weight of my hand!"

We turn, however, to the events in which Ken was personally involved. In the hope of bribing the Nonconformists to support him, James issued, in 1687, what was called a Declaration of Indulgence, repealing the penal laws against Nonconformists and Catholics, and the Acts which imposed a Sacramental test as a qualification for office in Church or State. So far as the principle of toleration was concerned, this might be regarded as a just and righteous measure; but in attempting to override the statutes of the realm, James was acting a most unconstitutional part, and dealing a fatal blow at English liberties. Once concede to the Crown a "dispensing power," and the laws made by Parliament became a sham and a nonentity. The Nonconformist leaders, therefore, threw in their lot with the Church of England, and rejected the sop which James had so ingeniously prepared for them. James then resolved to summon a Parliament, in the hope of extorting from it a repeal of the Test Act; but he soon found reason to conclude that, if elected, it would represent only too faithfully the spirit of the people. Whom the gods seek to destroy they first make mad, and with mad persistency he issued, on the 27th of April, 1688, a fresh Declaration of Indulgence, and ordered that it should be read on two successive Sundays in every cathedral and parish church in the kingdom. The royal command was disobeyed, however, by nearly all the bishops and clergy. In only four of the London churches was the Declaration read; and in those the congregations quitted their seats and departed at the opening sentences. Archbishop Sancroft and six of the Bishops of his province, the Bishops of Bath and Wells, Chichester, St. Asaph, Bristol, Ely and Peterborough, met at Lambeth, and signed a protest to the King, embodied in language which lacked neither moderation nor firmness, declining to publish an illegal ordinance. "It is a standard of rebellion," exclaimed the King in his passion; "I did not expect this from some of you," and having gone too far to recede, he committed the recalcitrant prelates to the Tower on the charge of libel. For once the Church was on the side of Freedom; and as the Bishops passed to their prison they were greeted with the cheers of sympathetic thousands. At its frowning gates the sentinels fell on their knees, and asked their blessing. The soldiers of the garrison loudly drank their healths. The tide of national feeling rolled in rapidly increasing volume from the capital to the furthest provinces; but James, though his Ministers trembled, refused to stay his steps. Like a man smitten with judicial blindness he hastened to his doom. Before judges who lived by the breath of his nostrils, and a jury carefully packed, the Bishops were brought to trial on the 29th of June; but neither judges nor jury durst withstand the popular enthusiasm, and a verdict of " Not guilty " was returned. These two words sealed the downfall of the Stuart dynasty.

When James II. abdicated Ken joined the Primate in maintaining that, so long as he lived, the throne could not be declared vacant; but that as he had governed ill, the nation could justly prohibit him from the exercise of government, and entrust it to a regency. He had abandoned the dogma of Passive Obedience, but still upheld the doctrine of Divine Right. He refused, therefore, in company with Sancroft and six other bishops, to take the oath of allegiance to William and Mary (1689). They were threatened with the deprivation of their sees; but were allowed a year's grace to consider their position; and Queen Mary employed Bishop Burnet to negotiate their submission, offering to dispense with the oath, and pass an act of indulgence. It is to be regretted that Ken and his brethren could not be induced to accept this reasonable concession. Eventually, as Bishop Turner engaged in an intrigue for King James's restoration, in which the other bishops were suspected of being involved, though there was certainly no evidence against Ken, the sentence of deprivation was put into execution, and Ken withdrew, for conscience sake, into an obscure retirement.

It is worth while to get at the motives which influenced him in maintaining this obstinate attitude, and we find them explained in a letter which he addressed to Bishop Burnet, on the 5th of October, 1689:—

"I am obliged to your lordship for the continued concern you express for me, and for the kind freedom you are pleased to take with me: and though I have already in public fully declared my mind to my diocese concerning the oath, to prevent my being misunderstood; yet, since you seem to expect it of me, I will give such an account, which, if it does not satisfy your lordship, will at least satisfy myself. I dare assure you, I never advised any-one to take the oath; though some, who came to talk insidiously with me, may have raised such a report. So far have I been from it, that I never would administer it to any one person whom I was to collate. And, therefore, before the act took place, I gave a particular commission to my Chancellor, who himself did not scruple it; so that he was authorised, not only to institute, but also to collate in my stead. If any came to discourse to me about taking the oath, I usually told them I durst not take it myself. I told them my reasons, if they urged me to it, and were of my own diocese; and then remitted them to their study and prayers, for further direction. 'Tis true, having been scandalized at many persons of our own coat, who for several years together preached up Passive Obedience to a much greater height than ever I did, it being a subject with which I very rarely meddled, and on a sudden, without the least acknowledgement of their past error, preached and acted the quite contrary, I did prepare a pastoral letter which, if I had some reason to alter my judgment, I thought to have published, at least that part of it on which I laid the greatest stress, to justify my conduct to my flock. . . .

"If your lordship gives credit to the many misrepresentations which are made of me, and which I being so used to can easily disregard, you may naturally enough be in pain for me; for to see one of your brethren throwing himself headlong into a wilful deprivation, not only of honour and of income, but of a good conscience also, are particulars out of which may be framed an idea very deplorable. But though I do daily in many things betray great infirmity, I thank God I cannot accuse myself of any insincerity; so that deprivation will not reach my conscience, and I am in no pain at all for myself."

Ken found an asylum at Longleat, the hospitable house of his early friend, Thomas Thynne, whither he carried his lute, the small Greek Testament which was his constant companion, the shroud which was to be his last garment, his "sorry horse" for his occasional journeys, and his income of twenty pounds a quarter—all that was left of his fortune. His later life presents few incidents that call for notice. In 1696, he was summoned before the Privy Council, on a charge of having been concerned in raising subscriptions for the poor Nonjurors; but he defended himself with manliness and success. In 1706, soon after the accession of Queen

Anne, he was invited to return to his diocese on the understanding that Bishop Kidder, who had succeeded him, should be removed to another see. In the following year Kidder accidently came to his death, in the episcopal palace at Wells, through the fall of a stack of chimneys in the fury of the Great Storm. Ken at the time was staying at his nephew's house at Salisbury, and met with a remarkable deliverance. There, too, the stack of chimneys was thrown down, but the beam which supported the roof broke their descent, so that nothing save the roof was damaged. Writing to Bishop Lloyd, Ken says: "I think I omitted to tell you the full of my deliverance in the late storm, for the house being surveyed the day following, the workmen found that the beam which supported the roof over my head was broken out to that degree, that it had but half an inch hold, so that it was a wonder it would hold together; for which signal and particular preservation God's holy name be ever praised!"

Hitherto Bishop Ken had considered himself Bishop of Bath and Wells *de jure*, not acknowledging the legality of his deprivation. But on Bishop Kidder's death he formally resigned, and it gave him much pleasure to see the mitre bestowed on his friend, Bishop Hooper. Queen Anne, when she found that he considered his physical infirmities a bar to his reinstatement, was graciously pleased to settle on him a pension of £200.

At Longleat, in the 73rd year of his age, passed away the saintly bishop. Before the end came, he had many painful warnings—general debility, rheumatic pains, and much oppression of breathing. These were followed by a fit of apoplexy, which rendered him for a time unconscious. On recovering his senses, he calmly assumed his shroud, and prepared for death in the true spirit of Christian heroism. With many prayers, and bestowing his blessing on his sorrowing friends, he entered into his rest between five and six o'clock on the morning of the 19th of March, 1711. He was interred in the churchyard at Frome.

Ken's poetical works were collected and published by Hawkins in four volumes—the first of which contained his hymns; the second, "Edmund, an Epic," and "Hymnarium; or, Hymns on the Attributes of God;" third, "Hymnothes, the Penitent;" and the fourth, "Preparatives for Death." To us the wonderful thing about these compositions is that they proceeded from the pen of the author of the "Morning" and "Evening" hymns. They are in the worst style of the school of Cowley; cumbrous in versification, loaded with grotesque and artificial imagery. It is said that he wrote his dreary epic, "Edmund," which is divided into fourteen books, to relieve the monotony of a sea-voyage. Probably he never intended it for the eyes of the public; and it would have been well for his memory if his biographer had allowed it to moulder in the dust of oblivion.

The four volumes, however, are not all rubbish; the barren tract is brightened with a few flowers. And not unworthy of preservation is his sketch of "A Christian Pastor," which seems to be a bit of unconscious self-portraiture:—

> "Give me the priest these graces shall possess:
> Of an ambassador the just address,
> A father's tenderness, a shepherd's care,
> A leader's courage, which the cross may bear;
> A ruler's awe, a watchman's wakeful eye,
> A pilot's skill, the helm in storms to ply;
> A prophet's inspiration from above;
> A teacher's knowledge and a Saviour's love.

> Of a mild, humble, and obliging heart,
> Who with his all will to the needy part;
> Distrustful of himself, in God confides,
> Daily himself among his flock divides;
> Of virtue uniform, and cheerful air,
> Fixed meditation, and incessant prayer;
> Who is all that he would have others be,
> From wilful sin, though not from frailty, free."

In the concluding lines, Ken's devout and simple piety finds due expression:—

> "E'er since I hung upon my mother's breast
> Thy love, my God, has me sustained and blest:
> My virtuous parents, tender of their child;
> My education pious, careful, mild;
> My teachers zealous to well-form my mind;
> My faithful friends and benefactors kind;
> My creditable station and good name;
> My life preserved from scandal and from shame;
> My understanding, memory, and health;
> Relations dear, and competance of wealth;
> All the vouchsafements Thou to me hast shown,
> All blessings, all deliverances unknown—
> Lord, when Thy blessings which all vot'ries share
> With my peculiar blessings I compare,
> I stand amazed at their unbounded store,
> And silently Thy liberal love adore."

A few words may be said in illustration of his character, which, however, offers no theme for the psychological analyst or the minute critic. It was simplicity itself; his life set it forth; and both text and comment he who ran might read. A man of clear intellect and direct purpose, Ken, when he had once determined on his duty, was not to be diverted from it. His judgment was sound, his courage high. From what he conceived to be the truth, no inducement could separate him; and his witness to it he was prepared always and everywhere to maintain. Hence we discern in him a true type of the Christian priest. His piety was profoundly sincere; an intelligent and reasonable piety, though with an ascetic touch about it; a loving and an unaffected piety, yet strong enough to sustain him in severe trials, and to encourage him to noble deeds—as when he repulsed a king's mistress, and surrendered the emoluments and dignities of the episcopate for conscience sake. He ruled his diocese firmly, yet with the gentle consideration of a loving nature; being in all things and at all times the father of his clergy, the friend and adviser and shepherd of his laity. As a preacher, he was distinguished by his fervour, his plainness of speech, and his boldness of utterance: and the glow of his devout enthusiasm sometimes warmed his language into eloquence. He was not a great scholar, and his credentials to the recollection of posterity are almost exclusively confined to his two celebrated hymns.

The Church of England at this period boasted of many divines who were rapidly rising into eminence as theologians or preachers. Dr. John Pearson, Bishop of Chester, who died in 1686, was already famous for his " Exposition of the Creed;" Dean Tillotson, 1630-1694, who, after the Revolution, became Archbishop of Canterbury, drew delighted congregations to St. Lawrence Jewry by his eloquent sermons; Dr. Sherlock, 1641-1707, was in the prime of manhood at Charles II.'s death, and had given evidence of scholarship and controversial ability; and Dr. Stillingfleet, 1635-1699, made Bishop of Chester in 1689, had produced his chief work, " Origines Sacræ; or, A Rational Account of the Grounds of Natural and Revealed Religion," as early as 1662.

We turn to the most renowned among the Nonconformists. Richard Baxter was born in 1615 at Rowton, in Shropshire; educated at Wroxeter; ordained in 1638;

and from 1640 to 1642 he officiated as pastor at Kidderminster. In the great religious and political struggle which divided England into two hostile parties, whose lines of separation are still far from being effaced, he supported the Parliament, and was present with the army as chaplain at the sieges of Bridgewater, Exeter, Bristol, and Worcester. But the polemics of officers and troopers were not to his taste, and from the vehement debates of Sergeant Moretext and Zephaniah Break-the-chains-of-Satan, he retired to Kidderminster, where, in 1653, he wrote that beautiful book of his, the consolation of so many anxious souls, " The Saint's Everlasting Rest." He boldly remonstrated with Cromwell on his assumption of the supreme power, and plainly told him that " the honest people of this land took their ancient monarchy to be a blessing and not an evil." After the Restoration he might well have abandoned this opinion, for the Act of Uniformity, passed in 1662, drove him out of the Established Church. He retired to Acton,* where he lived in the delights of lettered seclusion until the Act of Indulgence, in 1672, enabled him to return to London. Some passages in his " Paraphrase on the New Testament," which he published in 1685, were regarded as seditious, and he was arraigned before Judge Jeffreys. It was on the day on which Titus Oates was pilloried in Palace Yard that the venerable Nonconformist leader appeared in Westminster Hall. He asked that some little time might be allowed him to prepare his defence. " Not a minute," exclaimed the brutal Jeffreys, " to save his life! I can deal with saints as well as with sinners. There

* His house was near the church, but has long since been pulled down, and its site cannot now be identified.

stands Oates on one side of the pillory; and if Baxter stood on the other, the two greatest rogues in the kingdom would stand together."

Throughout the trial—if such a mockery of justice deserve the name—Jeffreys behaved with similar brutality. He browbeat and silenced Baxter's advocates, and when Baxter himself attempted to put in a word, overwhelmed him with ribald talk, mingled with quotations from "Hudibras." "My lord," said the aged divine, "I have been much blamed by Dissenters for speaking respectfully of bishops." "Baxter for bishops!" cried the Judge, "that's a merry conceit indeed. I know what you mean by bishops; rascals like yourself, Kidderminster bishops, factious, snivelling Presbyterians!" Again Baxter attempted to speak. "Richard, Richard," thundered the Judge, "dost thou think we will let thee poison the court? Richard, thou art an old knave. Thou hast written books enough to load a cart, and every book as full of sedition as an egg is full of meat. By the grace of God, I'll look after thee. I see a great many of your brotherhood waiting to know what will befall their mighty Don."

He was sentenced to pay 500 marks, and to be imprisoned in the King's Bench until the fine was paid. He lay in confinement for a year and a half, and then regained his liberty, partly through the exertions of Lord Powis, and partly because James II. desired to win over the Protestant Nonconformists. He was informed that if he chose to reside in London he might do so without fearing that the Five Mile Act would be enforced against him. But Baxter was not to be cajoled. He refused to join in any address of thanks for the Declaration of Indulgence, and strenuously exerted himself to promote a reconciliation between the Church and the Presbyterians. It was mainly through his influence that the two bodies stood side by side in the struggle against the Court. In the same moderate spirit he gave his assent, in 1689, to the Toleration Act, which enabled every dissenting minister to exercise his functions provided he declared his belief in some thirty-four of the thirty-nine Articles of the Church of England.

Two years later (on the 8th of December, 1691) he closed his long and blameless life, a life spent in the practice of moderation and the advocacy of charity. His separate writings are said to number 168. Of these, the "Saint's Everlasting Rest" and the "Call to the Unconverted" are still largely read among us. A deep interest also attaches to his autobiography—"A Narrative of the most Memorable Passages of my Life and Times"—which Coleridge rightly pronounces "an inestimable work." His own opinion of his writings is given with his usual frankness:—" I must confess," he says, " that my own judgment is, that fewer, well studied and polished, had been better; but the reader who can safely censure the books, is not fit to censure the author, unless he had been upon the places and acquainted with all the occasions and circumstances. Indeed, for 'The Saint's Rest,' I had four months' vacancy to write it, but in the midst of continual languishing and medicine; but, for the rest, I wrote them in the crowd of all my other employments, which would allow me no great leisure for polishing and exactness, or any ornament; so that I scarce ever wrote one sheet twice over, nor stayed to make any blots or interlinings, but was fain to let it go as it was first conceived: and when my own desire was rather to stay upon one thing long than run over many, some sudden occasion or other extorted almost all my writings from me; and the apprehensions of present usefulness or necessity prevailed against all other motives; so that the divines which were at hand with me still put me on, and approved of what I did, because they were moved by present necessities as well as I; but those that were far off, and felt not those nearer motives, did rather wish that I had taken the other way, and published a few elaborate writings; and I am ready myself to be of their mind, when I forget the case that I then stood in, and have lost the sense of former motives."

George Fox, the founder of the Society of Friends, or Quakers, must also be mentioned. He was the son of a weaver, and born at Drayton, in Leicestershire, in 1624. Apprenticed to a shoemaker who traded in wool and cattle, he devoted much of his time to the charge of sheep, and this solitary occupation enabled an excitable imagination to indulge in the wildest vagaries. He was about nineteen years old, when he was one day much disturbed by the love of drink displayed by two professedly religious friends whom he met at a fair. "I went away," he notes in his journal, "and, when I had done my business, returned home; but I did not go to bed that night, nor could I sleep; but sometimes walked up and down, and sometimes prayed, and cried to the Lord, who said unto me: 'Thou seest how young people go together into vanity, and old people into the earth; thou must forsake all, young and old, keep out of all, and be a stranger to all!'" Accepting this as a Divine command, he gave it his most rigid obedience; abandoned his trade and his home, and for several years wandered to and fro like a pilgrim in the desert. With his intellect too much disordered to enable him to apprehend things in their true relations, he fancied that he had celestial revelations, and, like Jeanne d'Arc, heard voices. "One morning," he says, "as I was sitting by the fire, a great cloud came over me, and a temptation beset me, and I sate still. And it was said, All things come by nature; and the Elements and Stars came over me, so that I was in a moment quite clouded with it; but inasmuch as I sate still and said nothing, the people of the house perceived nothing. And as I sate still under it and let it alone, a living hope rose in me, and a true voice arose in me which cried: There is a living God who made all things. And immediately the cloud and temptation vanished away, and the life rose over it all, and my heart was glad, and I praised the living God."

Confused and disgusted by the Babel of tongues which prevailed in the religious world, and the opposite views of Scriptural truth presented by the different denominations, he came to the conclusion that no living teachers could instruct him in Divine things, and that he must act upon the inspiration which came direct to him from heaven. "He argued that, as the division of languages began at Babel, and as the persecutors of Christ put on the cross an inscription in Latin, Greek, and Hebrew, the knowledge of languages, and more especially of Latin, Greek, and Hebrew, must be useless to a Christian minister." This is his confused utterance on the subject: "What they know they know naturally, who turn from the command and err from the spirit, whose fruit withers, who saith that Hebrew, Greek, and Latin is the original:

before Babell was, the earth was one of language ; and Nimrod, the cunning hunter before the Lord, which came out of cursed Ham's stock, the originall and builder of Babell, whom God confounded with many languages, and this they say is the original who erred from the spirit and command; and Pilate had his original Hebrew, Greek, and Latin, which crucified Christ and set over him."

It was about 1647 that he began to teach publicly in the neighbourhood of Duckenfield and Manchester, whence he made his way through the midland and northern counties. Teaching more confused and extravagant has seldom been put before men, and yet it found many to listen and assent, because it dwelt so much on those minute regulations and observances which ignorant minds most keenly appreciate and readily seize hold of. " One of the precious truths which were divinely revealed to this new apostle was, that it was falsehood and adulation to use the second person plural instead of the second person singular. Another was, that to talk of the month of March was to worship the bloodthirsty god Mars, and that to talk of Monday was to pay idolatrous homage to the moon. To say Good morning or Good evening was highly reprehensible; for those phrases evidently imported that God had made bad days and bad nights. A Christian was bound to face death itself rather than touch his hat to the greatest of mankind. When Fox was challenged to produce any Scriptural authority for this dogma, he cited the passage in which it is written that Shadrach, Meshach, and Abednego were thrown into the fiery furnace with their hats on; and, if his own narrative may be trusted, the Chief Justice of England was altogether unable to answer this argument except by crying out, 'Take him away, gaoler.' . . . Bowing he strictly prohibited, and, indeed, seemed to consider it as the effect of Satanical influence; for, as he observed, the woman in the Gospel, while she had a spirit of infirmity, was bowed together, and ceased to bow as soon as Divine power had liberated her from the tyranny of the Evil One."

His Scriptural expositions were, in their way, not less absurd and irrational. Passages of the most literal character he construed figuratively; and as figurative passages he construed not less literally, his theology was a curious jumble. Such as it was, however, he taught it everywhere, and with almost heroical persistency; even forcing his way into churches, and interrupting the service or the sermon with loud contradictions and vehement assertions of doctrine. By these exploits he soon acquired the notoriety which, no doubt, he coveted. His strange face, his strange chant, his immovable hat, and his leather breeches were known all over the country; and he boasts that wherever the rumour was heard, "The man in leather breeches is coming," hypocritical professors were seized with alarm, and hireling priests took to flight. He was repeatedly imprisoned; at Derby he languished in a wretched cell for a twelvemonth, and at Carlisle for six months experienced from his gaoler the most brutal treatment. At Ulverstone he underwent the following harsh experience:—

"The people were in a rage, and fell upon me in the steeple-house before the justice's face, knocked me down, kicked me, and trampled upon me. So great was the uproar, that some tumbled over their seats for fear. At last he came and took me from the people, led me out of the steeple-house, and put me into the hands of the constables and other officers, bidding them whip me, and put me out of the town. Many friendly people being come to the market, and some to the steeple-house to hear me, divers of these they knocked down also, and broke their heads, so that the blood ran down several; and Judge Fell's son running after to see what they would do with me, they threw him into a ditch of water, some of them crying: 'Knock the teeth out of his head!' When they had hauled me to the common moss-side, a multitude following, the constables and other officers gave me some blows over my back with willow-rods, and thrust me among the rude multitude, who, having furnished themselves with staves, hedge-stakes, holm or holly bushes, fell upon me, and beat me upon the head, arms, and shoulders, till they had deprived me of sense; so that I fell down upon the wet common. When I recovered again, and saw myself lying in a watery common, and the people standing about me, I lay still a little while, and the power of the Lord sprang through me, and the eternal refreshings revived me, so that I stood up again in the strengthening power of the Eternal God, and stretching out my arms amongst them, I said with a loud voice: 'Strike again! here are my arms, my head, and cheeks!' Then they began to fall out among themselves."

The extravagances of Fox were, of course, out-Heroded by some of his disciples. He tells us that one of them walked naked through Skipton declaring the truth; and that another was divinely moved to go naked during several years to market places, and to the houses of the clergy and gentry. Yet he complains that these outrageous manifestations of fanatical indecency were requited by an unbelieving generation with hooting, and pelting, and the horsewhip. But though he applauded the zeal of his followers, some remains of natural modesty prevented him from imitating it. He sometimes indeed would cast off his outer raiment, or his shoes; but the article of attire from which he obtained his popular nickname he was always careful, however, to wear in public.

Throughout the Protectorate, and the reign of Charles II., and into the reign of William III., this strange prophet—who could never speak intelligibly—continued to expound his views, and gradually succeeded in organising his followers into a new sect. With the help of the more educated among them, such as Robert Barclay, Samuel Fisher, and George Keith, he reduced into some degree of system and form his teachings, and began to enforce a severe discipline. Later in life he visited Ireland, and the young colonies in North America, where he spent nearly two years in making converts to his doctrines. He died in London, in 1690, aged 66. On the morning of the day appointed for his funeral, a great multitude assembled round the meeting-house in Gracechurch Street. Thence the corpse was conveyed to the Quaker burial-ground near Bunhill Fields. Several orators addressed the crowd which filled it—among these, not the least distinguished of Fox's disciples, William Penn.

William Penn, to whom we have made brief allusion in the opening chapter of this book, was the son of Sir William Penn, the famous Admiral, and was born on the 14th of October, 1644, in St. Catherine's, near the Tower of London. When about eleven years old he was sent to School at Chigwell, where, being on one occasion in his chamber alone, "he was so suddenly surprised with an inward comfort, and (as he thought) an external glory in the room, that he has many times said how from that time he had the seal of divinity and immortality; that there was also a God, and that the soul of man was capable of enjoying His divine communications." This mental delusion was the effect, no doubt, of an excited imagination, nourished by the boy's solitary pondering over his mother's religious books.

The Admiral, having fallen into disgrace through the failure of the expedition against Hispaniola, removed his family, in 1656, to Ireland, where he had considerable estates, and while professing to be employed in their cultivation, engaged in plots for the restoration of the Stuart dynasty. His son, meantime, had the advantage of receiving instruction from a private tutor, and profited so largely by it that, at the age of 16, he was sent to Oxford, and entered at Christ Church as a gentleman commoner (1660). There a measure of fame accrued to him very speedily through the brilliancy of his scholarship and his skill in all manly accomplishments. But by degrees Penn awoke to a perception of higher and holier things; his religious instinct was revolted by the unbridled licence of the companions among whom he was thrown; and he began to dream dreams of a Commonwealth of Saints which, in the coming years, he hoped to erect upon enduring foundations among the leafy wildernesses of the New World.

At Oxford, about this time, the doctrines of Fox, the Quaker apostle, were very eagerly discussed. As expounded by one Thomas Loe, or Lowe, they attracted the attention of Penn and his fellow-students; and the apparent simplicity which distinguished them naturally exercised a powerful influence upon minds alarmed and excited by the Court favour extended to Romanism. They went frequently to Thomas Loe's prelections, and refrained from attending the College services. For their contumacy they were fined. Breaking then into open rebellion they stripped off the surplice, the use of which was enjoined by the authorities; and were thereupon expelled from the University. Penn's father, a man of worldly nature and a great supporter of "the powers that be," was so enraged at this untoward event, that when his son presented himself at home, he caused him to be whipped, and finally turned out of doors. Still the young man held to his view of what was right, and received and answered letters from the Calvinist Owen, whom his father suspected of leading his son astray. After a while the elder Penn relented; and in the hope, natural to a worldly mind, that change of scene might efface the old impressions by exciting new, he sent him on his travels.

At Paris Penn was introduced to the Court of Louis XIV. He plunged into the wild vortex of fashionable life, and his father's worldly wisdom seemed justified by the eagerness with which this bright and accomplished young man threw himself into the current of dissipation. One night, as he was passing through a dark street, he was stopped by a French gallant, and commanded to draw and defend himself. What offence had he given? The Frenchman accused him of not having returned the salute of courtesy with which he had approached him. Penn replied that he had never seen him; but his adversary would accept of no excuse, and threatened to cut him down with his sword. At this insult Penn's patience broke its last bonds, and forgetting the doctrines of George Fox, he drew his blade rapidly, and assumed a defensive attitude. By this time a crowd had gathered, who expected that Penn, as in a few passes he had disarmed his quarrelsome adversary, would take his life, in accordance with the laws of the *duello;* but, greatly to their admiration, he returned him his sword with a polite bow, and unconcernedly went on his way.

Receiving instructions from his father to remain for awhile in France, and resume his studies, he selected for his tutor the eminent theologian, Mons. Ancyrault, of Saumur, and applying himself most earnestly to work, acquired with considerable rapidity a comprehensive knowledge of French literature, as well as a considerable acquaintance with the writings of the early theologians. He then recommenced his travels, and visited Italy, but was recalled to England, in 1664, on the outbreak of the war with Holland. He reached London in August, and seems to have created quite "a sensation" in "polite circles." Gossip Pepys, after receiving a visit from the accomplished young traveller, records in his Diary that "something of learning he hath got, but a great deal, if not too much, of the vanity of the French garb, and affected manner of speech and gait." He had grown a handsome man, and his manners were perfect in their easy grace. "Tall and well-set, his figure promised physical strength and hardihood of constitution. His face was mild, and almost womanly in its beauty; his eyes soft and full; his brow open and ample; his features well-defined and approaching to the ideal Greek in contour; the lines about his mouth were exquisitely sweet, and yet resolute in expression. Like Milton, he wore his hair long and parted in the centre of the forehead, from which it fell over his neck and shoulders in massive natural ringlets. In mien and manners he seemed formed by nature and stamped by art—a gentleman." Such, at least, is Mr. Hepworth Dixon's somewhat imaginative portrait of the future Quaker.

He entered himself as a student at Lincoln's Inn; but almost before he could settle down to legal studies, was summoned to accompany his father on board his flag-ship, the *Loyal Charles*, in March, 1665. His experience of a naval life was only of three weeks' duration; for on the 23rd of April he landed at Harwich with despatches for the King, and instead of returning to the fleet, he withdrew to his chambers in Lincoln's Inn. In the month of June the Great Plague began its fearful ravages in London—an event to rouse the conscience of the most frivolous, for in hardly any shape is death more hateful; in none are its accessories more painful. The *one* spot of deadly omen; the livid, swollen body; the death-agony; the roughly-made coffin; the plague-cart for the putrid corpse; the solemn bell that woke the echoes of the night; the horrid pit into which were huddled the ghastly remains of humanity—such circumstances as these might stimulate even the most thoughtless to reflection. Upon Penn's naturally contemplative mind they produced a deep, ever-enduring impression; and when his father returned to England, flushed with the honours of victory, he found the gay and graceful Cavalier transformed into the grave and serious student. Court festivities had given place to disputations with learned men. Love poems and gay sonnets had been abandoned for theological and political treatises; authors and legal professors of repute substituted for the courtiers and the frail beauties who displayed their meretricious charms at Whitehall. The change does not seem to have been to the Admiral's taste. He desired his son to be a prosperous man of the world, continuing in the path he himself had trodden with so much success, and raising the race of Penn to a yet higher point of affluence and pride. To wean his son from what he considered to be an irrational asceticism, he despatched him to Ireland in the autumn of 1665, furnished with introductions to the Duke of Ormond, whose vice-regal court was almost as brilliant as, and certainly more decent than, the court of Charles II.

Penn was cordially received, and the gaieties which surrounded him soon appeared to have the effect anticipated by his father. He resumed the habits and tastes of a young man of fashion. When an insurrection broke out among the military at Carrickfergus, he accompanied Lord Arran as a volunteer on the expedition intended to reduce them to obedience, and displayed a courage and an intrepedity which procured him from the Duke of Ormond the offer of a captaincy of foot. His father, however, would not allow him to accept it; and Penn betook himself to the paternal estate at Shangarry, near Cork. On a visit to the latter town, he heard that Thomas Loe, the Oxford Quaker, was to preach there; and recollections of his student-days induced him to be present. Loe's text was well adapted to Penn's peculiar mental condition:— "There is a faith that overcomes the world, and there is a faith that is overcome by the world." Penn felt that he himself had long hesitated in the border-land; had long wavered between light and darkness, morning and night, the world of faith and the world of unbelief. Loe's voice came to his uncertain soul like that of a messenger from Heaven; and shaking off the social fetters imposed by custom and tradition, he went home that night with a new inspiration kindling in his heart: William Penn had become a Quaker.

He thenceforth attended regularly the meetings of the Friends; but, one evening in November, 1667, a company of soldiers breaking in upon their secret assembly—for the Quakers were then enduring the ordeal of a severe persecution—Loe and his fellow-worshippers were made prisoners, and committed to the town jail. Penn lost no time in communicating with his friend the Earl of Ossory, son of the Duke of Ormond, and obtained a speedy release. But great was the amazement at Court, the ridicule in the world of fashion, the consternation of Sir William Penn, when it was thus made known that his son and heir had joined the despised followers of George Fox! He recalled him to England, and at first, observing no change in his attire, no precisian cut or rigid formality in his clothes, comforted himself with the hope that curiosity, and not belief, had attracted his son to the meeting-house. He soon noticed, however, that he forbore to remove his hat in the company of his friends and superiors, and on inquiring the reason, ascertained that his first alarms had been well-founded. He assailed him with sarcasm, but his son's convictions were too strong to be shaken by so feeble a weapon. He plied him with argument, but found him his master in Scriptural knowledge and logical reasoning. A third course remained, and the angry sea-captain adopted it: he turned him out of doors. After awhile he relented so far as to allow him to return to his house, but he would not admit him into his presence. Though gifted with strong affections, the young man, for conscience sake, bore the parental anger patiently. He had already begun to expound and defend, with pen and voice, the doctrines he had embraced; and in 1668 he published his first book, under the title of "Truth Exalted in a Short but Sure Testimony against all those Religions, Faiths, and Worships, that have been formed and followed in the darkness of Apostasy; and for that glorious light which is now risen and shines forth in the Life and Doctrine of the despised Quakers, as the alone good old way of Life and Salvation. Presented to Princes, Priests, and Peoples, that they may repent, believe, and obey. By William Penn, whom Divine Love constrains in an holy contempt to trample on Egypt's glory, not fearing the King's wrath, having beheld the Majesty of Him who is Invisible." This was shortly followed by a severe polemic, "The Guide Mistaken," in reply to John Clapham's attack upon the Quakers in his "Guide to True Religion;" and by a well-written argument in favour of the Unitarian view of The Godhead—"The Sandy Foundation Shaken" —which Mr. Pepys read, and found "so well writ, as I think it is too good for him to have writ it: it is a serious sort of book," he adds, "and not fit for everybody to read." So thought the authorities of the Church, and at their instance he was committed to the Tower, where he lingered in a solitary cell for nearly nine months, debarred from all intercourse with his family and friends. His books, however, supplied him with social converse; his pen proved an agreeable companion; and the fruit of his enforced seclusion appeared in that elaborate folio of his, "No Cross no Crown," in which he illustrates the value of suffering as an agent of moral purification, and the power of Christian endurance to win the Christian victory. His own endurance the Bishop of London tested by causing him to be informed that the Bishop had resolved he should die in his dungeon unless he recanted his errors. "I do not heed their threats," he replied; "I will weary out their malice. Neither great nor good things were ever attained without loss and hardship. The man that would reap and not labour must perish in disappointment." Shortly afterwards he published a vindication of himself and his religious opinions, entitled "Innocency with her Open Face," which produced a favourable impression on the public. At the Duke of York's intercession he obtained an unconditional release; and departed for Ireland to resume the management of his father's property at Shangarry Castle.

This was in October, 1669. In the following June he returned to England, and enjoyed the happiness of being reconciled to his father. It was in the same year that Parliament renewed the infamous Conventicle Act, which inflicted on every person attending a conventicle or meeting-house a fine of 5s. for the first, and 10s. for the second offence, while a much heavier penalty fell upon the officiating minister. The Quaker assemblies had hitherto been connived at, but the law was now enforced without distinction; and when Penn and his co-religionists repaired to their chapel in Gracechurch Street, on the 14th of August, they found a detachment of soldiers posted at the doors, who prohibited their entrance. Penn, taking off his hat, had begun to address them, when immediately some constables forced their way through the crowd, and arrested him and another, Captain William Mead, a city draper, who had served the Commonwealth with his sword. When Penn demanded their authority, they produced a warrant from the Lord Mayor, before whom the two prisoners were carried for examination. He ordered the Quaker to remove his hat, and on Penn's refusal, threatened to send him to Bridewell, and direct that he should be well whipped; but warned against so monstrous a proceeding, he committed him and his companion to the Black Dog, a "sponging-house" of ill repute, in Newgate Market, to await their trial at the Old Bailey.

This remarkable trial took place on the 1st of September; "remarkable," for it contributed in no small degree to secure the liberties of the subject. It pivoted, so to speak, on one great question. Undoubtedly, the Conventicle Act was a violation of principles laid down in the Great Charter; but it had been passed by Parliament and sanctioned by the Crown. Could the assent of the Crown and Parliament legalize a measure which violated the ancient constitution of the realm? No, said Penn, and claimed for every Englishman four fundamental rights as descending to him from the Saxon period:— 1, Security of Property; 2, Security of Person; 3, A voice in the making of all laws relating to Property or Person; and, 4, A share, by means of the jury, in the actual administration of the Civil Law. These rights had been attacked in Penn's person, and were vindicated by Penn's courageous action. He defended himself with great spirit and ability, though the Court seized every opportunity to browbeat and confuse him.

Thus said the Recorder, violently, in reply to Penn's calm request, that he would inform him by what law he was prosecuted, and on what law the indictment was grounded—

"You must not think that I am able to sum up so many years, and ever so many adjudged cases, which we call common law, to satisfy your curiosity."

PENN—"This answer, I am sure, is very short of my question; for if it be common, it should not be so very hard to produce."

RECORDER (angrily)—"Sir, will you plead to your indictment?"

PENN—"Shall I plead to an indictment that has no foundation in law? If it contain that law you say I have broken, why should you decline to produce it, since it will be impossible for the jury to determine, or agree to bring in their verdict, who have not the law produced by which they should measure the truth of the indictment?"

RECORDER (passionately)—"You are a saucy fellow; speak to the indictment."

PENN—"I say it is my place to speak to matters of law. I am arraigned a prisoner. My liberty, which is next to life itself, is now concerned. You are many against me, and it is hard if I must not make the best of my case. I say again, unless you show me and the people the law you ground your indictment upon, I shall take it for granted your proceedings are merely arbitrary. . . ."

RECORDER (waiving this critical point)—"The question is, whether you are guilty of this indictment?"

PENN—"The question is, not whether I am guilty of this indictment, but whether this indictment be legal. It is too general and imperfect an answer to say it is common law, unless we know both where and what it is; for where there is no law there is no transgression; and that law which is not in being, so far from being common law, is no law at all."

RECORDER—"You are an impertinent fellow. Will you teach the Court what law is? It is *lex non scripta*. That which many have studied thirty or forty years to know, would you have me tell you in a moment?"

PENN—"Certainly, if the common law be so hard to be understood, it is far from being very common; but if the Lord Coke in his Institutes be of any weight, he tells us that 'common law is common right,' and common right is the great charter privileges confirmed by various enactments."

RECORDER—"Sir, you are a very troublesome fellow, and it is not for the honour of the Court to allow you to go on. . . . My Lord, if you do not take some course with this pestilent fellow to stop his mouth, we shall not be able to do anything to-night."

LORD MAYOR—"Take him away! Take him away! Put him into the bale-dock!"

And in the midst of a vigorous appeal to the jury, he was forcibly removed to the extreme end of the Court, where he could neither see nor be seen.

The Recorder then proceeded —

"You, gentlemen of the jury, have heard what the indictment is; it is for preaching to the people and drawing a tumultuous company after them; and Mr. Penn was speaking. If they shall not be disturbed, you see they will go on. There are three or four witnesses have proved this—that Mr. Penn did preach there, that Mr. Mead did allow of it. After this, you have heard by substantial witnesses what is said against them. Now we are on matter of fact, which you are to keep and to observe, as what hath been fully sworn, at your peril."

Here Penn from the bale-dock interrupted, in his loudest tones —

"I appeal to the jury who are my judges, and to this great assembly, whether the proceedings of the Court are not most arbitrary, and void of all law, in offering to give the jury their charge in the absence of the prisoners? I say it is directly opposed and destructive to the right of every English prisoner, as declared by Coke in the 2nd Institute, 29, on the chapter of Magna Charta."

RECORDER (with an affectation of humour)—"Why, you *are* present. You *do* hear; do you not?"

PENN—"No, thanks to the Court that commanded me into the bale-dock. And you of the jury, take notice that I have not been heard; neither can you legally depart the Court before I have been fully heard, having at least ten or twelve material points to offer in order to invalidate the indictment."

RECORDER (furiously)—"Pull that fellow down! Pull him down! Take him to the hole. To hear him talk doth not become the honour of the Court."

After the prisoners had been "haled away" to the squalidest of all the squalid dens in England, the "hole" in Newgate, the Recorder commanded the jury to agree in their verdict according to the facts sworn. They retired for consideration; but instead of returning immediately, as the judges anticipated, tarried thirty minutes—sixty minutes—an hour and a half! Then entered eight of the jurors, saying that they could not agree. The Recorder demanded the attendance of the other four, and immediately poured out upon them a flood of vituperation.

The jury withdrew a second time; and after two hours' absence, returned with a verdict of "Guilty of speaking in Gracechurch Street." An attempt was made to coerce or cajole them into altering it to "unlawful speaking;" but they manfully refused. "We have given in our verdict; we can give no other." They were sent back a third time; whereupon they sent in a verdict, "Guilty of speaking to an assembly met together in Gracechurch Street." In a storm of passion, the Lord Mayor pronounced their foreman "an impudent, canting knave." The Recorder exclaimed, "You shall not be dismissed till you bring in a verdict which the Court will accept. You shall be locked up, without meat, drink, fire, and tobacco. You shall not think thus to abuse the Court. We will have a verdict, by the help of God, or you shall starve for it!"

Penn—"The jury, who are my judges, ought not to be thus menaced. Their verdict should be free—not forced."

Recorder—"Stop that fellow's mouth, or put him out of Court!"

Lord Mayor (addressing the jury)—"You have heard that he preached; that he gathered a company of tumultuous people; and that they not only disobey the martial power, but the civil also."

Penn—"That is a mistake. We did not make the tumult, but they that interrupted us. The jury cannot be so ignorant as to think we met there to disturb the peace, because it is well known that we are a peaceable people, never offering violence to any man, and were kept by force of arms out of our own house. You are Englishmen," he said to the jurors; "mind your privileges: give not away your rights."

The jury were then locked up, and the prisoners carried back to Newgate. The next morning (Sunday) the Court was again crowded, and with anxiety chequered by hope the public awaited the reappearance of the jurors. At seven o'clock their names were called over, and the Clerk once more inquired if they had agreed upon a verdict. They replied in the affirmative. " Guilty, or not guilty?"

"Guilty of speaking in Gracechurch Street."

LORD MAYOR—"To an unlawful assembly?"

BUSHEL—"No, my lord; we give no other verdict than we gave last night."

LORD MAYOR—"You are a factious fellow; I'll take a course with you."

BUSHEL—"I have done according to my conscience."

LORD MAYOR—"That conscience of yours would cut my throat."

BUSHEL—"No, my lord, it never shall."

LORD MAYOR—"But I will cut yours as soon as I can."

RECORDER (jestingly)—"He has inspired the jury; he has the spirit of divination; methinks he begins to affect *me!* I will have a positive verdict, or else you shall starve."

PENN—"I desire to ask the Recorder a question. Do you allow the verdict given of William Mead?"

RECORDER—"It cannot be a verdict, because you are indicted for conspiracy; and one being found 'Not Guilty' and not the other, it is no verdict."

PENN—"If 'Not Guilty' be no verdict, then you make of the jury and of the Great Charta a mere nose of wax."

MEAD—"How? Is 'Not Guilty' no verdict?"

RECORDER—"It is no verdict."

PENN—"I affirm that the consent of a jury is a verdict in law; and if William Mead be not guilty, it follows that I am clear, since you have indicted us for conspiracy, and I could not possibly conspire alone."

Once more the unfortunate jurors were compelled to retire—only to persist in the verdict already given. The Recorder, carried by his wrath beyond the bounds of decency, exclaimed—"Your verdict is nothing. You play upon the Court. I say you shall go and bring in another verdict, or you shall starve; and I will have you carted about the city as in Edward the Third's time."

FOREMAN—"We have given in our verdict, in which we are all agreed; if we give in another, it will be by force, to save our lives."

LORD MAYOR—"Take them up to their room."

OFFICER—"My lord, they will not go."

The jurors were constrained to withdraw—actual violence being used—and locked up without food and water. Exposed to this harsh treatment, some weaker minds wavered, and would have given way but for the courageous resolution of Bushel, and others like Bushel, who understood the importance of the question at issue. So when, on Monday morning, the Court once more summoned the jurors, there was not, though they had fasted two days and nights, a traitor or coward among them. Wan and worn were they, with hunger, fatigue, and a not unnatural anxiety, but determined to do justice to their fellow-men, arraigned, as they knew, on a false charge.

CLERK—"Gentlemen, are you agreed upon your verdict?"

JURY—"Yes."

CLERK—"Who shall speak for you?"

JURY—"Our foreman."

CLERK—"Look upon the prisoners. What say you: is

William Penn guilty of the matter whereof he stands indicted in manner and form, or not guilty?"

FOREMAN—"You have your verdict in writing."

CLERK—"I will read it."

RECORDER—"No, it is no verdict. The Court will not accept it."

FOREMAN—"If you will not accept of it, I desire to have it back again."

COURT—"The paper was no verdict, and no advantage shall be taken of you for it."

CLERK—How say you: is William Penn guilty or not guilty?"

FOREMAN (resolutely)—"*Not Guilty.*"

RECORDER—"I am sorry, gentlemen, you have followed your own judgments and opinions rather than the good advice which was given you. God keep my life out of your hands! But for this the Court fines you forty marks a man, and imprisonment in Newgate till the fines be paid."

PENN—"Being freed by the jury, I demand to be set at liberty."

LORD MAYOR—"No; you are in for your fines."

PENN—"Fines! What fines?"

LORD MAYOR—"For contempt of Court."

PENN—"I ask if it be according to the fundamental laws of England that any Englishman should be fined except by the judgment of his peers? Since it expressly contradicts the 14th and 29th chapters of the Great Charter of England, which says, 'No free man ought to be amerced except by the oath of good and lawful the vicinage.'"

RECORDER—"Take him away; put him out of the Court."

Penn—"I can never urge the fundamental laws of England, but you cry out, 'Take him away! take him away!' But this is no wonder, since the Spanish Inquisition sits so near the Recorder's heart. God, who is just, will judge you all for these things."

The prisoners and the jurors refusing to pay the fines so arbitrarily inflicted upon them, were removed to Newgate. The latter, at Penn's instigation, immediately brought an action against the Lord Mayor and the Recorder for having imprisoned them in defiance of law and justice. It was argued on the 9th of November, before the twelve judges, who unanimously decided in favour of the appellants. They were immediately released, and Penn went forth triumphant, having struck one effectual blow in vindication of the liberties of the subject.

"Son William," said Admiral Sir William Penn, as he lay on his death-bed, a man prematurely old—broken down by a life of action and adventure—"Son William, if you and your friends keep to your plain way of preaching, and also keep to your plain way of living, you will make an end of priests to the end of the world." In this prediction he was wrong, as latter-day prophets usually are; but his saying is worthy to be noted as a proof of the influence exercised upon the old sea-king's impetuous temper by his son's quiet steadiness in well-doing. He died on the 16th of September, ten days after his son's release, and was buried in the parish church of St. Mary Redclyffe, in the city of Bristol. On his deathbed he recommended his son to the favour of the Duke of York, and also solicited for him the King's protection. Penn was appointed sole executor, and inherited an estate valued at £1,500 per annum, in addition to claims on the

Crown for moneys lent and arrears of salary, amounting to about £15,000.

It was about this time that Penn made the acquaintance of Gulielma Maria, the fair daughter of Sir William Springett, a strict Puritan soldier, who died during the siege of Arundel Castle, a few weeks before his daughter's birth. She lived with her mother, who had married a second time, and chosen a man of worth and capacity, the celebrated Isaac Pennington, at Chalfont, in Buckinghamshire; in the immediate neighbourhood of the poet Milton, and Milton's friend and pupil, the Quaker Ellwood. Pennington was a follower of George Fox; and it was their mutual interest in the doctrines of the New Light that led to Penn's visit to Chalfont, and consequent introduction to his co-religionist's step-daughter, with whom he immediately fell in love. "She was a very desirable woman," says Ellwood, "whether regard was had to her outward person, which wanted nothing to render her comely; or to the endowments of her mind, which were very extraordinary and highly obliging; or to her outward fortune, which was fair." To Penn's grave and earnest attachment she responded with all the warmth of maidenhood.

The young Quaker, meanwhile, was active in his vocation. He published an exposure of the treatment to which he had been subjected at the Old Bailey, under the title of "Truth rescued from Imposture;" as well as a "Caveat against Popery," not less moderate in tone than cogent in reasoning. The former production roused against him some untiring enemies in the civic authorities, who eagerly watched for—and soon found—an opportunity to make their vengeance felt. Going from Chalfont to

London, he attended, as was his wont, the Quaker meeting-house in Wheeler Street; but while preparing to address the brethren, was seized by a troop of cavalry, and hurried off to the Tower. This was on the 5th of February, 1671. In the Tower he was confronted by his most determined persecutors, and subjected to a rigorous and insulting examination. An attempt was made to force upon him the oath of allegiance; but Penn refused to subscribe, on the ground that his conscience forbade him to take up any arms, whether for his Sovereign or against his own foes.

Sir John Robinson—"I am sorry you put me upon this severity. It is no pleasant work to me."

Penn—"These are but words. It is manifest that this is a prepense malice. Thou hast several times laid the meetings for me, and this day particularly."

Robinson—"No. I profess I could not tell you would be there."

Penn—"Thine own corporal told me that you had intelligence at the Tower that I should be at Wheeler Street to-day, almost as soon as I knew it myself. This is disingenuous and partial. I never gave thee occasion for such unkindness."

Robinson—"I knew no such thing; but if I had, I confess I should have sent for thee."

Penn—"That confession might have been spared. I do heartily believe it."

Robinson—"I vow, Mr. Penn, I am sorry for you. You are an ingenious gentleman, all the world must allow that; and you have a plentiful estate. Why should you render yourself unhappy by associating with such a simple people?"

Penn—"I confess I have made it my choice to relinquish the company of those that are ingeniously wicked, to converse with those who are more honestly simple."

Robinson—"I wish thee wiser."

Penn—"I wish *thee* better."

Robinson—"You have been as bad as other folks."

Penn—"When and where? I charge thee tell the company to my face."

Robinson—"Abroad, and at home too."

Sheldon—"No, no, Sir John. That's too much."

Penn—"I make this bold challenge to all men, justly to accuse me with ever having heard me swear, utter a curse, or speak one obscene word—much less that I make it my practice. Thy words shall be my burden, and I trample thy slander under my feet."

Eventually, Sir John Robinson committed him to Newgate for six months—a sentence which drew from Penn this noble declaration:—"I would have thee and all men know that I scorn that religion which is not worth suffering for, and able to sustain those that are afflicted for its sake. I leave you all," he added, "in perfect charity."

During his six months' imprisonment, Penn's intellect was very active, and he composed and published four polemical treatises:—"Truth rescued from Imposture," "The Great Case of Liberty of Conscience," "An Apology for the Quakers," and "A Postscript to Truth Exalted."

He was released in July, 1671, and, crossing over to the Continent, he visited Holland and Germany, making known the principles of the New Doctrine, and founding several small Quaker colonies. On his return to England, he renewed his suit to Gulielma Springett, and their marriage took place in February, 1672. After some months of domestic happiness at Rickmansworth, he returned to active life, and resumed his missionary labours, accompanied, sometimes by his wife, sometimes by the leaders of his sect, the enthusiastic Fox and the learned Barclay. With singular indefatigability of purpose, he wrote treatise after treatise, pamphlet upon pamphlet, all of a controversial character; of these he gave to the world no fewer than six-and-twenty, besides his two political essays, "On Oaths," and "England's Present Interest Considered." They may be read by the curious in the collected edition of Penn's works; but we cannot attribute to them that literary merit which is claimed for them by some of his fervent admirers, nor can we say that they are free from that intemperance of language which distinguishes the polemical writings of the period.

Penn's next occupation was to draw up a constitution for a Quaker colony settled in West New Jersey, in North America; for the time it was a singular concession to democratic ideas. While allowing the widest tolerance to different forms of religious belief, he was not less liberal in his political views; providing for the election of the people's representatives by vote by ballot, and conferring the franchise upon every adult man free from crime. Trial by jury was instituted; imprisonment for debt was disallowed; the maintenance of orphans was charged upon the State; and other not less wise and salutary enactments showed that the constitution-maker was far in advance, not only of his own, but of many succeeding generations. The colony proved completely successful, and attracted within its borders a constantly increasing number of settlers: the settlement in its result proving that the dreams of Harrington and Algernon Sidney, the fancies of Sir Thomas

More and Lord Bacon, were not so Utopian as the wits had imagined. It was the adumbration of that Christian commonwealth which Penn afterwards founded amid the pathless solitudes of Pennsylvania.

In 1677 we find him, accompanied by Fox and Barclay, visiting Holland and Germany, to encourage and reorganize the scattered settlements of the Friends, and diffuse the radiance of the New Light. We can trace the three Quaker Apostles to Rotterdam, Leyden, Hawerden, and Haarlem. After an absence of four months, Penn returned to England. Over the incidents of the next three years we must pass at a bound. His friendship with Algernon Sidney and his advocacy of civil and religious rights, gradually estranged from him the confidence and favour of Charles II. and the Duke of York; and it was not without difficulty that, in 1681, he obtained, in lieu of the large sum of money owing to him by the Crown, a grant of a large tract of unoccupied Crown-land in North America, covering 47,000 square miles, and extending 300 miles in length by 160 miles in breadth. On the 5th of March, however, he was summoned to attend the Council at Whitehall, and the charter which conveyed to him that noble domain was then signed and sealed. Penn had proposed to call the province, in allusion to its hilly character, *New Wales;* but as Secretary Blathwayte, a Welshman, objected to this use of his country's appellation, he substituted *Sylvania,* on account of its vast forests, and King Charles good-humouredly prefixed the syllable *Penn,* in compliment to the memory of his great Admiral. As Penn stood covered in the royal presence, he observed that Charles removed his hat. " Friend Charles," he exclaimed, " why dost thou not keep on thy hat?" " Because," retorted the King, with a smile, "it is the custom of this place for only one person to remain covered at a time!"

Having obtained his charter, the legislator assiduously addressed himself to the task of devising "a complete scheme of government," in which he had the assistance of Algernon Sidney. Penn at this time was residing with his family at Warminghurst, in Sussex, and it was there that the two law-givers carefully laid down those political principles which afterwards inspired the constitution of the United States. It was their object "to support power in reverence with the people, and to secure the people from the abuse of power; that they might be free by their just obedience, and the magistrates honourable for their just administration." They provided two legislative bodies, a council and an assembly, to be elected by the people. They instituted universal suffrage, vote by ballot, and payment of members. They required no property qualifications for their representatives; they divided the province into convenient electoral districts; they allowed the free exercise of every religious belief, and maintained by careful enactments the security of person and property.

As soon as the details of Penn's proposed scheme of government became known, numerous emigrants presented themselves to treat for lands in a state which promised to be so happily ruled, and before the end of the year were on their way to the New World. As early as April, Penn had despatched his cousin, Colonel Markham, as his lieutenant, to settle the boundary-lines, take possession of the province, and open up amicable negotiations with the Indians; a task which he executed with much dexterity.

Penn had determined that no arms should be borne in his new colony, and had resolved to trust, in his intercourse with the aborigines, to the power of truth, justice, and humanity.

Having attended the death-bed of his beloved mother, and completed such arrangements as in case of his own death might provide for the comfort of his wife and children, Penn took his departure from Deal on the 1st of September. Unfortunately a great disaster clouded his voyage at the outset. The small-pox broke out on board the crowded ship, and carried off upwards of thirty victims. On the 27th of October the *Welcome* arrived at Newcastle, a settlement in the Delaware territory which Penn had purchased from the Duke of York. His landing was the signal for a general rejoicing; men, women and children, Dutch, Germans, and English, flocked to the shore to welcome their governor, father, and friend. Next day, at a general assembly, the deeds and charters which had made Penn proprietor and governor of Pennsylvania, were read: after which, in a speech glowing with noble feeling, he explained his principles of government, promising to every person an equal and a fair share of political power and freedom of conscience. The governor and his companions then began their voyage up the river Delaware, with eager eyes surveying its wooded banks, and the vistas of shadowy valley and misty hill-top which were occasionally opened up through breaks in the far-spreading forest. The name of the Swede settlement of Optland he changed to that of Chester; and there he convoked the first General Assembly of Pennsylvania, to adopt, with such modifications and additions as might seem desirable, the constitution of which he was the author.

After visiting the capitals of the neighbouring provinces of New York, Maryland, and New Jersey, Penn proceeded to complete the organisation of his new settlement: dividing the land into lots, he sold it at 4d. per acre, with a reserve of 1s. per hundred acres as quit-rent, to form a revenue for the support of the governor and proprietor. Certain equal allotments were appropriated to his children; and two manors of ten thousand acres each reserved as a present for his patron, the Duke of York. A thousand acres, free of every charge, were set apart for the founder of the Society of Friends, George Fox.

For the capital of his state he selected an admirable site on a narrow neck of land, which extended between the two navigable rivers of the Delaware and Schuylkill. The banks were high, and open to genial winds; the soil was fertile, the air mild and salubrious. Here he marked out the plan of a noble city. Its area was to occupy twelve square miles; each river was to be overlooked by a street of bold design, and bordered by a public promenade; and these streets were to be linked together by the High Street, a splendid avenue, one hundred feet in width, to be lined with trees, and its houses enriched with gardens. A street of equal width, Broad Street, was to bisect the city from north to south, crossing High Street at a right-angle. At the junction-point of these four avenues was reserved a space of ten acres, for a public piazza or square, and other provisions were made to secure the healthiness and beauty of the new capital; which, in allusion to the great principle that underlay Penn's theory of government, the founder appropriately named *Philadelphia* (or Brotherly Love).

The new colony attracted to its shores a constant stream

of emigration. In a few months no fewer than twenty-three vessels disembarked their hundreds of adventurers at the mouth of the Delaware; and Penn could boast that, in Philadelphia, eighty houses and cottages were ready; that artisan, merchant, and trader were busy in buying and selling; that farms were springing up in fertile places; and that the land rescued from the wilderness already began to bloom with golden corn. At the end of three years the new city contained six hundred houses, and there were nearly as many thriving farms in the surrounding country.

The early part of Penn's career as a governor was marked by an interesting incident. Having arranged with the aboriginal Indians the terms of purchase of their lands, and concluded various treaties of peace and amity, he proposed to the native chiefs that a solemn conference should be held for the confirmation of the New Alliance.* The spot selected was a natural amphitheatre which ran gradually from the bank of the Delaware, in the immediate neighbourhood of the young city of Philadelphia, and to the Indians was known as *Shackamuxon*, or "the meeting-place of kings." Here a venerable elm, which already had endured the storms of a hundred and fifty winters—which now beheld the scattered houses of the white men, but was destined (for it flourished until 1810) to witness the growth of a mighty city on the bank of the sister-rivers—spread abroad its leafy shade. In the distance, against the deep blue heaven, was defined the undulating crest of a range of mountain heights; while the foreground was occupied by an immense forest of pine and cedar, stretching far away into the hunting-grounds of the red men. Surely the stage was not an inappropriate

* November 30, 1682.

one for the dramatic scene which was to be enacted upon it! As for the actors, they too presented some striking and unusual features. Chief among them stood William Penn, the Founder of the New Commonwealth, his only badge of authority a silken sash, but showing in his mien and bearing that he was a man among men, a born leader and ruler. His costume consisted of an outer coat reaching to the knee; a vest of nearly the same length; of trunks ample in dimensions, slashed at the sides, and tied at the knees with ribbons; of ruffles at the wrist, and a snowy fold of cambric round the neck, ending in a fall of lace; and a hat of cavalier shape, but innocent of feathers, surmounting a peruke of many curls. At his right hand stood Colonel Markham, his lieutenant; another trusty and trusted adherent, Pearson, on his left; and in the rear, a group of his principal followers. The Indian Sachems appeared in their native attire. A mantle of furs fell from the shoulder, the loins were girded with cloth, a head-dress of feathers waved in the wind, and the bright hues of their painted bodies glowed yet brighter in the sun. Taminent, their leader, having placed on his head a chaplet, into which a small horn was woven—a token that the place was thenceforth sacred, and the persons of all who assembled there inviolable—the Sachems seated themselves on the ground in order of seniority, and prepared, with their Indian taciturnity, to hear what Onas, as they had named the white chief, might wish to say to them. Penn spoke to them in their own language. His words were not many, but they were to the purpose, and testified to the anxiety felt by the white men to live with the red men in peace and good-will. He then produced the Treaty of Friendship, which declared that in all time to come "the children of Onas and the natives of the Lenni Lenapé" should be as brothers; that all roads and ways should be held as free and open; that if any white man injured a red man, or any red man inflicted harm upon a white man, the sufferer should lay his complaint before the proper authorities, and the case be investigated by twelve impartial men, and the injury buried "in a bottomless pit;" that the Lenni Lenapé and the white men should help each other in their time of need; and, lastly, that both should transmit to their descendants this chain of friendship, to the intent that it might yearly grow stronger and brighter, and be kept free from rust or blemish, so long as the water ran down the creeks and rivers, and the sun, moon, and stars gave light to earth.

Taminent immediately announced the assent of the Indian Sachems to this remarkable treaty; the only one, says Voltaire, the world has known that was never ratified by oath, and never broken.

Penn returned to England in August, 1684. He was summoned thither by urgent private affairs; and on his arrival was received with much favour by Charles II. and the Duke of York, the latter of whom, within a few months, succeeded to the throne. Penn was at once enrolled among the courtiers of the new sovereign. This is a period of his career which no honest biographer can regard with unmingled satisfaction; for we cannot think that Mr. Paget, in his "New Examen," with all his skill and enthusiasm, has succeeded in vindicating it completely from Macaulay's censures. It may be admitted, however, that he endeavoured to turn his influence to good account; that he pleaded the cause of Locke, who had been driven into exile for no other offence than that he was the friend of Shaftesbury; and had interceded on behalf of Monmouth's misguided partisans.

One of the unhappy victims of the "reign of terror" which prevailed after the victory of Sedgemoor was Henry Cornish, formerly a pensioner of Algernon Sidney, and latterly a friend of Penn. Having provoked the anger of Charles II. and his Court by the frankness and courage of his opinions, he had been accused of complicity in the Rye House Plot (1683), but on such untenable grounds that his persecutors were fain to withdraw the charge. After Monmouth's rebellion the attack was renewed, and supported by bribed witnesses. The mockery of a trial was played out; a verdict of Guilty extorted from a reluctant but timid jury; and the unfortunate man was hung upon a gibbet erected in front of his own house in Cheapside. He suffered with the calmness of a hero, protesting to the last his innocence. Penn, who had failed in his efforts to obtain a commutation of the cruel sentence, attended him to the scaffold. He was afterwards present at the last scene in the life of another victim of the King's tyranny, for whom he had also interceded, and in vain, Elizabeth Garnet. This admirable woman was an Anabaptist, who had devoted her time and fortune to the relief of the miserable inmates of the London prisons—anticipating by nearly a century and a half Mrs. Elizabeth Fry's noble work of charity—and after the battle of Sedgemoor had sheltered in her house a fugitive from that fatal field. He repaid her generosity by informing against her, earning his own wretched life by betraying his protectress. For this venial violation of the law she was arrested, tried, and burned alive at Tyburn.

Her sufferings, and the fortitude with which she endured them—calmly arranging the faggots and straw around her so as to increase the violence of the flames—produced a most painful impression upon the spectators, so that many were affected even to tears.

It was not long after these judicial murders that the perjury of the witnesses who had sworn away the life of Cornish was clearly proved. James seemed shocked that he had consented to the execution of an innocent man; restored his estates to his family; and sentenced his murderers to perpetual imprisonment.

The influence which Penn exercised over James II., and his daily attendance at Court, soon originated a report that he was a Papist in disguise. It is the misfortune of men in advance of their age that their best and wisest actions are always subjected to the most malignant construction, and Penn was in advance of his age on the question of religious tolerance. A strong bond of sympathy undoubtedly existed between the King and himself, because both were members of religious bodies which had been subjected to a common persecution and proscription. But this fact was not perceived or not understood by his contemporaries, and even the judicious and amiable Tillotson adopted the popular belief. A casual acquaintance asked Penn, one day, how it was that Barclay and himself were such ardent lovers of literature, when the Friends affected to despise it? Penn replied that it was probably owing, in his case, to his early education at Saumur. His interrogator had no ear for French, and went about repeating that the Quaker had acknowledged himself to have been educated at the famous Jesuit College of St. Omar! Penn laughed at these calumnies until they seemed in some measure countenanced by Tillotson, his intimate acquaintance, when he addressed him with his usual frankness, and so clearly and strongly vindicated his acceptance of the leading doctrines of Protestantism, that the divine averred his full conviction "that there was no just ground for his suspicion, and therefore did heartily beg his pardon for it."—(April 29th, 1686.)

It was at this time that James II. meditated a repeal of the Test Acts, which required from every candidate for public office a declaration of his adhesion to the Church of England; but finding his Parliament hostile to any measure which afforded relief to the Roman Catholics, he dispensed with these Acts by virtue of his own authority. Anxious in this critical state of affairs to obtain the support of William of Orange, who was regarded throughout Christendom as the champion and shield of Protestantism, he dispatched Penn to the Hague on a private and confidential mission. If the Prince would support James in the repeal of the Test Acts and the passing of an Act of Toleration, Penn was instructed to promise him assistance in his opposition to the aggressive power of France. But however liberal might be William's private views, he was not disposed to risk his chance of succession to the throne of England by openly contravening the feeling and opinion of the country; so that while expressing his willingness to accept an Act of Toleration, he objected to the proposed repeal of the Test Acts. In all ecclesiastical questions he was guided by Bishop Burnet, then an exile in Holland, who cherished a strong dislike for Penn, and chose to regard him as a "concealed Papist." "He was a talking, vain man," says the malicious prelate, "who had been long in the King's favour. He had such an opinion of his own faculty of persuading, that he thought none could stand before it; though he was singular in that opinion; for he had a tedious luscious way, that was not apt to overcome a man's reason, though it might tire his patience."

Having failed in his mission, Penn returned to England by way of Holland and Germany. He continued his attendance at Court, endeavouring to check the King in the arbitrary career on which he had unwisely entered, and striving to counteract the Jesuitical influence that so injuriously affected his actions. He showed him that Parliament would not consent to a revocation of the Test and Penal Acts, and that no concord could exist between him and his Parliament until he acted on more moderate counsels, and expelled from his Court the Jesuits and violent Papists who were urging him to his speedy ruin. When he issued his Declaration of Indulgence to all religious denominations, Penn warned him that to the popular mind it would seem only an ingenious device for the extension of more favour and the concession of greater power to the Papists, and that it was imperative he should not put it into operation without the sanction of the legislature. In the King's arbitrary interference with the rights of the Fellows of Magdalen College, Oxford, Penn boldly stood forward as their uncompromising advocate. When his honest expostulations were ignored, he would fain have retired to his commonwealth across "the western wave," and remained in England only at the urgent request of the King, who declared himself resolute to repeal the Penal Laws against religious sects, and establish toleration; "in which good work," he said, "he should have to rely much on Penn's help and counsel."

It is not within our province to dwell upon the events of the last few months of James's disastrous reign. When William III. arrived in the capital, those of the late King's councillors who had not betrayed him fled from the country, but Penn remained. He was conscious that he had done nothing but his duty, and believed that he had no reason to fear any man. He no longer, he said, owed allegiance to James as a King, but should still respect him as his friend and patron. His favour with the late King, however, had kept alive suspicion; and, being regarded as a Papist concealed under the mask of a Quaker, he was summoned before the Privy Council in December, 1688, and though no charge was proved against him, compelled to give security in £6,000 for his appearance on the first day of the following term. At Easter he appeared, but no accusers came forward, and "the judge in open court declared that he stood cleared and free of any charge that had been made against him."

This long friendship with the exiled King afforded his enemies, however, a foundation on which they continued to base their calumnies. In the spring of 1690, when the country was disturbed with alarms of a French invasion, he was suddenly arrested on the pretext that he was engaged in a treasonable correspondence with James Stuart. Being examined before William himself, he satisfactorily disproved the accusation; but was nevertheless bound over to appear in Trinity term, and answer any charges that might be preferred against him. At the appointed time he duly presented himself, but was immediately discharged.

For a third time in the same year he was exposed to persecution. He was accused of having joined in Lord Preston's conspiracy to restore the deposed monarch, and though the accusation was unsupported by a tittle of evidence, William profited by it to deprive him of the right of appointing a governor to his colony of Pennsylvania. At this very juncture Penn had engaged a ship to carry him to the New World; but the illness and death of George Fox detained him awhile in England. He attended his funeral, and over his grave delivered a glowing panegyric. Just as the crowd dispersed, and when Penn had left the ground, a posse of constables, armed with warrants, arrived to take him into custody on another charge of treason and conspiracy, preferred against him by William Fuller, the "Titus Oates" of the reign of William III. Weary of struggling against the malice of his foes, and unable through his conscientious scruples to deny "upon oath" the charges invented against him, Penn sought safety in seclusion. Meantime the King appointed Colonel Fletcher Governor of Pennsylvania—a soldier over the heads of peaceful Quakers!—and Penn's anxiety for the welfare of his young commonwealth increased daily. Nor did his domestic affairs fail to trouble him. In order that his colony might not be burdened with pecuniary liabilities, he had maintained the government out of his private means, expending not less than £120,000. His estates in Ireland had been confiscated; while, at home, his lands in Kent and Essex hardly sufficed to meet the immense claims advanced by a dishonest steward, John Forde, in whom he had placed his entire confidence. Locke now came to the front to repay the kindness shown to him by Penn in his days of prosperity, and interceded for his pardon. But the Quaker protested that he had done no wrong, and that, therefore, no pardon was needful. He threw himself, he said, upon the King's justice, not upon his mercy. He would not receive his liberty upon any conditions.

A greater affliction than all now befell him, for those whom Heaven loves most it chastens most. Worse than loss of fortune, loss of fame, or the wreck of his hopes and anticipations was the death of his loved and loving wife, Gulielma Maria, at Hoddesdon, in Hertfordshire, on the 23rd of February, 1693. Her husband's sufferings, sorrows, and misfortunes brought her to a premature grave, though a kind Providence spared her long enough to see the sunshine breaking through the heavy clouds and the bright dawn slow-reddening upon the stormy night.

The infamy of Fuller having been publicly demonstrated, and the House of Commons having branded him as a rogue, cheat, and false witness, many of Penn's most influential friends interfered to procure his restoration to the position of which he had been deprived upon Fuller's single and unsupported evidence. They pressed his case with so much earnestness that William summoned a Council at Westminster (in November, 1692), before whom Penn defended himself with such force and clearness that the King declared his entire satisfaction, and absolved him from all the charges at various times preferred against him. His enforced retirement, however, had not been without profit: its results were two works of widely different character, but of equal merit—"An Essay towards the Present and Future Peace of Europe" and "Some Fruits of Solitude."

We must pass rapidly over the next six years. Through

Queen Mary's generous action he was reinstated in his government of Pennsylvania; the military commission was revoked; and he was bound simply to maintain eighty men, fully armed and equipped, as the contingent to be furnished by his State, so long as the war with France lasted. In January, 1696, having found the need of a woman's gentle hand to keep order in his household, he married, at Bristol, Hannah Callowhill, by whom he had six children. In the following April he lost his eldest son (by his first wife), Springett, in the twenty-first year of his age. He seems to have been a young man of rare promise. After paying a brief visit to his Irish estates in the summer of 1698, Penn received intelligence of growing troubles and dissensions in Pennsylvania, which determined him to go there with a view to the reform of its administration. He embarked, with his wife and all his children, except William, the eldest surviving son, in September, 1699, and in December arrived at Philadelphia, where he was received with an enthusiastic welcome. The settlers hailed him as their father and friend, whose presence would compose all differences, and whose authority would reduce chaos into order. Nor were they disappointed in their expectations. With equal sagacity, judgment, and resolution he reformed the numerous abuses which had crept into the administration of the State, put down the contraband trade from which the colony had long been suffering, dismissed corrupt and incompetent officers, healed the jealousies of faction, and encouraged the development of commercial enterprise by many wise and liberal measures. Meanwhile, at his mansion of Pennsbury, he maintained a decorous state. He had his carriages, his horses, and his yacht, for Penn, though a

Quaker, was no Pharisaical precisian; he kept his cellar of rare wines; his house was splendidly furnished; he loved to see his table well supplied; his daughters dressed like gentlewomen; he himself was choice, though plain, in his attire; his gardens were planted with the most beautiful shrubs and flowers; and everywhere prevailed a spirit of calm contentment, due, no doubt, to the mild and genial influence of the master. "To innocent dances and country fairs," says Mr. Hepworth Dixon, "he not only made no objection, but countenanced them by his own and his family's presence. Those gentle charities which had distinguished him in England continued to distinguish him in Pennsylvania: he released the poor debtor from prison; he supported out of his private purse the sick and the destitute; many of the aged who were beyond labour and without friends were regular pensioners on his bounty to the extent of six shillings a fortnight: and there were numerous persons about him whom he had rescued from distress in England, and whom he supported, wholly or in part, until their own industry made them independent of his assistance."

While he was thus displaying his practical commonsense, and building up securely the structure of his new commonwealth, affairs in England were taking a direction entirely adverse to his just rights and legitimate interests. The English Government was developing a measure, necessary in itself though harsh in its incidence upon individuals, which proposed to annihilate the great colonial proprietaries and weld the separate states into a homogeneous colonial system. Such a measure must inevitably deprive Penn, and men like Penn, of the fruits of their pecuniary outlay, their labour, and their enterprise, by wresting from them the settlements which they had founded and carefully nursed into prosperity. The owners of Pennsylvanian property then in England succeeded, however, in procuring a postponement of the bill until Penn could return to plead their cause and his own; but they sent urgent messages to the founder of their colony to return to England at once if he would prevent an act of shameful spoliation.

Penn made haste to comply: he left Philadelphia on the 16th of September, 1701, and arrived in England about the middle of December. But in the interval a great change had taken place in the position of affairs. William III. was dead, and in the seat of that sagacious statesman-king sat the narrow-minded Anne. The Stuarts, however, had a hereditary liking for Penn, and Anne immediately welcomed him to her Court, and showed him in many ways her royal favour. No more was heard of the obnoxious Colonies Bill. Penn took up his residence at Knightsbridge, and afterwards, in 1706, at Brentford. There he was living in peace and contentment when the event occurred which overclouded his later years. He had long entrusted the management of his affairs to Philip Ford, a Quaker, who died in 1702, after having abused his master's generous confidence by wholesale fraud and embezzlement. "The lawyer," says Mr. Hepworth Dixon, "knew how to take advantage of his client's want of worldly prudence; and in an evil hour, when Penn needed money to go over to America the second time, he induced him to give him—as a mere matter of form—a deed of sale of the colony, on which he advanced him £2,800. This deed was considered by Penn, and professedly considered by Ford, as a mortgage. Ford received money on account of the province, and made such advances as the governor required; and it was not until the latter returned to England that the first suspicion of his steward's villany crossed his mind. He was loath to entertain it, and tried for a time to think himself deceived. But as soon as the old Quaker died his knavery came to the full light of day. Penn, from his uncertain remembrance of the various sums advanced and received, believed the mortgage—or deed of sale—to be nearly cancelled; but the funeral rites were hardly paid to the dead before the widow sent in a bill for £14,000, and threatened to seize and sell the province if it were not immediately paid."

A careful examination of the accounts and papers which Penn had fortunately preserved showed, however, that while Ford had received £17,859, he had paid on Penn's account only £16,200, so that his estate was indebted to Penn in a sum of £1,659. Desirous of sparing the Quaker community a public scandal, Penn proposed that the whole matter at dispute should be referred to arbitration; but Ford's representatives took advantage of the written instrument, the deed of sale, to enforce their unjust claim. On a thorough examination taking place, it appeared that Penn, on the said deed of sale, owed £4,303, which he offered to pay; but his enemies knew they had him in their power, as the deed was uncancelled, —threw the case into Chancery, obtained a verdict against him, attempted to arrest him while he was attending service in Gracechurch Street, and eventually drove him for security into the Fleet prison. He found lodgings in the Old Bailey, within what were then termed "the rules," or jurisdiction, of the Fleet. At length, to get free of his trials and anxieties, he consented, after a painful mental struggle, to mortgage his beloved Pennsylvania for the sum of £6,800, advanced by several friends, while he sold his Sussex estate at Warminghurst for £6,050.

The air of London disagreeing with his constitution, shaken as it was by confinement and severe mental suffering, Penn took a country house at Ruscombe, in Berkshire in 1710, and spent there his remaining years. In the early part of 1712 he was seized with a fit of paralysis, which seriously affected his intellectual powers. On his partial recovery he again directed his attention to his Western Commonwealth; but the effort proved too much for the enfeebled brain, and a second attack of paralysis resulted in October, 1712. Once more he recovered, slowly and imperfectly, but only to undergo a third and more violent shock, in the following December, which completely incapacitated him from any further exertion. At first his life seemed to be in imminent danger, but his wonderful constitution asserted itself, and he survived for some years, soothed by the indefatigable devotion of his wife and surrounded by the pious attentions of his friends. His memory was gone and his speech imperfect; but it was observed that the good man's affections remained unimpaired. In birds and flowers and children, in song and perfumes and bright colours, in things gentle and attractive, he showed a keen delight. It was the calm, sweet sunset of a long autumn day, which had opened with a radiant morning—had known clouds and the stress of storm at noon—and now slowly descended into the eternal sea with a tranquil glow and genial hush.

William Penn died, between two and three in the morning, on the 30th of July, 1718, in his seventy-fourth year. He was buried in the Quakers' cemetery at Jordans, near

Chalfont, by the side of his first wife and Springett, their eldest son. His second wife, with four more of his children, were afterwards interred in the same spot. No memorial marks the great Quaker's last resting-place; but it is under the fifth mound from the chapel door that William Penn lies.

In noticing the Men of Letters of the Restoration period it would be unpardonable to forget Sir Roger L'Estrange, one of the earliest of our political pamphleteers. Born in 1616, he fought as a loyal Cavalier during the Great Civil War; was captured by the army of the Parliament, tried, and condemned to death; and for four years lay in prison, expecting that each day would bring him the summons to the scaffold. It is said that at this time he wrote the poem—superior to his other compositions—entitled "The Liberty of the Imprisoned Royalists," from which we extract a few stanzas:—

> "Beat on, proud billows! Boreas blow!
>   Swell, curled waves, high as Jove's roof!
> Your incivility shall show
>   That innocence is tempest-proof.
> Though surly Nereis frown, my thoughts are calm;
> Then strike, Affliction, for thy wounds are balm.
>
> That which the world miscalls a gaol,
>   A private closet is to me,
> Whilst a good conscience is my bail,
>   And innocence my liberty.
> Locks, bars, walls, leanness, though together met,
> Make me no prisoner, but an anchoret. . . .
>
> Have you not seen the nightingale,
>   A pilgrim cooped into a cage,
> And heard her tell her wonted tale,
>   In that her narrow hermitage?
> Even then her charming melody doth prove
> That all her bars are trees, her cage a grove.

> I am the bird whom they combine
> Thus to deprive of liberty;
> But though they do my corps confine,
> Yet, maugre hate, my soul is free;
> And though I'm mured, yet I can chirp and sing,
> Disgrace to rebels, glory to my king!"

L'Estrange at length recovered his liberty, and had the good sense to keep free of political turmoil until the Restoration. In 1663 he was appointed licenser or censor of the press, and received a monopoly of the printing and publication of news. Of this monopoly he availed himself to produce his newspaper, *The Public Intelligencer*, which, in 1679, was succeeded by the *Observator*. He published also an interminable series of pamphlets, in which he appeared as the swash-buckler of the Court, defending any act of the Government with a prompt and audacious pen—generally lively and vigorous, and always abusive, vulgar, and unscrupulous. "L'Estrange," says Macaulay, "was by no means deficient in readiness and shrewdness; and his diction, though coarse, and disfigured by a mean and flippant jargon which then passed for wit in the green room and the tavern, was not without keenness and vigour. But his nature, at once ferocious and ignoble, showed itself in every line that he penned."

L'Estrange was not without some pretensions to scholarship, and translated, effectively if roughly, the Fables of Æsop, the Morals of Seneca (1678), Cicero's Offices (1680), Quevedo's Visions, the Annals of Josephus, and the Colloquies of Erasmus. He was knighted by James II., and died in 1704.

In reference to the newspapers of the period, the historian remarks:—"Nothing like the daily paper of our time existed or could exist. Neither the necessary capital nor the necessary skill was to be found. Freedom too was wanting, a want as fatal as that of either capital or skill. The press was not, indeed, at that moment under a general censorship. The licensing act, which had been passed soon after the Restoration, had expired in 1679. Any person might therefore print, at his own risk, a history, a sermon, or a poem, without the previous approbation of any officer; but the judges were unanimously of opinion that this liberty did not extend to Gazettes, and that, by the common law of England, no man, not authorised by the Crown, had a right to publish political news. While the Whig party was still formidable, the Government thought it expedient occasionally to connive at the violation of this rule. During the great battle of the Exclusion Bill, many newspapers were suffered to appear, the Protestant Intelligencer, the Current Intelligence, the Domestic Intelligencer, the True News, the London Mercury. None of these were published oftener than twice a week. None exceeded in size a single small leaf. The quantity of matter which one of them contained in a year was not more than is often found in two numbers of the Times. After the defeat of the Whigs it was no longer necessary for the King to be sparing in the use of that which all his judges had pronounced to be his undoubted prerogative. At the close of his reign no newspaper was suffered to appear without his allowance; and his allowance was given exclusively to the London Gazette.

"The London Gazette came out only on Mondays and

Thursdays. The contents generally were a royal proclamation, two or three Tory addresses, notices of two or three promotions, an account of a skirmish between the Imperial troops and the Janissaries on the Danube, a description of a highwayman, an announcement of a grand cockfight between two persons of honour, and an advertisement offering a reward for a strayed dog. The whole made up two pages of moderate size. Whatever was communicated respecting matters of the highest moment was communicated in the most meagre and formal style. . . . The most important Parliamentary debates, the most important State trials, recorded in our history, were passed over in profound silence. . . In the capital the coffee houses supplied in some measure the place of a journal. Thither the Londoners flocked, as the Athenians of old flocked to the market place, to hear whether there was any news. . . But people who lived at a distance from the great theatre of political contention could be regularly informed of what was passing there only by means of news-letters. To prepare such letters became a calling in London, as it now is among the natives of India. The news writer rambled from coffee-room to coffee-room, collecting reports, squeezed himself into the Sessions House at the Old Bailey if there was an interesting trial, nay, perhaps obtained admission to the gallery of Whitehall, and noticed how the King and Duke looked. In this way he gathered materials for weekly epistles destined to enlighten some county town or some bench of rustic magistrates. Such were the sources from which the inhabitants of the largest provincial cities, and the great body of the gentry and clergy, learned almost all that they know of the history of their own time."*

To the reign of Charles II. belongs no inconsiderable portion of the religious meditations and philosophical researches of Robert Boyle. The son of Richard Boyle, Earl of Cork, he was born at Lismore in 1627. He was educated at Eton and Geneva; travelled through Italy, returned to England soon after his father's death (in 1643); and with his widowed sister, Lady Ranelagh, taking charge of his household, devoted himself to study and especially to the practical application of the experimental sciences, Chemistry and Natural Philosophy. At his house assembled the professors of the new philosophy, whose co-operation resulted in the foundation of the Royal Society, and Boyle was not only one of its most active members, but a frequent contributor to its "Philosophical Transactions."

In 1660, Boyle appeared as an author, publishing a letter on "Seraphic Love," in which he expounded some of the principles of English Platonism, as approved by its apostle, Henry More. Soon afterwards he issued an interesting scientific treatise, "New Experiments Physico-mechanical, touching the Spring of the Air and its Effects, made for the most part in a New Pneumatical Engine"—this engine being Otto Guericke's air-pump, greatly enlarged by Boyle, with the help of his friend and assistant, Robert Hooke. In the following

* The elder Disraeli observes that "Sir Roger L'Estrange among his rivals was esteemed as the most perfect model of political writing. The temper of the man was factious, and the compositions of the author seem to us coarse, but I suspect they contain much idiomatic expression. His Æsop's Fables are a curious specimen of familiar style. Queen Mary showed a due contempt of him after the Revolution, by this anagram:—

"Roger L'Estrange,
Lye strange Roger!"

year he published some clear and intelligent considerations on the conduct of experiments, and the results of his persevering inquiry, in "Certain Physiological Essays." This was followed by "The Sceptical Chemist," directed against those self-sufficient philosophers who professed to find the true principles of things in salt, sulphur, and mercury. He gave to the world, in 1663, "Some Considerations touching the Usefulness of Experimental Natural Philosophy," "Experiments and Considerations touching Colours," and "Considerations touching the Style of the Holy Scriptures." His scientific work has a much more definite value than his theological, which is often jejune and commonplace; and his "Occasional Reflections upon Several Subjects: whereto is premised a Discourse about such kind of Thoughts," was admirably ridiculed by Swift in his "Meditations on a Broomstick." It is only fair to add, however, that this was written in his youth—to use his own expression, "in his infancy"—though not published until 1665. It would have been better for Boyle's fame if he had never published it at all.

Passing over the minor works which flowed from his indefatigable pen, we may note his "Excellency of Theology compared with Natural Philosophy, as both are the Objects of Men's Study" (1674), and his "Considerations about the Reconcilableness of Reason and Religion" (1675). These are both written in the devout strain natural to a man of his sincere and simple piety, whose pure and noble life was inspired throughout by a reverent sense of the Divine Love. Boyle refused to take orders because, he said, he could serve religion more effectually as a layman, and because, we imagine, his humility shrank from the acceptance of so high a responsibility. He printed at his own cost Dr. Pocock's translation into Arabic of the "De Veritate of Grotin's," and sent out a large number of copies for free distribution in the Levant. He also printed an Irish Bible. He was the first governor of a corporation for the Propagation of the Gospel; and as a director of the East India Company strongly advocated the duty of combining the diffusion of Christian truth with the extension of commercial interest. For six years he supplied Burnet with the means of preparing and publishing the first volume of his "History of the Reformation." Though a Churchman, he was a defender of the principle of religious tolerance. He declined the Presidency of the Royal Society in 1680, because he objected to the oaths required of whomsoever accepted the office; he also declined the Provostship of Eton, and more than once refused a peerage. His life of quiet study, persevering research, simple piety, and active charity—he gave to the poor a thousand pounds annually — came to a peaceful close in December, 1691.

To the works already mentioned as written by this amiable Christian philosopher we must add—"Considerations on the Style of the Holy Scriptures;" "A Free Discourse against Customary Swearing;" "A Discourse of Things above Reason;" "A Discourse of the High Veneration Man's Intellect owes to God, particularly for His Wisdom and Power;" "A Disquisition into the Final Causes of Natural Things;" and "The Christian Virtuoso, showing that, by being addicted to Experimental Philosophy, a Man is rather assisted than indisposed to be a Good Christian."

Some of our readers may be familiar, perhaps, with the following passage :—

"Let us consider the works of God, and observe the operations of his hands: let us take notice of and admire his infinite wisdom and goodness in the formation of them. No creature in this sublunary world is capable of so doing beside man; yet we are deficient herein: we content ourselves with the knowledge of the tongues, and a little skill in philology, or history perhaps, and antiquity, and neglect that which to me seems more material, I mean natural history and the works of creation. I do not discommend or derogate from those other studies; I should betray mine own ignorance and weakness should I do so; I only wish they might not altogether jostle out and exclude this. I wish that this might be brought in fashion among us; I wish men would be so equal and civil, as not to disparage, deride, and vilify those studies which themselves skill out of, or are not conversant in. No knowledge can be more pleasant than this, none that doth so satisfy and feed the soul; in comparison whereto that of words and phrases seems to me insipid and jejune. That learning, saith a wise and observant prelate, which consists only in the form and prelagogy of arts, or the critical notion upon words and phrases, hath in it this intrinsical imperfection, that it is only so far to be esteemed as it conduceth to the knowledge of things, being in itself but a kind of pedantry, apt to infect a man with such odd humours of pride, and affectation, and curiosity, as will render him unfit for any great employment. Words being but the images of matter, to be wholly given up to the study of these, what is it but Pygmalion's frenzy to fall in love with a picture or image. As for oratory, which is the best skill about words, that hath by some wise men been esteemed but a voluptuary art, like to cookery, which spoils wholesome meats, and helps unwholsome, by the variety of sauces, serving more to the pleasure of taste than the health of the body."

This is one of the earliest incentives and encouragements to the study of Nature to be met with in our literature, and it proceeded from the pen of John Ray, whose whole life was devoted to this study, and to the application of it as an evidence of the truth of the Christian Revelation. Natural theology is outlined—or, rather, its principles are suggested—in the works of Cudworth, Henry More, and Boyle; but it first assumed a definite form as a branch of Christian Apologetics in Ray's treatise, published in 1671, on "The Wisdom of God Manifested in the Works of the Creation." A quarter of a century later the argument was taken up and expounded by Denham in his "Physico-theology" and "Astro-theology;" and in the second year of the present century it was popularised by Paley in his "Natural Theology." It has not, perhaps, the value which was at one time attached to it by divines; but it must always be interesting, and the name of John Ray should, therefore, be remembered with respect.

Ray studied Nature for practical purposes also. He was the most eminent botanist of his age, and unquestionably one of the founders of the science. His two folios "Historia Plantarum," form a monument of well-directed labour—of keen observation, quick perception, and untiring industry—fully justifying the eulogium on its writer pronounced by White of Selborne:—"Our countryman, the excellent Mr. Ray, is th only describer that conveys some precise idea in every term or word, maintaining his superiority over his followers and imitators, in spite of the advantage of fresh discoveries and modern information."

John Ray was the son of a blacksmith, and born at Black Notley, in Essex, in 1628. He was educated at Braintree Grammar School, and thence removed to Cambridge, where he obtained a fellowship at Trinity. In 1651 he was appointed Greek Lecturer of his college, and afterwards Mathematical Reader. His botanical researches throughout the length and breadth of the country were gathered up in his Latin "Catalogue of the Plants of England and the adjacent Isles," published in 1670. Another of his more notable works was his "Collection of Proverbs, with Short Annotations," given to the world in the same year. At the age of 45, he married a lady twenty-four years younger than himself; and settling in his native place lived there a life of unassuming piety till his death in 1705.

We must pass over with a reference the names of the first English writers on Political Economy, such as Sir Josiah Child (1630-1699), who published in 1668, a "New Discourse on Trade;" and Sir William Petty (1623-1687), the physician, and founder of the noble family of Lansdowne, who, about the same time, compiled his treatise "On Taxes and Contributions." The greatest physician of the period was Thomas Sydenham, who, breaking loose from the antiquated traditions of the old school of empirics, applied to the treatment of disease the results of careful observation and individual diagnosis. His great principle is now accepted as the very foundation of the therapeutic art: that we must follow and encourage the processes by which Nature relieves herself of a disease, or else discover a specific. In the treatment of fevers he was the first English physician who made large use of Peruvian bark, or cinchona. He likewise introduced a much-needed reform into the treatment of smallpox. He was born in 1624, and died in 1689.

We have left to the last the greatest name in English Science, that of Sir Isaac Newton. It is impossible for us to do justice to the noble work which has placed him foremost among the philosophers of all time. That work, to be estimated aright, must be studied in his own marvellous writings, or in the comments of his followers and disciples, and especially in Sir David Brewster's "Life of Newton." A succinct summary of his great discoveries is provided in his epitaph:—"Here lies buried Isaac Newton, Knight, who, with an almost divine energy of mind, guided by the light of mathematics purely his own, first demonstrated the motions and figures of the planets, the paths of comets, and the causes of the tides; who discovered, what before his time no one had ever suspected, that rays of light are differently refrangible, and that is the cause of colours." The epitaph proceeds to define the philosopher's character. He was "a diligent, penetrating, and faithful interpreter of nature, antiquity, and the sacred writings. In his philosophy, he maintained the majesty of the Supreme Being; in his manners he expressed the simplicity of the Gospel. Let mortals congratulate themselves that the world has seen so great and excellent a man, the glory of human nature."

In a hackneyed line Young has told us that

"An undevout astronomer is mad."

No such aberration afflicted the reverent genius of Sir Isaac Newton, whose simple piety shed a pure and beautiful light over his whole life. He looked through Nature up to Nature's God, and every fresh advance that he made in a knowledge of the mysteries of creation did but intensify his faith in the wisdom and goodness of its Creator. His religious belief is thus stated by himself in an interesting document first published by Sir David Brewster, and we give it here because it contrasts so forcibly with the extravagance of modern sciolists and their cant about the Unknowable and the Unconditioned:—

"1. There is one God the Father, ever-living, omnipresent; omniscient, almighty, the maker of heaven and earth, and one Mediator between God and man, the man Christ Jesus.

"2. The Father is the invisible God whom no eye hath seen, nor eye can see. All other beings are sometimes visible.

"3. The Father hath life in Himself, and hath given the Son to have life in Himself.

"4. The Father is omniscient, and hath all knowledge originally in His own breast, and communicates knowledge of future things to Jesus Christ; and none in heaven or earth, or under the earth, is worthy to receive knowledge of future things immediately from the Father, but the Lamb. And, therefore, the testimony of Jesus is the spirit of prophecy, and Jesus is the Word or Prophet of God.

"5. The Father is immovable, no place being capable of becoming emptier or fuller of Him than it is by the eternal necessity of nature. All other things are movable from place to place.

"6. All the worship—whether of prayer, praise, or thanksgiving—which was due to the Father before the coming of Christ, is still due to Him. Christ came not to diminish the worship of His Father.

"7. Prayers are most prevalent when directed to the Father in the name of the Son.

"8. We are to return thanks to the Father alone for creating us, and giving us food and raiment and other blessings of this life, and whatsoever we are to thank Him for, or desire that He would do for us, we ask of Him immediately in the name of Christ.

"9. We need not pray to Christ to intercede for us. If we pray the Father aright, He will intercede.

"10. It is not necessary to salvation to direct our prayers to any other than the Father in the name of the Son.

"11. To give the name of God to angels or kings, is not against the First Commandment. To give the worship of the God of the Jews to angels or kings, is against it. The meaning of the commandment is, Thou shalt worship no other God but me.

"12. To us there is but one God, the Father, of Whom are all things, and one Lord Jesus Christ, by Whom are all things and we by Him. That is, we are to worship the Father alone as God Almighty, and Jesus alone as the Lord, the Messiah, the Great King, the Lamb of God Who was slain, and hath redeemed us with His blood, and made us kings and priests."

Newton was born at Woolsthorpe, in Lincolnshire, on Christmas Day, 1642. In his childhood he showed a strong bias towards the mechanical and mathematical sciences. He received his early education at the Grantham Grammar School, but at the age of fifteen was removed to take charge of the home farm on his father's small estate. His incompetency for this kind of work, however, was soon apparent, and he was sent back to school to fulfil the destiny marked out for him. Admitted as a sizar to Trinity College, Cambridge, in 1661, he became a Junior Fellow in 1667, and M.A. in 1668. In the following year he succeeded Dr. Baum in the Mathematical professorship. In 1672 he was admitted a Fellow of the Royal Society, and communicated to it his new theory of Light, which revolutionized the science of Optics. He was several times returned to Parliament as a member for the University which his genius adorned. In 1695 his great services were recognized by Government, who made him Warden of the Mint, and in 1703 by his scientific brethren, who elected him President of the Royal Society. In 1705 Queen Anne bestowed upon him the honour of knighthood. He lived into the last year of the reign of George I., dying on the 20th of March, 1727, scarcely three months before the King, at the venerable age of 84.

To the reign of Charles II. belong his two great discoveries, that of a new theory of Light, and that of the law of Gravitation; but it was not until 1687 that he published the "Philosophiæ Naturales Principia Mathematica," in which he revealed the secret of the power that binds together the several parts of the universe. The results of his minute optical investigations were embodied in his elaborate treatise, published in 1704, "Optics: or, a Treatise of the Refractions, Inflections, and Colours of Light." He was the author also of several profound mathematical works, and to his close study of the Hebrew prophets we owe his "Observations upon the Prophecies of Holy Writ, particularly the Prophecies of Daniel, and the Apocalypse of St. John." His "Historical Account of Two Notable Corruptions of Scripture" (1 John v. 7 and 1 Tim. iii. 16) testifies to the vigour and persistency of his Scriptural studies.

Newton made two important contributions to Chemistry, which constitute, as it were, the foundation-stones of its two great divisions. The first was pointing out a method of graduating thermometers, so that comparisons with each other might be possible in whatever part of the world observations with them were made. The second was by indicating the nature of chemical affinity, and showing that it consisted in an attraction by which the constituents of bodies were drawn towards each other and united; "thus destroying the previous hypothesis of the hooks, and points, and rings, and wedges, by means of which the different constituents of bodies were conceived to be kept together."

The last name we shall mention in our hasty retrospect is that of Sir Thomas Browne, the Norwich physician author of the "Religio Medici" (Religion of a Physician) 1642; "Pseudodoxia Epidemica" (Epidemic False Doctrines), or "Inquiries into Vulgar and Common Errors," 1646; and "Hydriotaphia, or Urn Burial; a Discourse on the Symbolical Urns lately found in Norfolk," 1658,—to which is appended "The Garden of Cyrus; or, The Quincuncial Lozenge, or Network Plantations of the Ancients, artificially, naturally, and mystically Considered." Browne, who obtained his doctor's degree at Leyden, settled as a medical practitioner at Norwich, and lived there a life of quiet usefulness and learned retirement. He was knighted in the reign of Charles II.

Few of our writers have more successfully embodied

grave and earnest thought in language of singular richness and dignity. On all his works he impresses the seal of his own individuality, and we are thus brought acquainted with a fine nature and an inquiring intellect, which invariably aims at lofty objects, though sometimes led astray by a weakness for fanciful speculation. Coleridge happily describes him as "rich in various knowledge, exuberant in conceptions and conceits; contemplative, imaginative, often truly great and magnificent in his style and diction, though doubtless, too often big, stiff, and *hyper-Latinistic*. He is a quiet and sublime enthusiast, with a strong tinge of the fantast: the humorist constantly mingling with, and flashing across, the philosopher, as the darting colours in shot-silk play upon the main dye." He belongs to the older school of writers, who had always something to say, and each of whom said it in his own manner—original, independent, self-reliant. He spake out of his fulness, and all his utterances were worth listening to because they were the utterances of a ripe and excellent genius, fed by observation, reflection, and study.

His characteristics are best appreciated from a careful study of the "Religio Medici," which has a remarkable psychological interest in the frankness of its self-revelations; but his other works also abound in evidence of the fulness and forcibleness of his intellectual gifts. They are sufficiently accessible, now-a-days, to any reader; but we cannot deny ourselves the pleasure of closing this chapter with a few quotations which shall illustrate the majestic beauty of his diction and the elevation of his thoughts.

As a commentary on the old text, *Vanitas Vanitatum*,

the following passage, with its subdued pathos and stately eloquence, is admirably impressive :—

"Darkness and light divide the course of time, and oblivion shares with memory a great part even of our living beings; we slightly remember our felicities, and the smartest strokes of affliction have but short smart upon us. Sense endureth no extremities, and sorrows destroy us or themselves. To creep into stones are fables. Afflictions induce callosities; miseries are slippery, or fall like snow upon upon us, which, notwithstanding, is no unhappy stupidity. To be ignorant of evils to come, and forgetful of evils past, is a merciful provision in nature whereby we digest the mixture of our few and evil days; and our delivered senses not relapsing into cutting remembrances, our sorrows are not kept raw by the edge of repetitions. A great part of antiquity contented their hopes of subsisting with a transmigration of their souls—a good way to continue their memories, while, having the advantage of plural successions, they could not but act something remarkable in such variety of beings; and, enjoying the fame of their passed selves, make accumulation of glories unto their last durations. Others, rather than be lost in the uncomfortable night of nothing, were content to recede into the common being, and make one particle of the public soul of all things, which was no more than to return into their unknown and divine original again. Egyptian ingenuity was more unsatisfied, contriving their bodies in sweet consistencies to attend the return of their souls. But all was vanity, feeding the wind; and folly. The Egyptian mummies which Cambyses or time hath spared, avarice now consumeth. Memory is become merchandise; Myzraim cures wounds, and Pharaoh is sold for balsams."

A beautiful thought upon Light:—

"Light, that makes things seen, makes some things invisible. Were it not for darkness, and the shadow of the earth, the noblest part of creation had remained unseen, and the stars of heaven as invisible as on the fourth day, when they were created above the horizon with the sun, and there was not an eye to behold them. The greatest mystery of religion is expressed by adumbration, and in the noblest part of Jewish types we find the cherubim shadowing the mercy-seat. Life itself is but the shadow of death, and souls departed but the shadows of the living. All things fall under this name. The sun itself is but the dark Simulacrum; and life but the shadow of God."

Art and Nature:—

"Nature is not at variance with art, nor Art with Nature —they being both the servants of His providence. Art is the perfection of Nature. Were the world now as it was the sixth day, there were yet a chaos. Nature hath made one world and Art another. In belief, all things are artificial, for Nature is the Art of God."

Study of Nature:—

"The world was made to be inhabited by beasts, but studied and contemplated by man; it is the debt of our reason we owe unto God, and the homage *we pay* for not being beasts; without this, the world is still as though it had not been, or as it was before the sixth day, when as yet there was not a creature that could conceive or say there was a world. The wisdom of God receives small honour from those vulgar heads that rudely stare about, and with a gross rusticity admire His works; those highly magnify Him whose judicious inquiry into His acts, and deliberate research into His creatures, return the duty of a devout and learned admiration."

In a wise largeness of soul he writes of Charity:—

"I hold not so narrow a conceit of this virtue as to conceive that to give alms is only to be charitable, or think a piece of liberality can comprehend the total of charity. Divinity hath wisely divided the acts thereof into many branches, and hath taught us in this narrow way many paths unto goodness: as many ways as we may do good, so many ways we may be charitable; there are infirmities, not only of body, but of soul and fortunes, which do require the merciful hand of our abilities. I cannot contemn a man for ignorance, but behold him with as much pity as I do Lazarus. It is no greater charity to clothe his body, than apparel the nakedness of his soul. It is an honourable object to see the reasons of other men wear our liveries, and their borrowed understandings do homage to the bounty of ours. It is the cheapest way of beneficence; and, like the natural charity of the sun, illuminates another without obscuring itself. To be reserved and caitiff in this part of goodness, is the sordidest piece of covetousness, and more contemptible than pecuniary avarice. To this, as calling myself a scholar, I am obliged by the duty of my condition: I make not, therefore, my head a grave, but a treasure of knowledge: I intend no monopoly, but a community in learning; I study not for my own sake only, but for theirs that study not for themselves. I envy no man that knows more than myself, but pity them that know less."

THE END.

www.ingramcontent.com/pod-product-compliance
Lightning Source LLC
Chambersburg PA
CBHW030550300426
44111CB00009B/921